DATE DUE

2 libs			
0 outs to 12/07			
100 bks cut this bk			

The History of the CONQUEST OF MEXICO

CLASSIC AMERICAN HISTORIANS

Paul M. Angle, GENERAL EDITOR

The History of the CONQUEST of MEXICO

by William H. Prescott

abridged and edited by C. Harvey Gardiner

THE UNIVERSITY OF CHICAGO PRESS *Chicago & London*

The History of the Conquest of Mexico was first published
in three volumes by Harper and Brothers in 1843.

Library of Congress Catalog Card Number: 66-20592
THE UNIVERSITY OF CHICAGO PRESS, CHICAGO & LONDON
The University of Toronto Press, Toronto 5, Canada
Abridged edition © 1966 by The University of Chicago
Published 1966. Printed in the United States of America

General Editor's Preface

FEW today read the great American historians. Few can. If a reader limited himself to those chosen for inclusion in this series—Prescott, Parkman, Bancroft, McMaster, Moses Coit Tyler, Henry Adams, Nicolay and Hay, and Rhodes—he would find himself straining his eyes eight hours a day for at least a year. This, in the modern world, is an impossible requirement.

Yet that the works of these men should remain unknown is deplorable. Something is better than nothing. From that conviction this series was born. But what should that "something" be? A series of condensations? How can one condense the sixteen volumes of Parkman, or the nine volumes of Henry Adams, into one volume without doing inexcusable violence to the whole? On the other hand, representative selections, each of substantial length, can convey a good idea of point of view, breadth of treatment, narrative skill, and style. This was the method chosen.

After this choice was made, the general editor came across a relevant pronouncement which John Hay made during the serialization of *Abraham Lincoln: A History*. "The only question," Hay wrote to Richard Watson Gilder, editor of the *Century*, "is whether you want the Life to run three years or four. If the former, you must take heroic measures. Leaving out a chapter here and there, or retrenching an adjective, will do no good. . . . You must cut great chunks of topics out. . . . Neither Nicolay nor I can write the work over again for the purpose of saving a half chapter here and there." Nor, we submit, can anyone else.

The books in this series were designed for reading, not research. All documentation, has therefore been eliminated.

Editors of individual volumes have used their discretion in retaining expository footnotes. Such footnotes as they have added are identified by their initials. The typographical style, punctuation, and spelling of the original texts have been followed.

PAUL M. ANGLE

Introduction

WILLIAM HICKLING PRESCOTT was born in Salem, Massachusetts, on May 4, 1796. There, to the north of Boston, he lived
the first twelve years of his life amid influences—physical, par-
ental, and otherwise—that significantly molded his entire life,
as man and writer.

Born with salt air in his nostrils, Prescott knew a lifetime
of enigmatic ties to the sea. When he sailed the sea, he detested
it; but when he contemplated it from successive summer residences, it inspired and colored much of his writing. Another
factor that insinuated itself into a permanent influence in his
life, the career of his grandfather Prescott, also defies precise measurement. However, Prescott entertained a lifelong
devotion to the achievements of his soldier-grandfather. Annual
visits to the Pepperell home of the hero of Bunker Hill early
fanned and forever sustained the love of truth, the relish for
heroism, and the dedication to the dramatic that permeates
his histories.

The historian's father, a stanch Federalist lawyer, significantly influenced the youngster in numerous ways. At Salem,
William Prescott was a co-founder of a library company and
likewise a co-founder of a good private school. The lawyer's
love of books prompted an early and ever-expanding library
in his household. And to all else, William Prescott's brilliant
success at the bar founded the fortune so necessary to the
subsidization of a scholarly minded son.

Catherine Hickling Prescott, the historian's mother, reinforced her husband's outlook and also introduced meaningful
influences of her own. To her marriage she brought a love of
travel and bright memories of distant places—of years spent
in the Azores and England, experiences which she had recorded

in her journal.[1] His mother's background tipped the scale and basically affected young William Hickling Prescott's itinerary when he initially went abroad and met the people and saw the things that first led him to interpret a foreign culture in journal entries and lengthy letters.[2]

William and Catherine Prescott, both book-lovers, established a family reading circle which met nightly around their dining room table. When he was very young, Will joined his parents there, as did Elizabeth (Lizzie), and Edward (Ned), his sister and brother who were four and eight years younger, respectively. For the lawyer, the reading circle was welcome relief from his workday diet of briefs and torts; for his wife, those hours helped to assuage an insatiable appetite for literature and the affairs of people. The younger Prescotts, joining their parents in laughter and tears over the triumphs and tragedies of the printed page, improved their reading abilities, widened their vocabularies, taxed their imaginations, and strengthened their memories. In the family reading circle—and he was a party to one for more than a half-century—William Hickling Prescott became addicted to the romantic as he met and admired the writings of Maria Edgeworth, Sir Walter Scott, and others.

In 1808 the Prescotts moved to Boston, the home of the historian for the remainder of his life. There, while preparing for entrance into Harvard, Will was subjected to the most significant intellectual discipline of all his schooling as he studied Latin and Greek with the Episcopalian rector John S. J. Gardiner. Later the Latin helped Prescott to learn other languages, but even earlier it led him to Italy, where he sup-

[1] Catherine Greene Hickling's revealing journal is in the William H. Prescott Papers, Massachusetts Historical Society. The 347-page record of her stay in the Azores and England covers the period between January 13, 1786 and September 30, 1789.

[2] William H. Prescott's journal for his European trip of 1815–17, along with his correspondence of that period, is in the William H. Prescott Papers, Massachusetts Historical Society. Representative letters of the period are in C. Harvey Gardiner (ed.), *The Papers of William Hickling Prescott* (Urbana: University of Illinois Press, 1964), pp. 5–12, 14–17, 18–20, 22–30.

plemented his love of ancient Rome with lively concern about Italian literature, especially epic poetry. The love of the epic so affected his best prose writing that his *Conquest of Mexico* often is admired as much for its literary elegance and epic proportions as for its historical substance.

The last of the accidental yet crucial influences of youthful years came during young William's junior year at Harvard. Then it was, during a food-tossing melee in commons, that a crust of bread hit him and permanently impaired the sight of his left eye. Even though he graduated from Harvard, in 1814, troubled vision interrupted his legal studies a few months later. Away he sailed, to the Azores and grandfather Hickling to avoid the rigors of the New England winter, then to London for medical attention.

The two years abroad made several things obvious: his vision would always be impaired; a career at the bar could not be; but his love of literature and the romantic in his nature were underscored by the premature grand tour which included many months in France and Italy as well as England and the Azores. In addition, western Europe became the focal point of his intellectual curiosity.

Upon his return to America, Prescott, in improving health, gave increasing attention to the idea of becoming a man of letters. For a few months, in the season of his marriage to Susan Amory in 1820, he edited a short-lived literary journal. Even after the journal folded, he continued to read widely and systematically studied foreign literatures and languages.[3] His book-loving parents not only consented to this regimen, they subsidized it. Next he wrote a succession of lengthy review articles on a multiplicity of themes for the *North American Review*.[4]

Gradually, in the decision-making decade of the 1820's, he

[3] Illustrative correspondence by Prescott, as editor of *Club-Room*, and successive programs of his literary studies are in *ibid.*, pp. 31–33, 34–35, 37–38, 40.

[4] Listings of all the review articles that Prescott published in the *North American Review*, between 1821 and 1850, are in William Charvat and

toyed with literary and historical themes that might become book-length research projects. At times, literary subjects, invariably related to Europe, captivated him. History, on the other hand, found him interested in both American and European subjects. As the balance swung in favor of history, he was much influenced by George Ticknor, a wealthy friend and fellow Bostonian. Ticknor's own immersion in Spanish literature, plus his Harvard lectures and private conversations on Spanish themes, drew Prescott toward Spain and an unmet people, an unseen land, and an unknown language.

The long effort to focus his intellectual endeavor was succeeded by a decade of difficult and dedicated labor before his first book, *The History of the Reign of Ferdinand and Isabella, the Catholic,* appeared—on Christmas Day, 1837.[5] Hailed on both sides of the Atlantic—Prescott, consciously in pursuit of a reputation in England, insisted upon simultaneous publication in England and America for every one of his histories,[6] the three-volume *Ferdinand and Isabella* achieved two significant results: it won its author an international reputation as an historian and man of letters, and it encouraged him to continue his historical labors on related Spanish-American themes, the conquests of Mexico and Peru.

By mid-1839, Prescott had outlined in great detail the organization and content of the *Conquest of Mexico.* He knew then the form it required and the mood the theme inspired in

---

Michael Kraus, *William Hickling Prescott; Representative Selections, with Introductions, Bibliography, and Notes* (New York: American Book Co., 1943), pp. cxxxi-cxxxiv and in Gardiner (ed.), *The Papers of William Hickling Prescott,* pp. xvii-xix.

[5] Prescott's own account of the procedures used in producing this and every other history from his hand is in William H. Prescott (C. Harvey Gardiner, ed.), *The Literary Memoranda of William Hickling Prescott* (2 vols.; Norman: University of Oklahoma Press, 1961). The publication and reception of *Ferdinand and Isabella* are detailed in C. Harvey Gardiner, "William Hickling Prescott: Launching a Bark," *The Americas,* XV, No. 3 (January, 1959), 221–234.

[6] A career-long account of Prescott's relations with his American and English publishers is in C. Harvey Gardiner, *Prescott and His Publishers* (Carbondale: Southern Illinois University Press, 1959).

him. "In short, the true way of conceiving the subject is," he wrote in his private memoranda, "not as a philosophical theme; but as an *epic in prose,* a romance of chivalry; as romantic and as chivalrous as any which Boiardo or Ariosto ever fabled,— and almost as marvellous; and which, while it combines all the picturesque features of the romantic school, is borne onward on a tide of destiny. . . . It is, without doubt, the most poetic subject ever offered to the pen of the historian. Is it, for that reason the best? At all events, being the most poetic, it must be regarded from this point of view, to be treated with full effect."[7]

Employing a succession of secretaries at home and many aides—booksellers, researchers, copyists, and others—abroad,[8] Prescott gave five years to the three-volume *History of the Conquest of Mexico.* For many reasons, the accolades bestowed upon his second history, published in 1843, outstripped those accorded the first.

Fanny Appleton Longfellow, the poet's wife, wrote in her diary, "It has the fascination of a romance and cannot be left. . . . Mr. Prescott seems to have seen it all with his own eyes as he makes his readers."[9] A general reader, Fanny had placed Prescott's book on her reading table alongside three-decker novels of the day. At a time when neither authors nor readers had as yet erected artificial barriers between literature and history, *The Conquest of Mexico* met the tests of both.

Like every other historical study by Prescott, *The Conquest of Mexico* is a significant and drama-laden segment of history which, with ample attention to historical background, he

[7] Prescott (Gardiner, ed.), *The Literary Memoranda of William Hickling Prescott,* II, 32–33. In modern times Archibald MacLeish's *Conquistador* (Boston and New York: Houghton Mifflin Co., 1932), a Pulitzer Prize-winning work, attests the poetic nature of the subject.

[8] The full services of one aide, and passing mention of numerous others, are in C. Harvey Gardiner, "Prescott's Most Indispensable Aide: Pascual de Gayangos," *The Hispanic American Historical Review,* XXXIX, No. 1 (February, 1959), 81–115.

[9] Fanny Appleton Longfellow (Edward Wagenknecht, ed.), *Mrs. Longfellow: Selected Letters and Journals of Fanny Appleton Longfellow (1817–1861)* (New York: Longmans, Green and Co., 1956), 103, 104.

treated fundamentally as biography. The opening section, a lengthy consideration of Aztec life in pre-Spanish years, so defied precision of statement and conclusion that Prescott justly termed it "the moonshine period of the old Aztecs."[10] The longer middle portion of the book, embracing the colorful conquest led by Cortés, especially demonstrates the author's genius for wedding truth and beauty, the truth of historical fact and the beauty of elegant style. The third and concluding part of his book, somewhat of an historical epilogue, affirms Prescott's penchant for biography by tracing Cortés' post-conquest career to its close.

In terms of narrative development, drama, and unity, *The Conquest of Mexico* easily assumed the epic form that the historian so much admired. Writing in an august British journal, S. M. Phillips compared Prescott's sketches of scenery to Scott, his battlepieces to Napier, and his views of disaster to Thucydides, and in every instance he lauded *The Conquest of Mexico*.[11] Prescott's telling of the conquest was not the first —nor was it the last, because, among other things, Prescott's own writing attracted novelists, poets, dramatists, and historians to the Mexican theme[12]—but this is certain: Prescott's is the classic account.

In the wake of the crescendo of scholarly and popular acclaim that greeted *The Conquest of Mexico,* Prescott wrote the two-volume companion work which appeared in 1847. Structurally

[10] Prescott (Gardiner, ed.), *The Literary Memoranda of William Hickling Prescott,* II, 49.

[11] [S. M. Phillips], "History of the Conquest of Mexico," *Edinburgh Review,* LXXXI (April, 1845), 229 (American edition).

[12] Illustrative of the inspirational quality of Prescott's book are the following: (1) Edward Maturin's *Montezuma; The Last of the Aztecs: a Romance* (2 vols.; New York: Paine & Burgess, 1845), which the author dedicated to Prescott; (2) William Henry Leatham's poem "Montezuma," written in England in 1844 and presently available in Roger Wolcott (ed.), *The Correspondence of William Hickling Prescott, 1833–1847* (Boston and New York: Houghton Mifflin Co., 1925), pp. 461, 504–7; (3) Lewis F. Thomas' *Cortez the Conqueror, A Tragedy in Five Acts* (Washington: B. W. Ferguson, 1857); and (4) Robert Anderson Wilson's *A New History of the Conquest of Mexico* (Philadelphia: James Challen & Son, 1859). Needless to say, the influence of Prescott's histories on other authors and literary forms, so strong during his lifetime, did not cease with his death.

a carbon copy of the *Mexico, The Conquest of Peru* once more permitted Prescott to trace the victory of civilized man over the barbarian, of the Christian over the pagan. But the longer interval of the conquest, its thematic disunity, and the unsavory character of Pizarro—not to be mentioned in the same breath with Cortés—made the writing of this work an unpleasant labor. While writing the two "conquests," in the period 1838–47, Prescott was at the height of his creative powers: his general health was best, his eyesight strongest, his disciplined use of time and energies—in Boston as well was as at the seashore and in the country—most manifest.

In 1847, he turned to a fourth great theme for which he had been amassing materials for years, the reign of Philip II, but Prescott was a changed man. The eyesight that had fluctuated between good and bad now went from bad to worse; his general health deteriorated; and often his social appetite so ate up his time that his scholarly nature suffered, even shrank. But more important than these factors, as one explains a creative man's passing his peak, were two others: the death of his father and the high level of his own reputation.

During pedestrian rambles and fireside chats—the historian, his wife, and their three children shared the home of the elder Prescotts, lawyer Prescott had been the historian's aide, confidant, and inspiration in ways and to lengths that defy enumeration and measurement.[13] His father's death, in December, 1844, occasioned the loss of one of the two great incentives the writer-son had for continuing his labors. Months after his father's death, during which he had written nothing, the historian wrote, "I must no longer delay to return to my studies, although my interest in them has much diminished, now that I have lost my best recompense of success in his approbation. . . ."[14]

[13] To strangers it might have appeared maudlin but the historian was in earnest when he dedicated *Ferdinand and Isabella* to his father with these words: "To the Honorable William Prescott, LL.D., the Guide of My Youth, My Best Friend in Riper Years, These Volumes, with the Warmest Feelings of Filial Affection, Are Respectfully Inscribed."

[14] Prescott (Gardiner, ed.), *The Literary Memoranda of William Hickling Prescott*, II, 137.

Meanwhile the historian's reputation had scaled the summit of public acclaim: publishers and acquaintances urged him to write on this and that subject; readers deluged him with requests for his autograph; admirers named literary societies for him; honorary memberships and invitations were heaped upon him; colleges at home and abroad conferred honorary degrees upon him; translators vied with one another in efforts to put his works before readers of German, Spanish, French, and Italian; and friends and unknowns deluged him with correspondence which he dutifully answered.[15] Reputation, not income, had been Prescott's primary reason for writing, and with that reputation won, why push one's self? Happy spirit that he was, Prescott enjoyed his fame, even as his fortune, manners, and tastes led him to enjoy the social whirl of Boston during the winters, the cooling Atlantic breezes at Nahant or Lynn during the summers, and the glorious pageant of nature at Pepperell every autumn.

Off and on during the twelve years between the publication of the *Peru* and his death, Prescott gave varying amounts of attention to Philip II. Lasting proof that he was unhappy at this work—yet the New Englander who could not accept idleness and the Bostonian who would not waste the investment he had made in research materials—is evident in the fact that he never formulated a firm, working outline for his study of Philip II. His wavering between a thorough, systematic survey of the entire reign and the presentation of dramatically colorful episodes meant that the unfinished three-volume *History of the Reign of Philip the Second* fulfilled neither hope.

Early in 1858 a warning of physical decline came in the form of an apoplectic stroke. After taking it easy for months, he gradually reentered society and resumed the endless labor on Philip II. Just when he seemed nearly restored, Prescott was felled by a second and fatal stroke, on January 28, 1859.

A circle of intimates sadly missed him, as witty conversa-

[15] Papers illustrative of all these forms of acclaim are in Gardiner (ed.), *The Papers of William Hickling Prescott.*

tionalist, diner-out, connoisseur of wines, clubman—as gentleman. A wider circle remembered him as the aide of struggling authors, contributor to orphanages, and as a co-founder of a fine school for the blind—as humanitarian. But most of all, and for the longest time, William Hickling Prescott would be, and still is, remembered for dramatically told, elegantly written, reliably recorded history—as historian and man of letters.

"We can confidently predict for it an extensive and permanent popularity," George S. Hillard wrote in 1843 as he reviewed *The Conquest of Mexico*.[16] Time—a century and a quarter of it—has fulfilled Hillard's prophecy because *The Conquest of Mexico* has been issued more than two hundred times, more often than any other Prescott title. Likewise it has been the most widely and frequently translated of his histories, having been made available to readers of at least ten languages.[17]

The Conquest of Mexico so captured the general reader that Harper and Brothers were able to send their author more than one hundred twenty newspaper 'puffs' during the first month of publication. Prescott's labor was condemned by very few of his contemporaries, among them fiery Theodore Parker and erratic Robert A. Wilson. Parker's condemnation of Prescott as no philosopher and not much of a historian left the historian unruffled and his following undiminished. Wilson's vitriolic effort to stamp Prescott's *Mexico* a colossal fiction boomeranged and hastened Wilson's own writing to the oblivion that time has consigned it.[18] During Prescott's lifetime the opinions of Parker and Wilson were but dissident ripples amid waves of approbation.

Decades later, toward the close of the nineteenth century,

[16] [George S. Hillard], "History of the Conquest of Mexico," *North American Review*, LVIII (January, 1844), 209.

[17] C. Harvey Gardiner, *William Hickling Prescott; An Annotated Bibliography of Published Works* (Washington, [1959]), pp. x, 57–128.

[18] Henry Steele Commager, *Theodore Parker* (Boston: The Beacon Press, 1936), p. 142; and Wilson, *A New History of the Conquest of Mexico*.

as the nature of both history and the historian changed, so too did the scholarly estimate of Prescott's works. The Boston patrician had been a foremost figure in a generation of magnificent amateurs that was followed by professional academicians of the scientific school. Increasingly encompassed by bulging files of bibliography cards and notes, the new breed of historian too often developed the myopia that induced uninspired paragraph-by-paragraph mastery of subject matter. Satisfied that the "facts," if gathered and spread before the reader, would speak for themselves, the new professional historian commonly published the results of his labor in drab vocabulary that guaranteed the distrust and disinterest of the general reader. This alienation of the wider reading public resulted in historians contenting themselves with writing for each other. Having separated history from literature, the scientific historians proceeded to exalt their own egos by attacking the work of their predecessors.[19] Prescott and his brilliant, literary minded, and romantically inclined company were labeled "literary historians" in a mood of condescension and disdain that equated the term with factual inadequacy.

In the same late nineteenth-century decades, certain scholarly disciplines, ancillary to history, so widened their activity and increased their body of knowledge as to promote criticism of the lengthy opening section of *The Conquest of Mexico.* Archaeology, ethnology, and anthropology found in Lewis H. Morgan, A. F. A. Bandelier, and others the leaders of a scientific assault on Prescott.[20] Their chiding and deriding of the romantic historian were essentially unfair in that the three fields that contributed much to our later knowledge of the pre-Columbian culture of the Aztecs had contributed very little prior to 1840. Judged by the lights of his day—and as Prescott repeatedly insisted that this be the rule for judging the

[19] David D. Van Tassel, *Recording America's Past: An Interpretation of the Development of Historical Studies in America 1607–1884* (Chicago: The University of Chicago Press, 1960), p. 173.

[20] Lewis H. Morgan, "Montezuma's Dinner," *North American Review,* CXXII (April, 1876), 265–308; and A. F. A. Bandelier, *The Romantic School of American Archaeology* (New York: Trow's Printing and Bookbinding Co., 1885).

conquest and the conquistador class, he himself deserves similar consideration—Prescott does not come off badly. His inability to anticipate the findings of later generations of archaeologists, ethnologists, and anthropologists can admit of no just criticism. Even today, despite a century of widening horizons, any student of the pre-conquest Aztec still walks in such a maze of uncertainty that he might properly employ Prescott's colorful phrase and term it "the moonshine period of the old Aztecs."[21]

In the twentieth century, history and literature are still more frequently apart than together—despite many prize competitions that try to wed them. Consequently modern evaluations of Prescott's *Mexico* have fallen, for the most part, into separate literary and historical channels. Harry Thurston Peck, the historian's third biographer, directed considerable attention to Prescott's style. "Regarded simply from the standpoint of literary criticism," Peck wrote, "*The Conquest of Mexico* is Prescott's masterpiece. More than that, it is one of the most brilliant examples which the English language possesses of literary art applied to historical narration."[22]

In the early 1940's, William Charvat emphasized, among others, these points: "his style was in harmony with his material;" "the characteristic pattern of his rhetoric is the single clause or sentence, followed by paired clauses in balance or antithesis or by a series of parallelisms." From a disciplined imagination Prescott drew many adjectives, "but such coloring was the prerogative of the romantic historian." "A lover of the concrete, Prescott turned naturally to metaphor when his subject led him into speculation." As regards diction, "Prescott's merit lay in precision rather than in originality or idiomatic quality." "In general, Prescott's style represents a modi-

[21] The most significant historical study of the Aztecs, Charles Gibson's *The Aztecs Under Spanish Rule; A History of the Indians of the Valley of Mexico 1519–1810* (Stanford: Stanford University Press, 1964)), treats the conquest and post-conquest periods, not the pre-conquest period that so troubled Prescott.
[22] Harry Thurston Peck, *William Hickling Prescott* (New York and London: Macmillan Co., 1905), p. 133.

fication of traditional prose rather than any radical departure from it. His syntax and diction, and his use of alliteration and metaphor seem a little old-fashioned, even for his time, but they give his prose dignity and an air of deliberate art."[23]

A decade later Donald A. Ringe's discussion of the artistry in *The Conquest of Mexico* focused on two interrelationships, those between theme and form and between theme and character, as well as on the employment of the usual literary techniques to reinforce and support the broader elements in the history. Contrasts between characters, the employment of anecdote, and the creation of suspense also characterize Prescott's artistry. A flexible, often rhythmic style, the piling up of sharp detail, and evocative description are other significant features of the writing which succeeds, in part, because of Prescott's ability "to achieve a variety of moods and tones." *"The Conquest of Mexico,"* the critic concludes, "is that rare type of book which satisfies the demands of both history and art."[24]

Frank Goodwyn, searching for the stylistic secrets of Prescott's astonishing success, focused, more so than most literary critics, upon individual techniques. "Perhaps the most powerful—certainly the most apparent—propellant of the Prescott style is the broad generalization." Analyzing the clarity, grace, and "constant forward impetus," Goodwyn richly illustrates the historian's use of simile, metaphor, alliteration, semi-figurative expressions, and rhythmic recurrence of stressed syllables. So considerable and so effective are the end results of Prescott's stylistic labors that Goodwyn concludes that "he certainly gave much conscious thought to the potentialities of both the sonic and the thematic content of language."[25]

---

[23] William Charvat, "Prescott's Style," in W. Charvat and M. Kraus, *Prescott; Representative Selections*, pp. lxxviii–lxxxvii, *passim*.

[24] Donald A. Ringe, "The Artistry of Prescott's 'The Conquest of Mexico'," *New England Quarterly*, XXVI (1953), 454–476., *passim*.

[25] Frank Goodwyn, "The Literary Style of William Hickling Prescott," *Inter-American Review of Bibliography*, IX (March, 1959), 16–39, *passim*.

Writing at greater length than any previous modern critic, but occasionally forcing Prescott into categories along with three other romantic historians, David Levin assessed *The Conquest of Mexico* from the standpoint of structure, characterization, and style. Of the first he says, "The great virtue of *The Conquest of Mexico* is its brilliant design." Prescott's characterization, on the other hand, is criticized for its frequent distortion, shallowness, and lack of sharp detail. Montezuma is considered to be out of focus and the unheroic qualities of Cortés too often excluded. "The triumph of excellent design over faulty detail is nowhere clearer than in Prescott's prose style." On the score of style, the critic says, "In *The Conquest of Mexico* it is often his organization, his control of the narrative, or his conception of a scene—rather than brilliant rhetoric or precise description—which contributed most to the effectiveness of a passage." "The main virtues of Prescott's style are its graceful balance, its frequently stately cadences, and its clarity." "The rhythms of this prose also require attention. Phrase, clause, and sentence consistently end with a firmly stressed word, emphasizing the almost orotund symmetry."

"The central weakness is inadequate attention to detail, a surprising insensitivity to precise meaning." His imagery is overworked, even monotonously repetitious in reference to battles. Among his flaws of language, Levin cites "cliché, abstract, unnecessary simile, and repetitious or unnecessary telling." "Prescott's most remarkable achievements in the history are the general scenes." "Prescott's style is better adapted to the tableau than to vigorous action."[26] Levin's criticism is noteworthy for its balanced consideration of merits and flaws. So many critics have overemphasized the former that Levin tends to emphasize the latter. Between the literary critic and the historian, however, this difference emerges: whereas Pres-

[26] David Levin, "History as Romantic Art: Structure, Characterization, and Style in *The Conquest of Mexico*," *The Hispanic American Historical Review*, XXXIX, No. 1 (February, 1959), 20–45, *passim*. This is also in Levin, *History as Romantic Art—Bancroft, Prescott, Motley, and Parkman* (Stanford: Stanford University Press, 1959), chap. vii.

cott made artistry the handmaid of history, Levin, Goodwyn, Ringe, Charvat, and others[27] incline to make history the hand-maid of artistry.

As literary critics have differed, yet agreed, in recent decades about *The Conquest of Mexico,* so too have the historians. In the 1890's, J. Franklin Jameson wrote, ". . . it may be doubted whether his critical insight was one of the most penetrating sort. Nor was he a profoundly philosophical historian, distinguished for searching analysis."[28] The shade of Theodore Parker and the canon of the scientific historian join forces in this terse evaluation.

Two decades later, on the eve of the first World War, G. P. Gooch wrote of Prescott, "He was more attracted by the con-crete aspects of life than by ideas. . . . He was not always criti-cal in the use of his authorities, nor was he a philosophic his-torian interested in social evolution. On the other hand, while Grote and Macaulay, Carlyle and Froude, Bancroft and Mot-ley made their histories vehicles of political and religious propa-ganda, his pages are free from hero-worship and party bias."[29] Far removed from the field of Latin American history him-self, Gooch, in reference to Prescott's use of his sources, em-phasizes the triumph, at times, of the romantic in the choice of authorities. More important still is the fact that any essen-tial imbalance in Prescott's *Mexico* derives from his over-weening dependence upon Spanish sources. The historian knew this and lamented repeatedly, in text and notes, his inability to delineate the Aztecs and relate the struggle from the Indian viewpoint.

Referring to both *The Conquest of Mexico* and *The Con-quest of Peru,* John Francis O'Hara wrote in 1931, "Prescott's classics . . . are still the broadest general treatment in their respective fields." This statement is as true today as when it

[27] See also Vittorio Gabrieli, "William H. Prescott (1796–1859) e la storia come arte," *Studi Americani,* IV (1958), 9–56.

[28] J. Franklin Jameson, *The History of Historical Writing in America* (Boston and New York: Houghton Mifflin Co., 1891), p. 117.

[29] G. P. Gooch, *History and Historians in the Nineteenth Century* (New York: Longmans, Green and Co., 1913), pp. 415–16.

was published. The same writer continued, "Monograph corrections of Prescott will continue to appear as new material is found and old material more impartially sifted."[30] Aside from the research on the Aztecs, which is essentially non-historical, the findings of the post-Prescott students of the conquest of Mexico have supported rather than attacked Prescott's account. Amplification, rather than challenge, has been the basic relationship between Prescott and the recent historical writing about Mexico in the era of the conquest.[31]

Henry Steele Commager, author of a particularly penetrating short assessment of Prescott as historian, insists, "Although he was essentially a literary historian, Prescott's reliance upon source material, conscientious research and critical acumen established standards of scholarship which justify the claim that he was the first American scientific historian." Concerning Prescott's defects Commager continues, "His history was narrative rather than analytical, descriptive rather than philosophical, and the brilliance of the coloring conceals a lack of depth. His concern was with politics, war and diplomacy rather than with social or economic institutions. . . ." Inasmuch as the modern historian's concern about social and economic institutions was in its infancy a half century after Prescott's death, this criticism is another based on subsequent developments and hindsight. Although the newest and the best of the most modern outlooks of the historian cannot be exhibited in Prescott's writing, some of the best of Prescott has come to influence modern historians. As Commager put it, "His observance of the most rigid standards did much to raise the level of historical scholarship in the United States. . . ."[32]

Affectionately terming Prescott the American Thucydides,

[30] George Matthew Dutcher *et al., A Guide to Historical Literature* (New York: Macmillan Co., 1931), p. 1066.

[31] This is evident, for example, in articles and books by Alfredo Chavero, G. R. G. Conway, Francisco Fernández del Castillo, C. Harvey Gardiner, Charles Gibson, Francisco A. de Icaza, Edmundo O'Gorman, Florentino Pérez Embid, and Henry R. Wagner.

[32] Henry Steele Commager, "William Hickling Prescott," in Edwin R. A. Seligman *et al.* (eds.), *Encyclopaedia of the Social Sciences* (15 vols.; New York: Macmillan Co., 1930–35), XII, 324.

Samuel Eliot Morison, another historian who has happily combined literary charm with historical accuracy, insists, ". . . he
was a master of *narrative*, which history essentially is, a fact
which too many modern historians have forgotten." "I shall
not attempt to analyze his style," Morison says, "because it is
to be enjoyed and admired, not plucked apart."[33]

Three criticisms of Prescott the historian deserve special
attention: his failure to delve personally into the archives and
collections from which materials were drawn, his failure to
travel in the countries related to his historical themes, and his
definition of the conquest. Perhaps Prescott would have seen
and employed more sources, his general health and eyesight
permitting, if he had personally plumbed, for example, the
archives of Spain. Some of the criticisms which have been
leveled at his historical method might have been reduced
thereby, but it is significant that his proportions and emphases
are sound without the additional data that personal recourse to
the archives might have supplied. It might be said that "the
genius of Prescott is not that of a physical giant reading every
document but rather that of one whose sensitive, critical faculties permitted him to produce whole cloth from a limited selection of historical threads."[34]

Despite his musing of 1822: ". . . I think, from obvious
reasons, every historian should be personally acquainted with
the country concerning which he is to write,"[35] Prescott never
traveled in Spain, Mexico, or Peru. In the first place, such travel
would have contradicted the social nature—that of the husband, parent, socialite in him—that kept him in the bosom of
his family in beloved Boston. But more than that is the fact
that prolonged and detailed firsthand experience in the lands
concerned would have disrupted the romantic in his literary

[33] Samuel Eliot Morison, "Prescott: the American Thucydides," *The
Atlanta Monthly*, CC, No. 5 (November, 1957), 167.
[34] C. H. Gardiner, "Prescott ante el mundo," *Revista Estudios Ameri-
canos*, núm. 101 (1960), 130. An English text of this paper was presented
at the meeting of the American Historical Association, in Washington,
D. C., on December 30, 1958.
[35] Gardiner (ed.), *The Papers of William Hickling Prescott*, 41.

nature, would have changed both the man and his histories. Prescott's avoidance of the lands of his masterworks represented his abhorrence of change.

The criticism that concerns Prescott's definition of the conquest brings the historian and the literary artist into conflict once more. Because he insisted upon good story line, indeed epic proportions, he intentionally avoided what, to his way of thinking, was a pitfall into which Washington Irving had fallen in writing his *Life and Voyages of Christopher Columbus.* That four-volume work had an early climax in the discovery of America and a long denouement in the tedious details of three subsequent voyages. "Irving," Prescott told himself in 1841, "should have abridged this part of his story; and instead of four volumes, have brought it into two."[36] As the historian fashioned his *Mexico* to avoid an early climax, he did two things: he curtailed his account of the post-conquest career of Cortés and he established the fall of Tenochtitlán, on August 13, 1521, as the end of the conquest. This latter decision does considerable violence to history, as everyone who has pursued the post-1521 career of Cortés, his captains, and his men readily knows. The widening conquest is closely related to the post-1521 campaigns of Gonzalo de Sandoval, Pedro de Alvarado, Cristóbal de Olid, and others.[37] In truth the dramatic conquest lost its original unity of action and then shaded imperceptibly into the rather prosaic period of settlement. Prescott had no love for a disjointed story that just petered out, and so he settled upon dimensions of the conquest which do violence to it both time and space. By abridging the conquest, Prescott's artistry triumphed at the expense of history.

[36] Prescott (Gardiner, ed.), *The Literary Memoranda of William Hickling Prescott,* II, 68.

[37] See the following biographies: C. Harvey Gardiner, *The Constant Captain: Gonzalo de Sandoval* (Carbondale: Southern Illinois University Press, 1961); John Eaghan Kelly, *Pedro de Alvarado, Conquistador* (Princeton: Princeton University Press, 1932); and Rafael Heliodoro Valle, *Cristóbal de Olid: Conquistador de México y Honduras* (México: Editorial Jus, 1950).

Modern specialists in Latin American history have also evaluated Prescott's *Conquest of Mexico*. Cline terms it a "literary and historiographical classic,´ still readable and useful. . . ."[38] R. A. Humphreys, a modern English judge of the American historian, insists, ". . . it is the measure of his success that after more than a hundred years there is still no narrative history of the Spanish conquest of America to equal his."[39] The leading American journal in the field of Latin American history, in an issue dedicated to Prescott on the centenary of his death, prefaced its tributes with these words, among others: "It may be said of his work as it may be said of few of his contemporaries that we still depend on it for some of our fundamental historical understanding. . . . He did much—and more than is commonly attributed to him—to establish canons of modern historical writing."[40]

The ultimate greatness of Prescott, the man and the historian, can be sensed from the following:

(1) he wedded history and literature, widening the historian's public and challenging succeeding generations of historians,

(2) he turned American interest to wider worlds in a period too given to narrow nationalism and isolation,

(3) he won the first significant international reputation ever accorded an American historian and simultaneously contributed to the internationalization of the nascent literature of his country,

(4) he is the most widely translated and frequently published of American historians,

(5) he introduced historical practices, for example, careful and full documentation, multi-archival research, and bio-

[38] American Historical Association, *Guide to Historical Literature* (New York: Macmillan Co., 1961), p. 669.
[39] R. A. Humphreys, "William Hickling Prescott: The Man and the Historian," *The Hispanic American Historical Review*, XXXIX, No. 1 (February, 1959), 10.
[40] *Ibid.*, unnumbered page.

bibliographical essays, which have basically enriched American historiography,

(6) he represents the self-educated and magnificent amateur historian at his best,

(7) he represents inspiring triumph over a vast array of obstacles,

(8) he is still considered the finest historian of the Hispanic world produced by the Anglo-Saxon world,

(9) he produced the classic accounts of the conquests of Mexico and Peru, and

(10) his works are alive today—published, bought, read, and enjoyed.[41]

The editorial practices adopted by the present editor for the pages that follow are intended to protect and project Prescott's work while facilitating the reading and enjoyment of it. To protect Prescott the artist and historian has meant that unity, balance, and narrative—major concerns of his at all times—have motivated the selection of materials. Moreover the protection of Prescott the artist and historian has meant that the selections are entirely in his own words. For the pleasure of the general reader, the mountainous notes, bibliographical essays, and appendixes have been omitted.

The section headings—Prescott terms them books, concisely stated and revelatory of the structuring of the book—have been retained as Prescott established and phrased them. For several reasons, however, the chapter headings have been restyled. Prescott's practice of enumerating the themes within a chapter, instead of deriving a single heading from them, has yielded to brief chapter headings. (These, in turn, have become a new table of contents.) An additional reason for restyling the chapter headings is the fact that some chapters have been consolidated.

[41] From the introduction of a forthcoming biography of Prescott by C. Harvey Gardiner.

In line with general editorial practice in this series Prescott's spelling of proper names and places has been retained. Where the difference between his form and the preferred modern form is sufficient to cause confusion, the modern form is given in a footnote. To this rule there is one exception: accent marks, which Prescott used sparingly, have been added in many instances. In keeping with the foregoing introduction, it has been thought desirable to retain the occasional minor error of fact which occurs in these selections.

C. HARVEY GARDINER

Contents

Contents

The History of the CONQUEST OF MEXICO

A sketch of William H. Prescott made by the English artist George Richmond in 1850.

AFTER discussing previous histories of the Conquest, especially those by Solís and Robertson, and the wealth of subsequently available pertinent material, Prescott sized up his theme and stated his approach to it.

Preface

AMONG the remarkable achievements of the Spaniards in the sixteenth century, there is no one more striking to the imagination than the conquest of Mexico. The subversion of a great empire by a handful of adventurers, taken with all its strange and picturesque accompaniments, has the air of romance rather than of sober history; and it is not easy to treat such a theme according to the severe rules prescribed by historical criticism. But, notwithstanding the seductions of the subject, I have conscientiously endeavoured to distinguish fact from fiction, and to establish the narrative on as broad a basis as possible of contemporary evidence. . . .

Although the subject of the work is, properly, only the Conquest of Mexico, I have prepared the way for it by such a view of the Civilization of the ancient Mexicans, as might acquaint the reader with the character of this extraordinary race, and enable him to understand the difficulties which the Spaniards had to encounter in their subjugation. . . .

The story of the Conquest terminates with the fall of the capital. Yet I have preferred to continue the narrative to the death of Cortés, relying on the interest which the development of his character in his military career may have excited in the reader. I am not insensible to the hazard I incur by such a course. The mind, previously occupied with one great idea, that of the subversion of the capital, may feel the prolongation of the story beyond that point superfluous, if not tedious; and may find it difficult, after the excitement caused by witnessing a great national catastrophe, to take an interest in the adventures of a private individual. Solís took the more politic course of concluding his narrative with the fall of Mexico, and thus leaves his readers with the full impression of that memorable event, undisturbed, on their minds. To prolong the narrative is to expose the historian to the error so much censured by the French critics in some of their most celebrated dramas, where the author by a premature *dénouement* has impaired the interest of his piece. It is the defect that necessarily attaches, though in a greater degree, to the history of Columbus, in which petty adventures among a group of islands make up the sequel of a life that opened with the magnificent discovery of a World; a defect, in short, which has required all the genius of Irving and the magical charm of his style perfectly to overcome.

Notwithstanding these objections, I have been induced to continue the narrative, partly from deference to the opinion of several Spanish scholars, who considered that the biography of Cortés had not been fully exhibited, and partly from the circumstance of my having such a body of original materials for this biography at my command. And I cannot regret that I have adopted this course; since, whatever lustre the Conquest may reflect on Cortés as a military achievement, it gives but an imperfect idea of his enlightened spirit, and of his comprehensive and versatile genius.

To the eye of the critic there may seem some incongruity in a plan which combines objects so dissimilar as those embraced by the present history; where the Introduction, occupied with the antiquities and origin of a nation, has somewhat the character of a *philosophic* theme, while the conclusion is strictly *biographical,* and the two may be supposed to match indifferently with the main body, a *historical* portion of the work. But I may hope that such objections will be found to have less weight in practice than in theory; and, if properly managed, that the general views of the Introduction will prepare the reader for the particulars of the Conquest, and that the great public events narrated in this will, without violence, open the way to the remaining personal history of the hero who is the soul of it.

Whatever incongruity may exist in other respects, I may hope that the *unity of interest,* the only unity held of much importance by modern critics, will be found still to be preserved.

The distance of the present age from the period of the narrative might be presumed to secure the historian from undue prejudice or partiality. Yet to American and English readers, acknowledging so different a moral standard from that of the sixteenth century, I may possibly be thought too indulgent to the errors of the Conquerors; while to a Spaniard, accustomed to the undiluted panegyric of Solís, I may be deemed to have dealt too hardly with them. To such I can only say, that, while, on the one hand, I have not hesitated to expose in their strongest colors the excesses of the Conquerors; on the other, I have given them the benefit of such mitigating reflections as might be suggested by the circumstances and the period in which they lived. I have endeavoured not only to present a picture true in itself, but to place it in its proper light, and to put the spectator in a proper point of view for seeing it to the best advantage. I have endeavoured, at the expense of some repetition, to surround him with the spirit of the times, and, in a word, to make him, if I may express myself, a contemporary of the sixteenth century. Whether, and how far, I have succeeded in this, he must determine. . . .

WILLIAM H. PRESCOTT

Boston, October 1, 1843

BOOK ONE

An Introductory View of the
Aztec Civilization

PRESCOTT began by indicating the geographical setting and identifying the primitive peoples of Anahuac, ancient Mexico. Turning to government, he focused attention not only on the laws and revenues but also on the most powerful elements in the political life of the natives.

I

The Power Structure

THE form of government differed in the different states of Anahuac. With the Aztecs and Tezcucans it was monarchical and nearly absolute. The two nations resembled each other so much, in their political institutions, that one of their historians has remarked, in too unqualified a manner indeed, that what is told of one may be always understood as applying to the other. I shall direct my inquiries to the Mexican polity, borrowing an illustration occasionally from that of the rival kingdom.

The government was an elective monarchy. Four of the principal nobles, who had been chosen by their own body in the preceding reign, filled the office of electors, to whom were added, with merely an honorary rank however, the two royal allies of Tezcuco and Tlacopan.* The sovereign was selected from the brothers of the deceased prince, or, in default of them, from his nephews. Thus the election was always restricted to the same family. The candidate preferred must have distinguished himself in war, though, as in the case of the last Montezuma, he were a member of the priesthood. This singular mode of supplying the throne had some advantages. The candidates received an education which fitted them for the royal dignity, while the age, at which they were chosen, not only secured the nation against the evils of minority, but afforded ample means for estimating their qualifications for the office. The result, at all events, was favorable; since the throne, as already noticed, was filled by a succession of able princes, well qualified to rule over a warlike and ambitious people. The scheme of election, however defective, argues a more refined and calculating policy than was to have been expected from a barbarous nation.

The new monarch was installed in his regal dignity with much parade of religious ceremony; but not until, by a victorious campaign, he had obtained a sufficient number of captives to grace his triumphal entry into the capital, and to furnish victims for the dark and bloody rites which stained the Aztec superstition. Amidst this pomp of human sacrifice, he was crowned. The crown, resembling a mitre in its form, and curiously ornamented with gold, gems, and feathers, was placed on his head by the lord of Tezcuco, the most powerful of his royal allies. The title of *King*, by which the earlier Aztec princes are distinguished by Spanish writers, is supplanted by that of *Emperor* in the later reigns, intimating, perhaps, his superiority over the confederated monarchies of Tlacopan and Tezcuco.

The Aztec princes, especially towards the close of the dynasty, lived in a barbaric pomp, truly Oriental. Their spacious palaces were provided with halls for the different councils, who aided the monarch in the transaction of business. The chief of these was a sort of privy council, composed in part, probably, of the four electors chosen by the nobles after the accession, whose places, when made vacant by death, were immediately supplied as before. It was the business of this body, so far as can be gathered from the very loose accounts given of it, to advise the king, in respect to the government of the provinces, the administration of the revenues, and, indeed, on all great matters of public interest.

In the royal buildings were accommodations, also, for a numerous body-guard of the sovereign, made up of the chief nobility. It is not easy to determine with precision, in these barbarian governments, the limits of the several orders. It is certain, there was a distinct class of nobles, with large landed possessions, who held the most important offices near the person of the prince, and engrossed the administration of the provinces and cities. Many of these could trace their descent from the founders of the Aztec monarchy. According to some writers of authority, there were thirty great *caciques*, who had their residence, at least a part of the year, in the capital, and who could muster a hundred thousand vassals each on their estates. Without relying on such wild statements, it is clear, from the testimony of the Conquerors, that the country was occupied by numerous powerful chieftains, who lived like independent princes on their domains. If it be true that the kings encouraged, or, indeed, exacted, the residence of these nobles in the capital, and required hostages in their absence, it is evident that their power must have been very formidable.

Their estates appear to have been held by various tenures, and to have been subject to different restrictions. Some of them, earned by their own good swords, or received as the recompense of public services, were held without any limitation, except that the possessors could not dispose of them to a plebeian. Others were entailed on the eldest male issue, and, in default of such, reverted to the crown. Most of them seem to have been burdened with the obligation of military service. The principal chiefs of Tezcuco, according to its chronicler, were expressly obliged to support their prince with their armed vassals, to attend his court, and aid him in the council. Some, instead of these services, were to provide for the repairs of his buildings, and to keep the royal demesnes in order, with an annual offering, by way of homage, of fruits and flowers. It was usual, if we are to believe historians, for a new king, on his accession, to confirm the investiture of estates derived from the crown.

It cannot be denied that we recognise, in all this, several features of the feudal system, which, no doubt, lose nothing of their effect, under the hands of the Spanish writers, who are fond of tracing analogies to European institutions. But such analogies lead sometimes to very erroneous conclusions. The obligation of military service, for instance, the most essential principle of a fief, seems to be naturally demanded by every government from its subjects. As to minor points of resemblance, they fall far short of that harmonious system of reciprocal service and protection, which embraced, in nice gradation, every order of a feudal monarchy. The kingdoms of Anahuac were, in their nature, despotic, attended, indeed, with many mitigating circumstances, unknown to the despotisms of the East; but it is chimerical to look for much in common—beyond a few accidental forms and ceremonies—with those aristocratic institutions of the Middle Ages, which made the court of every petty baron the precise image in miniature of that of his sovereign. . . .

BECAUSE one basically significant aspect of the Conquest, to Prescott, was the triumph of Christianity over paganism, he understandably directed considerable attention to native beliefs and practices.

II

Religion

IN contemplating the religious system of the Aztecs, one is struck with its apparent incongruity, as if some portion of it had emanated from a comparatively refined people, open to gentle influences, while the rest breathes a spirit of unmitigated ferocity. It naturally suggests the idea of two distinct sources, and authorizes the belief that the Aztecs had inherited from their predecessors a milder faith, on which was afterwards engrafted their own mythology. The latter soon became dominant, and gave its dark coloring to the creeds of the conquered nations,—which the Mexicans, like the ancient Romans, seem willingly to have incorporated into their own,—until the same funereal superstition settled over the farthest borders of Anahuac.

The Aztecs recognised the existence of a supreme Creator and Lord of the universe. They addressed him, in their prayers, as "the God by whom we live," "omnipresent, that knoweth all thoughts, and giveth all gifts," "without whom man is as nothing," "invisible, incorporeal, one God, of *perfect perfection* and purity," "under whose wings we find repose and a sure defence." These sublime attributes infer no inadequate conception of the true God. But the idea of unity—of a being, with whom volition is action, who has no need of inferior ministers to execute his purposes—was too simple, or too vast, for their understandings; and they sought relief, as usual, in a plurality of deities, who presided over the elements, the changes of the seasons, and the various occupations of man. Of these, there were thirteen principal deities, and more than two hundred inferior; to each of whom some special day, or appropriate festival, was consecrated.

At the head of all stood the terrible Huitzilopotchli, the Mexican Mars; although it is doing injustice to the heroic war-god of antiquity to identify him with this sanguinary monster. This was the patron deity of the nation. His fantastic image was loaded with costly ornaments. His temples were the most stately and august of the public edifices; and his altars reeked with the blood of human hecatombs in every city of the empire. Disastrous, indeed, must have been the influence of such a superstition on the character of the people.

A far more interesting personage in their mythology was Quetzalcoatl, god of the air, a divinity who, during his residence on earth, instructed the natives in the use of metals, in agriculture, and in the arts of government. He was one of those benefactors of their species, doubtless, who have been deified by the gratitude of posterity. Under him, the earth teemed with fruits and flowers, without the pains of culture. An ear of Indian corn was as much as a single man could carry. The cotton, as it grew, took, of its own accord, the rich dyes of human art. The air was filled with intoxicating perfumes and the sweet melody of birds. In short, these were the halcyon days, which find a place in the mythic systems of so many nations in the Old World. It was the *golden age* of Anahuac.

From some cause, not explained, Quetzalcoatl incurred the wrath of one of the principal gods, and was compelled to abandon the country. On his way, he stopped at the city of Cholula, where a temple was dedicated to his worship, the massy ruins of which still form one of the most interesting relics of antiquity in Mexico. When he reached the shores of the Mexican Gulf, he took leave of his followers, promising that he and his descendants would revisit them hereafter, and then, entering his wizard skiff, made of serpents' skins, embarked on the great ocean for the fabled land of Tlapallan. He was said to have been tall in stature, with a white skin, long, dark hair, and a flowing beard. The Mexicans looked confidently to the return of the benevolent deity; and this remarkable tradition, deeply cherished in their hearts, prepared the way, as we shall see hereafter, for the future success of the Spaniards.

We have not space for further details respecting the Mexican divinities, the attributes of many of whom were carefully defined, as they descended, in regular gradation, to the *penates* or household gods, whose little images were to be found in the humblest dwelling.

The Aztecs felt the curiosity, common to man in almost every stage of civilization, to lift the veil which covers the mysterious past, and the more awful future. They sought relief, like the nations of the Old Continent, from the oppressive idea of eternity, by breaking it up into distinct cycles, or periods of time, each of several thousand years' duration. There were four of these cycles, and at the end of each, by the agency of one of the elements, the human family was swept from the earth, and the sun blotted out from the heavens, to be again rekindled.

They imagined three separate states of existence in the future life. The wicked, comprehending the greater part of mankind, were to expiate their sins in a place of everlasting darkness. Another class, with no other merit than that of having died of certain diseases, capriciously selected, were to enjoy a negative existence of indolent contentment. The highest place was reserved, as in most warlike nations, for the heroes who fell in battle, or in sacrifice. They passed, at once, into the presence of the Sun, whom they accompanied with songs and choral dances, in the bright progress through the heavens; and, after some years, their spirits went to animate the clouds and singing birds of beautiful plumage, and to revel amidst the rich blossoms and odors of the gardens of paradise. Such was the heaven of the Aztecs; more refined in its character than that of the more polished pagan, whose elysium reflected only the martial sports, or sensual gratifications, of this life. In the destiny they assigned to the wicked, we discern similar traces of refinement; since the absence of all physical torture forms a striking contrast to the schemes of suffering so ingeniously devised by the fancies of the most enlightened nations. In all this, so contrary to the natural suggestions of the ferocious Aztec, we see the evidences of a higher civilization, inherited from their predecessors in the land.

Our limits will allow only a brief allusion to one or two of their most interesting ceremonies. On the death of a person, his corpse was dressed in the peculiar habiliments of his tutelar deity. It was strewed with pieces of paper, which operated as charms against the dangers of the dark road he was to travel. A throng of slaves, if he were rich, was sacrificed at his obsequies. His body was burned, and the ashes, collected in a vase, were preserved in one of the apartments of his house. Here we have successively the usages of the Roman Catholic, the Mussulman, the Tartar, and the Ancient Greek and Roman; curious coincidences, which may show how cautious we should be in adopting conclusions founded on analogy.

A more extraordinary coincidence may be traced with Christian rites, in the ceremony of naming their children. The lips and bosom of the infant were sprinkled with water, and "the Lord was implored to permit the holy drops to wash away the sin that was given to it before the foundation of the world; so that the child might be born anew." We are reminded of Christian morals, in more than one of their prayers, in which they used regular forms. "Wilt thou blot us out, O Lord, for ever? Is this punishment intended, not for our reformation, but for our destruction?" Again, "Impart to us, out of thy great mercy, thy gifts, which we are not worthy to receive through our own merits." "Keep peace with all," says another petition; "bear injuries with humility; God, who sees, will avenge you." But the most striking parallel with Scripture is in the remarkable declaration, that "he, who looks too curiously on a woman, commits adultery with his eyes." These pure and elevated maxims, it is true, are mixed up with others of a puerile, and even brutal character, arguing that confusion of the moral perceptions, which is natural in the twilight of civilization. One would not expect, however, to meet, in such a state of society, with doctrines as sublime as any inculcated by the enlightened codes of ancient philosophy.

But, although the Aztec mythology gathered nothing from the beautiful inventions of the poet, nor from the refinements of philosophy, it was much indebted, as I have noticed, to the priests, who endeavoured to dazzle the imagination of the people by the most formal and pompous ceremonial. The influence of the priesthood must be greatest in an imperfect state of civilization, where it engrosses all the scanty science of the time in its own body. This is particularly the case, when the science is of that spurious kind which is less occupied with the real phenomena of nature, than with the fanciful chimeras of human superstition. Such are the sciences of astrology and divination, in which the Aztec priests were well initiated; and, while they seemed to hold the keys of the future in their own hands, they impressed the ignorant people with sentiments of superstitious awe, beyond that which has probably existed in any other country,—even in ancient Egypt.

The sacerdotal order was very numerous; as may be inferred from the statement, that five thousand priests were, in some way or other, attached to the principal temple in the capital. The various ranks and functions of this multitudinous body were discriminated with great exactness. Those best instructed in music took the management of the choirs. Others arranged the festivals conformably to the calendar. Some superintended the education of youth, and others had charge of the hieroglyphical paintings and oral traditions; while the dismal rites of sacrifice were reserved for the chief dignitaries of the order. At the head of the whole establishment were two high-priests, elected from the order, as it would seem, by the king and principal nobles, without reference to birth, but solely for their qualifications, as shown by their previous conduct in a subordinate station. They were equal in dignity, and inferior only to the sovereign, who rarely acted without their advice in weighty matters of public concern.

The priests were each devoted to the service of some particular deity, and had quarters provided within the spacious precincts of their temple; at least, while engaged in immediate attendance there,—for they were allowed to marry, and have families of their own. In this monastic residence they lived in all the stern severity of conventual discipline. Thrice during the day, and once at night, they were called to prayers. They were frequent in their ablutions and vigils, and mortified the flesh by fasting and cruel penance,—drawing blood from their bodies by flagellation, or by piercing them with the thorns of the aloe; in short, by practising all those austerities to which fanaticism (to borrow the strong language of the poet) has resorted, in every age of the world,

"In hopes to merit heaven by making earth a hell."

The great cities were divided into districts, placed under the charge of a sort of parochial clergy, who regulated every act of religion within their precincts. It is remarkable that they administered the rites of confession and absolution. The secrets of the confessional were held inviolable, and penances were imposed of much the same kind as those enjoined by the Roman Catholic Church. There were two remarkable peculiarities in the Aztec ceremony. The first was, that, as the repetition of an offence, once atoned for, was deemed inexpiable, confession was made but once in a man's life, and was usually deferred to a late period of it, when the penitent unburdened his conscience, and settled, at once, the long arrears of iniquity. Another peculiarity was, that priestly absolution was received in place of the legal punishment of offences, and authorized an acquittal in case of arrest. Long after the Conquest, the simple natives, when they came under the arm of the law, sought to escape by producing the certificate of their confession.

One of the most important duties of the priesthood was that of education, to which certain buildings were appropriated within the inclosure of the principal temple. Here the youth of both sexes, of the higher and middling orders, were placed

at a very tender age. The girls were intrusted to the care of
priestesses; for women were allowed to exercise sacerdotal
functions, except those of sacrifice. In these institutions the
boys were drilled in the routine of monastic discipline; they
decorated the shrines of the gods with flowers, fed the sacred
fires, and took part in the religious chants and festivals. Those
in the higher school—the *Calmecac,* as it was called—were initiated in their traditionary lore, the mysteries of hieroglyphics,
the principles of government, and such branches of astronomical and natural science as were within the compass of the
priesthood. The girls learned various feminine employments,
especially to weave and embroider rich coverings for the altars
of the gods. Great attention was paid to the moral discipline
of both sexes. The most perfect decorum prevailed; the offences
were punished with extreme rigor, in some instances with death
itself. Terror, not love, was the spring of education with the
Aztecs.

At a suitable age for marrying, or for entering into the world,
the pupils were dismissed, with much ceremony, from the convent, and the recommendation of the principal often introduced
those most competent to responsible situations in public life.
Such was the crafty policy of the Mexican priests, who, by re-
serving to themselves the business of instruction, were enabled
to mould the young and plastic mind according to their own
wills, and to train it early to implicit reverence for religion and
its ministers; a reverence which still maintained its hold on the
iron nature of the warrior, long after every other vestige of education had been effaced by the rough trade to which he was
devoted.

To each of the principal temples, lands were annexed for
the maintenance of the priests. These estates were augmented
by the policy or devotion of successive princes, until, under
the last Montezuma, they had swollen to an enormous extent,
and covered every district of the empire. The priests took the
management of their property into their own hands; and they
seem to have treated their tenants with the liberality and

indulgence characteristic of monastic corporations. Besides
the large supplies drawn from this source, the religious order
was enriched with the first-fruits, and such other offerings as
piety or superstition dictated. The surplus beyond what was
required for the support of the national worship was distributed
in alms among the poor; a duty strenuously prescribed by their
moral code. Thus we find the same religion inculcating lessons
of pure philanthropy, on the one hand, and of merciless extermi-
nation, as we shall soon see, on the other. The inconsistency
will not appear incredible to those who are familiar with the history of the Roman Catholic Church, in the early ages of the
Inquisition.

The Mexican temples—*teocallis,* "houses of God," as they
were called—were very numerous. There were several hundred
in each of the principal cities, many of them, doubtless, very
humble edifices. They were solid masses of earth, cased with
brick, or stone, and in their form somewhat resembled the
pyramidal structures of ancient Egypt. The bases of many of
them were more than a hundred feet square, and they towered
to a still greater height. They were distributed into four or five
stories, each of smaller dimensions than that below. The ascent
was by a flight of steps, at an angle of the pyramid, on the outside. This led to a sort of terrace, or gallery, at the base of the
second story, which passed quite round the building to another
flight of stairs, commencing also at the same angle as the preceding and directly over it, and leading to a similar terrace; so that
one had to make the circuit of the temple several times, before
reaching the summit. In some instances the stairway led directly up the centre of the western face of the building. The top
was a broad area, on which were erected one or two towers,
forty or fifty feet high, the sanctuaries in which stood the sacred
images of the presiding deities. Before these towers stood the
dreadful stone of sacrifice, and two lofty altars, on which fires
were kept, as inextinguishable as those in the temple of Vesta.
There were said to be six hundred of these altars, on smaller
buildings within the inclosure of the great temple of Mexico,

which, with those on the sacred edifices in other parts of the city, shed a brilliant illumination over its streets, through the darkest night.

From the construction of their templès, all religious services were public. The long processions of priests, winding round their massive sides, as they rose higher and higher towards the summit, and the dismal rites of sacrifice performed there, were all visible from the remotest corners of the capital, impressing on the spectator's mind a superstitious veneration for the mysteries of his religion, and for the dread ministers by whom they were interpreted.

This impression was kept in full force by their numerous festivals. Every month was consecrated to some protecting deity; and every week, nay, almost every day, was set down in their calendar for some appropriate celebration; so that it is difficult to understand how the ordinary business of life could have been compatible with the exactions of religion. Many of their ceremonies were of a light and cheerful complexion, consisting of the national songs and dances, in which both sexes joined. Processions were made of women and children crowned with garlands and bearing offerings of fruits, the ripened maize, or the sweet incense of copal and other odoriferous gums, while the altars of the deity were stained with no blood save that of animals. Those were the peaceful rites derived from their Toltec predecessors, on which the fierce Aztecs engrafted a superstition too loathsome to be exhibited in all its nakedness, and one over which I would gladly draw a veil altogether, but that it would leave the reader in ignorance of their most striking institution, and one that had the greatest influence in forming the national character.

Human sacrifices were adopted by the Aztecs early in the fourteenth century, about two hundred years before the Conquest. Rare at first, they became more frequent with the wider extent of their empire; till, at length, almost every festival was closed with this cruel abomination. These religious ceremonials were generally arranged in such a manner as to afford a type of the most prominent circumstances in the character or history of the deity who was the object of them. A single example will suffice.

One of their most important festivals was that in honor of the god Tezcatlipoca, whose rank was inferior only to that of the Supreme Being. He was called "the soul of the world," and supposed to have been its creator. He was depicted as a handsome man, endowed with perpetual youth. A year before the intended sacrifice, a captive, distinguished for his personal beauty, and without a blemish on his body, was selected to represent this deity. Certain tutors took charge of him, and instructed him how to perform his new part with becoming grace and dignity. He was arrayed in a splendid dress, regaled with incense and with a profusion of sweet-scented flowers, of which the ancient Mexicans were as fond as their descendants at the present day. When he went abroad, he was attended by a train of royal pages, and, as he halted in the streets to play some favorite melody, the crowd prostrated themselves before him, and did him homage as the representative of their good deity. In this way he led an easy, luxurious life, till within a month of his sacrifice. Four beautiful girls, bearing the names of the principal goddesses, were then selected to share the honors of his bed; and with them he continued to live in idle dalliance, feasted at the banquets of the principal nobles, who paid him all the honors of a divinity.

At length the fatal day of sacrifice arrived. The term of his short-lived glories was at an end. He was stripped of his gaudy apparel, and bade adieu to the fair partners of his revelries. One of the royal barges transported him across the lake to a temple which rose on its margin, about a league from the city. Hither the inhabitants of the capital flocked, to witness the consummation of the ceremony. As the sad procession wound up the sides of the pyramid, the unhappy victim threw away his gay chaplets of flowers, and broke in pieces the musical instruments with which he had solaced the hours of captivity. On the summit he was received by six priests, whose long and matted locks flowed disorderly over their sable robes, covered with hieroglyphic scrolls of mystic import. They led him to the sacrificial stone, a huge block of jasper, with its upper surface somewhat convex. On this the prisoner was stretched. Five priests secured his head and his limbs; while the sixth, clad in a scarlet mantle, emblematic of his bloody office, dexterously opened the breast of the wretched victim with a sharp razor of *itztli,*—a volcanic substance, hard as flint,—and, inserting his hand in the wound, tore out the palpitating heart. The minister of death, first holding this up towards the sun, an object of worship throughout Anahuac, cast it at the feet of the deity to whom the temple was devoted, while the multitudes below prostrated themselves in humble adoration. The tragic story of this prisoner was expounded by the priests as the type of human destiny, which, brilliant in its commencement, too often closes in sorrow and disaster. . . .

AN admirer of the intellectual achievements of the Aztecs, Prescott assessed, among other things, their hieroglyphical writing and manuscripts, their system of arithmetical notation, and their calendar.

III

Learning

THE Aztecs had various emblems for expressing such things as, from their nature, could not be directly represented by the painter; as, for example, the years, months, days, the seasons, the elements, the heavens, and the like. A "tongue" denoted speaking; a "foot-print," travelling; a "man sitting on the ground," an earthquake. These symbols were often very arbitrary, varying with the caprice of the writer; and it requires a nice discrimination to interpret them, as a slight change in the form or position of the figure intimated a very different meaning. An ingenious writer asserts that the priests devised secret symbolic characters for the record of their religious mysteries. It is possible. But the researches of Champollion lead to the conclusion, that the similar opinion, formerly entertained respecting the Egyptian hieroglyphics, is without foundation.

Lastly, they employed, as above stated, phonetic signs, though these were chiefly confined to the names of persons and places; which, being derived from some circumstance, or characteristic quality, were accommodated to the hieroglyphical system. Thus the town *Cimatlan* was compounded of *cimatl,* a "root," which grew near it, and *tlan,* signifying "near"; *Tlaxcallan* meant "the place of bread," from its rich fields of corn; *Huexotzinco,* "a place surrounded by willows." The names of persons were often significant of their adventures and achievements. That of the great Tezcucan prince, Nezahualcoyotl, signified "hungry fox," intimating his sagacity, and his

distresses in early life. The emblems of such names were no
sooner seen, than they suggested to every Mexican the person
and place intended; and, when painted on their shields, or
embroidered on their banners, became the armorial bearings,
by which city and chieftain were distinguished, as in Europe,
in the age of chivalry.

But, although the Aztecs were instructed in all the varieties
of hieroglyphical painting, they chiefly resorted to the clumsy
method of direct representation. Had their empire lasted, like
the Egyptian, several thousand, instead of the brief space of
two hundred years, they would, doubtless, like them, have
advanced to the more frequent use of the phonetic writing.
But, before they could be made acquainted with the capabilities
of their own system, the Spanish Conquest, by introducing the
European alphabet, supplied their scholars with a more perfect
contrivance for expressing thought, which soon supplanted the
ancient pictorial character.

Clumsy as it was, however, the Aztec picture-writing seems
to have been adequate to the demands of the nation, in their
imperfect state of civilization. By means of it were recorded all
their laws, and even their regulations for domestic economy;
their tribute-rolls, specifying the imposts of the various towns;
their mythology, calendars, and rituals; their political annals,
carried back to a period long before the foundation of the city.
They digested a complete system of chronology, and could
specify with accuracy the dates of the most important events
in their history; the year being inscribed on the margin, against
the particular circumstance recorded. It is true, history, thus
executed, must necessarily be vague and fragmentary. Only a
few leading incidents could be presented. But in this it did not
differ much from the monkish chronicles of the dark ages,
which often dispose of years in a few brief sentences;—quite
long enough for the annals of barbarians.

In order to estimate aright the picture-writing of the Aztecs,
one must regard it in connexion with oral tradition, to which
it was auxiliary. In the colleges of the priests the youth were

instructed in astronomy, history, mythology, &c.; and those who were to follow the profession of hieroglyphical painting were taught the application of the characters appropriated to each of these branches. In an historical work, one had charge of the chronology, another of the events. Every part of the labor was thus mechanically distributed. The pupils, instructed in all that was before known in their several departments, were prepared to extend still further the boundaries of their imperfect science. The hieroglyphics served as a sort of stenography, a collection of notes, suggesting to the initiated much more than could be conveyed by a literal interpretation. This combination of the written and the oral comprehended what may be called the literature of the Aztecs.

Their manuscripts were made of different materials—of cotton cloth, or skins nicely prepared; of a composition of silk and gum; but, for the most part, of a fine fabric from the leaves of the aloe, *agave Americana,* called by the natives, *maguey,* which grows luxuriantly over the table-lands of Mexico. A sort of paper was made from it, resembling somewhat the Egyptian *papyrus,* which, when properly dressed and polished, is said to have been more soft and beautiful than parchment. Some of the specimens, still existing, exhibit their original freshness, and the paintings on them retain their brilliancy of colors. They were sometimes done up into rolls, but more frequently into volumes, of moderate size, in which the paper was shut up, like a folding-screen, with a leaf or tablet of wood at each extremity, that gave the whole, when closed, the appearance of a book. The length of the strips was determined only by convenience. As the pages might be read and referred to separately, this form had obvious advantages over the rolls of the ancients. . . .

A few of the Mexican manuscripts have found their way, from time to time, to Europe, and are carefully preserved in the public libraries of its capitals. They are brought together in the magnificent work of Lord Kingsborough; but not one is there from Spain. The most important of them, for the light it throws on the Aztec institutions, is the Mendoza Codex; which, after its mysterious disappearance for more than a century, has at length reappeared in the Bodleian library at Oxford. It has been several times engraved. The most brilliant in coloring, probably, is the Borgian collection, in Rome. The most curious, however, is the Dresden Codex, which has excited less attention than it deserves. Although usually classed among Mexican manuscripts, it bears little resemblance to them in its execution; the figures of objects are more delicately drawn, and the characters, unlike the Mexican, appear to be purely arbitrary, and are possibly phonetic. Their regular arrangement is quite equal to the Egyptian. The whole infers a much higher civilization than the Aztec, and offers abundant food for curious speculation.

Some few of these maps have interpretations annexed to them, which were obtained from the natives after the Conquest. The greater part are without any, and cannot now be unriddled. Had the Mexicans made free use of a phonetic alphabet, it might have been originally easy, by mastering the comparatively few signs employed in this kind of communication, to have got a permanent key to the whole. A brief inscription has furnished a clue to the vast labyrinth of Egyptian hieroglyphics. But the Aztec characters, representing individuals, or, at most, species, require to be made out separately; a hopeless task, for which little aid is to be expected from the vague and general tenor of the few interpretations now existing. There was, as already mentioned, until late in the last century, a professor in the University of Mexico, especially devoted to the study of the national picture-writing. But, as this was with a view to legal proceedings, his information, probably, was limited to deciphering titles. In less than a hundred years after the Conquest, the knowledge of the hieroglyphics had so far declined, that a diligent Tezcucan writer complains he could find in the country only two persons, both very aged, at all competent to interpret them.

It is not probable, therefore, that the art of reading these picture-writings will ever be recovered; a circumstance certainly to be regretted. Not that the records of a semi-civilized people would be likely to contain any new truth or discovery important to human comfort or progress; but they could scarcely fail to throw some additional light on the previous history of the nation, and that of the more polished people who before occupied the country. This would be still more probable, if any literary relics of their Toltec predecessors were preserved; and, if report be true, an important compilation from this source was extant at the time of the invasion, and may have perhaps contributed to swell the holocaust of Zumárraga. It is no great stretch of fancy, to suppose that such records might reveal the successive links in the mighty chain of migration of the primitive races, and, by carrying us back to the seat of their possessions in the Old World, have solved the mystery which has so long perplexed the learned, in regard to the settlement and civilization of the New.

Besides the hieroglyphical maps, the traditions of the country were embodied in the songs and hymns, which, as already mentioned, were carefully taught in the public schools. These were various, embracing the mythic legends of a heroic age, the warlike achievements of their own, or the softer tales of love and pleasure. Many of them were composed by scholars and persons of rank, and are cited as affording the most authentic record of events. The Mexican dialect was rich and expressive, though inferior to the Tezcucan, the most polished of the idioms of Anahuac. None of the Aztec compositions have survived, but we can form some estimate of the general state of poetic culture from the odes which have come down to us from the royal house of Tezcuco. Sahagún has furnished us with translations of their more elaborate prose, consisting of prayers and public discourses, which give a favorable idea of their eloquence, and show that they paid much attention to rhetorical effect. They are said to have had, also, something like theatrical exhibitions, of a pantomimic sort, in which the faces of the performers were covered with masks, and the figures of birds or animals were frequently represented; an imitation, to which they may have been led by the familiar delineation of such objects in their hieroglyphics. In all this we see the dawning of a literary culture, surpassed, however, by their attainments in the severer walks of mathematical science.

They devised a system of notation in their arithmetic, sufficiently simple. The first twenty numbers were expressed by a corresponding number of dots. The first five had specific names; after which they were represented by combining the fifth with one of the four preceding; as five and one for six, five and two for seven, and so on. Ten and fifteen had each a separate name, which was also combined with the first four, to express a higher quantity. These four, therefore, were the radical characters of their oral arithmetic, in the same manner as they were of the written with the ancient Romans; a more simple arrangement, probably, than any existing among Europeans. Twenty was expressed by a separate hieroglyphic,—a flag. Larger sums were reckoned by twenties, and, in writing, by repeating the number of flags. The square of twenty, four hundred, had a separate sign, that of a plume, and so had the cube of twenty, or eight thousand, which was denoted by a purse, or sack. This was the whole arithmetical apparatus of the Mexicans, by the combination of which they were enabled to indicate any quantity. For greater expedition, they used to denote fractions of the larger sums by drawing only a part of the object. Thus, half or three fourths of a plume, or of a purse, represented that proportion of their respective sums, and so on. With all this, the machinery will appear very awkward to us, who perform our operations with so much ease, by means of the Arabic, or rather, Indian ciphers. It is not much more awkward, however, than the system pursued by the great mathematicians of antiquity, unacquainted with the brilliant invention, which has given a new aspect to mathematical science, of determining the value, in a great measure, by the relative position of the figures.

In the measurement of time, the Aztecs adjusted their civil

year by the solar. They divided it into eighteen months of twenty days each. Both months and days were expressed by peculiar hieroglyphics,—those of the former often intimating the season of the year, like the French months, at the period of the Revolution. Five complementary days, as in Egypt, were added, to make up the full number of three hundred and sixty-five. They belonged to no month, and were regarded as peculiarly unlucky. A month was divided into four weeks, of five days each, on the last of which was the public fair, or market day. This arrangement, differing from that of the nations of the Old Continent, whether of Europe or Asia, has the advantage of giving an equal number of days to each month, and of comprehending entire weeks, without a fraction, both in the months and in the year.

As the year is composed of nearly six hours more than three hundred and sixty-five days, there still remained an excess, which, like other nations who have framed a calendar, they provided for by intercalation; not, indeed, every fourth year, as the Europeans, but at longer intervals, like some of the Asiatics. They waited till the expiration of fifty-two vague years, when they interposed thirteen days, or rather twelve and a half, this being the number which had fallen in arrear. Had they inserted thirteen, it would have been too much, since the annual excess over three hundred and sixty-five is about eleven minutes less than six hours. But, as their calendar, at the time of the Conquest, was found to correspond with the European, (making allowance for the subsequent Gregorian reform,) they would seem to have adopted the shorter period of twelve days and a half, which brought them, within an almost inappreciable fraction, to the exact length of the tropical year, as established by the most accurate observations. Indeed, the intercalation of twenty-five days, in every hundred and four years, shows a nicer adjustment of civil to solar time than is presented by any European calendar; since more than five centuries must elapse, before the loss of an entire day. Such was the astonishing precision displayed by the Aztecs, or, perhaps, by their more polished Toltec predecessors, in these computations, so difficult as to have baffled, till a comparatively recent period, the most enlightened nations of Christendom!

THE primitive agriculture of the Aztecs, however basic to their culture, did not draw the attention that their mechanical arts, commerce, and manners received.

IV

Economic Endeavors and Social Forms

THE Mexicans were as well acquainted with the mineral, as with the vegetable treasures of their kingdom. Silver, lead, and tin they drew from the mines of Tasco; copper from the mountains of Zacotollan. These were taken, not only from the crude masses on the surface, but from veins wrought in the solid rock, into which they opened extensive galleries. In fact, the traces of their labors furnished the best indications for the early Spanish miners. Gold, found on the surface, or gleaned from the beds of rivers, was cast into bars, or, in the form of dust, made part of the regular tribute of the southern provinces of the empire. The use of iron, with which the soil was impregnated, was unknown to them. Notwithstanding its abundance, it demands so many processes to prepare it for use, that it has commonly been one of the last metals pressed into the service of man. The age of iron has followed that of brass, in fact as well as in fiction.

They found a substitute in an alloy of tin and copper; and, with tools made of this bronze, could cut not only metals, but, with the aid of a silicious dust, the hardest substances, as basalt, porphyry, amethysts, and emeralds. They fashioned these last, which were found very large, into many curious and fantastic forms. They cast, also, vessels of gold and silver, carving them with their metallic chisels in a very delicate manner. Some of the silver vases were so large that a man could not encircle them with his arms. They imitated very nicely the figures of animals, and, what was extraordinary, could mix the metals in such a manner, that the feathers of a bird, or the scales of a fish, should be alternately of gold and silver. The Spanish goldsmiths admitted their superiority over themselves in these ingenious works.

They employed another tool, made of *itztli*, or obsidian, a dark transparent mineral, exceedingly hard, found in abundance in their hills. They made it into knives, razors, and their serrated swords. It took a keen edge, though soon blunted. With this they wrought the various stones and alabasters employed in the construction of their public works and principal dwellings. I shall defer a more particular account of these to the body of the narrative, and will only add here that the entrances and angles of the buildings were profusely ornamented with images, sometimes of their fantastic deities, and frequently of animals. The latter were executed with great accuracy. "The former," according to Torquemada, "were the hideous reflection of their own souls. And it was not till after they had been converted to Christianity, that they could model the true figure of a man." The old chronicler's facts are well founded, whatever we may think of his reasons. The allegorical phantasms of his religion, no doubt, gave a direction to the Aztec artist, in his delineation of the human figure; supplying him with an imaginary beauty in the personification of divinity itself. As these superstitions lost their hold on his mind, it opened to the influences of a purer taste; and, after the Conquest, the Mexicans furnished many examples of correct, and some of beautiful portraiture.

Sculptured images were so numerous, that the foundations of the cathedral in the *plaza mayor*, the great square of Mexico, are said to be entirely composed of them. This spot may, indeed, be regarded as the Aztec forum,—the great depository of the treasures of ancient sculpture, which now lie hid in its bosom. Such monuments are spread all over the capital, however, and a new cellar can hardly be dug, or foundation laid, without turning up some of the mouldering relics of barbaric art. But they are little heeded, and, if not wantonly broken in pieces at once, are usually worked into the rising wall, or supports of the new edifice. Two celebrated bas-reliefs, of the last Montezuma and his father, cut in the solid rock, in the beautiful groves of Chapoltepec, were deliberately destroyed, as late as the last century, by order of the government! The monuments of the barbarian meet with as little respect from civilized man, as those of the civilized man from the barbarian.

The most remarkable piece of sculpture yet disinterred is the great calendar-stone. . . . It consists of dark porphyry, and, in its original dimensions, as taken from the quarry, is computed to have weighed nearly fifty tons. It was transported from the mountains beyond Lake Chalco, a distance of many leagues, over a broken country intersected by water-courses and canals. In crossing a bridge which traversed one of these latter, in the capital, the supports gave way, and the huge mass was precipitated into the water, whence it was with difficulty recovered. The fact, that so enormous a fragment of porphyry could be thus safely carried for leagues, in the face of such obstacles, and without the aid of cattle,—for the Aztecs, as already mentioned, had no animals of draught,—suggests to us no mean ideas of their mechanical skill, and of their machinery; and implies a degree of cultivation, little inferior to that demanded for the geometrical and astronomical science displayed in the inscriptions on this very stone.

The ancient Mexicans made utensils of earthen ware for the ordinary purposes of domestic life, numerous specimens of which still exist. They made cups and vases of a lackered or painted wood, impervious to wet and gaudily colored. Their dyes were obtained from both mineral and vegetable substances. Among them was the rich crimson of the cochineal, the modern rival of the famed Tyrian purple. It was introduced into Europe from Mexico, where the curious little insect was nourished with great care on plantations of cactus, since fallen into neglect. The natives were thus enabled to give a brilliant coloring to the webs, which were manufactured of every degree of fineness, from the cotton raised in abundance throughout the warmer regions of the country. They had the art, also, of interweaving with these the delicate hair of rabbits and other animals, which made a cloth of great warmth as well as beauty, of a kind altogether original; and on this they often laid a rich embroidery, of birds, flowers, or some other fanciful device.

But the art in which they most delighted was their *plumaje,* or feather-work. With this they could produce all the effect of a beautiful mosaic. The gorgeous plumage of the tropical birds, especially of the parrot tribe, afforded every variety of color; and the fine down of the humming-bird, which revelled in swarms among the honeysuckle bowers of Mexico, supplied them with soft aërial tints that gave an exquisite finish to the picture. The feathers, pasted on a fine cotton web, were wrought into dresses for the wealthy, hangings for apartments, and ornaments for the temples. No one of the American fabrics excited such admiration in Europe, whither numerous specimens were sent by the Conquerors. It is to be regretted that so graceful an art should have been suffered to fall into decay.

There were no shops in Mexico, but the various manufactures and agricultural products were brought together for sale in the great market-places of the principal cities. Fairs were held there every fifth day, and were thronged by a numerous concourse of persons, who came to buy or sell from all the neighbouring country. A particular quarter was allotted to each kind of article. The numerous transactions were conducted without confusion, and with entire regard to justice, under the inspection of magistrates appointed for the purpose. The traffic was carried on partly by barter, and partly by means of a regulated currency, of different values. This consisted of transparent quills of gold dust; of bits of tin, cut in the form of a T; and of bags of cacao, containing a specified number of grains. "Blessed money," claims Peter Martyr, "which exempts its possessors from avarice, since it cannot be long hoarded, nor hidden under ground!"

There did not exist in Mexico that distinction of castes found
among the Egyptian and Asiatic nations. It was usual, however,
for the son to follow the occupation of his father. The different
trades were arranged into something like guilds; having, each,
a particular district of the city appropriated to it, with its own
chief, is own tutelar deity, its peculiar festivals, and the like.
Trade was held in avowed estimation by the Aztecs. "Apply
thyself, my son," was the advice of an aged chief, "to agriculture, or to feather-work, or some other honorable calling. Thus
did your ancestors before you. Else, how would they have provided for themselves and their families? Never was it heard,
that nobility alone was able to maintain its possessor." Shrewd
maxims, that must have sounded somewhat strange in the ear
of a Spanish *hidalgo!*

But the occupation peculiarly respected was that of the
merchant. It formed so important and singular a feature of
their social economy, as to merit a much more particular notice
that it has received from historians. The Aztec merchant was a
sort of itinerant trader, who made his journeys to the remotest
borders of Anahuac, and to the countries beyond, carrying with
him merchandise of rich stuffs, jewelry, slaves, and other valuable commodities. The slaves were obtained at the great market
of Azcapozalco, not many leagues from the capital, where fairs
were regularly held for the sale of these unfortunate beings.
They were brought thither by their masters, dressed in their
gayest apparel, and instructed to sing, dance, and display their
little stock of personal accomplishments, so as to recommend
themselves to the purchaser. Slave-dealing was an honorable
calling among the Aztecs.

With this rich freight, the merchant visited the different
provinces, always bearing some present of value from his own
sovereign to their chiefs, and usually receiving others in return,
with a permission to trade. Should this be denied him, or
should he meet with indignity or violence, he had the means
of resistance in his power. He performed his journeys with a
number of companions of his own rank, and a large body of

inferior attendants who were employed to transport the goods. Fifty or sixty pounds were the usual load for a man. The whole caravan went armed, and so well provided against sudden hostilities, that they could make good their defence, if necessary, till reinforced from home. In one instance, a body of these militant traders stood a siege of four years in the town of Ayotlán, which they finally took from the enemy. Their own government, however, was always prompt to embark in a war on this ground, finding it a very convenient pretext for extending the Mexican empire. It was not unusual to allow the merchants to raise levies themselves, which were placed under their command. It was, moreover, very common for the prince to employ the merchants as a sort of spies, to furnish him information of the state of the countries through which they passed, and the dispositions of the inhabitants towards himself.

Thus their sphere of action was much enlarged beyond that of a humble trader, and they acquired a high consideration in the body politic. They were allowed to assume insignia and devices of their own. Some of their number composed what is called by the Spanish writers a council of finance; at least, this was the case in Tezcuco. They were much consulted by the monarch, who had some of them constantly near his person; addressing them by the title of "uncle," which may remind one of that of *primo,* or "cousin," by which a grandee of Spain is saluted by his sovereign. They were allowed to have their own courts, in which civil and criminal cases, not excepting capital, were determined; so that they formed an independent community, as it were, of themselves. And, as their various traffic supplied them with abundant stores of wealth, they enjoyed many of the most essential advantages of an hereditary aristocracy.

That trade should prove the path to eminent political preferment in a nation but partially civilized, where the names of soldier and priest are usually the only titles to respect, is certainly an anomaly in history. It forms some contrast to the standard of the more polished monarchies of the Old World, in which rank is supposed to be less dishonored by a life of idle ease or frivolous pleasure, than by those active pursuits which promote equally the prosperity of the state and of the individual. If civilization corrects many prejudices, it must be allowed that it creates others.

We shall be able to form a better idea of the actual refinement of the natives, by penetrating into their domestic life and observing the intercourse between the sexes. We have fortunately the means of doing this. We shall there find the ferocious Aztec frequently displaying all the sensibility of a cultivated nature; consoling his friends under affliction, or congratulating them on their good fortune, as on occasion of a marriage, or of the birth or baptism of a child, when he was punctilious in his visits, bringing presents of costly dresses and ornaments, or the more simple offering of flowers, equally indicative of his sympathy. The visits, at these times, though regulated with all the precision of Oriental courtesy, were accompanied by expressions of the most cordial and affectionate regard.

The discipline of children, especially at the public schools, as stated in a previous chapter, was exceedingly severe. But after she had come to a mature age, the Aztec maiden was treated by her parents with a tenderness, from which all reserve seemed banished. In the counsels to a daughter about to enter into life, they conjured her to preserve simplicity in her manners and conversation, uniform neatness in her attire, with strict attention to personal cleanliness. They inculcated modesty, as the great ornament of a woman, and implicit reverence for her husband; softening their admonitions by such endearing epithets, as showed the fulness of a parent's love.

Polygamy was permitted among the Mexicans, though chiefly confined, probably, to the wealthiest classes. And the obligations of the marriage vow, which was made with all the formality of a religious ceremony, were fully recognised, and impressed on both parties. The women are described by the Spaniards as pretty, unlike their unfortunate descendants, of the present day, though with the same serious and rather melancholy cast of countenance. Their long black hair, covered, in some parts of the country, by a veil made of the fine web of the *pita,* might generally be seen wreathed with flowers, or, among the richer people, with strings of precious stones, and pearls from the Gulf of California. They appear to have been treated with much consideration by their husbands; and passed their time in indolent tranquillity, or in such feminine occupations as spinning, embroidery, and the like; while their maidens beguiled the hours by the rehearsal of traditionary tales and ballads.

The women partook equally with the men of social festivities and entertainments. These were often conducted on a large scale, both as regards the number of guests and the costliness of the preparations. Numerous attendants, of both sexes, waited at the banquet. The halls were scented with perfumes, and the courts strewed with odoriferous herbs and flowers, which were distributed in profusion among the guests, as they arrived. Cotton napkins and ewers of water were placed before them, as they took their seats at the board; for the venerable ceremony of ablution, before and after eating, was punctiliously observed by the Aztecs. Tobacco was then offered to the company, in pipes, mixed up with aromatic substances, or in the form of cigars, inserted in tubes of tortoise-shell or silver. They compressed the nostrils with the fingers, while they inhaled the smoke, which they frequently swallowed. Whether the women, who sat apart from the men at table, were allowed the indulgence of the fragrant weed, as in the most polished circles of modern Mexico, is not told us. It is a curious fact, that the Aztecs also took the dried leaf in the pulverized form of snuff.

The table was well provided with substantial meats, especially game; among which the most conspicuous was the turkey, erroneously supposed, as its name imports, to have come originally from the East. These more solid dishes were flanked by others of vegetables and fruits, of every delicious variety found on the North American continent. The different viands were prepared in various ways, with delicate sauces and seasoning, of which the Mexicans were very fond. . . .

The Aztec character was perfectly original and unique. It was made up of incongruities apparently irreconcilable. It blended into one the marked peculiarities of different nations, not only of the same phase of civilization, but as far removed from each other as the extremes of barbarism and refinement. It may find a fitting parallel in their own wonderful climate, capable of producing, on a few square leagues of surface, the boundless variety of vegetable forms, which belong to the frozen regions of the North, the temperate zone of Europe, and the burning skies of Arabia and Hindostan!

BOOK TWO

Discovery of Mexico

HAVING described the land to be invaded and the people to be encountered, Prescott introduced the Spanish leader who, in the wake of Francisco Hernández de Córdoba and Juan de Grijalva, would lead the third Spanish expedition westward from Cuba.

I

Cortés and His Project

HERNANDO CORTÉS was born at Medellín, a town in the southeast corner of Estremadura, in 1485. He came of an ancient and respectable family; and historians have gratified the national vanity by tracing it up to the Lombard kings, whose descendants crossed the Pyrenees, and established themselves in Aragon under the Gothic monarchy. This royal genealogy was not found out till Cortés had acquired a name which would confer distinction on any descent, however noble. His father, Martín Cortés de Monroy, was a captain of infantry, in moderate circumstances, but a man of unblemished honor; and both he and his wife, Doña Catalina Pizarro Altamirano, appear to have been much regarded for their excellent qualities.

In his infancy Cortés is said to have had a feeble constitution, which strengthened as he grew older. At fourteen, he was sent to Salamanca, as his father, who conceived great hopes from his quick and showy parts, proposed to educate him for the law, a profession which held out better inducements to the young aspirant than any other. The son, however, did not conform to these views. He showed little fondness for books, and, after loitering away two years at college, returned home, to the great chagrin of his parents. Yet his time had not been wholly misspent, since he had laid up a little store of Latin, and learned to write good prose, and even verses "of some estimation, considering"—as an old writer quaintly remarks—

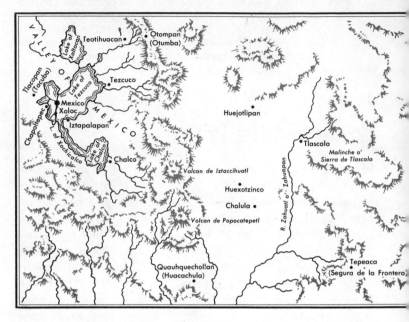

Adapted from William H. Prescott's *The History of the Conquest of Mexico.*

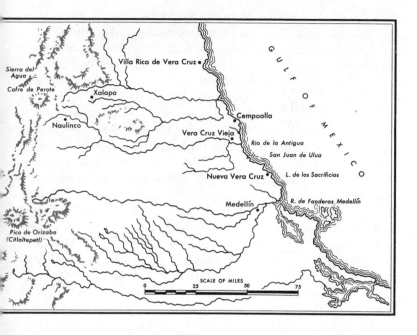

Sierra del Agua

Cofre de Perote

Villa Rica de Vera Cruz •

Xalapa

Naulinco

Cempoalla

Vera Cruz Vieja

Rio de la Antigua

San Juan de Ulua

Nueva Vera Cruz •

L. de los Sacrificios

Medellín

R. de Fanderas Medellín

Pico de Orizaba
(Citlaltepetl)

GULF OF MEXICO

SCALE OF MILES

0   25   50   75

"Cortés as the author." He now passed his days in the idle, unprofitable manner of one who, too wilful to be guided by others, proposes no object to himself. His buoyant spirits were continually breaking out in troublesome frolics and capricious humors, quite at variance with the orderly habits of his father's household. He showed a particular inclination for the military profession, or rather for the life of adventure to which in those days it was sure to lead. And when, at the age of seventeen, he proposed to enrol himself under the banners of the Great Captain, his parents, probably thinking a life of hardship and hazard abroad preferable to one of idleness at home, made no objection.

The youthful cavalier, however, hesitated whether to seek his fortunes under that victorious chief, or in the New World, where gold as well as glory was to be won, and where the very dangers had a mystery and romance in them inexpressibly fascinating to a youthful fancy. It was in this direction, accordingly, that the hot spirits of that day found a vent, especially from that part of the country where Cortés lived, the neighbourhood of Seville and Cádiz, the focus of nautical enterprise. He decided on this latter course, and an opportunity offered in the splendid armament fitted out under Don Nicolás de Ovando, successor to Columbus. An unlucky accident defeated the purpose of Cortés.

As he was scaling a high wall, one night, which gave him access to the apartment of a lady with whom he was engaged in an intrigue, the stones gave way, and he was thrown down with much violence and buried under the ruins. A severe contusion, though attended with no other serious conquences, confined him to his bed till after the departure of the fleet.

Two years longer he remained at home, profiting little, as it would seem, from the lesson he had received. At length he availed himself of another opportunity presented by the departure of a small squadron of vessels bound to the Indian islands. He was nineteen years of age, when he bade adieu to his native shores in 1504,—the same year in which Spain lost the best and greatest in her long line of princes, Isabella the Catholic.

The vessel in which Cortés sailed was commanded by one Alonso Quintero. The fleet touched at the Canaries, as was common in the outward passage. While the other vessels were detained there taking in supplies, Quintero secretly stole out by night from the island, with the design of reaching Hispaniola, and securing the market, before the arrival of his companions. A furious storm, which he encountered, however, dismasted his ship, and he was obliged to return to port and refit. The convoy consented to wait for their unworthy partner, and after a short detention they all sailed in company again. But the faithless Quintero, as they drew near the Islands, availed himself once more of the darkness of the night, to leave the squadron with the same purpose as before. Unluckily for him, he met with a succession of heavy gales and head winds, which drove him from his course, and he wholly lost his reckoning. For many days the vessel was tossed about, and all on board were filled with apprehensions, and no little indignation against the author of their calamities. At length they were cheered one morning with the sight of a white dove, which, wearied by its flight, lighted on the topmast. The biographers of Cortés speak of it as a miracle. Fortunately it was no miracle, but a very natural occurrence, showing incontestably that they were near land. In a short time, by taking the direction of the bird's flight, they reached the island of Hispaniola; and, on coming into port, the worthy master had the satisfaction to find his companions arrived before him, and their cargoes already sold.

Immediately on landing, Cortés repaired to the house of the governor, to whom he had been personally known in Spain. Ovando was absent on an expedition into the interior, but the young man was kindly received by the secretary, who assured him there would be no doubt of his obtaining a liberal grant of land to settle on. "But I came to get gold," replied Cortés, "not to till the soil, like a peasant."

On the governor's return, Cortés consented to give up his

roving thoughts, at least for a time, as the other labored to convince him that he would be more likely to realize his wishes from the slow, indeed, but sure, returns of husbandry, where the soil and the laborers were a free gift to the planter, than by taking his chance in the lottery of adventure, in which there were so many blanks to a prize. He accordingly received a grant of land, with a *repartimiento* of Indians, and was appointed notary of the town or settlement of Açua. His graver pursuits, however, did not prevent his indulgence of the amorous propensities which belong to the sunny clime where he was born; and this frequently involved him in affairs of honor, from which, though an expert swordsman, he carried away scars that accompanied him to his grave. He occasionally, moreover, found the means of breaking up the monotony of his way of life by engaging in the military expeditions, which, under the command of Ovando's lieutenant, Diego Velásquez, were employed to suppress the insurrections of the natives. In this school the young adventurer first studied the wild tactics of Indian warfare; he became familiar with toil and danger, and with those deeds of cruelty which have too often, alas! stained the bright scutcheons of the Castilian chivalry in the New World. He was only prevented by illness—a most fortunate one, on this occasion—from embarking in Nicuessa's expedition, which furnished a tale of woe, not often matched in the annals of Spanish discovery. Providence reserved him for higher ends.

At length, in 1511, when Velásquez undertook the conquest of Cuba, Cortés willingly abandoned his quiet life for the stirring scenes there opened, and took part in the expedition. He displayed, throughout the invasion, an activity and courage that won him the approbation of the commander; while his free and cordial manners, his good-humor, and lively sallies of wit made him the favorite of the soldiers. "He gave little evidence," says a contemporary, "of the great qualities which he afterwards showed." It is probable these qualities were not known to himself; while to a common observer his careless manners and jocund repartees might well seem incompatible with any thing serious or profound; as the real depth of the current is not suspected under the light play and sunny sparkling of the surface.

After the reduction of the island, Cortés seems to have been held in great favor by Velásquez, now appointed its governor. According to Las Casas, he was made one of his secretaries. He still retained the same fondness for gallantry, for which his handsome person afforded obvious advantages, but which had more than once brought him into trouble in earlier life. Among the families who had taken up their residence in Cuba was one of the name of Xuárez,* from Granada in Old Spain. It consisted of a brother, and four sisters remarkable for their beauty. With one of them, named Catalina, the susceptible heart of the young soldier became enamoured. How far the intimacy was carried is not quite certain. But it appears he gave his promise to marry her,—a promise, which, when the time came, and reason, it may be, had got the better of passion, he showed no alacrity in keeping. He resisted, indeed, all remonstrances to this effect, from the lady's family, backed by the governor, and somewhat sharpened, no doubt, in the latter by the particular interest he took in one of the fair sisters, who is said not to have repaid it with ingratitude.

Whether the rebuke of Velásquez, or some other cause of disgust, rankled in the breast of Cortés, he now became cold toward his patron, and connected himself with a disaffected party tolerably numerous in the island. They were in the habit of meeting at his house and brooding over their causes of discontent, chiefly founded, it would appear, on what they conceived an ill requital of their services in the distribution of lands and offices. It may well be imagined, that it could have been no easy task for the ruler of one of these colonies, however discreet and well intentioned, to satisfy the indefinite cravings of speculators and adventurers, who swarmed like so many famished harpies, in the track of discovery in the New World.

The malecontents determined to lay their grievances before

*Suárez. C. H. G.

the higher authorities in Hispaniola, from whom Velásquez had received his commission. The voyage was one of some hazard, as it was to be made in an open boat, across an arm of the sea eighteen leagues wide; and they fixed on Cortés, with whose fearless spirit they were well acquainted, as the fittest man to undertake it. The conspiracy got wind, and came to the governor's ears before the departure of the envoy, whom he instantly caused to be seized, loaded with fetters, and placed in strict confinement. It is even said, he would have hung him, but for the interposition of his friends. The fact is not incredible. The governors of these little territories, having entire control over the fortunes of their subjects, enjoyed an authority far more despotic than that of the sovereign himself. They were generally men of rank and personal consideration; their distance from the mother country withdrew their conduct from searching scrutiny, and, when that did occur, they usually had interest and means of corruption at command, sufficient to shield them from punishment. The Spanish colonial history, in its earlier stages, affords striking instances of the extraordinary assumption and abuse of powers by these petty potentates; and the sad fate of Vásquez Núñez de Balboa, the illustrious discoverer of the Pacific, though the most signal, is by no means a solitary example, that the greatest services could be requited by persecution and an ignominious death.

The governor of Cuba, however, although irascible and suspicious in his nature, does not seem to have been vindictive, nor particularly cruel. In the present instance, indeed, it may well be doubted whether the blame would not be more reasonably charged on the unfounded expectations of his followers than on himself.

Cortés did not long remain in durance. He contrived to throw back one of the bolts of his fetters; and, after extricating his limbs, succeeded in forcing open a window with the irons so as to admit of his escape. He was lodged on the second floor of the building, and was able to let himself down to the pavement without injury, and unobserved. He then made the best of his way to a neighbouring church, where he claimed the privilege of sanctuary.

Velásquez, though incensed at his escape, was afraid to violate the sanctity of the place by employing force. But he stationed a guard in the neighbourhood, with orders to seize the fugitive, if he should forget himself so far as to leave the sanctuary. In a few days this happened. As Cortés was carelessly standing without the walls in front of the building, an *alguacil* suddenly sprung on him from behind and pinioned his arms, while others rushed in and secured him. This man, whose name was Juan Escudero, was afterwards hung by Cortés for some offence in New Spain.

The unlucky prisoner was again put in irons, and carried on board a vessel to sail the next morning for Hispaniola, there to undergo his trial. Fortune favored him once more. He succeeded, after much difficulty and no little pain, in passing his feet through the rings which shackled them. He then came cautiously on deck, and, covered by the darkness of the night, stole quietly down the side of the ship into a boat that lay floating below. He pushed off from the vessel with as little noise as possible. As he drew near the shore, the stream became rapid and turbulent. He hesitated to trust his boat to it; and as he was an excellent swimmer prepared to breast it himself, and boldly plunged into the water. The current was strong, but the arm of a man struggling for life was stronger; and after buffeting the waves till he was nearly exhausted, he succeeded in gaining a landing; when he sought refuge in the same sanctuary which had protected him before. The facility with which Cortés a second time effected his escape may lead one to doubt the fidelity of his guards; who perhaps looked on him as the victim of persecution, and felt the influence of those popular manners which seem to have gained him friends in every society into which he was thrown.

For some reason not explained,—perhaps from policy,—he now relinquished his objections to the marriage with Catalina Xuárez. He thus secured the good offices of her family.

Soon afterwards the governor himself relented, and became reconciled to his unfortunate enemy. A strange story is told in connexion with this event. It is said, his proud spirit refused to accept the proffers of reconciliation made him by Velásquez; and that one evening, leaving the sanctuary, he presented himself unexpectedly before the latter in his own quarters, when on a military excursion at some distance from the capital. The governor, startled by the sudden apparition of his enemy completely armed before him, with some dismay inquired the meaning of it. Cortés answered by insisting on a full explanation of his previous conduct. After some hot discussion the interview terminated amicably; the parties embraced, and, when a messenger arrived to announce the escape of Cortés, he found him in the apartments of his Excellency, where, having retired to rest, both were actually sleeping in the same bed! The anecdote is repeated without distrust by more than one biographer of Cortés. It is not very probable, however, that a haughty, irascible man like Velásquez should have given such uncommon proofs of condescension and familiarity to one, so far beneath him in station, with whom he had been so recently in deadly feud; nor, on the other hand, that Cortés should have had the silly temerity to brave the lion in his den, where a single nod would have sent him to the gibbet,—and that, too, with as little compunction or fear of consequences, as would have attended the execution of an Indian slave.

The reconciliation with the governor, however brought about, was permanent. Cortés, though not reëstablished in the office of secretary, received a liberal *repartimiento* of Indians, and an ample territory in the neighbourhood of St. Jago,* of which he was soon after made *alcalde*. He now lived almost wholly on his estate, devoting himself to agriculture with more zeal than formerly. He stocked his plantation with different kinds of cattle, some of which were first introduced by him into Cuba. He wrought, also, the gold mines which fell to his share, and which in this island promised better returns than those in His-

* Santiago. C.H.G.

paniola. By this course of industry he found himself, in a few years, master of some two or three thousand *castellanos,* a large sum for one in his situation. "God, who alone knows at what cost of Indian lives it was obtained," exclaims Las Casas, "will take account of it!" His days glided smoothly away in these tranquil pursuits, and in the society of his beautiful wife, who, however ineligible as a connexion, from the inferiority of her condition, appears to have fulfilled all the relations of a faithful and affectionate partner. Indeed, he was often heard to say at this time, as the good bishop above quoted remarks, "that he lived as happily with her as if she had been the daughter of a duchess." Fortune gave him the means in after life of verifying the truth of his assertion.

Such was the state of things, when Alvarado returned with the tidings of Grijalva's discoveries, and the rich fruits of his traffic with the natives. The news spread like wildfire throughout the island; for all saw in it the promise of more important results than any hitherto obtained. The governor, as already noticed, resolved to follow up the track of discovery with a more considerable armament; and he looked around for a proper person to share the expense of it, and to take the command.

Several hidalgos presented themselves, whom, from want of proper qualifications, or from his distrust of their assuming an independence of their employer, he, one after another, rejected. There were two persons in St. Jago in whom he placed great confidence,—Amador de Lares, the *contador,* or royal treasurer, and his own secretary, Andrés de Duero. Cortés was also in close intimacy with both these persons; and he availed himself of it to prevail on them to recommend him as a suitable person to be intrusted with the expedition. It is said, he reinforced the proposal, by promising a liberal share of the proceeds of it. However this may be, the parties urged his selection by the governor with all the eloquence of which they were capable. That officer had had ample experience of the capacity and courage of the candidate. He knew, too, that he had acquired a fortune which would enable him to coöperate materially in fitting out the armament. His popularity in the island would speedily attract followers to his standard. All past animosities had long since been buried in oblivion, and the confidence he was now to repose in him would insure his fidelity and gratitude. He lent a willing ear, therefore, to the recommendation of his counsellors, and, sending for Cortés, announced his purpose of making him Captain-General of the Armada.

Cortés had now attained the object of his wishes,—the object for which his soul had panted, ever since he had set foot in the New World. He was no longer to be condemned to a life of mercenary drudgery; nor to be cooped up within the precincts of a petty island. But he was to be placed on a new and independent theatre of action, and a boundless perspective was opened to his view, which might satisfy not merely the wildest cravings of avarice, but, to a bold, aspiring spirit like his, the far more importunate cravings of ambition. He fully appreciated the importance of the late discoveries, and read in them the existence of the great empire in the far West, dark hints of which had floated, from time to time, to the Islands, and of which more certain glimpses had been caught by those who had reached the continent. This was the country intimated to the "Great Admiral" in his visit to Honduras in 1502, and which he might have reached, had he held on a northern course, instead of striking to the south in quest of an imaginary strait. As it was, "he had but opened the gate," to use his own bitter expression, "for others to enter." The time had at length come, when they were to enter it; and the young adventurer, whose magic lance was to dissolve the spell which had so long hung over these mysterious regions, now stood ready to assume the enterprise.

From this hour the deportment of Cortés seemed to undergo a change. His thoughts, instead of evaporating in empty levities or idle flashes of merriment, were wholly concentrated on the great object to which he was devoted. His elastic spirits were shown cheering and stimulating the companions of his toilsome duties, and he was roused to a generous enthusiasm, of which even those who knew him best had not conceived him capable. He applied at once all the money in his possession to fitting out the armament. He raised more by the mortgage of his estates, and by giving his obligations to some wealthy merchants of the place, who relied for their reimbursement on the success of the expedition; and, when his own credit was exhausted, he availed himself of that of his friends.

The funds thus acquired he expended in the purchase of vessels, provisions, and military stores, while he invited recruits by offers of assistance to such as were too poor to provide for themselves, and by the additional promise of a liberal share of the anticipated profits.

All was now bustle and excitement in the little town of St. Jago. Some were busy in refitting the vessels and getting them ready for the voyage; some in providing naval stores; others in converting their own estates into money in order to equip themselves; every one seemed anxious to contribute in some way or other to the success of the expedition. Six ships, some of them of a large size, had already been procured; and three hundred recruits enrolled themselves in the course of a few days, eager to seek their fortunes under the banner of this daring and popular chieftain.

How far the governor contributed towards the expenses of the outfit is not very clear. If the friends of Cortés are to be believed, nearly the whole burden fell on him; since, while he supplied the squadron without remuneration, the governor sold many of his own stores at an exorbitant profit. Yet it does not seem probable that Velásquez, with such ample means at his command, should have thrown on his deputy the burden of the expedition, nor that the latter—had he done so—could have been in a condition to meet these expenses, amounting, as we are told, to more than twenty thousand gold ducats. Still it cannot be denied that an ambitious man like Cortés, who was to reap all the glory of the enterprise, would very naturally be less solicitous to count the gains of it, than his employer, who, inactive at home, and having no laurels to win, must look on the pecuniary profits as his only recompense. The question gave rise, some years later, to a furious litigation between the parties, with which it is not necessary at present to embarrass the reader.

It is due to Velásquez to state that the instructions delivered by him for the conduct of the expedition cannot be charged with a narrow or mercenary spirit. The first object of the voyage was to find Grijalva, after which the two commanders were to proceed in company together. Reports had been brought back by Córdova, on his return from the first visit to Yucatan, that six Christians were said to be lingering in captivity in the interior of the country. It was supposed they might belong to the party of the unfortunate Nicuessa, and orders were given to find them out, if possible, and restore them to liberty. But the great object of the expedition was barter with the natives. In pursuing this, special care was to be taken that they should receive no wrong, but be treated with kindness and humanity. Cortés was to bear in mind, above all things, that the object which the Spanish monarch had most at heart was the conversion of the Indians. He was to impress on them the grandeur and goodness of his royal master, to invite them "to give in their allegiance to him, and to manifest it by regaling him with such comfortable presents of gold, pearls, and precious stones as, by showing their own good-will, would secure his favor and protection." He was to make an accurate survey of the coast, sounding its bays and inlets for the benefit of future navigators. He was to acquaint himself with the natural products of the country, with the character of its different races, their institutions and progress in civilization; and he was to send home minute accounts of all these, together with such articles as he should obtain in his intercourse with them. Finally, he was to take *the most careful care* to omit nothing that might redound to the service of God or his sovereign.

Such was the general tenor of the instructions given to Cortés, and they must be admitted to provide for the interests of science and humanity, as well as for those which had reference only to a commercial speculation. It may seem strange, considering the discontent shown by Velásquez with his former captain, Grijalva, for not colonizing, that no directions should have been given to that effect here. But he had not yet received from Spain the warrant for investing his agents with such powers; and that which had been obtained from the Hierony-mite fathers in Hispaniola conceded only the right to traffic with the natives. The commission at the same time recognised the authority of Cortés as Captain-General of the expedition.

II

Final Preparations

THE importance given to Cortés by his new position, and, perhaps, a somewhat more lofty bearing, gradually gave uneasiness
to the naturally suspicious temper of Velásquez, who became
apprehensive that his officer, when away where he would have
the power, might also have the inclination, to throw off his dependence on him altogether. An accidental circumstance at this
time heightened these suspicions. A mad fellow, his jester,
one of those crack-brained wits,—half wit, half fool,—who
formed in those days a common appendage to every great man's
establishment, called out to the governor, as he was taking his
usual walk one morning with Cortés towards the port, "Have
a care, master Velásquez, or we shall have to go a hunting,
some day or other, after this same captain of ours!" "Do you
hear what the rogue says?" exclaimed the governor to his
companion. "Do not heed him," said Cortés, "he is a saucy
knave, and deserves a good whipping." The words sunk deep,
however, in the mind of Velásquez,—as, indeed, true jests are
apt to stick.

There were not wanting persons about his Excellency, who
fanned the latent embers of jealousy into a blaze. These worthy
gentlemen, some of them kinsmen of Velásquez, who probably
felt their own deserts somewhat thrown into the shade by the
rising fortunes of Cortés, reminded the governor of his ancient
quarrel with that officer, and of the little probability that af-
fronts so keenly felt at the time could ever be forgotten. By
these and similar suggestions, and by misconstructions of the
present conduct of Cortés, they wrought on the passions of
Velásquez to such a degree, that he resolved to intrust the expedition to other hands.

He communicated his design to his confidential advisers,
Lares and Duero, and these trusty personages reported it with-

Vol. I, pp. 251–64.

out delay to Cortés, although, "to a man of half his penetration," says Las Casas, "the thing would have been readily devined from the governor's altered demeanour." The two functionaries advised their friend to expedite matters as much as possible, and to lose no time in getting his fleet ready for sea, if he would retain the command of it. Cortés showed the same prompt decision on this ocassion, which more than once afterwards in a similar crisis gave the direction to his destiny.

He had not yet got his complement of men, nor of vessels; and was very inadequately provided with supplies of any kind. But he resolved to weigh anchor that very night. He waited on his officers, informed them of his purpose, and probably of the cause of it; and at midnight, when the town was hushed in sleep, they all went quietly on board, and the little squadron dropped down the bay. First, however, Cortés had visited the person whose business it was to supply the place with meat, and relieved him of all his stock on hand, notwithstanding his complaint that the city must suffer for it on the morrow, leaving him, at the same time, in payment, a massive gold chain of much value, which he wore round his neck.

Great was the amazement of the good citizens of St. Jago, when, at dawn, they saw that the fleet, which they knew was so ill prepared for the voyage, had left its moorings and was busily getting under way. The tidings soon came to the ears of his Excellency, who, springing from his bed, hastily dressed himself, mounted his horse, and, followed by his retinue, galloped down to the quay. Cortés, as soon as he descried their approach, entered an armed boat, and came within speaking distance of the shore. "And is it thus you part from me!" exclaimed Velásquez; "a courteous way of taking leave, truly!" "Pardon me," answered Cortés, "time presses, and there are some things that should be done before they are even thought of. Has your Excellency any commands?" But the mortified governor had no commands to give; and Cortés, politely waving his hand, returned to his vessel, and the little fleet instantly made sail for the port of Macaca, about fifteen leagues distant. (November 18, 1518.) Velásquez rode back to his house to digest his chagrin as he best might; satisfied, probably, that he had made at least two blunders; one in appointing Cortés to the command, —the other in attempting to deprive him of it. For, if it be true, that, by giving our confidence by halves, we can scarcely hope to make a friend, it is equally true, that, by withdrawing it when given, we shall make an enemy.

This clandestine departure of Cortés has been severely criticized by some writers, especially by Las Casas. Yet much may be urged in vindication of his conduct. He had been appointed to the command by the voluntary act of the governor, and this had been fully ratified by the authorities of Hispaniola. He had at once devoted all his resources to the undertaking, incurring, indeed, a heavy debt in addition. He was now to be deprived of his commission, without any misconduct having been alleged or at least proved against him. Such an event must overwhelm him in irretrievable ruin, to say nothing of the friends from whom he had so largely borrowed, and the followers who had embarked their fortunes in the expedition on the faith of his commanding it. There are few persons, probably, who, under these circumstances, would have felt called tamely to acquiesce in the sacrifice of their hopes to a groundless and arbitrary whim. The most to have been expected from Cortés was, that he should feel obliged to provide faithfully for the interests of his employer in the conduct of the enterprise. How far he felt the force of this obligation will appear in the sequel.

From Macaca, where Cortés laid in such stores as he could obtain from the royal farms, and which, he said, he considered as "a loan from the king," he proceded to Trinidad; a more considerable town, on the southern coast of Cuba. Here he landed, and, erecting his standard in front of his quarters, made proclamation, with liberal offers to all who would join the expedition. Volunteers came in daily, and among them more than a hundred of Grijalva's men, just returned from their voyage, and willing to follow up the discovery under an enterprising leader. The fame of Cortés attracted, also, a number of cavaliers of family and distinction, some of whom, having accompanied Grijalva, brought much information valuable for the present expedition. Among these hidalgos may be mentioned Pedro de Alvarado and his brothers, Cristóval de Olid, Alonso de Ávila, Juan Velásquez de León, a near relation of the governor, Alonso Hernández de Puertocarrero, and Gonzalo de Sandoval,—all of them men who took a most important part in the Conquest. Their presence was of great moment, as giving consideration to the enterprise; and, when they entered the little camp of adventurers, the latter turned out to welcome them amidst lively strains of music and joyous salvos of artillery.

Cortés meanwhile was active in purchasing military stores and provisions. Learning that a trading vessel laden with grain and other commodities for the mines was off the coast, he ordered out one of his caravels to seize her and bring her into port. He paid the master in bills for both cargo and ship, and even persuaded this man, named Sedeño, who was wealthy, to join his fortunes to the expedition. He also despatched one of his officers, Diego de Ordaz, in quest of another ship, of which he had tidings, with instructions to seize it in like manner, and to meet him with it off Cape St. Antonio, the westerly point of the island. By this he effected another object, that of getting rid of Ordaz, who was one of the governor's household, and an inconvenient spy on his own actions.

While thus occupied, letters from Velásquez were received by the commander of Trinidad, requiring him to seize the person of Cortés and to detain him, as he had been deposed from the command of the fleet, which was given to another. This functionary communicated his instructions to the principal officers in the expedition, who counselled him not to make the attempt, as it would undoubtedly lead to a commotion among the soldiers, that might end in laying the town in ashes. Verdugo thought it prudent to conform to this advice.

As Cortés was willing to strengthen himself by still further reinforcements, he ordered Alvarado with a small body of men to march across the country to the Havana, while he himself would sail round the westerly point of the island, and meet him there with the squadron. In this port he again displayed his standard, making the usual proclamation. He caused all the large guns to be brought on shore, and, with the small arms and crossbows, to be put in order. As there was abundance of cotton raised in this neighbourhood, he had the jackets of the soldiers thickly quilted with it, for a defence against the Indian arrows, from which the troops in the former expeditions had grievously suffered. He distributed his men into eleven companies, each under the command of an experienced officer; and it was observed, that, although several of the cavaliers in the service were the personal friends and even kinsmen of Velásquez, he appeared to treat them all with perfect confidence.

His principal standard was of black velvet embroidered with gold, and emblazoned with a red cross amidst flames of blue and white, with this motto in Latin beneath; "Friends, let us follow the Cross; and under this sign, if we have faith, we shall conquer." He now assumed more state in his own person and way of living, introducing a greater number of domestics and officers into his household, and placing it on a footing becoming a man of high station. This state he maintained through the rest of his life.

Cortés at this time was thirty-three, or perhaps thirty-four years of age. In stature he was rather above the middle size. His complexion was pale; and his large dark eye gave an expression of gravity to his countenance, not to have been expected in one of his cheerful temperament. His figure was slender, at least until later life; but his chest was deep, his shoulders broad, his frame muscular and well proportioned. It presented the union of agility and vigor which qualified him to excel in fencing, horsemanship, and the other generous exercises of chivalry. In his diet he was temperate, careless of what he ate, and drinking little; while to toil and privation he seemed perfectly indifferent. His dress, for he did not disdain the impression produced by such adventitious aids, was such as to set off his handsome person to advantage; neither gaudy nor striking, but rich. He wore few ornaments, and usually the same; but those were of great price. His manners, frank and soldierlike, concealed a most cool and calculating spirit. With his gayest humor there mingled a settled air of resolution, which made those who approached him feel they must obey; and which infused something like awe into the attachment of his most devoted followers. Such a combination, in which love was tempered by authority, was the one probably best calculated to inspire devotion in the rough and turbulent spirits among whom his lot was to be cast.

The character of Cortés seems to have undergone some change with change of circumstances; or, to speak more correctly, the new scenes in which he was placed called forth qualities which before lay dormant in his bosom. There are some hardy natures that require the heats of excited action to unfold their energies; like the plants, which, closed to the mild influence of a temperate latitude, come to their full growth, and give forth their fruits, only in the burning atmosphere of the tropics. —Such is the portrait left to us by his contemporaries of this remarkable man; the instrument selected by Providence to scatter terror among the barbarian monarchs of the Western World, and lay their empires in the dust.

Before the preparations were fully completed at the Havana, the commander of the place, Don Pedro Barba, received despatches from Velásquez ordering him to apprehend Cortés, and to prevent the departure of his vessels; while another epistle from the same source was delivered to Cortés himself, requesting him to postpone his voyage till the governor could communicate with him, as he proposed, in person. "Never," exclaims Las Casas, "did I see so little knowledge of affairs shown, as in this letter of Diego Velásquez,—that he should have imagined, that a man, who had so recently put such an affront on him, would defer his departure at his bidding!" It was, indeed, hoping to stay the flight of the arrow by a word, after it had left the bow.

The Captain-General, however, during his short stay, had

entirely conciliated the good-will of Barba. And, if that officer
had had the inclination, he knew he had not the power, to enforce his principal's orders, in the face of a resolute soldiery, incensed at this ungenerous persecution of their commander, and
"all of whom," in the words of the honest chronicler who bore
part in the expedition, "officers and privates, would have cheer-
fully laid down their lives for him." Barba contented himself,
therefore, with explaining to Velásquez the impracticability of
the attempt, and at the same time endeavoured to tranquillize
his apprehensions by asserting his own confidence in the fidelity
of Cortés. To this the latter added a communication of his own,
couched "in the soft terms he knew so well how to use," in which
he implored his Excellency to rely on his devotion to his interests, and concluded with the comfortable assurance that he
and the whole fleet, God willing, would sail on the following
morning.

Accordingly on the 10th of February, 1519, the little squadron got under way, and directed its course towards Cape St.
Antonio, the appointed place of rendezvous. When all were
brought together, the vessels were found to be eleven in number; one of them, in which Cortés himself went, was a hundred
tons, burden, three others were from seventy to eighty tons;
the remainder were caravels and open brigantines. The whole
was put under the direction of Antonio de Alaminos, as chief
pilot; a veteran navigator, who had acted as pilot to Columbus
in his last voyage, and to Córdova and Grijalva in the former
expeditions to Yucatan.

Landing on the Cape and mustering his forces, Cortés found
they amounted to one hundred and ten mariners, five hundred
and fifty-three soldiers, including thirty-two crossbowmen, and
thirteen arquebusiers, besides two hundred Indians of the
island, and a few Indian women for menial offices. He was
provided with ten heavy guns, four lighter pieces called falconets, and with a good supply of ammunition. He had besides
sixteen horses. They were not easily procured; for the difficulty
of transporting them across the ocean in the flimsy craft of

that day made them rare and incredibly dear in the Islands. But Cortés rightfully estimated the importance of cavalry, however small in number, both for their actual service in the field, and for striking terror into the savages. With so paltry a force did he enter on a Conquest which even his stout heart must have shrunk from attempting with such means, had he but foreseen half its real difficulties!

Before embarking, Cortés addressed his soldiers in a short but animated harangue. He told them they were about to enter on a noble enterprise, one that would make their name famous to after ages. He was leading them to countries more vast and opulent than any yet visited by Europeans. "I hold out to you a glorious prize," continued the orator, "but it is to be won by incessant toil. Great things are achieved only by great exertions, and glory was never the reward of sloth. If I have labored hard and staked my all on this undertaking, it is for the love of that renown, which is the noblest recompense of man. But, if any among you covet riches more, be but true to me, as I will be true to you and to the occasion, and I will make you masters of such as our countrymen have never dreamed of! You are few in number, but strong in resolution; and, if this does not falter, doubt not but that the Almighty, who has never deserted the Spaniard in his contest with the infidel, will shield you, though encompassed by a cloud of enemies; for your cause is a *just cause,* and you are to fight under the banner of the Cross. Go forward, then," he concluded, "with alacrity and confidence, and carry to a glorious issue the work so auspiciously begun."

The rough eloquence of the general, touching the various chords of ambition, avarice, and religious zeal, sent a thrill through the bosoms of his martial audience; and receiving it with acclamations, they seemed eager to press forward under a chief who was to lead them not so much to battle, as to triumph.

Cortés was well satisfied to find his own enthusiasm so largely shared by his followers. Mass was then celebrated with the solemnities usual with the Spanish navigators, when entering on their voyages of discovery. The fleet was placed under the immediate protection of St. Peter, the patron saint of Cortés; and weighing anchor, took its departure on the eighteenth day of February, 1519, for the coast of Yucatan.

AFTER crossing the channel between Cuba and the continent, the fleet came together off the island of Cozumel, at the northeast corner of Yucatan. Natives were met, but the efforts of the missionaries to convert them to Christianity failed. However, the finding of Jerónimo de Aguilar, a Spaniard who had been shipwrecked on Yucatan, was most helpful because he provided Cortés with an interpreter. As the expedition moved along the coast of modern Campeche and Tabasco, natives were seen and fought and rivers explored. Then came the day when Cortés led his men in their first great battle.

III

Coastal Probings

AT the first glimmering of light he mustered his army, and declared his purpose not to abide, cooped up in the town, the assault of the enemy, but to march at once against him. For he well knew that the spirits rise with action, and that the attacking party gathers a confidence from the very movement, which is not felt by the one who is passively, perhaps anxiously, awaiting the assault. The Indians were understood to be encamped on a level ground a few miles distant from the city, called the plain of Ceutla. The general commanded that Ordaz should march with the foot, including the artillery, directly across the country, and attack them in front, while he himself would fetch a circuit with the horse, and turn their flank when thus engaged, or fall upon their rear.

These dispositions being completed, the little army heard mass and then sallied forth from the wooden walls of Tabasco. It was Lady-day, the twenty-fifth of March,—long memorable in the annals of New Spain. The district around the town was chequered with patches of maize, and, on the lower level, with plantations of cacao,—supplying the beverage, and perhaps the coin of the country, as in Mexico. These plantations, requiring constant irrigation, were fed by numerous canals and reservoirs of water, so that the country could not be traversed without great toil and difficulty. It was, however, intersected by a narrow path or causeway, over which the cannon could be dragged.

The troops advanced more than a league on their laborious march, without descrying the enemy. The weather was sultry, but few of them were embarrassed by the heavy mail worn by the European cavaliers at that period. Their cotton jackets, thickly quilted, afforded a tolerable protection against the arrows of the Indian, and allowed room for the freedom and activity of movement essential to a life of rambling adventure in the wilderness.

At length they came in sight of the broad plains of Ceutla, and beheld the dusky lines of the enemy stretching, as far as the eye could reach, along the edge of the horizon. The Indians had shown some sagacity in the choice of their position; and, as the weary Spaniards came slowly on, floundering through the morass, the Tabascans set up their hideous battle-cries, and discharged volleys of arrows, stones, and other missiles, which rattled like hail on the shields and helmets of the assailants. Many were severely wounded, before they could gain the firm ground, where they soon cleared a space for themselves, and opened a heavy fire of artillery and musketry on the dense columns of the enemy, which presented a fatal mark for the balls. Numbers were swept down at every discharge; but the bold barbarians, far from being dismayed, threw up dust and leaves to hide their losses, and, sounding their war instruments, shot off fresh flights of arrows in return.

They even pressed closer on the Spaniards, and, when driven off by a vigorous charge, soon turned again, and, rolling back like the waves of the ocean, seemed ready to overwhelm the little band by weight of numbers. Thus cramped, the latter had scarcely room to perform their necessary evolutions, or even to work their guns with effect.

The engagement had now lasted more than an hour, and the Spaniards, sorely pressed, looked with great anxiety for the arrival of the horse,—which some unaccountable impediments must have detained,—to relieve them from their perilous position. At this crisis, the furthest columns of the Indian army were seen to be agitated and thrown into a disorder that rapidly spread through the whole mass. It was not long before the ears of the Christians were saluted with the cheering war-cry of "San Jago and San Pedro!" and they beheld the bright helmets and swords of the Castilian chivalry flashing back the rays of the morning sun, as they dashed through the ranks of the enemy, striking to the right and left, and scattering dismay around them. The eye of faith, indeed, could discern the patron Saint of Spain, himself, mounted on his grey war-horse, heading the rescue and trampling over the bodies of the fallen infidels!

The approach of Cortés had been greatly retarded by the broken nature of the ground. When he came up, the Indians were so hotly engaged, that he was upon them before they observed his approach. He ordered his men to direct their lances at the faces of their opponents, who, terrified at the monstrous apparition,—for they supposed the rider and the horse, which they had never before seen, to be one and the same,—were seized with a panic. Ordaz availed himself of it to command a general charge along the line, and the Indians, many of them throwing away their arms, fled without attempting further resistance.

Cortés was too content with the victory, to care to follow it up by dipping his sword in the blood of the fugitives. He drew off his men to a copse of palms which skirted the place, and under their broad canopy the soldiers offered up thanksgivings to the Almighty for the victory vouchsafed them. The field of battle was made the site of a town, called, in honor of the day on which the action took place, *Santa María de la Vitoria,* long afterwards the capital of the Province. The number of those who fought or fell in the engagement is altogether doubtful.

Nothing, indeed, is more uncertain than numerical estimates of barbarians. And they gain nothing in probability, when they come, as in the present instance, from the reports of their enemies. Most accounts, however, agree that the Indian force consisted of five squadrons of eight thousand men each. There is more discrepancy as to the number of slain, varying from one to thirty thousand! In this monstrous discordance, the common disposition to exaggerate may lead us to look for truth in the neighbourhood of the smallest number. The loss of the Christians was inconsiderable; not exceeding—if we receive their own reports, probably, from the same causes, much diminishing the truth—two killed and less than a hundred wounded! We may readily comprehend the feelings of the Conquerors, when they declared, that "Heaven must have fought on their side, since their own strength could never have prevailed against such a multitude of enemies!"

The fleet held its course so near the shore, that the inhabitants could be seen on it; and, as it swept along the winding borders of the Gulf, the soldiers, who had been on the former expedition with Grijalva, pointed out to their companions the memorable places on the coast. Here was the *Río de Alvarado,* named after the gallant adventurer, who was present, also, in this expedition; there the *Río de Vanderas,* in which Grijalva had carried on so lucrative a commerce with the Mexicans; and there the *Isla de los Sacrificios,* where the Spaniards first saw the vestiges of human sacrifice on the coast. Puertocarrero, as he listened to these reminiscences of the sailors, repeated the words of the old ballad of Montesinos, "Here is France, there is Paris, and there the waters of the Duero," &c. "But I advise you," he added, turning to Cortés, "to look out only for the rich lands, and the best way to govern them." "Fear not," replied his commander, "if Fortune but favors me as she did Orlando, and I have such gallant gentlemen as you for my companions, I shall understand myself very well."

The fleet had now arrived off San Juan de Ulua, the island

so named by Grijalva. The weather was temperate and serene, and crowds of natives were gathered on the shore of the main land, gazing at the strange phenomenon, as the vessels glided along under easy sail on the smooth bosom of the waters. It was the evening of Thursday in Passion Week. The air came pleasantly off the shore, and Cortés, liking the spot, thought he might safely anchor under the lee of the island, which would shelter him from the *nortes* that sweep over these seas with fatal violence in the winter, sometimes even late in the spring.

The ships had not been long at anchor, when a light pirogue, filled with natives, shot off from the neighbouring continent, and steered for the general's vessel, distinguished by the royal ensign of Castile floating from the mast. The Indians came on board with a frank confidence, inspired by the accounts of the Spaniards spread by their countrymen who had traded with Grijalva. They brought presents of fruits and flowers and little ornaments of gold, which they gladly exchanged for the usual trinkets. Cortés was baffled in his attempts to hold a conversation with his visiters by means of the interpreter, Aguilar, who was ignorant of the language; the Mayan dialects, with which he was conversant, bearing too little resemblance to the Aztec. The natives supplied the deficiency, as far as possible, by the uncommon vivacity and significance of their gestures,— the hieroglyphics of speech,—but the Spanish commander saw with chagrin the embarrassments he must encounter in future for want of a more perfect medium of communication. In this dilemma, he was informed that one of the female slaves given to him by the Tabascan chiefs was a native Mexican, and understood the language. Her name—that given to her by the Spaniards—was Marina; and, as she was to exercise a most important influence on their fortunes, it is necessary to acquaint the reader with something of her character and history.

She was born at Painalla, in the province of Coatzacualco, on the south-eastern borders of the Mexican empire. Her father, a rich and powerful cacique, died when she was very young. Her mother married again, and, having a son, she conceived the infamous idea of securing to this offspring of her second union Marina's rightful inheritance. She accordingly feigned that the latter was dead, but secretly delivered her into the hands of some itinerant traders of Xicallanco. She availed herself, at the same time, of the death of a child of one of her slaves, to substitute the corpse for that of her own daughter, and celebrated the obsequies with mock solemnity. These particulars are related by the honest old soldier, Bernal Díaz, who knew the mother, and witnessed the generous treatment of her afterwards by Marina. By the merchants the Indian maiden was again sold to the cacique of Tabasco, who delivered her, as we have seen, to the Spaniards.

From the place of her birth she was well acquainted with the Mexican tongue, which, indeed, she is said to have spoken with great elegance. Her residence in Tabasco familiarized her with the dialects of that country, so that she could carry on a conversation with Aguilar, which he in turn rendered into the Castilian. Thus a certain, though somewhat circuitous channel was opened to Cortés for communicating with the Aztecs; a circumstance of the last importance to the success of his enterprise. It was not very long, however, before Marina, who had a lively genius, made herself so far mistress of the Castilian as to supersede the necessity of any other linguist. She learned it the more readily, as it was to her the language of love.

Cortés, who appreciated the value of her services from the first, made her his interpreter, then his secretary, and, won by her charms, his mistress. She had a son by him, Don Martín Cortés, *comendador* of the Military Order of St. James, less distinguished by his birth than his unmerited persecutions.

Marina was at this time in the morning of life. She is said to have possessed uncommon personal attractions, and her open, expressive features indicated her generous temper. She always remained faithful to the countrymen of her adoption; and her knowledge of the language and customs of the Mexicans, and often of their designs, enabled her to extricate the Spaniards, more than once, from the most embarrassing and perilous situations. She had her errors, as we have seen. But they should be rather charged to the defects of early education, and to the evil influence of him to whom in the darkness of her spirit she looked with simple confidence for the light to guide her. All agree that she was full of excellent qualities, and the important services which she rendered the Spaniards have made her memory deservedly dear to them; while the name of Malinche—the name by which she is still known in Mexico—was pronounced with kindness by the conquered races, with whose misfortunes she showed an invariable sympathy.

With the aid of his two intelligent interpreters, Cortés entered into conversation with his Indian visiters. He learned that they were Mexicans, or rather subjects of the great Mexican empire, of which their own province formed one of the comparatively recent conquests. The country was ruled by a powerful monarch, called Moctheuzoma, or by Europeans more commonly Montezuma, who dwelt on the mountain plains of the interior, nearly seventy leagues from the coast; their own province was governed by one of his nobles, named Teuhtlile, whose residence was eight leagues distant. Cortés acquainted them in turn with his own friendly views in visiting their country, and with his desire of an interview with the Aztec governor. He then dismissed them loaded with presents, having first ascertained that there was abundance of gold in the interior, like the specimens they had brought.

Cortés, pleased with the manners of the people, and the goodly reports of the land, resolved to take up his quarters here for the present. The next morning, April 21, being Good Friday, he landed, with all his force, on the very spot where now stands the modern city of Vera Cruz. . . .

IN the Easter season Cortés met and exchanged gifts with Montezuma's emissaries. It was a time when the Indians and the Spaniards were fashioning estimates of each other. Discontent in the cumbersome and recently enlarged native empire and more than a little confusion beset Montezuma.

IV

A Dilemma

SUCH was the condition of the Aztec monarchy, on the arrival of Cortés;—the people disgusted with the arrogance of the sovereign; the provinces and distant cities outraged by fiscal exactions; while potent enemies in the neighbourhood lay watching the hour when they might assail their formidable rival with advantage. Still the kingdom was strong in its internal resources, in the will of its monarch, in the long habitual deference to his authority,—in short, in the terror of his name, and in the valor and discipline of his armies, grown grey in active service, and well drilled in all the tactics of Indian warfare. The time had now come, when these imperfect tactics and rude weapons of the barbarian were to be brought into collision with the science and enginery of the most civilized nations of the globe.

During the latter years of his reign, Montezuma had rarely taken part in his military expeditions, which he left to his captains, occupying himself chiefly with his sacerdotal functions. Under no prince had the priesthood enjoyed greater consideration and immunities. The religious festivals and rites were celebrated with unprecedented pomp. The oracles were consulted on the most trivial occasions; and the sanguinary deities were propitiated by hecatombs of victims dragged in triumph to the capital from the conquered or rebellious provinces. The religion, or, to speak correctly, the superstition of Montezuma proved a principal cause of his calamities.

In a preceding chapter I have noticed the popular traditions respecting Quetzalcoatl, that deity with a fair complexion and flowing beard, so unlike the Indian physiognomy, who, after fulfilling his mission of benevolence among the Aztecs, embarked on the Atlantic Sea for the mysterious shores of Tlapallan. He promised, on his departure, to return at some future day with his posterity, and resume the possession of his empire. That day was looked forward to with hope or with apprehension, according to the interest of the believer, but with general confidence throughout the wide borders of Anahuac. Even after the Conquest, it still lingered among the Indian races, by whom it was as fondly cherished, as the advent of their king Sebastian continued to be by the Portuguese, or that of the Messiah by the Jews.

A general feeling seems to have prevailed in the time of Montezuma, that the period for the return of the deity, and the full accomplishment of his promise, was near at hand. This conviction is said to have gained ground from various preternatural occurrences, reported with more or less detail by all the most ancient historians. In 1510, the great lake of Tezcuco, without the occurrence of a tempest, or earthquake, or any other visible cause, became violently agitated, overflowed its banks, and, pouring into the streets of Mexico, swept off many of the buildings by the fury of the waters. In 1511, one of the turrets of the great temple took fire, equally without any apparent cause, and continued to burn in defiance of all attempts to extinguish it. In the following years, three comets were seen; and not long before the coming of the Spaniards a strange light broke forth in the east. It spread broad at its base on the horizon, and rising in a pyramidal form tapered off as it approached the zenith. It resembled a vast sheet or flood of fire, emitting sparkles, or, as an old writer expresses it, "seemed thickly powdered with stars." At the same time, low voices were heard in the air, and doleful wailings, as if to announce some strange, mysterious calamity! The Aztec monarch, terrified at the apparitions in the heavens, took counsel of Nezahualpilli, who was a great proficient in the subtle science of astrology. But the royal sage cast a deeper cloud over his spirit, by reading in these prodigies the speedy downfall of the empire.

Such are the strange stories reported by the chroniclers, in which it is not impossible to detect the glimmerings of truth. Nearly thirty years had elapsed since the discovery of the Islands by Columbus, and more than twenty since his visit to the American continent. Rumors, more or less distinct, of this wonderful appearance of the white men, bearing in their hands the thunder and the lightning, so like in many respects to the traditions of Quetzalcoatl, would naturally spread far and wide among the Indian nations. Such rumors, doubtless, long before the landing of the Spaniards in Mexico, found their way up the grand plateau, filling the minds of men with anticipations of the near coming of the period when the great deity was to return and receive his own again.

In the excited state of their imaginations, prodigies became a familiar occurrence. Or rather, events not very uncommon in themselves, seen through the discolored medium of fear, were easily magnified into prodigies; and the accidental swell of the lake, the appearance of a comet, and the conflagration of a building were all interpreted as the special annunciations of Heaven. Thus it happens in those great political convulsions which shake the foundations of society,—the mighty events that cast their shadows before them in their coming. Then it is that the atmosphere is agitated with the low, prophetic murmurs, with which Nature, in the moral as in the physical world, announces the march of the hurricane;

> "When from the shores
> And forest-rustling mountains comes a voice,
> That, solemn sounding, bids the world prepare!"

When tidings were brought to the capital, of the landing of Grijalva on the coast, in the preceding year, the heart of Montezuma was filled with dismay. He felt as if the destinies which had so long brooded over the royal line of Mexico were to be accomplished, and the sceptre was to pass away from his house for ever. Though somewhat relieved by the departure of the Spaniards, he caused sentinels to be stationed on the heights; and, when the Europeans returned under Cortés, he doubtless received the earliest notice of the unwelcome event. It was by his orders, however, that the provincial governor had prepared so hospitable a reception for them. The hieroglyphical report of these strange visiters, now forwarded to the capital, revived all his apprehensions. He called, without delay, a meeting of his principal counsellors, including the kings of Tezcuco and Tlacopan, and laid the matter before them. . . .

WHILE Montezuma pondered the nature of the Spaniards—were they invaders to be expelled or gods to be welcomed?—the Spaniards, marveling at the wealth indicated by the Aztec presents, took steps to establish themselves in the land.

V

A Base for Operations

THERE is no situation which tries so severely the patience and discipline of the soldier, as a life of idleness in camp, where his thoughts, instead of being bent on enterprise and action, are fastened on himself and the inevitable privations and dangers of his condition. This was particularly the case in the present instance, where, in addition to the evils of a scanty subsistence, the troops suffered from excessive heat, swarms of venomous insects, and the other annoyances of a sultry climate. They were, moreover, far from possessing the character of regular forces, trained to subordination under a commander whom they had long been taught to reverence and obey. They were soldiers of fortune, embarked with him in an adventure in which all seemed to have an equal stake, and they regarded their captain—the captain of a day—as little more than an equal.

There was a growing discontent among the men at their longer residence in this strange land. They were still more dissatisfied on learning the general's intention to remove to the neighbourhood of the port discovered by Montejo. "It was time to return," they said, "and report what had been done to the governor of Cuba, and not linger on these barren shores until they had brought the whole Mexican empire on their heads!" Cortés evaded their importunities as well as he could, assuring them there was no cause for despondency. "Every thing so far had gone on prosperously, and, when they had taken up a more favorable position, there was no reason to doubt they might still continue the same profitable intercourse with the natives."

While this was passing, five Indians made their appearance in the camp one morning, and were brought to the general's tent. Their dress and whole appearance were different from those of the Mexicans. They wore rings of gold, and gems of a bright blue stone in their ears and nostrils, while a gold leaf delicately wrought was attached to the under lip. Marina was unable to comprehend their language, but, on her addressing them in Aztec, two of them, it was found, could converse in that tongue. They said they were natives of Cempoalla, the chief town of the Totonacs, a powerful nation who had come upon the great plateau many centuries back, and, descending its eastern slope, settled along the sierras and broad plains which skirt the Mexican Gulf towards the north. Their country was one of the recent conquests of the Aztecs, and they experienced such vexatious oppressions from their conquerors as made them very impatient of the yoke. They informed Cortés of these and other particulars. The fame of the Spaniards had reached their master, who sent these messengers to request the presence of the wonderful strangers in his capital.

This communication was eagerly listened to by the general, who, it will be remembered, was possessed of none of those facts, laid before the reader, respecting the internal condition of the kingdom, which he had no reason to suppose other than strong and united. An important truth now flashed on his mind; as his quick eye descried in this spirit of discontent a potent lever, by the aid of which he might hope to overturn this barbaric empire.—He received the mission of the Totonacs most graciously, and, after informing himself, as far as possible, of their dispositions and resources, dismissed them with presents, promising soon to pay a visit to their lord.

Meanwhile, his personal friends, among whom may be particularly mentioned Alonso Hernández Puertocarrero, Christóval de Olid, Alonso de Ávila, Pedro de Alvarado and his brothers, were very busy in persuading the troops to take such measures as should enable Cortés to go forward in those ambitious plans, for which he had no warrant from the powers of Velásquez. "To return now," they said, "was to abandon the enterprise on the threshold, which, under such a leader, must conduct to glory and incalculable riches. To return to Cuba would be to surrender to the greedy governor the little gains they had already got. The only way was to persuade the general to establish a permanent colony in the country, the government of which would take the conduct of matters into its own hands, and provide for the interests of its members. It was true, Cortés had no such authority from Velásquez. But the interests of the Sovereigns, which were paramount to every other, imperatively demanded it."

These conferences could not be conducted so secretly, though held by night, as not to reach the ears of the friends of Velásquez. They remonstrated against the proceedings, as insidious and disloyal. They accused the general of instigating them; and, calling on him to take measures without delay for the return of the troops to Cuba, announced their own intention to depart, with such followers as still remained true to the governor.

Cortés, instead of taking umbrage at this high-handed proceeding, or even answering in the same haughty tone, mildly replied, "that nothing was further from his desire than to exceed his instructions. He, indeed, preferred to remain in the country, and continue his profitable intercourse with the natives. But, since the army thought otherwise, he should defer to their opinion, and give orders to return, as they desired." On the following morning, proclamation was made for the troops to hold themselves in readiness to embark at once on board the fleet, which was to sail for Cuba.

Great was the sensation caused by their general's order. Even many of those before clamorous for it, with the usual caprice of men whose wishes are too easily gratified, now regretted it. The partisans of Cortés were loud in their remonstrances.

"They were betrayed by the general," they cried, and, thronging round his tent, called on him to countermand his orders. "We came here," said they, "expecting to form a settlement, if the state of the country authorized it. Now it seems you have no warrant from the governor to make one. But there are interests, higher than those of Velásquez, which demand it. These territories are not his property, but were discovered for the Sovereigns; and it is necessary to plant a colony to watch over their interests, instead of wasting time in idle barter, or, still worse, of returning, in the present state of affairs, to Cuba. If you refuse," they concluded, "we shall protest against your conduct as disloyal to their Highnesses."

Cortés received this remonstrance with the embarrassed air of one by whom it was altogether unexpected. He modestly requested time for deliberation, and promised to give his answer on the following day. At the time appointed, he called the troops together, and made them a brief address. "There was no one," he said, "if he knew his own heart, more deeply devoted than himself to the welfare of his sovereigns, and the glory of the Spanish name. He had not only expended his all, but incurred heavy debts, to meet the charges of this expedition, and had hoped to reimburse himself by continuing his traffic with the Mexicans. But, if the soldiers thought a different course advisable, he was ready to postpone his own advantage to the good of the state." He concluded by declaring his willingness to take measures for settling a colony *in the name of the Spanish sovereigns,* and to nominate a magistracy to preside over it.

For the *alcaldes* he selected Puertocarrero and Montejo, the former cavalier his fast friend, and the latter the friend of Velásquez, and chosen for that very reason; a stroke of policy which perfectly succeeded. The *regidores, alguacil,* treasurer, and other functionaries, were then appointed, all of them his personal friends and adherents. They were regularly sworn into office, and the new city received the title of *Villa Rica de Vera Cruz,* "The Rich Town of the True Cross"; a name which was considered as happily intimating that union of spiritual and temporal interests to which the arms of the Spanish adventurers in the New World were to be devoted. Thus, by a single stroke of the pen, as it were, the camp was transformed into a civil community, and the whole frame-work and even title of the city were arranged, before the site of it had been settled.

The new municipality were not slow in coming together; when Cortés presented himself, cap in hand, before that august body, and, laying the powers of Velásquez on the table, respectfully tendered the resignation of his office of Captain-General, "which, indeed," he said, "had necessarily expired, since the authority of the governor was now superseded by that of the magistracy of Villa Rica de Vera Cruz." He then, with a profound obeisance, left the apartment.

The council, after a decent time spent in deliberation, again requested his presence. "There was no one," they said, "who, on mature reflection, appeared to them so well qualified to take charge of the interests of the community, both in peace and in war, as himself; and they unanimously named him, in behalf of their Catholic Highnesses, Captain-General and Chief Justice of the colony." He was further empowered to draw, on his own account, one fifth of the gold and silver which might hereafter be obtained by commerce or conquest from the natives. Thus clothed with supreme civil and military jurisdiction, Cortés was not backward in exerting his authority. He found speedy occasion for it.

The transactions above described had succeeded each other so rapidly, that the governor's party seemed to be taken by surprise, and had formed no plan of opposition. When the last measure was carried however, they broke forth into the most indignant and opprobrious invectives, denouncing the whole as a systematic conspiracy against Velásquez. These accusations led to recrimination from the soldiers of the other side, until from words they nearly proceeded to blows. Some of the principal cavaliers, among them Velásquez de León, a kinsman of the governor, Escobar, his page, and Diego de Ordaz, were so active in instigating these turbulent movements, that Cortés took the bold measure of putting them all in irons, and sending them on board the vessels. He then dispersed the common file by detaching many of them with a strong party under Alvarado to forage the neighbouring country, and bring home provisions for the destitute camp.

During their absence, every argument that cupidity or ambition could suggest was used to win the refractory to his views. Promises, and even gold, it is said, were liberally lavished; till, by degrees, their understandings were opened to a clearer view of the merits of the case. And when the foraging party reappeared with abundance of poultry and vegetables, and the cravings of the stomach—that great laboratory of disaffection, whether in camp or capital—were appeased, good-humor returned with good cheer, and the rival factions embraced one another as companions in arms, pledged to a common cause. Even the high-mettled hidalgos on board the vessels did not long withstand the general tide of reconciliation, but one by one gave in their adhesion to the new government. What is more remarkable is that this forced conversion was not a hollow one, but from this time forward several of these very cavaliers became the most steady and devoted partisans of Cortés.

Such was the address of this extraordinary man, and such the ascendency which in a few months he had acquired over these wild and turbulent spirits! By this ingenious transformation of a military into a civil community, he had secured a new and effectual basis for future operations. He might now go forward without fear of check or control from a superior,—at least from any other superior than the Crown, under which alone he held his commission. In accomplishing this, instead of incurring the charge of usurpation, or of transcending his legitimate powers, he had transferred the responsibility, in a great measure, to those who had imposed on him the necessity of action. By this step, moreover, he had linked the fortunes of his followers indissolubly with his own. They had taken their chance with him, and, whether for weal or for woe, must abide the consequences. He was no longer limited to the narrow concerns of a sordid traffic, but, sure of their coöperation, might now boldly meditate, and gradually disclose, those lofty schemes which he had formed in his own bosom for the conquest of an empire. . . .

ARRIVING in Cempoalla, the Spaniards saw their first sizable Indian community. Employing his interpreters with its natives and the neighboring Totonacs, Cortés diplomatically set about winning his first Indian allies. While making the most of a divide-and-conquer technique, he reinforced Spanish identification with the land by selecting a site for the town of Vera Cruz. Soon another Aztec embassy came down to the coast and waited upon Cortés. Once more the gifts received multiplied Spanish desire to plunge into the interior. But before that could be undertaken, the Spanish commander had to consolidate his following and promote his own cause.

VI

The Die Is Cast

CORTÉS now resolved to put a plan in execution which he had been some time meditating. He knew that all the late acts of the colony, as well as his own authority, would fall to the ground without the royal sanction. He knew, too, that the interest of Velásquez, which was great at court, would, so soon as he was acquainted with his secession, be wholly employed to circumvent and crush him. He resolved to anticipate his movements, and to send a vessel to Spain, with despatches addressed to the emperor himself, announcing the nature and extent of his discoveries, and to obtain, if possible, the confirmation of his proceedings. In order to conciliate his master's good-will, he further proposed to send him such a present, as should suggest lofty ideas of the importance of his own services to the crown. To effect this, the royal fifth he considered inadequate. He conferred with his officers, and persuaded them to relinquish their share of the treasure. At his instance, they made a similar application to the soldiers; representing that it was the earnest wish of the general, who set the example by resigning his own fifth, equal to the share of the crown. It was but little that each man was asked to surrender, but the whole would make a present worthy of the monarch for whom it was intended. By this sacrifice, they might hope to secure his indulgence for the past, and his favor for the future; a temporary sacrifice, that would be well repaid by the security of the rich possessions which awaited them in Mexico. A paper was then circulated among the soldiers, which, all who were disposed to relinquish their shares, were requested to sign. Those who declined should have their claims respected, and receive the amount due to them. No one refused to sign; thus furnishing another example of the extraordinary power obtained by Cortés over these rapacious spirits, who, at his call, surrendered up the very treasures which had been the great object of their hazardous enterprise!

He accompanied this present with a letter to the emperor, in which he gave a full account of all that had befallen him since his departure from Cuba; of his various discoveries, battles, and traffic with the natives; their conversion to Christianity; his strange perils and sufferings; many particulars respecting the lands he had visited, and such as he could collect in regard to the great Mexican monarchy and its sovereign. He stated his difficulties with the governor of Cuba, the proceedings of the army in reference to colonization, and besought the emperor to confirm their acts, as well as his own authority, expressing his entire confidence that he should be able, with the aid of his brave followers, to place the Castilian crown in possession of this great Indian empire!

This was the celebrated *First Letter,* as it is called, of Cortés, which has hitherto eluded every search that has been made for it in the libraries of Europe. Its existence is fully established by references to it, both in his own subsequent letters, and in the writings of contemporaries. Its general purport is given by his chaplain, Gómara. The importance of the document has doubtless been much overrated; and, should it ever come to light, it will probably be found to add little of interest to the matter contained in the letter from Vera Cruz, which has formed the basis of the preceding portion of our narrative. He had no sources of information beyond those open to the authors of the latter document. He was even less full and frank in his communications, if it be true, that he suppressed all notice of the discoveries of his two immediate predecessors.

The magistrates of the Villa Rica, in their epistle, went over the same ground with Cortés; concluding with an emphatic representation of the misconduct of Velásquez, whose venality, extortion, and selfish devotion to his personal interests, to the exclusion of those of his sovereigns as well as of his own followers, they placed in a most clear and unenviable light. They implored the government not to sanction his interference with the new colony, which would be fatal to its welfare, but to commit the undertaking to Hernando Cortés, as the man most capable, by his experience and conduct, of bringing it to a glorious termination.

With this letter went also another in the name of the citizen-soldiers of Villa Rica, tendering their dutiful submission to the sovereigns, and requesting the confirmation of their proceedings, above all, that of Cortés as their general.

The selection of the agents for the mission was a delicate matter, as on the result might depend the future fortunes of the colony and its commander. Cortés intrusted the affair to two cavaliers on whom he could rely; Francisco de Montejo, the ancient partisan of Velásquez, and Alonso Hernández de Puertocarrero. The latter officer was a near kinsman of the count of Medellín, and it was hoped his high connexions might secure a favorable influence at court.

Together with the treasure, which seemed to verify the assertion that "the land teemed with gold as abundantly as that whence Solomon drew the same precious metal for his temple," several Indian manuscripts were sent. Some were of cotton, others of the Mexican *agave*. Their unintelligible characters, says a chronicler, excited little interest in the Conquerors. As evidence of intellectual culture, however, they formed higher objects of interest to a philosophic mind, than those costly fabrics which attested only the mechanical ingenuity of the nation. Four Indian slaves were added as specimens of the natives. They had been rescued from the cages in which they were confined for sacrifice. One of the best vessels of the fleet was selected for the voyage, manned by fifteen seamen, and placed under the direction of the pilot Alaminos. He was directed to hold his course through the Bahama channel, north of Cuba, or Fernandina, as it was then called, and on no account to touch at that island, or any other in the Indian ocean. With these instructions, the good ship took its departure on the 26th of July, freighted with the treasures and the good wishes of the community of the Villa Rica de Vera Cruz.

After a quick run the emissaries made the island of Cuba, and, in direct disregard of orders, anchored before Marien, on the northern side of the island. This was done to accommodate Montejo, who wished to visit a plantation owned by him in the neighbourhood. While off the port, a sailor got on shore, and, crossing the island to St. Jago, the capital, spread everywhere tidings of the expedition, until they reached the ears of Velásquez. It was the first intelligence which had been received of the armament since its departure; and, as the governor listened to the recital, it would not be easy to paint the mingled emotions of curiosity, astonishment, and wrath which agitated his bosom. In the first sally of passion, he poured a storm of invective on the heads of his secretary and treasurer, the friends of Cortés, who had recommended him as the leader of the expedition. After somewhat relieving himself in this way, he despatched two fast-sailing vessels to Marien with orders to seize the rebel ship, and, in case of her departure, to follow and overtake her.

But before the ships could reach that port, the bird had flown, and was far on her way across the broad Atlantic. Stung with mortification at this fresh disappointment, Velásquez wrote letters of indignant complaint to the government at home, and to the fathers of St. Jerome, in Hispaniola, demanding redress. He obtained little satisfaction from the last. He resolved, however, to take it into his own hands, and set about making formidable preparations for another squadron, which should be more than a match for that under his rebellious officer. He was indefatigable in his exertions, visiting every part of the island, and straining all his resources to effect his purpose. The preparations were on a scale that necessarily consumed many months.

Meanwhile the little vessel was speeding her prosperous way across the waters; and, after touching at one of the Azores, came safely into the harbour of St. Lucar, in the month of October. However long it may appear, in the more perfect nautical science of our day, it was reckoned a fair voyage for that. Of what befell the commissioners on their arrival, their reception at court, and the sensation caused by their intelligence, I defer the account to a future chapter.

Shortly after the departure of the commissioners, an affair occurred of a most unpleasant nature. A number of persons, with the priest Juan Díaz at their head, ill-affected, from some cause or other, towards the administration of Cortés, or not relishing the hazardous expedition before them, laid a plan to seize one of the vessels, make the best of their way to Cuba, and report to the governor the fate of the armament. It was conducted with so much secrecy, that the party had got their provisions, water, and every thing necessary for the voyage, on board, without detection; when the conspiracy was betrayed, on the very night they were to sail, by one of their own number, who repented the part he had taken in it. The general caused the persons implicated to be instantly apprehended. An examination was instituted. The guilt of the parties was placed beyond a doubt. Sentence of death was passed on two of the ringleaders; another, the pilot, was condemned to lose his feet, and several others to be whipped. The priest, probably the most guilty of the whole, claiming the usual benefit of clergy, was permitted to escape. One of those condemned to the gallows was named Escudero, the very alguacil who, the reader may remember, so stealthily apprehended Cortés before the sanctuary in Cuba. The general, on signing the death-warrants, was heard to exclaim, "Would that I had never learned to write!" It was not the first time, it was remarked, that the exclamation had been uttered in similar circumstances.

The arrangements being now finally settled at the Villa Rica, Cortés sent forward Alvarado, with a large part of the army, to Cempoalla, where he soon after joined them with the remainder. The late affair of the conspiracy seems to have made a deep impression on his mind. It showed him, that there were timid spirits in the camp on whom he could not rely, and who, he feared, might spread the seeds of disaffection among their companions. Even the more resolute, on any occasion of disgust or disappointment hereafter, might falter in purpose, and, getting possession of the vessels, abandon the enterprise. This was already too vast, and the odds were too formidable, to authorize expectation of success with diminution of numbers. Experience showed that this was always to be apprehended, while means of escape were at hand. The best chance for success was to cut off these means.—He came to the daring resolution to destroy the fleet, without the knowledge of his army.

When arrived at Cempoalla, he communicated his design to a few of his devoted adherents, who entered warmly into his views. Through them he readily persuaded the pilots, by means of those golden arguments which weigh more than any other with ordinary minds, to make such a report of the condition of the fleet as suited his purpose. The ships, they said, were grievously racked by the heavy gales they had encountered, and, what was worse, the worms had eaten into their sides and bottoms until most of them were not sea-worthy, and some, indeed, could scarcely now be kept afloat.

Cortés received the communication with surprise; "for he could well dissemble," observes Las Casas, with his usual friendly comment, "when it suited his interests." "If it be so," he exclaimed, "we must make the best of it! Heaven's will be done!" He then ordered five of the worst conditioned to be dismantled, their cordage, sails, iron, and whatever was mova-

ble, to be brought on shore, and the ships to be sunk. A survey
was made of the others, and, on a similar report, four more were
condemned in the same manner. Only one small vessel remained!

When the intelligence reached the troops in Cempoalla, it
caused the deepest consternation. They saw themselves cut
off by a single blow from friends, family, country! The stoutest
hearts quailed before the prospect of being thus abandoned on
a hostile shore, a handful of men arrayed against a formidable
empire. When the news arrived of the destruction of the five
vessels first condemned, they had acquiesced in it as a necessary measure, knowing the mischievous activity of the insects
in these tropical seas. But, when this was followed by the loss
of the remaining four, suspicions of the truth flashed on their
minds. They felt they were betrayed. Murmurs, at first deep,
swelled louder and louder, menacing open mutiny. "Their
general," they said, "had led them like cattle to be butchered
in the shambles!" The affair wore a most alarming aspect. In
no situation was Cortés ever exposed to greater danger from
his soldiers.

His presence of mind did not desert him at this crisis. He
called his men together, and, employing the tones of persuasion
rather than authority, assured them, that a survey of the ships
showed they were not fit for service. If he had ordered them
to be destroyed, they should consider, also, that his was the
greatest sacrifice, for they were his property,—all, indeed, he
possessed in the world. The troops, on the other hand, would
derive one great advantage from it, by the addition of a hundred
able-bodied recruits, before required to man the vessels. But,
even if the fleet had been saved, it could have been of little
service in their present expedition; since they would not need
it if they succeeded, while they would be too far in the interior
to profit by it if they failed. He besought them to turn their
thoughts in another direction. To be thus calculating chances
and means of escape was unworthy of brave souls. They had
set their hands to the work; to look back, as they advanced,

would be their ruin. They had only to resume their former confidence in themselves and their general, and success was certain. "As for me," he concluded, "I have chosen my part. I will remain here, while there is one to bear me company. If there be any so craven, as to shrink from sharing the dangers of our glorious enterprise, let them go home, in God's name. There is still one vessel left. Let them take that and return to Cuba. They can tell there, how they have deserted their commander and their comrades, and patiently wait till we return loaded with the spoils of the Aztecs."

The politic orator had touched the right chord in the bosoms of the soldiers. As he spoke, their resentment gradually died away. The faded visions of future riches and glory, rekindled by his eloquence, again floated before their imaginations. The first shock over, they felt ashamed of their temporary distrust. The enthusiasm for their leader revived, for they felt that under his banner only they could hope for victory; and, as he concluded, they testified the revulsion of their feelings by making the air ring with their shouts, "To Mexico! to Mexico!"

The destruction of his fleet by Cortés is, perhaps, the most remarkable passage in the life of this remarkable man. History, indeed, affords examples of a similar expedient in emergencies somewhat similar; but none where the chances of success were so precarious, and defeat would be so disastrous. Had he failed, it might well seem an act of madness. Yet it was the fruit of deliberate calculation. He had set fortune, fame, life itself, all upon the cast, and must abide the issue. There was no alternative in his mind but to succeed or perish. The measure he adopted greatly increased the chance of success. But to carry it into execution, in the face of an incensed and desperate soldiery, was an act of resolution that has few parallels in history.

BOOK THREE

March to Mexico

ESTABLISHING a garrison at Vera Cruz, and naming Juan de Escalante its commander, Cortés began preparations for the march into the interior.

I

Marching Inland

THE forces reserved for the expedition amounted to about four hundred foot and fifteen horse, with seven pieces of artillery. He obtained, also, thirteen hundred Indian warriors, and a thousand *tamanes,* or porters, from the cacique of Cempoalla, to drag the guns, and transport the baggage. He took forty more of their principal men as hostages, as well as to guide him on the way, and serve him by their counsels among the strange tribes he was to visit. They were, in fact, of essential service to him throughout the march.

The remainder of his Spanish force he left in garrison at Villa Rica de Vera Cruz, the command of which he had intrusted to the alguacil, Juan de Escalante, an officer devoted to his interests. The selection was judicious. It was important to place there a man who would resist any hostile interference from his European rivals, on the one hand, and maintain the present friendly relations with the natives, on the other. Cortés recommended the Totonac chiefs to apply to this officer, in case of any difficulty, assuring them that, so long as they remained faithful to their new sovereign and religion, they should find a sure protection in the Spaniards.

Before marching, the general spoke a few words of encouragement to his own men. He told them, they were now to embark, in earnest, on an enterprise which had been the great object of their desires; and that the blessed Saviour would carry them victorious through every battle with their enemies. "Indeed," he added, "this assurance must be our stay, for every other refuge is now cut off, but that afforded by the Providence of

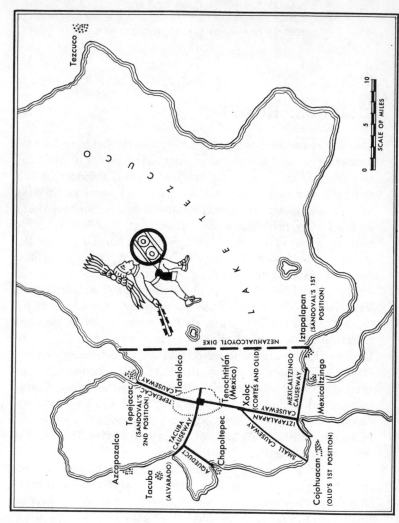

Adapted from C. Harvey Gardiner's *Naval Power in the Conquest of Mexico*

God, and your own stout hearts." He ended by comparing
their achievements to those of the ancient Romans, "in phrases
of honeyed eloquence far beyond any thing I can repeat," says
the brave and simple-hearted chronicler who heard them.
Cortés was, indeed, master of that eloquence which went to the
soldiers' hearts. For their sympathies were his, and he shared
in that romantic spirit of adventure which belonged to them.
"We are ready to obey you," they cried as with one voice. "Our
fortunes, for better or worse, are cast with yours." Taking leave,
therefore, of their hospitable Indian friends, the little army,
buoyant with high hopes and lofty plans of conquest, set
forward on the march to Mexico.

It was the sixteenth of August, 1519. During the first day,
their road lay through the *tierra caliente,* the beautiful land
where they had been so long lingering; the land of the vanilla,
cochineal, cacao, (not till later days of the orange and the
sugar cane) products which, indigenous to Mexico, have now
become the luxuries of Europe; the land where the fruits and
the flowers chase one another in unbroken circle through the
year; where the gales are loaded with perfumes till the sense
aches at their sweetness; and the groves are filled with many-
colored birds, and insects whose enamelled wings glisten like
diamonds in the bright sun of the tropics. Such are the magical
splendors of this paradise of the senses. Yet Nature, who generally works in a spirit of compensation, has provided one here;
since the same burning sun, which quickens into life these
glories of the vegetable and animal kingdoms, calls forth the
pestilent *malaria,* with its train of bilious disorders, unknown
to the cold skies of the North. The season in which the Spaniards were there, the rainy months of summer, was precisely
that in which the *vómito* rages with greatest fury; when the
European stranger hardly ventures to set his foot on shore, still
less to linger there a day. We find no mention made of it in
the records of the Conquerors, nor any notice, indeed, of an uncommon mortality. The fact doubtless corroborates the theory
of those who postpone the appearance of the yellow fever till

long after the occupation of the country by the whites. It proves, at least, that, if existing before, it must have been in a very much mitigated form.

After some leagues of travel over roads made nearly impassable by the summer rains, the troops began the gradual ascent—more gradual on the eastern than the western declivities of the Cordilleras—which leads up to the table-land of Mexico. At the close of the second day, they reached Xalapa, a place still retaining the same Aztec name, that it has communicated to the drug raised in its environs, the medicinal virtues of which are now known throughout the world. This town stands midway up the long ascent, at an elevation where the vapors from the ocean, touching in their westerly progress, maintain a rich verdure throughout the year. Though somewhat infected with these marine fogs, the air is usually bland and salubrious. The wealthy resident of the lower regions retires here for safety in the heats of summer, and the traveller hails its groves of oak with delight, as announcing that he is above the deadly influence of the *vómito*. From this delicious spot, the Spaniards enjoyed one of the grandest prospects in nature. Before them was the steep ascent,—much steeper after this point,—which they were to climb. On the right rose the *Sierra Madre*, girt with its dark belt of pines, and its long lines of shadowy hills stretching away in the distance. To the south, in brilliant contrast, stood the mighty Orizaba, with his white robe of snow descending far down his sides, towering in solitary grandeur, the giant spectre of the Andes. Behind them, they beheld, unrolled at their feet, the magnificent *tierra caliente*, with its gay confusion of meadows, streams, and flowering forests, sprinkled over with shining Indian villages; while a faint line of light on the edge of the horizon told them that there was the ocean, beyond which were the kindred and country—they were many of them never more to see.

Still winding their way upward, amidst scenery as different as was the temperature from that of the regions below, the army passed through settlements containing some hundreds of inhabitants each, and on the fourth day reached a "strong town," as Cortés terms it, standing on a rocky eminence, supposed to be that now known by the Mexican name of Naulinco. Here they were hospitably entertained by the inhabitants, who were friends of the Totonacs. Cortés endeavoured, through father Olmedo, to impart to them some knowledge of Christian truths, which were kindly received, and the Spaniards were allowed to erect a cross in the place, for the future adoration of the natives. Indeed, the route of the army might be tracked by these emblems of man's salvation, raised wherever a willing population of Indians invited it, suggesting a very different idea from what the same memorials intimate to the traveller in these mountain solitudes in our day.

The troops now entered a rugged defile, the Bishop's Pass, as it is called, capable of easy defence against an army. Very soon they experienced a most unwelcome change of climate. Cold winds from the mountains, mingled with rain, and, as they rose still higher, with driving sleet and hail, drenched their garments, and seemed to penetrate to their very bones. The Spaniards, indeed, partially covered by their armor and thick jackets of quilted cotton were better able to resist the weather, though their long residence in the sultry regions of the valley made them still keenly sensible to the annoyance. But the poor Indians, natives of the *tierra caliente,* with little protection in the way of covering, sunk under the rude assault of the elements, and several of them perished on the road.

The aspect of the country was as wild and dreary as the climate. Their route wound along the spur of the huge Cofre de Perote, which borrows its name, both in Mexican and Castilian, from the coffer-like rock on its summit. It is one of the great volcanoes of New Spain. It exhibits now, indeed, no vestige of a crater on its top, but abundant traces of volcanic action at its base, where acres of lava, blackened scoriæ, and cinders, proclaim the convulsions of nature, while numerous shrubs and mouldering trunks of enormous trees, among the crevices, attest the antiquity of these events. Working their toilsome way across this scene of desolation, the path often led them along the borders of precipices, down whose sheer depths of two or three thousand feet the shrinking eye might behold another climate, and see all the glowing vegetation of the tropics choking up the bottom of the ravines.

After three days of this fatiguing travel, the way-worn army emerged through another defile, the *Sierra del Agua*. They soon came upon an open reach of country, with a genial climate, such as belongs to the temperate latitudes of southern Europe. They had reached the level of more than seven thousand feet above the ocean, where the great sheet of table-land spreads out for hundreds of miles along the crests of the Cordilleras. The country showed signs of careful cultivation, but the products were, for the most part, not familiar to the eyes of the Spaniards. Fields and hedges of the various tribes of the cactus, the towering organum, and plantations of aloes with rich yellow clusters of flowers on their tall stems, affording drink and clothing to the Aztec, were everywhere seen. The plants of the torrid and temperate zones had disappeared, one after another, with the ascent into these elevated regions. The glossy and dark-leaved banana, the chief, as it is the cheapest, aliment of the countries below, had long since faded from the landscape. The hardy maize, however, still shone with its golden harvests in all the pride of cultivation, the great staple of the higher, equally with the lower terraces of the plateau.

Suddenly the troops came upon what seemed the environs of a populous city, which, as they entered it, appeared to surpass even that of Cempoalla in the size and solidity of its structures. These were of stone and lime, many of them spacious and tolerably high. There were thirteen *teocallis* in the place; and in the suburbs they had seen a receptacle, in which, according to Bernal Díaz, were stored a hundred thousand skulls of human victims, all piled and ranged in order! He reports the number as one he had ascertained by counting them himself. Whatever faith we may attach to the precise accuracy of his figures, the result is almost equally startling.

The Spaniards were destined to become familiar with this appalling spectacle, as they approached nearer to the Aztec capital.

The lord of the town ruled over twenty thousand vassals. He was tributary to Montezuma, and a strong Mexican garrison was quartered in the place. He had probably been advised of the approach of the Spaniards, and doubted how far it would be welcome to his sovereign. At all events, he gave them a cold reception, the more unpalatable after the extraordinary sufferings of the last few days. To the inquiry of Cortés, whether he were subject to Montezuma, he answered, with real of affected surprise, "Who is there that is not a vassal to Montezuma?" The general told him, with some emphasis, that he was not. He then explained whence and why he came, assuring him that he served a monarch who had princes for his vassals as powerful as the Aztec monarch himself.

The cacique in turn fell nothing short of the Spaniard, in the pompous display of the grandeur and resources of the Indian emperor. He told his guest that Montezuma could muster thirty great vassals, each master of a hundred thousand men! His revenues were immense, as every subject, however poor, paid something. They were all expended on his magnificent state, and in support of his armies. These were continually in the field, while garrisons were maintained in most of the large cities of the empire. More than twenty thousand victims, the fruit of his wars, were annually sacrificed on the altars of his gods! His capital, the cacique said, stood in a lake, in the centre of a spacious valley. The lake was commanded by the emperor's vessels, and the approach to the city was by means of causeways, several miles long, connected in parts by wooden bridges, which, when raised, cut off all communication with the country. Some other things he added, in answer to the queries of his guest, in which, as the reader may imagine, the crafty, or credulous cacique varnished over the truth with a lively coloring of romance. Whether romance, or reality, the Spaniards could not determine. The particulars they gleaned were not of a kind to tranquillize their minds, and might well have made bolder hearts than theirs pause, ere they advanced. But far from it. "The words which we heard," says the stout old cavalier, so often quoted, "however they may have filled us with wonder, made us—such is the temper of the Spaniard—only the more earnest to prove the adventure, desperate as it might appear."

In a further conversation Cortés inquired of the chief, whether his country abounded in gold, and intimated a desire to take home some, as specimens to his sovereign. But the Indian lord declined to give him any, saying it might displease Montezuma. "Should he command it," he added, "my gold, my person, and all I possess, shall be at your disposal." The general did not press the matter further. . . .

As they trudged west across the coastal plain and then up through the eastern mountain range of Mexico, the Spaniards experienced conditions unlike any encountered elsewhere in the New World. The scenery was picturesque but the march was an arduous one, despite the aid in the baggage train from the Indian allies. Approaching Tlaxcala, that fiercely militant island of independence in a sea of Aztec dominion, Cortés sent an Indian embassy forward. But the people who had jealously maintained their freedom in the face of constant Aztec pressures were not to be won by words. Instead, one desperate battle followed another.

II

At War with Tlaxcala

THEY had not proceeded far, when they were met by the two remaining Cempoallan envoys, who with looks of terror informed the general that they had been treacherously seized and confined, in order to be sacrificed at an approaching festival of the Tlascalans, but in the night had succeeded in making their escape. They gave the unwelcome tidings, also, that a large force of the natives was already assembled to oppose the progress of the Spaniards.

Soon after, they came in sight of a body of Indians, about a thousand, apparently, all armed and brandishing their weapons, as the Christians approached, in token of defiance. Cortés, when he had come within hearing, ordered the interpreters to proclaim that he had no hostile intentions; but wished only to be allowed a passage through their country, which he had entered as a friend. This declaration he commanded the royal notary, Godoy, to record on the spot, that, if blood were shed, it might not be charged on the Spaniards. This pacific proclamation was met, as usual on such occasions, by a shower of darts, stones, and arrows, which fell like rain on the Spaniards, rattling on their stout harness, and in some instances penetrating to the skin. Galled by the smart of their wounds, they called on the general to lead them on, till he sounded the well known battle-cry, "St. Jago, and at them!"

The Indians maintained their ground for a while with spirit, when they retreated with precipitation, but not in disorder. The Spaniards, whose blood was heated by the encounter, followed up their advantage with more zeal than prudence, suffering the wily enemy to draw them into a narrow glen or defile, intersected by a little stream of water, where the broken ground was impracticable for artillery, as well as for the movements of cavalry. Pressing forward with eagerness, to extricate themselves from their perilous position, to their great dismay, on turning an abrupt angle of the pass, they came in presence of a numerous army, choking up the gorge of the valley, and stretching far over the plains beyond. To the astonished eyes of Cortés, they appeared a hundred thousand men, while no account estimates them at less than thirty thousand.

They presented a confused assemblage of helmets, weapons, and many-colored plumes, glancing bright in the morning sun, and mingled with banners, above which proudly floated one that bore as a device the heron on a rock. It was the well known ensign of the house of Titcala, and, as well as the white and yellow stripes on the bodies, and the like colors on the feather-mail of the Indians, showed that they were the warriors of Xicotencatl.

As the Spaniards came in sight, the Tlascalans set up a hideous war-cry, or rather whistle, piercing the ear with its shrillness, and which, with the beat of their melancholy drums, that could be heard for half a league or more, might well have filled the stoutest heart with dismay. This formidable host came rolling on towards the Christians, as if to overwhelm them by their very numbers. But the courageous band of warriors, closely serried together and sheltered under their strong panoplies, received the shock unshaken, while the broken masses of the enemy, chafing and heaving tumultuously around them, seemed to recede only to return with new and accumulated force.

Cortés, as usual, in the front of danger, in vain endeavoured, at the head of the horse, to open a passage for the infantry. Still his men, both cavalry and foot, kept their array unbroken, offering no assailable point to their foe. A body of the Tlascalans, however, acting in concert, assaulted a soldier named Moran, one of the best riders in the troop. They succeeded in dragging him from his horse, which they despatched with a thousand blows. The Spaniards, on foot, made a desperate effort to rescue their comrade from the hands of the enemy,—and from the horrible doom of the captive. A fierce struggle now began over the body of the prostrate horse. Ten of the Spaniards were wounded, when they succeeded in retrieving the unfortunate cavalier from his assailants, but in so disastrous a plight that he died on the following day. The horse was borne off in triumph by the Indians, and his mangled remains were sent, a strange trophy, to the different towns of Tlascala. The circumstance troubled the Spanish commander, as it divested the animal of the supernatural terrors with which the superstition of the natives had usually surrounded it. To prevent such a consequence, he had caused the two horses, killed on the preceding day, to be secretly buried on the spot.

The enemy now began to give ground gradually, borne down by the riders, and trampled under the hoofs of their horses. Through the whole of this sharp encounter, the Indian allies were of great service to the Spaniards. They rushed into the water, and grappled their enemies, with the desperation of men who felt that "their only safety was in the despair of safety." "I see nothing but death for us," exclaimed a Cempoallan chief to Marina; "we shall never get through the pass alive." "The God of the Christians is with us," answered the intrepid woman; "and He will carry us safely through."

Amidst the din of battle, the voice of Cortés was heard, cheering on his soldiers. "If we fail now," he cried, "the cross of

Christ can never be planted in this land. Forward, comrades! When was it ever known that a Castilian turned his back on a foe?" Animated by the words and heroic bearing of their general, the soldiers, with desperate efforts, at length succeeded in forcing a passage through the dark columns of the enemy, and emerged from the defile on the open plain beyond.

Here they quickly recovered their confidence with their superiority. The horse soon opened a space for the manœuvres of the artillery. The close files of their antagonists presented a sure mark; and the thunders of the ordnance vomiting forth torrents of fire and sulphurous smoke, the wide desolation caused in their ranks, and the strangely mangled carcasses of the slain, filled the barbarians with consternation and horror. They had no weapons to cope with those terrible engines, and their clumsy missiles, discharged from uncertain hands, seemed to fall ineffectual on the charmed heads of the Christians. What added to their embarrassment was, the desire to carry off the dead and wounded from the field, a general practice among the people of Anahuac, but which necessarily exposed them, while thus employed, to still greater loss.

Eight of their principal chiefs had now fallen; and Xicotencatl, finding himself wholly unable to make head against the Spaniards in the open field, ordered a retreat. Far from the confusion of a panic-struck mob, so common among barbarians, the Tlascalan force moved off the ground with all the order of a well disciplined army. Cortés, as on the preceding day, was too well satisfied with his present advantage to desire to follow it up. It was within an hour of sunset, and he was anxious before nightfall to secure a good position, where he might refresh his wounded troops, and bivouac for the night. . . .

> XICOTENCATL *the younger, leading the Tlaxcalan forces, regrouped and returned to plague the Spaniards.*

As a battle was now inevitable, Cortés resolved to march out and meet the enemy in the field. This would have a show

of confidence, that might serve the double purpose of intimi-
dating the Tlascalans, and inspiriting his own men, whose enthusiasm might lose somewhat of its heat, if compelled to await
the assault of their antagonists, inactive in their own intrenchments. The sun rose bright on the following morning, the 5th
of September, 1519, an eventful day in the history of the Spanish Conquest. The general reviewed his army, and gave them,
preparatory to marching, a few words of encouragement and
advice. The infantry he instructed to rely on the point rather
than the edge of their swords, and to endeavour to thrust their
opponents through the body. The horsemen were to charge at
half speed, with their lances aimed at the eyes of the Indians.
The artillery, the arquebusiers, and crossbow-men, were to
support one another, some loading while others discharged
their pieces, that there should be an unintermitted firing kept
up through the action. Above all, they were to maintain their
ranks close and unbroken, as on this depended their preservation.

They had not advanced a quarter of a league, when they
came in sight of the Tlascalan army. Its dense array stretched
far and wide over a vast plain or meadow ground, about six
miles square. Its appearance justified the report which had
been given of its numbers. Nothing could be more picturesque
than the aspect of these Indian battalions, with the naked bodies of the common soldiers gaudily painted, the fantastic helmets of the chiefs glittering with gold and precious stones, and
the glowing panoplies of feather-work, which decorated their
persons. Innumerable spears and darts tipped with points of
transparent *itztli,* or fiery copper, sparkled bright in the morning sun, like the phosphoric gleams playing on the surface of
a troubled sea, while the rear of the mighty host was dark with
the shadows of banners, on which were emblazoned the armorial
bearings of the great Tlascalan and Otomie chieftains. Among
these, the white heron on the rock, the cognizance of the house
of Xicotencatl, was conspicuous, and, still more, the golden
eagle with outspread wings, in the fashion of a Roman *signum,*

richly ornamented with emeralds and silver-work, the great standard of the republic of Tlascala.

The common file wore no covering except a girdle round the loins. Their bodies were painted with the appropriate colors of the chieftain whose banner they followed. The feather-mail of the higher class of warriors exhibited, also, a similar selection of colors for the like object, in the same manner as the color of the tartan indicates the peculiar clan of the Highlander. The caciques and principal warriors were clothed in a quilted cotton tunic, two inches thick, which, fitting close to the body, protected, also, the thighs and the shoulders. Over this the wealthier Indians wore cuirasses of thin gold plate, or silver. Their legs were defended by leathern boots or sandals, trimmed with gold. But the most brilliant part of their costume was a rich mantle of the *plumaje* or feather-work, embroidered with curious art, and furnishing some resemblance to the gorgeous surcoat worn by the European knight over his armor in the Middle Ages. This graceful and picturesque dress was surmounted by a fantastic head-piece made of wood or leather, representing the head of some wild animal, and frequently displaying a formidable array of teeth. With this covering the warrior's head was enveloped, producing a most grotesque and hideous effect. From the crown floated a splendid panache of the richly variegated plumage of the tropics, indicating, by its form and colors, the rank and family of the wearer. To complete their defensive armor, they carried shields or targets, made sometimes of wood covered with leather, but more usually of a light frame of reeds quilted with cotton, which were preferred, as tougher and less liable to fracture than the former. They had other bucklers, in which the cotton was covered with an elastic substance, enabling them to be shut up in a more compact form, like a fan or umbrella. These shields were decorated with showy ornaments, according to the taste or wealth of the wearer, and fringed with a beautiful pendant of feather-work.

Their weapons were slings, bows and arrows, javelins, and darts. They were accomplished archers, and would discharge two or even three arrows at a time. But they most excelled in throwing the javelin. One species of this, with a thong attached to it, which remained in the slinger's hand, that he might recall the weapon, was especially dreaded by the Spaniards. These various weapons were pointed with bone, or the mineral *itztli,* (obsidian,) the hard vitreous substance, already noticed, as capable of taking an edge like a razor, though easily blunted. Their spears and arrows were also frequently headed with copper. Instead of a sword, they bore a two-handed staff, about three feet and a half long, in which, at regular distances, were inserted, transversely, sharp blades of *itztli,*—a formidable weapon, which, an eyewitness assures us, he had seen fell a horse at a blow.

Such was the costume of the Tlascalan warrior, and, indeed, of that great family of nations generally, who occupied the plateau of Anahuac. Some parts of it, as the targets and the cotton mail or *escaupil,* as it was called in Castilian, were so excellent, that they were subsequently adopted by the Spaniards, as equally effectual in the way of protection, and superior, on the score of lightness and convenience, to their own. They were of sufficient strength to turn an arrow, or the stroke of a javelin, although impotent as a defense against fire-arms. But what armor is not? Yet it is probably no exaggeration to say, that, in convenience, gracefulness, and strength, the arms of the Indian warrior were not very inferior to those of the polished nations of antiquity.

As soon as the Castilians came in sight, the Tlascalans set up their yell of defiance, rising high above the wild barbaric minstrelsy of shell, atabal, and trumpet, with which they proclaimed their triumphant anticipations of victory over the paltry forces of the invaders. When the latter had come within bowshot, the Indians hurled a tempest of missiles, that darkened the sun for a moment as with a passing cloud, strewing the earth around with heaps of stones and arrows. Slowly and steadily the little band of Spaniards held on its way amidst this arrowy shower, until it had reached what appeared the proper distance for delivering its fire with full effect. Cortés then halted, and, hastily forming his troops, opened a general well-directed fire along the whole line. Every shot bore its errand of death; and the ranks of the Indians were mowed down faster than their comrades in the rear could carry off their bodies, according to custom, from the field. The balls in their passage through the crowded files, bearing splinters of the broken harness, and mangled limbs of the warriors, scattered havoc and desolation in their path. The mob of barbarians stood petrified with dismay, till, at length, galled to desperation by their intolerable suffering, they poured forth simultaneously their hideous war-shriek, and rushed impetuously on the Christians.

On they came like an avalanche, or mountain torrent, shaking the solid earth, and sweeping away every obstacle in its path. The little army of Spaniards opposed a bold front to the overwhelming mass. But no strength could withstand it. They faltered, gave way, were borne along before it, and their ranks were broken and thrown into disorder. It was in vain the general called on them to close again and rally. His voice was drowned by the din of the fight and the fierce cries of the assailants. For a moment, it seemed that all was lost. The tide of the battle had turned against them, and the fate of the Christians was sealed.

But every man had that within his bosom, which spoke louder than the voice of the general. Despair gave unnatural energy to his arm. The naked body of the Indian afforded no resistance to the sharp Toledo steel; and with their good swords, the Spanish infantry at length succeeded in staying the human torrent. The heavy guns from a distance thundered on the flank of the assailants, which, shaken by the iron tempest, was thrown into disorder. Their very numbers increased the confusion, as they were precipitated on the masses in front. The horse at the same moment, charging gallantly under Cortés, followed up the advantage, and at length compelled the tumultuous throng to fall back with greater precipitation and disorder than that with which they had advanced.

More than once in the course of the action, a similar assault was attempted by the Tlascalans, but each time with less spirit, and greater loss. They were too deficient in military science to profit by the vast superiority in numbers. They were distributed into companies, it is true, each serving under its own chieftain and banner. But they were not arranged by rank and file, and moved in a confused mass, promiscuously heaped together. They knew not how to concentrate numbers on a given point, or even how to sustain an assault, by employing successive detachments to support and relieve one another. A very small part only of their array could be brought into contact with an enemy inferior to them in amount of forces. The remainder of the army, inactive and worse than useless, in the rear, served only to press tumultuously on the advance, and embarrass its movements by mere weight of numbers, while, on the least alarm, they were seized with a panic and threw the whole body into inextricable confusion. It was, in short, the combat of the ancient Greeks and Persians over again.

Still, the great numerical superiority of the Indians might have enabled them, at a severe cost of their own lives, indeed, to wear out, in time, the constancy of the Spaniards, disabled by wounds and incessant fatigue. But, fortunately for the latter, dissensions arose among their enemies. A Tlascalan chieftain, commanding one of the great divisions, had taken umbrage at the haughty demeanour of Xicotencatl, who had charged him with misconduct or cowardice in the late action. The injured cacique challenged his rival to single combat. This did not take place. But, burning with resentment, he chose the present occasion to indulge it, by drawing off his forces, amounting to ten thousand men, from the field. He also persuaded another of the commanders to follow his example.

Thus reduced to about half his original strength, and that greatly crippled by the losses of the day, Xicotencatl could

no longer maintain his ground against the Spaniards. After
disputing the field with admirable courage for four hours, he
retreated and resigned it to the enemy. The Spaniards were too
much jaded, and too many were disabled by wounds, to allow
them to pursue; and Cortés, satisfied with the decisive victory
he had gained, returned in triumph to his position on the hill
of Tzompach. . . .

NEVER before had Tlaxcalans met such men on the field of battle. After a succession of bloody defeats, the Tlaxcalan elders who advocated peace with the invaders prevailed. However, even as negotiations with the recent enemy got underway, Cortés had to face mounting discontent in his own ranks. Most of his men bore numerous wounds; and as they thought about plunging deeper into the country, they increasingly favored the idea of withdrawing before they all found graves in the hostile land. The capitulation of the Tlaxcalans, however, afforded the respite which enabled Cortés to weather this storm.

III

Peace with Tlaxcala

ALL thoughts of further resistance being abandoned, the four delegates of the Tlascalan republic were now allowed to proceed on their mission. They were speedily followed by Xicotencatl himself, attended by a numerous train of military retainers. As they drew near the Spanish lines, they were easily recognised by the white and yellow colors of their uniforms, the livery of the house of Titcala. The joy of the army was great at this sure intimation of the close of hostilities; and it was with difficulty that Cortés was enabled to restore the men to tranquillity, and the assumed indifference which it was proper to maintain in presence of an enemy.

The Spaniards gazed with curious eye on the valiant chief who had so long kept his enemies at bay, and who now advanced with the firm and fearless step of one who was coming rather to bid defiance than to sue for peace. He was rather above the middle size, with broad shoulders, and a muscular frame intimating great activity and strength. His head was large, and his countenance marked with the lines of hard service rather than of age, for he was but thirty-five. When he entered the pres-

ence of Cortés, he made the usual salutation, by touching the
ground with his hand, and carrying it to his head; while the
sweet incense of aromatic gums rolled up in clouds from the
censers carried by his slaves.

Far from a pusillanimous attempt to throw the blame on
the senate, he assumed the whole responsibility of the war. He
had considered the white men, he said, as enemies, for they
came with the allies and vassals of Montezuma. He loved his
country, and wished to preserve the independence which she
had maintained through her long wars with the Aztecs. He had
been beaten. They might be the strangers, who, it had been so
long predicted, would come from the east, to take possession
of the country. He hoped they would use their victory with
moderation, and not trample on the liberties of the republic.
He came now in the name of his nation, to tender their obedience to the Spaniards, assuring them they would find his countrymen as faithful in peace as they had been firm in war.

Cortés, far from taking umbrage, was filled with admiration
at the lofty spirit which thus disdained to stoop beneath misfortunes. The brave man knows how to respect bravery in another. He assumed, however, a severe aspect, as he rebuked the
chief for having so long persisted in hostilities. Had Xicotencatl
believed the word of the Spaniards, and accepted their proffered
friendship sooner, he would have spared his people much suffering, which they well merited by their obstinacy. But it was
impossible, continued the general, to retrieve the past. He was
willing to bury it in oblivion, and to receive the Tlascalans as
vassals to the emperor, his master. If they proved true, they
should find him a sure column of support; if false, he would
take such vengeance on them as he had intended to take on
their capital, had they not speedily given in their submission.—'
It proved an ominous menace for the chief to whom it was
addressed.

The cacique then ordered his slaves to bring forward some
trifling ornaments of gold and feather-embroidery, designed as
presents. They were of little value, he said, with a smile, for

the Tlascalans were poor. They had little gold, not even cotton, nor salt. The Aztec emperor had left them nothing but their freedom and their arms. He offered this gift only as a token of his good-will. "As such I receive it," answered Cortés, "and, coming from the Tlascalans, set more value on it, than I should from any other source, though it were a house full of gold";—a politic, as well as magnanimous reply, for it was by the aid of this good-will, that he was to win the gold of Mexico.

Thus ended the bloody war with the fierce republic of Tlascala, during the course of which, the fortunes of the Spaniards, more than once, had trembled in the balance. Had it been persevered in but a little longer, it must have ended in their confusion and ruin, exhausted as they were by wounds, watching, and fatigues, with the seeds of disaffection rankling among themselves. As it was, they came out of the fearful contest with untarnished glory. To the enemy, they seemed invulnerable, bearing charmed lives, proof alike against the accidents of fortune and the assaults of man. No wonder that they indulged a similar conceit in their own bosoms, and that the humblest Spaniard should have fancied himself the subject of a special interposition of Providence, which shielded him in the hour of battle, and reserved him for a higher destiny.

While the Tlascalans were still in the camp, an embassy was announced from Montezuma. Tidings of the exploits of the Spaniards had spread far and wide over the plateau. The emperor, in particular, had watched every step of their progress, as they climbed the steeps of the Cordilleras, and advanced over the broad table-land, on their summit. He had seen them, with great satisfaction, take the road to Tlascala, trusting, that, if they were mortal men, they would find their graves there. Great was his dismay, when courier after courier brought him intelligence of their successes, and that the most redoubtable warriors on the plateau had been scattered like chaff, by the swords of this handful of strangers.

His superstitious fears returned in full force. He saw in the Spaniards "the men of destiny," who were to take possession of his sceptre. In his alarm and uncertainty, he sent a new embassy to the Christian camp. It consisted of five great nobles of his court, attended by a train of two hundred slaves. They brought with them a present, as usual, dictated partly by fear, and, in part, by the natural munificence of his disposition. It consisted of three thousand ounces of gold, in grains, or in various manufactured articles, with several hundred mantles and dresses of embroidered cotton, and the picturesque featherwork. As they laid these at the feet of Cortés, they told him, they had come to offer the congratulations of their master on the late victories of the white men. The emperor only regretted that it would not be in his power to receive them in his capital, where the numerous population was so unruly, that their safety would be placed in jeopardy. The mere intimation of the Aztec emperor's wishes, in the most distant way, would have sufficed with the Indian nations. It had very little weight with the Spaniards; and the envoys, finding this puerile expression of them ineffectual, resorted to another argument, offering a tribute in their master's name to the Castilian sovereign, provided the Spaniards would relinquish their visit to his capital. This was a greater error; it was displaying the rich casket with one hand, which he was unable to defend with the other. Yet the author of this pusillanimous policy, the unhappy victim of superstition, was a monarch renowned among the Indian nations for his intrepidity and enterprise,—the terror of Anahuac!

Cortés, while he urged his own sovereign's commands as a reason for disregarding the wishes of Montezuma, uttered expressions of the most profound respect for the Aztec prince, and declared that if he had not the means of requiting his munificence, as he could wish, at present, he trusted *to repay him, at some future day, with good works!*

The Mexican ambassadors were not much gratified with finding the war at an end, and a reconciliation established between their mortal enemies and the Spaniards. The mutual disgust of the two parties with each other was too strong to be repressed even in the presence of the general, who saw with satisfaction the evidences of jealousy, which, undermining the strength of the Indian emperor, was to prove the surest source of his own success.

Two of the Aztec mission returned to Mexico, to acquaint their sovereign with the state of affairs in the Spanish camp. The others remained with the army, Cortés being willing that they should be personal spectators of the deference shown him by the Tlascalans. Still he did not hasten his departure for their capital. Not that he placed reliance on the injurious intimations of the Mexicans respecting their good faith. Yet he was willing to put this to some longer trial, and, at the same time, to reëstablish his own health more thoroughly, before his visit. Meanwhile, messengers daily arrived from the city, pressing his journey, and were finally followed by some of the aged rulers of the republic, attended by a numerous retinue, impatient of his long delay. They brought with them a body of five hundred *tamanes,* or *men of burden,* to drag his cannon, and relieve his own forces from this fatiguing part of their duty. It was impossible to defer his departure longer; and after mass, and a solemn thanksgiving to the great Being who had crowned their arms with triumph, the Spaniards bade adieu to the quarters which they had occupied for nearly three weeks on the hill of Tzompach. The strong tower, or *teocalli,* which commanded it, was called, in commemoration of their residence, "the tower of victory"; and the few stones, which still survive of its ruins, point out to the eye of the traveller a spot ever memorable in history for the courage and constancy of the early Conquerors.

The city of Tlascala, the capital of the republic of the same name, lay at the distance of about six leagues from the Spanish camp. The road led into a hilly region, exhibiting in every arable patch of ground the evidence of laborious cultivation. Over a deep *barranca,* or ravine, they crossed on a bridge of stone, which, according to tradition,—a slippery authority,— is the same still standing, and was constructed originally for

the passage of the army. They passed some considerable towns
on their route, where they experienced a full measure of Indian
hospitality. As they advanced, the approach to a populous city
was intimated by the crowds who flocked out to see and welcome the strangers; men and women in their picturesque
dresses, with bunches and wreaths of roses, which they gave to
the Spaniards, or fastened to the necks and caparisons of their
horses, in the same manner as at Cempoalla. Priests, with their
white robes, and long matted tresses floating over them, mingled
in the crowd, scattering volumes of incense from their burning
censers. In this way, the multitudinous and motley procession
defiled through the gates of the ancient capital of Tlascala. It
was the twenty-third of September, 1519, the anniversary of
which is still celebrated by the inhabitants, as a day of jubilee.

The press was now so great, that it was with difficulty the
police of the city could clear a passage for the army; while the
azoteas, or flat terraced roofs of the buildings, were covered
with spectators, eager to catch a glimpse of the wonderful
strangers. The houses were hung with festoons of flowers, and
arches of verdant boughs, intertwined with roses and honeysuckle, were thrown across the streets. The whole population
abandoned itself to rejoicing; and the air was rent with songs
and shouts of triumph mingled with the wild music of the national instruments, that might have excited apprehensions in
the breasts of the soldiery, had they not gathered their peaceful import from the assurance of Marina, and the joyous countenances of the natives.

With these accompaniments, the procession moved along
the principal streets to the mansion of Xicotencatl, the aged
father of the Tlascalan general, and one of the four rulers of the
republic. Cortés dismounted from his horse, to receive the old
chieftain's embrace. He was nearly blind; and satisfied, as far
as he could, a natural curiosity respecting the person of the
Spanish general, by passing his hand over his features. He then
led the way to a spacious hall in his palace, where a banquet
was served to the army. In the evening, they were shown to

their quarters, in the buildings and open ground surrounding one of the principal *teocallis;* while the Mexican ambassadors, at the desire of Cortés, had apartments assigned them next to his own, that he might the better watch over their safety, in this city of their enemies.

Tlascala was one of the most important and populous towns on the table-land. Cortés, in his letter to the Emperor, compares it to Granada, affirming, that it was larger, stronger, and more populous than the Moorish capital, at the time of the conquest, and quite as well built. But, notwithstanding we are assured by a most respectable writer at the close of the last century, that its remains justify the assertion, we shall be slow to believe that its edifices could have rivalled those monuments of Oriental magnificence, whose light, aërial forms still survive after the lapse of ages, the admiration of every traveller of sensibility and taste. The truth is, that Cortés, like Columbus, saw objects through the warm medium of his own fond imagination, giving them a higher tone of coloring and larger dimensions than were strictly warranted by the fact. It was natural that the man who had made such rare discoveries should unconsciously magnify their merits to his own eyes, and to those of others.

The houses were built, for the most part, of mud or earth; the better sort of stone and lime, or bricks dried in the sun. They were unprovided with doors or windows, but in the apertures for the former hung mats fringed with pieces of copper or something which, by its tinkling sound, would give notice of any one's entrance. The streets were narrow and dark. The population must have been considerable, if, as Cortés asserts, thirty thousand souls were often gathered in the market on a public day. These meetings were a sort of fairs, held, as usual in all great towns, every fifth day, and attended by the inhabitants of the adjacent country, who brought there for sale every description of domestic produce and manufacture, with which they were acquainted. They peculiarly excelled in pottery, which was considered as equal to the best in Europe. It is a

further proof of civilized habits, that the Spaniards found barbers' shops, and baths both of vapor and hot water, familiarly
used by the inhabitants. A still higher proof of refinement may
be discerned in a vigilant police which repressed every thing
like disorder among the people.

The city was divided into four quarters, which might rather
be called so many separate towns, since they were built at different times, and separated from each other by high stone walls,
defining their respective limits. Over each of these districts
ruled one of the four great chiefs of the republic, occupying
his own spacious mansion, and surrounded by his own immediate vassals. Strange arrangement,—and more strange, that it
should have been compatible with social order and tranquillity! The ancient capital, through one quarter of which flowed
the rapid current of the Zahuatl, stretched along the summits
and sides of hills, at whose base are now gathered the miserable remains of its once flourishing population. Far beyond, to
the south-east, extended the bold sierra of Tlascala, and the
huge Malinche, crowned with the usual silver diadem of the
highest Andes, having its shaggy sides clothed with dark-green
forests of firs, gigantic sycamores, and oaks whose towering
stems rose to the height of forty or fifty feet, unincumbered by a
branch. The clouds, which sailed over from the distant Atlantic,
gathered round the lofty peaks of the sierra, and, settling into
torrents, poured over the plains in the neighbourhood of the
city, converting them, at such seasons, into swamps. Thunder
storms, more frequent and terrible here, than in other parts of
the table-land, swept down the sides of the mountains, and
shook the frail tenements of the capital to their foundations.
But, although the bleak winds of the sierra gave an austerity
to the climate, unlike the sunny skies and genial temperature of
the lower regions, it was far more favorable to the development
of both the physical and moral energies. A bold and hardy
peasantry was nurtured among the recesses of the hills, fit
equally to cultivate the land in peace, and to defend it in war.
Unlike the spoiled child of Nature, who derives such facilities

of subsistence from her too prodigal hand, as supersede the necessity of exertion on his own part, the Tlascalan earned his bread — from a soil not ungrateful, it is true—by the sweat of his brow. He led a life of temperance and toil. Cut off by his long wars with the Aztecs from commercial intercourse, he was driven chiefly to agricultural labor, the occupation most propitious to purity of morals and sinewy strength of constitution. His honest breast glowed with the patriotism,—or local attachment to the soil, which is the fruit of its diligent culture; while he was elevated by a proud consciousness of independence, the natural birthright of the child of the mountains.— Such was the race with whom Cortés was now associated, for the achievement of his great work.

Some days were given by the Spaniards to festivity, in which they were successively entertained at the hospitable boards of the four great nobles, in their several quarters of the city. Amidst these friendly demonstrations, however, the general never relaxed for a moment his habitual vigilance, or the strict discipline of the camp; and he was careful to provide for the security of the citizens by prohibiting, under severe penalties, any soldier from leaving his quarters without express permission. Indeed, the severity of his discipline provoked the remonstrance of more than one of his officers, as a superfluous caution; and the Tlascalan chiefs took some exception at it, as inferring an unreasonable distrust of them. But, when Cortés explained it, as in obedience to an established military system, they testified their admiration, and the ambitious young general of the republic proposed to introduce it, if possible, into his own ranks.

The Spanish commander, having assured himself of the loyalty of his new allies, next proposed to accomplish one of the great objects of his mission, their conversion to Christianity. By the advice of father Olmedo, always opposed to precipitate measures, he had deferred this till a suitable opportunity presented itself for opening the subject. Such a one occurred when the chiefs of the state proposed to strengthen the alliance with the Spaniards, by the intermarriage of their daughters with Cortés and his officers. He told them, this could not be, while they continued in the darkness of infidelity. Then, with the aid of the good friar, he expounded as well as he could the doctrines of the Faith; and, exhibiting the image of the Virgin with the infant Redeemer, told them that there was the God, in whose worship alone they would find salvation, while that of their own false idols would sink them in eternal perdition.

It is unnecessary to burden the reader with a recapitulation of his homily, which contained, probably, dogmas quite as incomprehensible to the untutored Indian, as any to be found in his own rude mythology. But, though it failed to convince his audience, they listened with a deferential awe. When he had finished, they replied, they had no doubt that the God of the Christians must be a good and a great God, and as such they were willing to give him a place among the divinities of Tlascala. The polytheistic system of the Indians, like that of the ancient Greeks, was of that accommodating kind which could admit within its elastic folds the deities of any other religion, without violence to itself. But every nation, they continued, must have its own appropriate and tutelary deities. Nor could they, in their old age, abjure the service of those who had watched over them from youth. It would bring down the vengeance of their gods, and of their own nation, who were as warmly attached to their religion as their liberties, and would defend both with the last drop of their blood!

It was clearly inexpedient to press the matter further, at present. But the zeal of Cortés, as usual, waxing warm by opposition, had now mounted too high for him to calculate obstacles; nor would he have shrunk, probably, from the crown of martyrdom in so good a cause. But, fortunately, at least for the success of his temporal cause, this crown was not reserved for him.

The good monk, his ghostly adviser, seeing the course things were likely to take, with better judgment interposed to prevent it. He had no desire, he said, to see the same scenes acted over again as at Cempoalla. He had no relish for forced conversions. They could hardly be lasting. The growth of an hour might well die with the hour. Of what use was it to overturn the altar, if the idol remained enthroned in the heart? or to destroy the idol itself, if it were only to make room for another? Better to wait patiently the effect of time and teaching to soften the heart and open the understanding, without which there could be no assurance of a sound and permanent conviction. These rational views were enforced by the remonstrances of Alvarado, Velásquez de León, and those in whom Cortés placed most confidence; till, driven from his original purpose, the military polemic consented to relinquish the attempt at conversion, for the present, and to refrain from a repetition of the scenes, which, considering the different mettle of the population, might have been attended with very different results from those at Cozumel and Cempoalla.

In the course of our narrative, we have had occasion to witness more than once the good effects of the interposition of father Olmedo. Indeed, it is scarcely too much to say, that his discretion in spiritual matters contributed as essentially to the success of the expedition, as did the sagacity and courage of Cortés in temporal. He was a true disciple in the school of Las Casas. His heart was unscathed by that fiery fanaticism which sears and hardens whatever it touches. It melted with the warm glow of Christian charity. He had come out to the New World, as a missionary among the heathen, and he shrunk from no sacrifice, but that of the welfare of the poor benighted flock to whom he had consecrated his days. If he followed the banners of the warrior, it was to mitigate the ferocity of war, and to turn the triumphs of the Cross to a good account for the natives themselves, by the spiritual labors of conversion. He afforded the uncommon example—not to have been looked for, certainly, in a Spanish monk of the sixteenth century—of enthusiasm controlled by reason, a quickening zeal tempered by the mild spirit of toleration.

But, though Cortés abandoned the ground of conversion for the present, he compelled the Tlascalans to break the fetters of the unfortunate victims reserved for sacrifice; an act of humanity unhappily only transient in its effects, since the prisons were filled with fresh victims, on his departure.

He also obtained permission for the Spaniards to perform the services of their own religion unmolested. A large cross was erected in one of the great courts or squares. Mass was celebrated every day in the presence of the army and of crowds of natives, who, if they did not comprehend its full import, were so far edified, that they learned to reverence the religion of their conquerors. The direct interposition of Heaven, however, wrought more for their conversion than the best homily of priest or soldier. Scarcely had the Spaniards left the city,—the tale is told on very respectable authority,—when a thin, transparent cloud descended and settled like a column on the cross, and, wrapping it round in its luminous folds, continued to emit a soft, celestial radiance through the night, thus proclaiming the sacred character of the symbol, on which was shed the halo of divinity!

The principle of toleration in religious matters being established, the Spanish general consented to receive the daughters of the caciques. Five or six of the most beautiful of the Indian maidens were assigned to as many of his principal officers, after they had been cleansed from the stains of infidelity by the waters of baptism. They received, as usual, on this occasion, good Castilian names, in exchange for the barbarous nomenclature of their own vernacular. Among them, Xicotencatl's daughter, Doña Luisa, as she was called after her baptism, was a princess of the highest estimation and authority in Tlascala. She was given by her father to Alvarado, and their posterity intermarried with the noblest families of Castile. The frank and joyous manners of this cavalier made him a great favorite with the Tlascalans; and his bright, open countenance, fair complexion, and golden locks, gave him the name of *Tonatiuh*, the "Sun." The Indians often pleased their fancies by fastening a *sobriquet,* or some characteristic epithet on the Spaniards. As Cortés was always attended, on public occasions, by Doña Marina, or Malinche, as she was called by the natives, they distinguished him by the same name. By these epithets, originally bestowed in Tlascala, the two Spanish captains were popularly designated among the Indian nations.

While these events were passing, another embassy arrived from the court of Mexico. It was charged, as usual, with a costly donative of embossed gold plate, and rich embroidered stuffs of cotton and feather-work. The terms of the message might well argue a vacillating and timid temper in the monarch, did they not mask a deeper policy. He now invited the Spaniards to his capital, with the assurance of a cordial welcome. He besought them to enter into no alliance with the base and barbarous Tlascalans; and he invited them to take the route of the friendly city of Cholula, where arrangements, according to his orders, were made for their reception.

The Tlascalans viewed with deep regret the general's proposed visit to Mexico. Their reports fully confirmed all he had before heard of the power and ambition of Montezuma. His armies, they said, were spread over every part of the continent. His capital was a place of great strength, and as, from its insular position, all communication could be easily cut off with the adjacent country, the Spaniards, once entrapped there, would be at his mercy. His policy, they represented, was as insidious, as his ambition was boundless. "Trust not his fair words," they said, "his courtesies, and his gifts. His professions are hollow, and his friendships are false." When Cortés remarked, that he hoped to bring about a better understanding between the emperor and them, they replied, it would be impossible; however smooth his words, he would hate them at heart.

They warmly protested, also, against the general's taking the route of Cholula. The inhabitants, not brave in the open field, were more dangerous from their perfidy and craft. They were Montezuma's tools, and would do his bidding. The Tlascalans seemed to combine with this distrust a superstitious dread of the ancient city, the head-quarters of the religion of Anahuac. It was here that the god Quetzalcoatl held the pristine seat of his empire. His temple was celebrated throughout the land, and the priests were confidently believed to have the power, as they themselves boasted, of opening an inundation from the foundations of his shrine, which should bury their enemies in the deluge. The Tlascalans further reminded Cortés, that, while so many other and distant places had sent to him at Tlascala, to testify their good-will, and offer their allegiance to his sovereigns, Cholula, only six leagues distant, had done neither.—The last suggestion struck the general more forcibly than any of the preceding. He instantly despatched a summons to the city, requiring a formal tender of its submission. . . .

As word spread of the Spanish victories, embassies came to Tlaxcala to wait upon Cortés. The delegation from Cholula, the religious seat of the Aztec realm, was composed of such insignificant persons that the Tlaxcalans renewed their warning to Cortés about Cholulan perfidy. When Cortés and his men set out for that place, his contingent of Indian allies included thousands of Tlaxcalans. As he entered Cholula, Cortés left most of the Tlaxcalans outside that city. A few days after their entry, the Spaniards noticed the arrival of messengers from Montezuma.

IV

The Massacre at Cholula

FROM this time, the deportment of their Cholulan hosts underwent a visible alteration. They did not visit the quarters as before, and, when invited to do so, excused themselves on pretence of illness. The supply of provisions was stinted, on the ground that they were short of maize. These symptoms of alienation, independently of temporary embarrassment, caused serious alarm in the breast of Cortés, for the future. His apprehensions were not allayed by the reports of the Cempoallans, who told him, that in wandering round the city, they had seen several streets barricadoed, the *azoteas,* or flat roofs of the houses, loaded with huge stones and other missiles, as if preparatory to an assault, and in some places they had found holes covered over with branches, and upright stakes planted within, as if to embarrass the movements of the cavalry. Some Tlascalans coming in, also, from their camp, informed the general, that a great sacrifice, mostly of children, had been offered up in a distant quarter of the town, to propitiate the favor of the gods, apparently for some intended enterprise. They added, that they had seen numbers of the citizens leaving the city with their women and children, as if to remove them to a place of safety. These tidings confirmed the worst suspicions of Cortés, who had no doubt that some hostile scheme was in agitation. If he had felt any, a discovery by Marina, the good angel of the expedition, would have turned these doubts into certainty.

The amiable manners of the Indian girl had won her the regard of the wife of one of the caciques, who repeatedly urged Marina to visit her house, darkly intimating that in this way she would escape the fate that awaited the Spaniards. The interpreter, seeing the importance of obtaining further intelligence at once, pretended to be pleased with the proposal, and affected, at the same time, great discontent with the white men, by whom she was detained in captivity. Thus throwing the credulous Cholulan off her guard, Marina gradually insinuated herself into her confidence, so far as to draw from her a full account of the conspiracy.

It originated, she said, with the Aztec emperor, who had sent rich bribes to the great caciques, and to her husband among others, to secure them in his views. The Spaniards were to be assaulted as they marched out of the capital, when entangled in its streets, in which numerous impediments had been placed to throw the cavalry into disorder. A force of twenty thousand Mexicans was already quartered at no great distance from the city, to support the Cholulans in the assault. It was confidently expected that the Spaniards, thus embarrassed in their movements, would fall an easy prey to the superior strength of their enemy. A sufficient number of prisoners was to be reserved to grace the sacrifices of Cholula; the rest were to be led in fetters to the capital of Montezuma.

While this conversation was going on, Marina occupied herself with putting up such articles of value and wearing apparel as she proposed to take with her in the evening, when she could escape unnoticed from the Spanish quarters to the house of her Cholulan friend, who assisted her in the operation. Leaving her visiter thus employed, Marina found an opportunity to steal away for a few moments, and, going to the general's apartment, disclosed to him her discoveries. He immediately caused the cacique's wife to be seized, and, on examination, she fully confirmed the statement of his Indian mistress.

The intelligence thus gathered by Cortés filled him with the deepest alarm. He was fairly taken in the snare. To fight or to fly seemed equally difficult. He was in a city of enemies, where every house might be converted into a fortress, and where such embarrassments were thrown in the way, as might render the manœuvres of his artillery and horse nearly impracticable. In addition to the wily Cholulans, he must cope, under all these disadvantages, with the redoubtable warriors of Mexico. He was like a traveller who has lost his way in the darkness among precipices, where any step may dash him to pieces, and where to retreat or to advance is equally perilous.

He was desirous to obtain still further confirmation and particulars of the conspiracy. He accordingly induced two of the priests in the neighbourhood, one of them a person of much influence in the place, to visit his quarters. By courteous treatment, and liberal largesses of the rich presents he had received from Montezuma,—thus turning his own gifts against the giver, —he drew from them a full confirmation of the previous report. The emperor had been in a state of pitiable vacillation since the arrival of the Spaniards. His first orders to the Cholulans were, to receive the strangers kindly. He had recently consulted his oracles anew, and obtained for answer, that Cholula would be the grave of his enemies; for the gods would be sure to support him in avenging the sacrilege offered to the Holy City. So confident were the Aztecs of success, that numerous manacles, or poles with thongs which served as such, were already in the place to secure the prisoners.

Cortés, now feeling himself fully possessed of the facts, dismissed the priests, with injunctions of secrecy, scarcely necessary. He told them it was his purpose to leave the city on the following morning, and requested that they would induce some of the principal caciques to grant him an interview in his quarters. He then summoned a council of his officers, though, as it seems, already determined as to the course he was to take.

The members of the council were differently affected by the startling intelligence, according to their different characters. The more timid, disheartened by the prospect of obstacles which seemed to multiply as they drew nearer the Mexican capital, were for retracing their steps, and seeking shelter in the friendly city of Tlascala. Others, more persevering, but prudent, were for taking the more northerly route, originally recommended by their allies. The greater part supported the general, who was ever of opinion that they had no alternative but to advance. Retreat would be ruin. Half-way measures were scarcely better; and would infer a timidity which must discredit them with both friend and foe. Their true policy was to rely on themselves; to strike such a blow, as should intimidate their enemies, and show them that the Spaniards were as incapable of being circumvented by artifice, as of being crushed by weight of numbers and courage in the open field.

When the caciques, persuaded by the priests, appeared before Cortés, he contented himself with gently rebuking their want of hospitality, and assured them the Spaniards would be no longer a burden to their city, as he proposed to leave it early on the following morning. He requested, moreover, that they would furnish a reinforcement of two thousand men to transport his artillery and baggage. The chiefs, after some consultation, acquiesced in a demand which might in some measure favor their own designs.

On their departure, the general summoned the Aztec ambassadors before him. He briefly acquainted them with his detection of the treacherous plot to destroy his army, the contrivance of which, he said, was imputed to their master, Montezuma. It grieved him much, he added, to find the emperor implicated in so nefarious a scheme, and that the Spaniards must now march as enemies against the prince, whom they had hoped to visit as a friend.

The ambassadors, with earnest protestations, asserted their entire ignorance of the conspiracy; and their belief that Montezuma was equally innocent of a crime, which they charged wholly on the Cholulans. It was clearly the policy of Cortés to keep on good terms with the Indian monarch; to profit as long as possible by his good offices; and to avail himself of his fancied security—such feelings of security as the general could inspire him with—to cover his own future operations. He affected to give credit, therefore, to the assertion of the envoys, and declared his unwillingness to believe, that a monarch, who had rendered the Spaniards so many friendly offices, would now consummate the whole by a deed of such unparalleled baseness. The discovery of their twofold duplicity, he added, sharpened his resentment against the Cholulans, on whom he would take such vengeance as should amply requite the injuries done both to Montezuma and the Spaniards. He then dismissed the ambassadors, taking care, notwithstanding this show of confidence, to place a strong guard over them, to prevent communication with the citizens.

That night was one of deep anxiety to the army. The ground they stood on seemed loosening beneath their feet, and any moment might be the one marked for their destruction. Their vigilant general took all possible precautions for their safety, increasing the number of the sentinels, and posting his guns in such a manner as to protect the approaches to the camp. His eyes, it may well be believed, did not close during the night. Indeed, every Spaniard lay down in his arms, and every horse stood saddled and bridled, ready for instant service. But no assault was meditated by the Indians, and the stillness of the hour was undisturbed except by the occasional sounds heard in a populous city, even when buried in slumber, and by the hoarse cries of the priests from the turrets of the *teocallis,* proclaiming through their trumpets the watches of the night.

With the first streak of morning light, Cortés was seen on horseback, directing the movements of his little band. The strength of his forces he drew up in the great square or court, surrounded partly by buildings, as before noticed, and in part by a high wall. There were three gates of entrance, at each of which he placed a strong guard. The rest of his troops, with his

great guns, he posted without the inclosure, in such a manner
as to command the avenues and secure those within from interruption in their bloody work. Orders had been sent the night
before to the Tlascalan chiefs to hold themselves ready, at a
concerted signal, to march into the city and join the Spaniards.

The arrangements were hardly completed, before the Cholulan caciques appeared, leading a body of levies, *tamanes,*
even more numerous than had been demanded. They were
marched, at once, into the square, commanded, as we have seen,
by the Spanish infantry which was drawn up under the walls.
Cortés then took some of the caciques aside. With a stern air,
he bluntly charged them with the conspiracy, showing that he
was well acquainted with all the particulars. He had visited
their city, he said, at the invitation of the emperor; had come
as a friend; had respected the inhabitants and their property;
and, to avoid all cause of umbrage, had left a great part of his
forces without the walls. They had received him with a show
of kindness and hospitality, and, reposing on this, he had been
decoyed into the snare, and found this kindness only a mask
to cover the blackest perfidy.

The Cholulans were thunderstruck at the accusation. An
undefined awe crept over them, as they gazed on the mysterious
strangers, and felt themselves in the presence of beings who
seemed to have the power of reading the thoughts scarcely
formed in their bosoms. There was no use in prevarication or
denial before such judges. They confessed the whole, and endeavoured to excuse themselves by throwing the blame on
Montezuma. Cortés, assuming an air of higher indignation at
this, assured them that the pretence should not serve, since,
even if well founded, it would be no justification; and he would
now make such an example of them for their treachery, that
the report of it should ring throughout the wide borders of
Anahuac!

The fatal signal, the discharge of an arquebuse, was then
given. In an instant every musket and crossbow was levelled
at the unfortunate Cholulans in the court-yard, and a frightful

volley poured into them as they stood crowded together like a herd of deer in the centre. They were taken by surprise, for they had not heard the preceding dialogue with the chiefs. They made scarcely any resistance to the Spaniards, who followed up the discharge of their pieces by rushing on them with their swords; and, as the half-naked bodies of the natives afforded no protection, they hewed them down with as much ease as the reaper mows down the ripe corn in harvest time. Some endeavoured to scale the walls, but only afforded a surer mark to the arquebusiers and archers. Others threw themselves into the gateways, but were received on the long pikes of the soldiers who guarded them. Some few had better luck in hiding themselves under the heaps of slain with which the ground was soon loaded.

While this work of death was going on, the countrymen of the slaughtered Indians, drawn together by the noise of the massacre, had commenced a furious assault on the Spaniards from without. But Cortés had placed his battery of heavy guns in a position that commanded the avenues, and swept off the files of the assailants as they rushed on. In the intervals between the discharges, which, in the imperfect state of the science in that day, were much longer than in ours, he forced back the press by charging with the horse into the midst. The steeds, the guns, the weapons of the Spaniards were all new to the Cholulans. Notwithstanding the novelty of the terrific spectacle, the flash of fire-arms mingling with the deafening roar of the artillery as its thunders reverberated among the buildings, the despairing Indians pushed on to take the places of their fallen comrades.

While this fierce struggle was going forward, the Tlascalans, hearing the concerted signal, had advanced with quick pace into the city. They had bound, by order of Cortés, wreaths of sedge round their heads, that they might the more surely be distinguished from the Cholulans. Coming up in the very heat of the engagement, they fell on the defenceless rear of the townsmen, who, trampled down under the heels of the Castilian cavalry on one side, and galled by their vindictive enemies on the other, could no longer maintain their ground. They gave way, some taking refuge in the nearest buildings, which, being partly of wood, were speedily set on fire. Others fled to the temples. One strong party, with a number of priests at its head, got possession of the great *teocalli*. There was a vulgar tradition, already alluded to, that, on removal of part of the walls, the god would send forth an inundation to overwhelm his enemies. The superstitious Cholulans with great difficulty succeeded in wrenching away some of the stones in the walls of the edifice. But dust, not water, followed. Their false god deserted them in the hour of need. In despair they flung themselves into the wooden turrets that crowned the temple, and poured down stones, javelins, and burning arrows on the Spaniards, as they climbed the great staircase, which, by a flight of one hundred and twenty steps, scaled the face of the pyramid. But the fiery shower fell harmless on the steel bonnets of the Christians, while they availed themselves of the burning shafts to set fire to the wooden citadel, which was speedily wrapt in flames. Still the garrison held out, and though quarter, *it is said*, was offered, only one Cholulan availed himself of it. The rest threw themselves headlong from the parapet, or perished miserably in the flames.

All was now confusion and uproar in the fair city which had so lately reposed in security and peace. The groans of the dying, the frantic supplications of the vanquished for mercy, were mingled with the loud battle-cries of the Spaniards as they rode down their enemy, and with the shrill whistle of the Tlascalans, who gave full scope to the long cherished rancor of ancient rivalry. The tumult was still further swelled by the incessant rattle of musketry, and the crash of falling timbers, which sent up a volume of flame that outshone the ruddy light of morning, making all together a hideous confusion of sights and sounds, that converted the Holy City into a Pandemonium. As resistance slackened, the victors broke into the houses and sacred places, plundering them of whatever valuables they contained, plate, jewels, which were found in some quantity, wearing apparel and provisions, the two last coveted even more than the former by the simple Tlascalans, thus facilitating a division of the spoil much to the satisfaction of their Christian confederates. Amidst this universal license, it is worthy of remark, the commands of Cortés were so far respected that no violence was offered to women or children, though these, as well as numbers of the men, were made prisoners to be swept into slavery by the Tlascalans. These scenes of violence had lasted some hours, when Cortés, moved by the entreaties of some Cholulan chiefs, who had been reserved from the massacre, backed by the prayers of the Mexican envoys, consented, out of regard, as he said, to the latter, the representatives of Montezuma, to call off the soldiers, and put a stop, as well as he could, to further outrage. Two of the caciques were, also, permitted to go to their countrymen with assurances of pardon and protection to all who would return to their obedience.

These measures had their effect. By the joint efforts of Cortés and the caciques, the tumult was with much difficulty appeased. The assailants, Spaniards and Indians, gathered under their respective banners, and the Cholulans, relying on the assurance of their chiefs, gradually returned to their homes.

The first act of Cortés was, to prevail on the Tlascalan chiefs to liberate their captives. Such was their deference to the Spanish commander that they acquiesced, though not without murmurs, contenting themselves, as they best could, with the rich spoil rifled from the Cholulans, consisting of various luxuries long since unknown in Tlascala. His next care was to cleanse the city from its loathsome impurities, particularly from the dead bodies which lay festering in heaps in the streets and great square. The general, in his letter to Charles the Fifth, admits three thousand slain, most accounts say six, and some swell the amount yet higher. As the eldest and principal cacique was among the number, Cortés assisted the Cholulans in installing a successor in his place. By these pacific measures confidence was gradually restored. The people in the environs, reassured, flocked into the capital to supply the place of the diminished population. The markets were again opened; and the usual avocations of an orderly, industrious community were resumed. Still, the long piles of black and smouldering ruins proclaimed the hurricane which had so lately swept over the city, and the walls surrounding the scene of slaughter in the great square, which were standing more than fifty years after the event, told the sad tale of the Massacre of Cholula.

This passage in their history is one of those that have left a dark stain on the memory of the Conquerors. Nor can we contemplate at this day, without a shudder, the condition of this fair and flourishing capital thus invaded in its privacy, and delivered over to the excesses of a rude and ruthless soldiery. But, to judge the action fairly, we must transport ourselves to the age when it happened. The difficulty that meets us in the outset is, to find a justification of the right of conquest, at all. But it should be remembered, that religious infidelity, at this period, and till a much later, was regarded—no matter whether founded on ignorance or education, whether hereditary or acquired, heretical or Pagan—as a sin to be punished with fire and faggot in this world, and eternal suffering in the next. This doctrine, monstrous as it is, was the creed of the Romish, in other words, of the Christian Church,—the basis of the Inquisition, and of those other species of religious persecutions, which have stained the annals, at some time or other, of nearly every nation in Christendom. Under this code, the territory of the heathen, wherever found, was regarded as a sort of religious waif, which, in default of a legal proprietor, was claimed and taken possession of by the Holy See, and as such was freely given away by the head of the Church, to any temporal potentate whom he pleased, that would assume the burden of conquest. Thus, Alexander the Sixth generously granted a large portion of the Western hemisphere to the Spaniards, and of the Eastern to the Portuguese. These lofty pretensions of the successors of the humble fisherman of Galilee, for from being nominal, were acknowledged and appealed to as conclusive in controversies between nations.

With the right of conquest, thus conferred, came, also, the obligation, on which it may be said to have been founded, to retrieve the nations sitting in darkness from eternal perdition. This obligation was acknowledged by the best and the bravest, the gownsman in his closet, the missionary, and the warrior in the crusade. However much it may have been debased by temporal motives and mixed up with worldly considerations of ambition and avarice, it was still active in the mind of the Christian conqueror. We have seen how far paramount it was to every calculation of personal interest in the breast of Cortés. The concession of the Pope, then, founded on, and enforcing, the imperative duty of conversion, was the assumed basis—and, in the apprehension of that age, a sound one—of the right of conquest.

This right could not, indeed, be construed to authorize any unnecessary act of violence to the natives. The present expedition, up to the period of its history at which we are now arrived, had probably been stained with fewer of such acts than almost any similar enterprise of the Spanish discoverers in the New World. Throughout the campaign, Cortés had prohibited all wanton injuries to the natives, in person or property, and had punished the perpetrators of them with exemplary severity. He had been faithful to his friends, and, with perhaps a single exception, not unmerciful to his foes. Whether from policy or principle, it should be recorded to his credit; though, like every sagacious mind, he may have felt, that principle and policy go together.

He had entered Cholula as a friend, at the invitation of the Indian emperor, who had a real, if not avowed, control over the state. He had been received as a friend, with every demonstration of goodwill; when, without any offence of his own or his followers, he found they were to be the victims of an insidious plot,—that they were standing on a mine which might be sprung at any moment, and bury them all in its ruins. His safety, as he truly considered, left no alternative but to anticipate the blow of his enemies. Yet who can doubt that the punishment thus inflicted was excessive,—that the same end might

have been attained by directing the blow against the guilty
chiefs, instead of letting it fall on the ignorant rabble, who but
obeyed the commands of their masters? But when was it ever
seen, that fear, armed with power, was scrupulous in the exercise
of it? or that the passions of a fierce soldiery, inflamed by conscious injuries, could be regulated in the moment of explosion?

We shall, perhaps, pronounce more impartially on the conduct of the Conquerors, if we compare it with that of our own
contemporaries under somewhat similar circumstances. The
atrocities at Cholula were not so bad as those inflicted on the
descendants of these very Spaniards, in the late war of the
Peninsula, by the most polished nations of our time; by the
British at Badajoz, for example,—at Taragona, and a hundred
other places, by the French. The wanton butchery, the ruin of
property, and, above all, those outrages worse than death, from
which the female part of the population were protected at
Cholula, show a catalogue of enormities quite as black as those
imputed to the Spaniards, and without the same apology for
resentment,—with no apology, indeed, but that afforded by
a brave and patriotic resistance. The consideration of these
events, which, from their familiarity, make little impression
on our senses, should render us more lenient in our judgments
of the past, showing, as they do, that man in a state of excitement, savage or civilized, is much the same in every age. It may
teach us,—it is one of the best lessons of history,—that, since
such are the *inevitable* evils of war, even among the most
polished people, those who hold the destinies of nations in
their hands, whether rulers or legislators, should submit to
every sacrifice, save that of honor, before authorizing an appeal
to arms. The extreme solicitude to avoid these calamities, by
the aid of peaceful congresses and impartial mediation, is, on
the whole, the strongest evidence, stronger than that afforded
by the progress of science and art, of our boasted advance in
civilization.

It is far from my intention to vindicate the cruel deeds of
the old Conquerors. Let them lie heavy on their heads. They

were an iron race, who periled life and fortune in the cause; and, as they made little account of danger and suffering for themselves, they had little sympathy to spare for their unfortunate enemies. But, to judge them fairly, we must not do it by the lights of our own age. We must carry ourselves back to theirs, and take the point of view afforded by the civilization of their time. Thus only can we arrive at impartial criticism in reviewing the generations that are past. We must extend to them the same justice which we shall have occasion to ask from Posterity, when, by the light of a higher civilization, it surveys the dark or doubtful passages in our own history, which hardly arrest the eye of the contemporary....

Once more Montezuma's emissaries waited upon Cortés, bearing gifts and trying to dissuade him and his men from visiting the Aztec capital. But all was in vain. When quiet returned to Cholula and it was time to resume the march westward, Cortés found that the Cempoallans, weary of campaigning, wanted to return to their homes on the coast. As they turned east, shouldering their loot, the loyal Tlaxcalans continued with the Spaniards. Through the mountain pass they trudged, Popocatepetl on their left and Ixtaccíhuatl on their right.

V

Into the Valley of Mexico

THEY had not advanced far, when, turning an angle of the sierra, they suddenly came on a view which more than compensated the toils of the preceding day. It was that of the Valley of Mexico, or Tenochtitlán, as more commonly called by the natives; which, with its picturesque assemblage of water, woodland, and cultivated plains, its shining cities and shadowy hills, was spread out like some gay and gorgeous panorama before them. In the highly rarefied atmosphere of these upper regions, even remote objects have a brilliancy of coloring and a distinctness of outline which seem to annihilate distance. Stretching far away at their feet, were seen noble forests of oak, sycamore, and cedar, and beyond, yellow fields of maize and the towering maguey, intermingled with orchards and blooming gardens; for flowers, in such demand for their religious festivals, were even more abundant in this populous valley than in other parts of Anahuac. In the centre of the great basin were beheld the lakes, occupying then a much larger portion of its surface than at present; their borders thickly studded with towns and hamlets, and, in the midst,—like some Indian empress with her coronal of pearls,—the fair city of Mexico, with her white towers and pyramidal temples, reposing, as it were, on the bosom of the waters,—the far-famed "Venice of the Aztecs." High over all rose the royal hill of Chapoltepec, the residence of the Mexican monarchs, crowned with the same grove of gigantic cypresses, which at this day fling their broad shadows over the land. In the distance beyond the blue waters of the lake, and nearly screened by intervening foliage, was seen a shining speck, the rival capital of Tezcuco, and, still further on, the dark belt of porphyry, girdling the Valley around, like a rich setting which Nature had devised for the fairest of her jewels.

Such was the beautiful vision which broke on the eyes of the Conquerors. And even now, when so sad a change has come over the scene; when the stately forests have been laid low, and the soil, unsheltered from the fierce radiance of a tropical sun, is in many places abandoned to sterility; when the waters have retired, leaving a broad and ghastly margin white with the incrustation of salts, while the cities and hamlets on their borders have mouldered into ruins;—even now that desolation broods over the landscape, so indestructible are the lines of beauty which Nature has traced on its features, that no traveller, however cold, can gaze on them with any other emotions than those of astonishment and rapture.

What, then, must have been the emotions of the Spaniards, when, after working their toilsome way into the upper air, the cloudy tabernacle parted before their eyes, and they beheld these fair scenes in all their pristine magnificence and beauty! It was like the spectacle which greeted the eyes of Moses from the summit of Pisgah, and, in the warm glow of their feelings, they cried out, "It is the promised land!". . . .

ACROSS *the Valley they marched. The invaders paused on the southern shore of Lake Texcoco in the city of Iztapalapa.*

With the first faint streak of dawn, the Spanish general was up, mustering his followers. They gathered, with beating hearts,

under their respective banners, as the trumpet sent forth its
spirit-stirring sounds across water and woodland, till they died
away in distant echoes among the mountains. The sacred
flames on the altars of numberless *teocallis,* dimly seen through
the grey mists of morning, indicated the site of the capital, till
temple, tower, and palace were fully revealed in the glorious
illumination which the sun, as he rose above the eastern barrier, poured over the beautiful Valley. It was the eighth of
November, 1519; a conspicuous day in history, as that on
which the Europeans first set foot in the capital of the Western
World.

Cortés with his little body of horse formed a sort of advanced
guard to the army. Then came the Spanish infantry, who in
a summer's campaign had acquired the discipline, and the
weather-beaten aspect, of veterans. The baggage occupied the
centre; and the rear was closed by the dark files of Tlascalan
warriors. The whole number must have fallen short of seven
thousand; of which less than four hundred were Spaniards.

For a short distance, the army kept along the narrow tongue
of land that divides the Tezcucan from the Chalcan waters,
when it entered on the great dike, which, with the exception
of an angle near the commencement, stretches in a perfectly
straight line across the salt floods of Tezcuco to the gates of
the capital. It was the same causeway, or rather the basis of
that, which still forms the great southern avenue of Mexico.
The Spaniards had occasion more than ever to admire the
mechanical science of the Aztecs, in the geometrical precision
with which the work was executed, as well as the solidity of
its construction. It was composed of huge stones well laid in
cement; and wide enough, throughout its whole extent, for
ten horsemen to ride abreast.

They saw, as they passed along, several large towns, resting
on piles, and reaching far into the water,—a kind of architecture which found great favor with the Aztecs, being in imitation
of that of their metropolis. The busy population obtained a
good subsistence from the manufacture of salt, which they

extracted from the waters of the great lake. The duties on the traffic in this article were a considerable source of revenue to the crown.

Everywhere the Conquerors beheld the evidence of a crowded and thriving population, exceeding all they had yet seen. The temples and principal buildings of the cities were covered with a hard white stucco, which glistened like enamel in the level beams of the morning. The margin of the great basin was more thickly gemmed, than that of Chalco, with towns and hamlets. The water was darkened by swarms of canoes filled with Indians, who clambered up the sides of the causeway, and gazed with curious astonishment on the strangers. And here, also, they beheld those fairy islands of flowers, over-shadowed occasionally by trees of considerable size, rising and falling with the gentle undulation of the billows. At the distance of half a league from the capital, they encountered a solid work or curtain of stone, which traversed the dike. It was twelve feet high, was strengthened by towers at the extremities, and in the centre was a battlemented gate-way, which opened a passage to the troops. It was called the Fort of Xoloc, and became memorable in aftertimes as the position occupied by Cortés in the famous siege of Mexico.

Here they were met by several hundred Aztec chiefs, who came out to announce the approach of Montezuma, and to welcome the Spaniards to his capital. They were dressed in the fanciful gala costume of the country, with the *maxtlatl*, or cotton sash, around their loins, and a broad mantle of the same material, or of the brilliant feather-embroidery, flowing gracefully down their shoulders. On their necks and arms they displayed collars and bracelets of turquoise mosaic, with which delicate plumage was curiously mingled, while their ears, under-lips, and occasionally their noses, were garnished with pendants formed of precious stones, or crescents of fine gold. As each cacique made the usual formal salutation of the country separately to the general, the tedious ceremony delayed the march more than an hour. After this, the army experienced no further interruption till it reached a bridge near the gates of the city. It was built of wood, since replaced by one of stone, and was thrown across an opening of the dike, which furnished an outlet to the waters, when agitated by the winds, or swollen by a sudden influx in the rainy season. It was a draw-bridge; and the Spaniards, as they crossed it, felt how truly they were committing themselves to the mercy of Montezuma, who, by thus cutting off their communications with the country, might hold them prisoners in his capital.

In the midst of these unpleasant reflections, they beheld the glittering retinue of the emperor emerging from the great street which led then, as it still does, through the heart of the city. Amidst a crowd of Indian nobles, preceded by three officers of state, bearing golden wands, they saw the royal palanquin blazing with burnished gold. It was borne on the shoulders of nobles, and over it a canopy of gaudy feather-work, powdered with jewels, and fringed with silver, was supported by four attendants of the same rank. They were bare-footed, and walked with a slow, measured pace, and with eyes bent on the ground. When the train had come within a convenient distance, it halted, and Montezuma, descending from his litter, came forward leaning on the arms of the lords of Tezcuco and Iztapalapan, his nephew and brother, both of whom, as we have seen, had already been made known to the Spaniards. As the monarch advanced under the canopy, the obsequious attendants strewed the ground with cotton tapestry, that his imperial feet might not be contaminated by the rude soil. His subjects of high and low degree, who lined the sides of the causeway, bent forward with their eyes fastened on the ground as he passed, and some of the humbler class prostrated themselves before him. Such was the homage paid to the Indian despot, showing that the slavish forms of Oriental adulation were to be found among the rude inhabitants of the Western World.

Montezuma wore the girdle and ample square cloak, *tilmatli*, of his nation. It was made of the finest cotton, with the embroidered ends gathered in a knot round his neck. His feet were defended by sandals having soles of gold, and the leathern thongs which bound them to his ankles were embossed with the same metal. Both the cloak and sandals were sprinkled with pearls and precious stones, among which the emerald and the *chalchivitl*—a green stone of higher estimation than any other among the Aztecs—were conspicuous. On his head he wore no other ornament than a *panache* of plumes of the royal green which floated down his back, the badge of military, rather than of regal, rank.

He was at this time about forty years of age. His person was tall and thin, but not ill-made. His hair, which was black and straight, was not very long; to wear it short was considered unbecoming persons of rank. His beard was thin; his complexion somewhat paler than is often found in his dusky, or rather copper colored race. His features, though serious in their expression, did not wear the look of melancholy, indeed, of dejection, which characterizes his portrait, and which may well have settled on them at a later period. He moved with dignity, and his whole demeanour, tempered by an expression of benignity not to have been anticipated from the reports circulated of his character, was worthy of a great prince.—Such is the portrait left to us of the celebrated Indian emperor, in this his first interview with the white men.

The army halted as he drew near. Cortés, dismounting, threw his reins to a page, and, supported by a few of the principal cavaliers, advanced to meet him. The interview must have been one of uncommon interest to both. In Montezuma, Cortés beheld the lord of the broad realms he had traversed, whose magnificence and power had been the burden of every tongue. In the Spaniard, on the other hand, the Aztec prince saw the strange being whose history seemed to be so mysteriously connected with his own; the predicted one of his oracles; whose achievements proclaimed him something more than human. But, whatever may have been the monarch's feelings, he so far suppressed them as to receive his guest with princely courtesy, and to express his satisfaction at personally seeing him in his capital. Cortés responded by the most profound expressions of respect, while he made ample acknowledgments for the substantial proofs which the emperor had given the Spaniards of his munificence. He then hung round Montezuma's neck a sparkling chain of colored crystal, accompanying this with a movement as if to embrace him, when he was restrained by the two Aztec lords, shocked at the menaced profanation of the sacred person of their master. After the interchange of these civilities, Montezuma appointed his brother to conduct the Spaniards to their residence in the capital, and again entering his litter was borne off amidst prostrate crowds in the same state in which he had come. The Spaniards quickly followed, and with colors flying and music playing soon made their entrance into the southern quarter of Tenochtitlán.

Here, again, they found fresh cause for admiration in the grandeur of the city, and the superior style of its architecture. The dwellings of the poorer class were, indeed, chiefly of reeds and mud. But the great avenue through which they were now marching was lined with the houses of the nobles, who were encouraged by the emperor to make the capital their residence. They were built of a red porous stone drawn from quarries in the neighbourhood, and, though they rarely rose to a second story, often covered a large space of ground. The flat roofs, *azoteas*, were protected by stone parapets, so that every house was a fortress. Sometimes these roofs resembled parterres of flowers, so thickly were they covered with them, but more frequently these were cultivated in broad terraced gardens, laid out between the edifices. Occasionally a great square or marketplace intervened, surrounded by its porticos of stone and stucco; or a pyramidal temple reared its colossal bulk, crowned with its tapering sanctuaries, and altars blazing with inextinguishable fires. The great street facing the southern causeway, unlike most others in the place, was wide, and extended some miles in nearly a straight line, as before noticed, through the centre of the city. A spectator standing at one end of it, as his eye ranged along the deep vista of temples, terraces, and gardens, might clearly discern the other, with the blue mountains in the distance, which, in the transparent atmosphere of the table-land, seemed almost in contact with the buildings.

But what most impressed the Spaniards was the throngs of people who swarmed through the streets and on the canals, filling every door-way and window, and clustering on the roofs of the buildings. "I well remember the spectacle," exclaims Bernal Díaz; "it seems now, after so many years, as present to my mind, as if it were but yesterday." But what must have been the sensations of the Aztecs themselves, as they looked on the portentous pageant! as they heard, now for the first time, the well-cemented pavement ring under the iron tramp of the horses,—the strange animals which fear had clothed in such supernatural terrors; as they gazed on the children of the East, revealing their celestial origin in their fair complexions; saw the bright falchions and bonnets of steel, a metal to them unknown, glancing like meteors in the sun, while sounds of unearthly music—at least, such as their rude instruments had never wakened—floated in the air! But every other emotion was lost in that of deadly hatred, when they beheld their detested enemy, the Tlascalan, stalking, in defiance, as it were, through their streets, and staring around with looks of ferocity and wonder, like some wild animal of the forest, who had strayed by chance from his native fastnesses into the haunts of civilization.

As they passed down the spacious street, the troops repeatedly traversed bridges suspended above canals, along which they saw the Indian barks gliding swiftly with their little cargoes of fruits and vegetables for the markets of Tenochtitlán. At length, they halted before a broad area near the centre of the city, where rose the huge pyramidal pile dedicated to the patron war-god of the Aztecs, second only, in size, as well as sanctity, to the temple of Cholula, and covering the same ground now in part occupied by the great cathedral of Mexico.

Facing the western gate of the inclosure of the temple, stood
a low range of stone buildings, spreading over a wide extent
of ground, the palace of Axayacatl, Montezuma's father, built
by that monarch about fifty years before. It was appropriated
as the barracks of the Spaniards. The emperor himself was in
the court-yard, waiting to receive them. Approaching Cortés,
he took from a vase of flowers, borne by one of his slaves, a
massy collar, in which the shell of a species of craw-fish, much
prized by the Indians, was set in gold, and connected by heavy
links of the same metal. From this chain depended eight ornaments, also of gold, made in resemblance of the same shell-fish,
a span in length each, and of delicate workmanship; for the
Aztec goldsmiths were confessed to have shown skill in their
craft, not inferior to their brethren of Europe. Montezuma,
as he hung the gorgeous collar round the general's neck, said,
"This palace belongs to you, Malinche," (the epithet by which
he always addressed him,) "and your brethren. Rest after your
fatigues, for you have much need to do so, and in a little while
I will visit you again." So saying, he withdrew with his attendants, evincing, in this act, a delicate consideration not to have
been expected in a barbarian.

Cortés' first care was to inspect his new quarters. The building, though spacious, was low, consisting of one floor, except,
indeed, in the centre, where it rose to an additional story. The
apartments were of great size, and afforded accommodations,
according to the testimony of the Conquerors themselves, for
the whole army! The hardy mountaineers of Tlascala were,
probably, not very fastidious, and might easily find a shelter
in the out-buildings, or under temporary awnings in the ample
court-yards. The best apartments were hung with gay cotton
draperies, the floors covered with mats or rushes. There were,
also, low stools made of single pieces of wood elaborately carved,
and in most of the apartments beds made of the palm-leaf,
woven into a thick mat, with coverlets, and sometimes canopies
of cotton. These mats were the only beds used by the natives,
whether of high or low degree.

After a rapid survey of this gigantic pile, the general assigned his troops their respective quarters, and took as vigilant precautions for security, as if he had anticipated a siege, instead of a friendly entertainment. The place was encompassed by a stone wall of considerable thickness, with towers or heavy buttresses at intervals, affording a good means of defence. He planted his cannon so as to command the approaches, stationed his sentinels along the works, and, in short, enforced in every respect as strict military discipline as had been observed in any part of the march. He well knew the importance to his little band, at least for the present, of conciliating the goodwill of the citizens; and, to avoid all possibility of collision, he prohibited any soldier from leaving his quarters without orders, under pain of death. Having taken these precautions, he allowed his men to partake of the bountiful collation which had been prepared for them.

They had been long enough in the country to become reconciled to, if not to relish, the peculiar cooking of the Aztecs. The appetite of the soldier is not often dainty, and on the present occasion it cannot be doubted that the Spaniards did full justice to the savory productions of the royal kitchen. During the meal they were served by numerous Mexican slaves, who were, indeed, distributed through the palace, anxious to do the bidding of the strangers. After the repast was concluded, and they had taken their *siesta,* not less important to a Spaniard than food itself, the presence of the emperor was again announced.

Montezuma was attended by a few of his principal nobles. He was received with much deference by Cortés; and, after the parties had taken their seats, a conversation commenced between them, through the aid of Doña Marina, while the cavaliers and Aztec chieftains stood around in respectful silence.

Montezuma made many inquiries concerning the country of the Spaniards, their sovereign, the nature of his government, and especially their own motives in visiting Anahuac. Cortés explained these motives by the desire to see so distinguished a

monarch, and to declare to him the true Faith professed by
the Christians. With rare discretion, he contented himself with
dropping this hint, for the present, allowing it to ripen in the
mind of the emperor, till a future conference. The latter asked,
whether those white men, who in the preceding year had landed
on the eastern shores of his empire, were their countrymen. He
showed himself well informed of the proceedings of the Spaniards from their arrival in Tabasco to the present time, information of which had been regularly transmitted in the hieroglyphical paintings. He was curious, also, in regard to the rank
of his visiters in their own country; inquiring, if they were the
kinsmen of the sovereign. Cortés replied, they were kinsmen
of one another, and subjects of their great monarch, who held
them all in peculiar estimation. Before his departure, Montezuma made himself acquainted with the names of the principal
cavaliers, and the position they occupied in the army.

At the conclusion of the interview, the Aztec prince commanded his attendants to bring forward the presents prepared
for his guests. They consisted of cotton dresses, enough to
supply every man, it is said, including the allies, with a suit!
And he did not fail to add the usual accompaniment of gold
chains and other ornaments, which he distributed in profusion
among the Spaniards. He then withdrew with the same ceremony with which he had entered, leaving every one deeply
impressed with his munificence, and his affability so unlike
what they had been taught to expect, by, what they now considered, an invention of the enemy.

That evening, the Spaniards celebrated their arrival in
the Mexican capital by a general discharge of artillery. The
thunders of the ordnance reverberating among the buildings
and shaking them to their foundations, the stench of the sul-
phureous vapor that rolled in volumes above the walls of the
encampment, reminding the inhabitants of the explosions of
the great *volcán*, filled the hearts of the superstitious Aztecs
with dismay. It proclaimed to them, that their city held in
its bosom those dread beings whose path had been marked

with desolation, and who could call down the thunderbolts to consume their enemies! It was doubtless the policy of Cortés to strengthen this superstitious feeling as far as possible, and to impress the natives, at the outset, with a salutary awe of the supernatural powers of the Spaniards.

On the following morning, the general requested permission to return the emperor's visit, by waiting on him in his palace. This was readily granted, and Montezuma sent his officers to conduct the Spaniards to his presence. Cortés dressed himself in his richest habit, and left the quarters attended by Alvarado, Sandoval, Velásquez, and Ordaz, together with five or six of the common file.

The royal habitation was at no great distance. It stood on the ground, to the south-west of the cathedral, since covered in part by the *Casa del Estado,* the palace of the dukes of Monteleone, the descendants of Cortés. It was a vast, irregular pile of low stone buildings, like that garrisoned by the Spaniards. So spacious was it, indeed, that, as one of the Conquerors assures us, although he had visited it more than once, for the express purpose, he had been too much fatigued each time by wandering through the apartments ever to see the whole of it. It was built of the red porous stone of the country, *tetzontli,* was ornamented with marble, and on the façade over the principal entrance were sculptured the arms or device of Montezuma, an eagle bearing an ocelot in his talons.

In the courts through which the Spaniards passed, fountains of crystal water were playing, fed from the copious reservoir on the distant hill of Chapoltepec, and supplying in their turn more than a hundred baths in the interior of the palace. Crowds of Aztec nobles were sauntering up and down in these squares, and in the outer halls, loitering away their hours in attendance on the court. The apartments were of immense size, though not lofty. The ceilings were of various sorts of odoriferous wood ingeniously carved; the floors covered with mats of the palm-leaf. The walls were hung with cotton richly stained, with the skins of wild animals, or gorgeous draperies of feather-work wrought in imitation of birds, insects, and flowers, with the nice art and glowing radiance of colors that might compare with the tapestries of Flanders. Clouds of incense rolled up from censers, and diffused intoxicating odors through the apartments. The Spaniards might well have fancied themselves in the voluptuous precincts of an Eastern harem, instead of treading the halls of a wild barbaric chief in the Western World.

On reaching the hall of audience, the Mexican officers took off their sandals, and covered their gay attire with a mantle of *nequén,* a coarse stuff made of the fibres of the maguey, worn only by the poorest classes. This act of humiliation was imposed on all, except the members of his own family, who approached the sovereign. Thus bare-footed, with down-cast eyes, and formal obeisance, they ushered the Spaniards into the royal presence.

They found Montezuma seated at the further end of a spacious saloon, and surrounded by a few of his favorite chiefs. He received them kindly, and very soon Cortés, without much ceremony, entered on the subject which was uppermost in his thoughts. He was fully aware of the importance of gaining the royal convert, whose example would have such an influence on the conversion of his people. The general, therefore, prepared to display the whole store of his theological science, with the most winning arts of rhetoric he could command, while the interpretation was conveyed through the silver tones of Marina, as inseparable from him, on these occasions, as his shadow.

He set forth, as clearly as he could, the ideas entertained by the Church in regard to the holy mysteries of the Trinity, the Incarnation, and the Atonement. From this he ascended to the origin of things, the creation of the world, the first pair, paradise, and the fall of man. He assured Montezuma, that the idols he worshipped were Satan under different forms. A sufficient proof of it was the bloody sacrifices they imposed, which he contrasted with the pure and simple rite of the mass. Their worship would sink him in perdition. It was to snatch his soul, and the souls of his people, from the flames of eternal fire by opening to them a purer faith, that the Christians had come to his land. And he earnestly besought him not to neglect the occasion, but to secure his salvation by embracing the Cross, the great sign of human redemption.

The eloquence of the preacher was wasted on the insensible heart of his royal auditor. It, doubtless, lost somewhat of its efficacy, strained through the imperfect interpretation of so recent a neophyte as the Indian damsel. But the doctrines were too abstruse in themselves to be comprehended at a glance by the rude intellect of a barbarian. And Montezuma may have, perhaps, thought it was not more monstrous to feed on the flesh of a fellow-creature, than on that of the Creator himself. He was, besides, steeped in the superstitions of his country from his cradle. He had been educated in the straitest sect of her religion; had been himself a priest before his election to the throne; and was now the head both of the religion and the state. Little probability was there that such a man would be open to argument or persuasion, even from the lips of a more practised polemic than the Spanish commander. How could he abjure the faith that was intertwined with the dearest affections of his heart, and the very elements of his beings? How could he be false to the gods who had raised him to such prosperity and honors, and whose shrines were intrusted to his especial keeping?

He listened, however, with silent attention, until the general had concluded his homily. He then replied, that he knew the Spaniards had held this discourse wherever they had been. He doubted not their God was, as they said, a good being. His gods, also, were good to him. Yet what his visiter said of the creation of the world was like what he had been taught to believe. It was not worth while to discourse further of the matter. His ancestors, he said, were not the original proprietors of the land. They had occupied it but a few ages, and had been led there by a great Being, who, after giving them laws and ruling over the nation for a time, had withdrawn to the regions where

the sun rises. He had declared, on his departure, that he or
his descendants would again visit them and resume his empire.
The wonderful deeds of the Spaniards, their fair complexions,
and the quarter whence they came, all showed they were his descendants. If Montezuma had resisted their visit to his capital,
it was because he had heard such accounts of their cruelties,—
that they sent the lightning to consume his people, or crushed
them to pieces under the hard feet of the ferocious animals on
which they rode. He was now convinced that these were idle
tales; that the Spaniards were kind and generous in their natures; they were mortals, of a different race, indeed, from the
Aztecs, wiser, and more valiant,—and for this he honored
them.

"You, too," he added, with a smile, "have been told, perhaps,
that I am a god, and dwell in palaces of gold and silver. But
you see it is false. My houses, though large, are of stone and
wood like those of others; and as to my body," he said, baring
his tawny arm, "you see it is flesh and bone like yours. It is
true, I have a great empire inherited from my ancestors; lands,
and gold, and silver. But your sovereign beyond the waters is,
I know, the rightful lord of all. I rule in his name. You, Malinche, are his ambassador; you and your brethren shall share these
things with me. Rest now from your labors. You are here in
your own dwellings, and every thing shall be provided for your
subsistence. I will see that your wishes shall be obeyed in the
same way as my own." As the monarch concluded these words,
a few natural tears suffused his eyes, while the image of ancient
independence, perhaps, flitted across his mind.

Cortés, while he encouraged the idea that his own sovereign
was the great Being indicated by Montezuma, endeavoured to
comfort the monarch by the assurance that his master had no
desire to interfere with his authority, otherwise than, out of
pure concern for his welfare, to effect his conversion and that
of his people to Christianity. Before the emperor dismissed his
visiters he consulted his munificent spirit, as usual, by distributing rich stuffs and trinkets of gold among them, so that the

poorest soldier, says Bernal Díaz, one of the party, received at least two heavy collars of the precious metal for his share. The iron hearts of the Spaniards were touched with the emotion displayed by Montezuma, as well as by his princely spirit of liberality. As they passed him, the cavaliers, with bonnet in hand, made him the most profound obeisance, and "on the way home," continues the same chronicler, "we could discourse of nothing but the gentle breeding and courtesy of the Indian monarch, and of the respect we entertained for him."

Speculation of a graver complexion must have pressed on the mind of the general, as he saw around him the evidences of a civilization, and consequently power, for which even the exaggerated reports of the natives—discredited from their apparent exaggeration—had not prepared him. In the pomp and burdensome ceremonial of the court, he saw that nice system of subordination and profound reverence for the monarch which characterize the semi-civilized empires of Asia. In the appearance of the capital, its massy, yet elegant architecture, its luxurious social accommodations, its activity in trade, he recognised the proofs of the intellectual progress, mechanical skill, and enlarged resources of an old and opulent community; while the swarms in the streets attested the existence of a population capable of turning these resources to the best account.

In the Aztec he beheld a being unlike either the rude republican Tlascalan, or the effeminate Cholulan; but combining the courage of the one with the cultivation of the other. He was in the heart of a great capital, which seemed like an extensive fortification, with its dikes and its draw-bridges, where every house might be easily converted into a castle. Its insular position removed it from the continent, from which, at the mere nod of the sovereign, all communication might be cut off, and the whole warlike population be at once precipitated on him and his handful of followers. What could superior science avail against such odds?

As to the subversion of Montezuma's empire, now that he had seen him in his capital, it must have seemed a more doubtful enterprise than ever. The recognition which the Aztec prince had made of the feudal supremacy, if I may so say, of the Spanish sovereign, was not to be taken too literally. Whatever show of deference he might be disposed to pay the latter, under the influence of his present—perhaps temporary—delusion, it was not to be supposed that he would so easily relinquish his actual power and possessions, or that his people would consent to it. Indeed, his sensitive apprehensions in regard to this very subject, on the coming of the Spaniards, were sufficient proof of the tenacity with which he clung to his authority. It is true that Cortés had a strong lever for future operations in the superstitious reverence felt for himself both by prince and people. It was undoubtedly his policy to maintain this sentiment unimpaired in both, as far as possible. But, before settling any plan of operations, it was necessary to make himself personally acquainted with the topography and local advantages of the capital, the character of its population, and the real nature and amount of its resources. With this view, he asked the emperor's permission to visit the principal public edifices.

BOOK FOUR

Residence in Mexico

CURIOSITY, fear, and the wonder of it all led the Spaniards to hasten their acquaintance with the island-city in which they were quartered. Home of possibly 300,000 people, Tenochtitlán was Montezuma's capital.

I

Tenochtitlán

NOT content with the spacious residence of his father, Montezuma erected another on a yet more magnificent scale. It occupied, as before mentioned, the ground partly covered by the private dwellings on one side of the *plaza mayor* of the modern city. This building, or, as it might more correctly be styled, pile of buildings, spread over an extent of ground so vast, that, as one of the Conquerors assures us, its terraced roof might have afforded ample room for thirty knights to run their courses in a regular tourney. I have already noticed its interior decorations, its fanciful draperies, its roofs inlaid with cedar and other odoriferous woods, held together without a nail, and, probably, without a knowledge of the arch, its numerous and spacious apartments, which Cortés, with enthusiastic hyperbole, does not hesitate to declare superior to any thing of the kind in Spain.

Adjoining the principal edifice were others devoted to various objects. One was an armory, filled with the weapons and military dresses worn by the Aztecs, all kept in the most perfect order, ready for instant use. The emperor was himself very expert in the management of the *maquahuitl*, or Indian sword, and took great delight in witnessing athletic exercises, and the mimic representation of war by his young nobility. Another building was used as a granary, and others as warehouses for the different articles of food and apparel contributed by the districts charged with the maintenance of the royal household.

There were, also, edifices appropriated to objects of quite

another kind. One of these was an immense aviary, in which birds of splendid plumage were assembled from all parts of the empire. Here was the scarlet cardinal, the golden pheasant, the endless parrot-tribe with their rainbow hues, (the royal green predominant,) and that miniature miracle of nature, the humming-bird, which delights to revel among the honeysuckle bowers of Mexico. Three hundred attendants had charge of this aviary, who made themselves acquainted with the appropriate food of its inmates, oftentimes procured at great cost, and in the moulting season were careful to collect the beautiful plumage, which, with its many-colored tints, furnished the materials for the Aztec painter.

A separate building was reserved for the fierce birds of prey; the voracious vulture-tribes and eagles of enormous size, whose home was in the snowy solitudes of the Andes. No less than five hundred turkeys, the cheapest meat in Mexico, were allowed for the daily consumption of these tyrants of the feathered race.

Adjoining this aviary was a menagerie of wild animals gathered from the mountain forests, and even from the remote swamps of the *tierra caliente*. The resemblance of the different species to those in the Old World, with which no one of them, however, was identical, led to a perpetual confusion in the nomenclature of the Spaniards, as it has since done in that of better instructed naturalists. The collection was still further swelled by a great number of reptiles and serpents remarkable for their size and venomous qualities, among which the Spaniards beheld the fiery little animal "with the castanets in his tail," the terror of the American wilderness. The serpents were confined in long cages lined with down or feathers, or in troughs of mud and water. The beasts and birds of prey were provided with apartments large enough to allow of their moving about, and secured by a strong lattice-work, through which light and air were freely admitted. The whole was placed under the charge of numerous keepers, who acquainted themselves with the habits of their prisoners, and provided for their comfort and cleanliness. With what deep interest would the enlightened naturalist of that day—an Oviedo, or a Martyr, for example— have surveyed this magnificent collection, in which the various tribes which roamed over the Western wilderness, the unknown races of an unknown world, were brought into one view! How would they have delighted to study the peculiarities of these new species, compared with those of their own hemisphere, and thus have risen to some comprehension of the general laws by which Nature acts in all her works! The rude followers of Cortés did not trouble themselves with such refined speculations. They gazed on the spectacle with a vague curiosity not un- mixed with awe; and, as they listened to the wild cries of the ferocious animals and the hissings of the serpents, they almost fancied themselves in the infernal regions.

I must not omit to notice a strange collection of human mon- sters, dwarfs, and other unfortunate persons, in whose organiza- tion Nature had capriciously deviated from her regular laws. Such hideous anomalies were regarded by the Aztecs as a suitable appendage of state. It is even said, they were in some cases the result of artificial means, employed by unnatural parents desirous to secure a provision for their offspring by thus qualifying them for a place in the royal museum!

Extensive gardens were spread out around these buildings, filled with fragrant shrubs and flowers, and especially with me- dicinal plants. No country has afforded more numerous species of these last, than New Spain; and their virtues were perfectly understood by the Aztecs, with whom medical botany may be said to have been studied as a science. Amidst this labyrinth of sweet-scented groves and shrubberies, fountains of pure water might be seen throwing up their sparkling jets, and scattering refreshing dews over the blossoms. Ten large tanks, well stocked with fish, afforded a retreat on their margins to various tribes of water-fowl, whose habits were so carefully consulted, that some of these ponds were of salt water, as that which they most loved to frequent. A tessellated pavement of marble inclosed the ample basins, which were overhung by light and fanciful pavilions, that admitted the perfumed breezes of the gardens, and offered a grateful shelter to the monarch and his mistresses in the sultry heats of summer.

But the most luxurious residence of the Aztec monarch, at that season, was the royal hill of Chapoltepec, a spot consecrated, moreover, by the ashes of his ancestors. It stood in a westerly direction from the capital, and its base was, in his day, washed by the waters of the Tezcuco. On its lofty crest of porphyritic rock, there now stands the magnificent, though desolate, castle erected by the young viceroy Gálvez, at the close of the seventeenth century. The view from its windows is one of the finest in the environs of Mexico. The landscape is not disfigured here, as in many other quarters, by the white and barren patches, so offensive to the sight; but the eye wanders over an unbroken expanse of meadows and cultivated fields, waving with rich harvests of European grain. Montezuma's gardens stretched for miles around the base of the hill. Two statues of that monarch and his father, cut in *bas relief* in the porphyry, were spared till the middle of the last century; and the grounds are still shaded by gigantic cypresses, more than fifty feet in circumference, which were centuries old at the time of the Conquest. The place is now a tangled wilderness of wild shrubs, where the myrtle mingles its dark, glossy leaves with the red berries and delicate foliage of the pepper-tree. Surely, there is no spot better suited to awaken meditation on the past; none, where the traveller, as he sits under those stately cypresses grey with the moss of ages, can so fitly ponder on the sad destinies of the Indian races and the monarch who once held his courtly revels under the shadow of their branches.

The domestic establishment of Montezuma was on the same scale of barbaric splendor as every thing else about him. He could boast as many wives as are found in the harem of an Eastern sultan. They were lodged in their own apartments, and provided with every accommodation, according to their ideas, for personal comfort and cleanliness. They passed their hours in the usual feminine employments of weaving and embroidery, especially in the graceful feather-work, for which such rich materials were furnished by the royal aviaries. They conducted themselves with strict decorum, under the supervision of certain aged females, who acted in the respectable capacity of duennas, in the same manner as in the religious houses attached to the *teocallis*. The palace was supplied with numerous baths, and Montezuma set the example, in his own person, of frequent ablutions. He bathed at least once, and changed his dress four times, it is said, every day. He never put on the same apparel a second time, but gave it away to his attendants. Queen Elizabeth, with a similar taste for costume, showed a less princely spirit in hoarding her discarded suits. Her wardrobe was, probably, somewhat more costly than that of the Indian emperor.

Besides his numerous female retinue, the halls and antechambers were filled with nobles in constant attendance on his person, who served also as a sort of body-guard. It had been usual for plebeians of merit to fill certain offices in the palace. But the haughty Montezuma refused to be waited upon by any but men of noble birth. They were not unfrequently the sons of the great chiefs, and remained as hostages in the absence of their fathers; thus serving the double purpose of security and state.

His meals the emperor took alone. The well-matted floor of a large saloon was covered with hundreds of dishes. Sometimes Montezuma himself, but more frequently his steward, indicated those which he preferred, and which were kept hot by means of chafing-dishes. The royal bill of fare comprehended, besides domestic animals, game from the distant forests, and fish which, the day before, was swimming in the Gulf of Mexico! They were dressed in manifold ways, for the Aztec *artistes*, as we have already had occasion to notice, had penetrated deep into the mysteries of culinary science.

The meats were served by the attendant nobles, who then resigned the office of waiting on the monarch to maidens selected for their personal grace and beauty. A screen of richly gilt and carved wood was drawn around him, so as to conceal him from vulgar eyes during the repast. He was seated on a cushion, and the dinner was served on a low table covered with a delicate cotton cloth. The dishes were of the finest ware of Cholula. He had a service of gold, which was reserved for religious celebrations. Indeed, it would scarcely have comported with even his princely revenues to have used it on ordinary occasions, when his table equipage was not allowed to appear a second time, but was given away to his attendants. The saloon was lighted by torches made of a resinous wood, which sent forth a sweet odor and, probably, not a little smoke, as they burned. At his meal, he was attended by five or six of his ancient counsellors, who stood at a respectful distance, answering his questions, and occasionally rejoiced by some of the viands with which he complimented them from his table.

This course of solid dishes was succeeded by another of sweetmeats and pastry, for which the Aztec cooks, provided with the important requisites of maize-flour, eggs, and the rich sugar of the aloe, were famous. Two girls were occupied at the further end of the apartment, during dinner, in preparing fine rolls and wafers, with which they garnished the board from time to time. The emperor took no other beverage than the *chocolatl,* a potation of chocolate, flavored with vanilla and other spices, and so prepared as to be reduced to a froth of the consistency of honey, which gradually dissolved in the mouth. This beverage, if so it could be called, was served in golden goblets, with spoons of the same metal or of tortoise-shell finely wrought. The emperor was exceedingly fond of it, to judge from the quantity,—no less than fifty jars or pitchers being prepared for his own daily consumption! Two thousand more were allowed for that of his household.

The general arrangement of the meal seems to have been not very unlike that of Europeans. But no prince in Europe could boast a dessert which could compare with that of the Aztec emperor. For it was gathered fresh from the most opposite climes; and his board displayed the products of his own temperate region, and the luscious fruits of the tropics, plucked, the day previous, from the green groves of the *tierra caliente,* and transmitted with the speed of steam, by means of couriers, to the capital. It was as if some kind fairy should crown our banquets with the spicy products that but yesterday were growing in a sunny isle of the far-off Indian seas!

After the royal appetite was appeased, water was handed to him by the female attendants in a silver basin, in the same manner as had been done before commencing his meal; for the Aztecs were as constant in their ablutions, at these times, as any nation of the East. Pipes were then brought, made of a varnished and richly gilt wood, from which he inhaled, sometimes through the nose, at others through the mouth, the fumes of an intoxicating weed, "called *tobacco*," mingled with liquid-amber. While this soothing process of fumigation was going on, the emperor enjoyed the exhibitions of his mountebanks and jugglers, of whom a regular corps was attached to the palace. No people, not even those of China or Hindostan, surpassed the Aztecs in feats of agility and legerdemain.

Sometimes he amused himself with his jester; for the Indian monarch had his jesters, as well as his more refined brethren of Europe, at that day. Indeed, he used to say, that more instruction was to be gathered from them than from wiser men, for they dared to tell the truth. At other times, he witnessed the graceful dances of his women, or took delight in listening to music,—if the rude minstrelsy of the Mexicans deserve that name,—accompanied by a chant, in slow and solemn cadence, celebrating the heroic deeds of great Aztec warriors, or of his own princely line.

When he had sufficiently refreshed his spirits with these diversions, he composed himself to sleep, for in his *siesta* he was as regular as a Spaniard. On awakening, he gave audience to ambassadors from foreign states, or his own tributary cities, or to such caciques as had suits to prefer to him. They were introduced by the young nobles in attendance, and, whatever might be their rank, unless of the blood royal, they were obliged to submit to the humiliation of shrouding their rich dresses under the coarse mantle of *nequén,* and entering barefooted, with downcast eyes, into the presence. The emperor addressed few and brief remarks to the suitors, answering them generally by his secretaries; and the parties retired with the same reverential obeisance, taking care to keep their faces turned towards the monarch. Well might Cortés exclaim, that no court, whether of the Grand Seignior or any other infidel, ever displayed so pompous and elaborate a ceremonial!

Besides the crowd of retainers already noticed, the royal household was not complete without a host of artisans constantly employed in the erection or repair of buildings, besides a great number of jewellers and persons skilled in working metals, who found abundant demand for their trinkets among the dark-eyed beauties of the harem. The imperial mummers and jugglers were also very numerous, and the dancers belonging to the palace occupied a particular district of the city, appropriated exclusively to them.

The maintenance of this little host, amounting to some thousands of individuals, involved a heavy expenditure, requiring accounts of a complicated, and, to a simple people, it might well be, embarrassing nature. Every thing, however, was conducted with perfect order; and all the various receipts and disbursements were set down in the picture-writing of the country. The arithmetical characters were of a more refined and conventional sort than those for narrative purposes; and a separate apartment was filled with hieroglyphical legers, exhibiting a complete view of the economy of the palace. The care of all this was intrusted to a treasurer, who acted as a sort of major-domo in the household, having a general superintendence over all its concerns. This responsible office, on the arrival of the Spaniards, was in the hands of a trusty cacique named Tapia.

Such is the picture of Montezuma's domestic establishment and way of living, as delineated by the Conquerors and their immediate followers, who had the best means of information;

too highly colored, it may be, by the proneness to exaggerate, which was natural to those who first witnessed a spectacle so striking to the imagination, so new and unexpected. I have thought it best to present the full details, trivial though they may seem to the reader, as affording a curious picture of manners, so superior in point of refinement to those of the other Aboriginal tribes on the North American continent. Nor are they, in fact, so trivial, when we reflect, that, in these details of private life, we possess a surer measure of civilization, than in those of a public nature. . . .

On drawing near to the *tianguez*, or great market, the Spaniards were astonished at the throng of people pressing towards it, and, on entering the place, their surprise was still further heightened by the sight of the multitudes assembled there, and the dimensions of the inclosure, thrice as large as the celebrated square of Salamanca. Here were met together traders from all parts, with the products and manufactures peculiar to their countries; the goldsmiths of Azcapozalco; the potters and jewellers of Cholula, the painters of Tezcuco, the stone-cutters of Tenajocán, the hunters of Xilotepec, the fishermen of Cuitlahuac, the fruiterers of the warm countries, the mat and chairmakers of Quauhtitlan, and the florists of Xochimilco,—all busily engaged in recommending their respective wares, and in chaffering with purchasers.

The market-place was surrounded by deep porticos, and the several articles had each its own quarter allotted to it. Here might be seen cotton piled up in bales, or manufactured into dresses and articles of domestic use, as tapestry, curtains, coverlets, and the like. The richly stained and nice fabrics reminded Cortés of the *alcaycería*, or silk-market of Granada. There was the quarter assigned to the goldsmiths, where the purchaser might find various articles of ornament or use formed of the precious metals, or curious toys, such as we have already had occasion to notice, made in imitation of birds and fishes, with scales and feathers alternately of gold and silver, and with movable heads and bodies. These fantastic little trinkets were often garnished with precious stones, and showed a patient, puerile ingenuity in the manufacture, like that of the Chinese.

In an adjoining quarter were collected specimens of pottery coarse and fine, vases of wood elaborately carved, varnished or gilt, of curious and sometimes graceful forms. There were also hatchets made of copper alloyed with tin, the substitute, and, as it proved, not a bad one, for iron. The soldier found here all the implements of his trade. The casque fashioned into the head of some wild animal, with its grinning defences of teeth, and bristling crest dyed with the rich tint of the cochineal; the *escaupil,* or quilted doublet of cotton, the rich surcoat of feather-mail, and weapons of all sorts, copper-headed lances and arrows, and the broad *maquahuitl,* the Mexican sword, with its sharp blades of *itztli.* Here were razors and mirrors of this same hard and polished mineral which served so many of the purposes of steel with the Aztecs. In the square were also to be found booths occupied by barbers, who used these same razors in their vocation. For the Mexicans, contrary to the popular and erroneous notions respecting the Aborigines of the New World, had beards, though scanty ones. Other shops or booths were tenanted by apothecaries, well provided with drugs, roots, and different medicinal preparations. In other places, again, blank books or maps for the hieroglyphical picture-writing were to be seen, folded together like fans, and made of cotton, skins, or more commonly the fibres of the agave, the Aztec papyrus.

Under some of the porticos they saw hides raw and dressed, and various articles for domestic or personal use made of the leather. Animals, both wild and tame, were offered for sale, and near them, perhaps, a gang of slaves, with collars round their necks, intimating they were likewise on sale,—a spectacle unhappily not confined to the barbarian markets of Mexico, though the evils of their condition were aggravated there by the consciousness that a life of degradation might be consummated at any moment by the dreadful doom of sacrifice.

The heavier materials for building, as stone, lime, timber, were considered too bulky to be allowed a place in the square, and were deposited in the adjacent streets on the borders of the canals. It would be tedious to enumerate all the various articles, whether for luxury or daily use, which were collected from all quarters in this vast bazaar. I must not omit to mention, however, the display of provisions, one of the most attractive features of the *tianguez;* meats of all kinds, domestic poultry, game from the neighbouring mountains, fish from the lakes and streams, fruits in all the delicious abundance of these temperate regions, green vegetables, and the unfailing maize. There was many a viand, too, ready dressed, which sent up its savory steams provoking the appetite of the idle passenger; pastry, bread of the Indian corn, cakes, and confectionary. Along with these were to be seen cooling or stimulating beverages, the spicy foaming *chocolatl,* with its delicate aroma of vanilla, and the inebriating *pulque,* the fermented juice of the aloe. All these commodities, and every stall and portico, were set out, or rather smothered, with flowers, showing, on a much greater scale, indeed, a taste similar to that displayed in the markets of modern Mexico. Flowers seem to be the spontaneous growth of this luxuriant soil; which, instead of noxious weeds, as in other regions, is ever ready, without the aid of man, to cover up its nakedness with this rich and variegated livery of Nature.

I will spare the reader the repetition of all the particulars enumerated by the bewildered Spaniards, which are of some interest as evincing the various mechanical skill and the polished wants, resembling those of a refined community, rather than of a nation of savages. It was the *material* civilization, which belongs neither to the one nor the other. The Aztec had plainly reached that middle station, as far above the rude races of the New World as it was below the cultivated communities of the Old.

As to the numbers assembled in the market, the estimates differ, as usual. The Spaniards often visited the place, and no one states the amount at less than forty thousand! Some carry it much higher. Without relying too much on the arithmetic of the Conquerors, it is certain that on this occasion, which occurred every fifth day, the city swarmed with a motley crowd of strangers, not only from the vicinity, but from many leagues around; the causeways were thronged, and the lake was darkened by canoes filled with traders flocking to the great *tianguez*. It resembled, indeed, the periodical fairs in Europe, not as they exist now, but as they existed in the Middle Ages, when, from the difficulties of intercommunication, they served as the great central marts for commercial intercourse, exercising a most important and salutary influence on the community.

The exchanges were conducted partly by barter, but more usually in the currency of the country. This consisted of bits of tin stamped with a character like a T, bags of cacao, the value of which was regulated by their size, and lastly quills filled with gold dust. Gold was part of the regular currency, it seems, in both hemispheres. In their dealings it is singular that they should have had no knowledge of scales and weights. The quantity was determined by measure and number.

The most perfect order reigned throughout this vast assembly. Officers patrolled the square, whose business it was to keep the peace, to collect the duties imposed on the different articles of merchandise, to see that no false measures or fraud of any kind were used, and to bring offenders at once to justice. A court of twelve judges sat in one part of the *tianguez*, clothed with those ample and summary powers, which, in despotic countries, are often delegated even to petty tribunals. The extreme severity with which they exercised these powers, in more than one instance, proves that they were not a dead letter.

The *tianguez* of Mexico was naturally an object of great interest, as well as wonder, to the Spaniards. For in it they saw converged into one focus, as it were, all the rays of civilization scattered throughout the land. Here they beheld the various evidences of mechanical skill, of domestic industry, the multiplied resources, of whatever kind, within the compass of the natives. It could not fail to impress them with high ideas of the magnitude of these resources, as well as of the commercial activity and social subordination by which the whole community was knit together; and their admiration is fully evinced by the minuteness and energy of their descriptions.

From this bustling scene, the Spaniards took their way to the great *teocalli,* in the neighbourhood of their own quarters. It covered, with the subordinate edifices, as the reader has already seen, the large tract of ground now occupied by the cathedral, part of the market-place, and some of the adjoining streets. It was the spot which had been consecrated to the same object, probably, ever since the foundation of the city. The present building, however, was of no great antiquity, having been constructed by Ahuitzotl, who celebrated its dedication in 1486, by that hecatomb of victims, of which such incredible reports are to be found in the chronicles.

It stood in the midst of a vast area, encompassed by a wall of stone and lime, about eight feet high, ornamented on the outer side by figures of serpents, raised in relief, which gave it the name of the *coatepantli,* or "wall of serpents." This emblem was a common one in the sacred sculpture of Anahuac, as well as of Egypt. The wall, which was quadrangular, was pierced by huge battlemented gateways, opening on the four principal streets of the capital. Over each of the gates was a kind of arsenal, filled with arms and warlike gear; and, if we may credit the report of the Conquerors, there were barracks adjoining, garrisoned by ten thousand soldiers, who served as a sort of military police for the capital, supplying the emperor with a strong arm in case of tumult or sedition.

The *teocalli* itself was a solid pyramidal structure of earth and pebbles, coated on the outside with hewn stones probably of the light, porous kind employed in the buildings of the city. It was probably square, with its sides facing the cardinal points. It was divided into five bodies or stories, each one receding so as to be of smaller dimensions than that immediately below it; the usual form of the Aztec *teocallis,* as already described, and bearing obvious resemblance to some of the primitive pyramidal structures in the Old World. The ascent was by a flight of steps on the outside, which reached to the narrow terrace or platform at the base of the second story, passing quite round the building, when a second stairway conducted to a similar landing at the base of the third. The breadth of this walk was just so much space as was left by the retreating story next above it. From this construction the visiter was obliged to pass round the whole edifice four times, in order to reach the top. This had a most imposing effect in the religious ceremonials, when the pompous procession of priests with their wild minstrelsy came sweeping round the huge sides of the pyramid, as they rose higher and higher, in the presence of gazing multitudes, towards the summit.

The dimensions of the temple cannot be given with any certainty. The Conquerors judged by the eye, rarely troubling themselves with any thing like an accurate measurement. It was, probably, not much less than three hundred feet square at the base; and, as the Spaniards counted a hundred and fourteen steps, was, probably, less than one hundred feet in height.

When Cortés arrived before the *teocalli,* he found two priests and several caciques commissioned by Montezuma to save him the fatigue of the ascent by bearing him on their shoulders, in the same manner as had been done to the emperor. But the general declined the compliment, preferring to march up at the head of his men. On reaching the summit, they found it a vast area, paved with broad flat stones. The first object that met their view was a large block of jasper, the peculiar shape of which showed it was the stone on which the bodies of the unhappy victims were stretched for sacrifice. Its convex surface, by raising the breast, enabled the priest to perform his diabolical task more easily, of removing the heart. At the other end of the area were two towers or sanctuaries, consisting of three stories, the lower one of stone and stucco, the two upper

of wood elaborately carved. In the lower division stood the
images of their gods; the apartments above were filled with
utensils for their religious services, and with the ashes of
some of their Aztec princes, who had fancied this airy sepulchre.
Before each sanctuary stood an altar with that undying fire
upon it, the extinction of which boded as much evil to the
empire, as that of the Vestal flame would have done to ancient
Rome. Here, also, was the huge cylindrical drum made of serpents' skins, and struck only on extraordinary occasions, when
it sent forth a melancholy sound that might be heard for
miles,—a sound of woe in after-times to the Spaniards.

Montezuma, attended by the high-priest, came forward to
receive Cortés as he mounted the area. "You are weary, Malinche," said he to him, "with climbing up our great temple." But
Cortés, with a politic vaunt, assured him "the Spaniards were
never weary"! Then, taking him by the hand, the emperor
pointed out the localities of the neighbourhood. The temple
on which they stood, rising high above all other edifices in the
capital, afforded the most elevated as well as central point of
view. Below them, the city lay spread out like a map, with
its streets and canals intersecting each other at right angles,
its terraced roofs blooming like so many parterres of flowers.
Every place seemed alive with business and bustle; canoes were
glancing up and down the canals, the streets were crowded with
people in their gay, picturesque costume, while from the market-
place, they had so lately left, a confused hum of many sounds
and voices rose upon the air. They could distinctly trace the
symmetrical plan of the city, with its principal avenues issuing,
as it were, from the four gates of the *coatepantli;* and connecting
themselves with the causeways, which formed the grand entrances to the capital. This regular and beautiful arrangement
was imitated in many of the inferior towns, where the great
roads converged towards the chief *teocalli,* or cathedral, as to
a common focus. They could discern the insular position of the
metropolis, bathed on all sides by the salt floods of the Tezcuco,
and in the distance the clear fresh waters of the Chalco; far

beyond stretched a wide prospect of fields and waving woods, with the burnished walls of many a lofty temple rising high above the trees, and crowning the distant hill-tops. The view reached in an unbroken line to the very base of the circular range of mountains, whose frosty peaks glittered as if touched with fire in the morning ray; while long, dark wreaths of vapor, rolling up from the hoary head of Popocatepetl, told that the destroying element was, indeed, at work in the bosom of the beautiful Valley.

Cortés was filled with admiration at this grand and glorious spectacle, and gave utterance to his feelings in animated language to the emperor, the lord of these flourishing domains. His thoughts, however, soon took another direction; and, turning to father Olmedo, who stood by his side, he suggested that the area would afford a most conspicuous position for the Christian Cross, if Montezuma would but allow it to be planted there. But the discreet ecclesiastic, with the good sense which on these occasions seems to have been so lamentably deficient in his commander, reminded him, that such a request, at present, would be exceedingly ill-timed, as the Indian monarch had shown no dispositions as yet favorable to Christianity.

Cortés then requested Montezuma to allow him to enter the sanctuaries, and behold the shrines of his gods. To this the latter, after a short conference with the priests, assented, and conducted the Spaniards into the building. They found themselves in a spacious apartment incrusted on the sides with stucco, on which various figures were sculptured, representing the Mexican calendar, perhaps, or the priestly ritual. At one end of the saloon was a recess with a roof of timber richly carved and gilt. Before the altar in this sanctuary, stood the colossal image of Huitzilopotchli, the tutelary deity and war-god of the Aztecs. His countenance was distorted into hideous lineaments of symbolical import. In his right hand he wielded a bow, and in his left a bunch of golden arrows, which a mystic legend had connected with the victories of his people. The huge folds of a serpent, consisting of pearls and precious stones, were coiled round his waist, and the same rich materials were profusely sprinkled over his person. On his left foot were the delicate feathers of the humming-bird, which, singularly enough, gave its name to the dread deity. The most conspicuous ornament was a chain of gold and silver hearts alternate, suspended round his neck, emblematical of the sacrifice in which he most delighted. A more unequivocal evidence of this was afforded by three human hearts smoking and almost palpitating, as if recently torn from the victims, and now lying on the altar before him!

The adjoining sanctuary was dedicated to a milder deity. This was Tezcatlipoca, next in honor to that invisible Being, the Supreme God, who was represented by no image, and confined by no temple. It was Tezcatlipoca who created the world, and watched over it with a providential care. He was represented as a young man, and his image, of polished black stone, was richly garnished with gold plates and ornaments; among which a shield, burnished like a mirror, was the most characteristic emblem, as in it he saw reflected all the doings of the world. But the homage to this god was not always of a more refined and merciful character than that paid to his carnivorous brother; for five bleeding hearts were also seen in a golden platter on his altar.

The walls of both these chapels were stained with human gore. "The stench was more intolerable," exclaims Díaz, "than that of the slaughterhouses in Castile!" And the frantic forms of the priests, with their dark robes clotted with blood, as they flitted to and fro, seemed to the Spaniards to be those of the very ministers of Satan!

From this foul abode they gladly escaped into the open air; when Cortés, turning to Montezuma, said, with a smile, "I do not comprehend how a great and wise prince, like you, can put faith in such evil spirits as these idols, the representatives of the Devil! If you will but permit us to erect here the true Cross, and place the images of the blessed Virgin and her Son in your sanctuaries, you will soon see how your false gods will shrink before them!"

Montezuma was greatly shocked at this sacrilegious address. "These are the gods," he answered, "who have led the Aztecs on to victory since they were a nation, and who send the seed-time and harvest in their seasons. Had I thought you would have offered them this outrage, I would not have admitted you into their presence."

Cortés, after some expressions of concern at having wounded the feelings of the emperor, took his leave. Montezuma remained, saying that he must expiate, if possible, the crime of exposing the shrines of the divinities to such profanation by the strangers. . . .

II

The Kidnapping of Montezuma

THE Spaniards had been now a week in Mexico. During this time, they had experienced the most friendly treatment from the emperor. But the mind of Cortés was far from easy. He felt that it was quite uncertain how long this amiable temper would last. A hundred circumstances might occur to change it. He might very naturally feel the maintenance of so large a body too burdensome on his treasury. The people of the capital might become dissatisfied at the presence of so numerous an armed force within their walls. Many causes of disgust might arise betwixt the soldiers and the citizens. Indeed, it was scarcely possible that a rude, licentious soldiery, like the Spaniards, could be long kept in subjection without active employment. The danger was even greater with the Tlascalans, a fierce race now brought into daily contact with the nation who held them in loathing and detestation. Rumors were already rife among the allies, whether well-founded or not, of murmurs among the Mexicans, accompanied by menaces of raising the bridges.

Even should the Spaniards be allowed to occupy their present quarters unmolested, it was not advancing the great object of the expedition. Cortés was not a whit nearer gaining the capital, so essential to his meditated subjugation of the country; and any day he might receive tidings that the Crown, or, what he most feared, the governor of Cuba, had sent a force of superior strength to wrest from him a conquest but half achieved. Disturbed by these anxious reflections, he resolved to extricate himself from his embarrassment by one bold stroke. But he first submitted the affair to a council of the officers in whom he most confided, desirous to divide with them the responsibility of the act, and, no doubt, to interest them more heartily in its execution, by making it in some measure the result of their combined judgments.

When the general had briefly stated the embarrassments of their position, the council was divided in opinion. All admitted the necessity of some instant action. One party were for retiring secretly from the city, and getting beyond the causeways before their march could be intercepted. Another advised that it should be done openly, with the knowledge of the emperor, of whose good-will they had had so many proofs. But both these measures seemed alike impolitic. A retreat under these circumstances, and so abruptly made, would have the air of a flight. It would be construed into distrust of themselves; and any thing like timidity on their part would be sure not only to bring on them the Mexicans, but the contempt of their allies, who would, doubtless, join in the general cry.

As to Montezuma, what reliance could they place on the protection of a prince so recently their enemy, and who, in his altered bearing, must have taken counsel of his fears, rather than his inclinations?

Even should they succeed in reaching the coast, their situation would be little better. It would be proclaiming to the world, that, after all their lofty vaunts, they were unequal to the enterprise. Their only hopes of their sovereign's favor, and of pardon for their irregular proceedings, were founded on success. Hitherto, they had only made the discovery of Mexico; to retreat would be to leave conquest and the fruits of it to another.—In short, to stay and to retreat seemed equally disastrous.

In this perplexity, Cortés proposed an expedient, which none but the most daring spirit, in the most desperate extremity, would have conceived. This was, to march to the royal palace, and bring Montezuma to the Spanish quarters, by fair means if they could persuade him, by force if necessary,—at all events, to get possession of his person. With such a pledge, the Spaniards would be secure from the assault of the Mexicans, afraid by acts of violence to compromise the safety of their prince. If he came by his own consent, they would be deprived of all apology for doing so. As long as the emperor remained among the Spaniards, it would be easy, by allowing him a show of sovereignty, to rule in his name, until they had taken measures for securing their safety, and the success of their enterprise. The idea of employing a sovereign as a tool for the government of his own kingdom, if a new one in the age of Cortés, is certainly not so in ours.

A plausible pretext for the seizure of the hospitable monarch —for the most barefaced action seeks to veil itself under some show of decency—was afforded by a circumstance of which Cortés had received intelligence at Cholula. He had left, as we have seen, a faithful officer, Juan de Escalante, with a hundred and fifty men in garrison at Vera Cruz, on his departure for the capital. He had not been long absent, when his lieutenant received a message from an Aztec chief named Quauhpopoca, governor of a district to the north of the Spanish settlement, declaring his desire to come in person and tender his allegiance to the Spanish authorities at Vera Cruz. He requested that four of the white men might be sent to protect him against certain unfriendly tribes through which his road lay. This was not an uncommon request, and excited no suspicion in Escalante. The four soldiers were sent; and on their arrival two of them were murdered by the false Aztec. The other two made their way back to the garrison.

The commander marched at once, with fifty of his men, and several thousand Indian allies, to take vengeance on the cacique. A pitched battle followed. The allies fled from the redoubted Mexicans. The few Spaniards stood firm, and with the aid of their fire-arms and the blessed Virgin, who was distinctly seen hovering over their ranks in the van, they made good the field against the enemy. It cost them dear, however; since seven or eight Christians were slain, and among them the gallant Escalante himself, who died of his injuries soon after his return to the fort. The Indian prisoners captured in the battle spoke of the whole proceeding as having taken place at the instigation of Montezuma.

One of the Spaniards fell into the hands of the natives, but soon after perished of his wounds. His head was cut off and sent to the Aztec emperor. It was uncommonly large and covered with hair; and, as Montezuma gazed on the ferocious features, rendered more horrible by death, he seemed to read in them the dark lineaments of the destined destroyers of his house. He turned from it with a shudder, and commanded that it should be taken from the city, and not offered at the shrine of any of his gods.

Although Cortés had received intelligence of this disaster at Cholula, he had concealed it within his own breast, or communicated it to very few only of his most trusty officers, from apprehension of the ill effect it might have on the spirits of the common soldiers.

The cavaliers whom Cortés now summoned to the council were men of the same mettle with their leader. Their bold, chivalrous spirits seemed to court danger for its own sake. If one or two, less adventurous, were startled by the proposal he made, they were soon overruled by the others, who, no doubt, considered that a desperate disease required as desperate a remedy.

That night, Cortés was heard pacing his apartment to and fro, like a man oppressed by thought, or agitated by strong emotion. He may have been ripening in his mind the daring scheme for the morrow. In the morning the soldiers heard mass as usual, and father Olmedo invoked the blessing of Heaven on their hazardous enterprise. Whatever might be the cause in which he was embarked, the heart of the Spaniard was cheered with the conviction that the Saints were on his side!

Having asked an audience from Montezuma, which was readily granted, the general made the necessary arrangements for his enterprise. The principal part of his force was drawn up in the court-yard, and he stationed a considerable detachment in the avenues leading to the palace, to check any attempt at rescue by the populace. He ordered twenty-five or thirty of the soldiers to drop in at the palace, as if by accident, in groups of three or four at a time, while the conference was going on with Montezuma. He selected five cavaliers, in whose courage and coolness he placed most trust, to bear him company; Pedro de Alvarado, Gonzalo de Sandoval, Francisco de Lujo, Velásquez de León, and Alonso de Ávila,—brilliant names in the annals of the Conquest. All were clad, as well as the common soldiers, in complete armor, a circumstance of too familiar occurrence to excite suspicion.

The little party were graciously received by the emperor, who soon, with the aid of the interpreters, became interested in a sportive conversation with the Spaniards, while he indulged his natural munificence by given them presents of gold and jewels. He paid the Spanish general the particular compliment of offering him one of his daughters as his wife; an honor which the latter respectfully declined, on the ground that he was already accommodated with one in Cuba, and that his religion forbade a plurality.

When Cortés perceived that a sufficient number of his soldiers were assembled, he changed his playful manner, and with a serious tone briefly acquainted Montezuma with the treacherous proceedings in the *tierra caliente,* and the accusation of him as their author. The emperor listened to the charge with surprise; and disavowed the act, which he said could only have been imputed to him by his enemies. Cortés expressed his belief in his declaration, but added, that, to prove it true, it would be necessary to send for Quauhpopoca and his accomplices, that they might be examined and dealt with according to their deserts. To this Montezuma made no objection. Taking from his wrist, to which it was attached, a precious stone, the royal signet, on which was cut the figure of the War-god, he gave it to one of his nobles, with orders to show it to the Aztec governor, and require his instant presence in the capital, together with all those who had been accessory to the murder of the Spaniards. If he resisted, the officer was empowered to call in the aid of the neighbouring towns, to enforce the mandate.

When the messenger had gone, Cortés assured the monarch that this prompt compliance with his request convinced him of his innocence. But it was important that his own sovereign should be equally convinced of it. Nothing would promote this so much as for Montezuma to transfer his residence to the palace occupied by the Spaniards, till on the arrival of Quauhpopoca the affair could be fully investigated. Such an act of condescension would, of itself, show a personal regard for the Spaniards, incompatible with the base conduct alleged against him, and would fully absolve him from all suspicion!

Montezuma listened to this proposal, and the flimsy reasoning with which it was covered, with looks of profound amazement. He became pale as death; but in a moment, his face flushed with resentment, as, with the pride of offended dignity, he exclaimed, "When was it ever heard that a great prince, like myself, voluntarily left his own palace to become a prisoner in the hands of strangers!"

Cortés assured him he would not go as a prisoner. He would experience nothing but respectful treatment from the Spaniards; would be surrounded by his own household, and hold intercourse with his people as usual. In short, it would be but a change of residence, from one of his palaces to another, a circumstance of frequent occurrence with him.—It was in vain. "If I should consent to such a degradation," he answered, "my subjects never would!" When further pressed, he offered to give up one of his sons and of his daughters to remain as hostages with the Spaniards, so that he might be spared this disgrace.

Two hours passed in this fruitless discussion, till a high-mettled cavalier, Velásquez de León, impatient of the long delay, and seeing that the attempt, if not the deed, must ruin them, cried out, "Why do we waste words on this barbarian? We have gone too far to recede now. Let us seize him, and, if he resists, plunge our swords into his body!" The fierce tone and menacing gestures, with which this was uttered, alarmed the monarch, who inquired of Marina what the angry Spaniard said. The interpreter explained it in as gentle a manner as she could, beseeching him "to accompany the white men to their quarters, where he would be treated with all respect and kindness, while to refuse them would but expose himself to violence, perhaps to death." Marina, doubtless, spoke to her sovereign as she thought, and no one had better opportunity of knowing the truth than herself.

This last appeal shook the resolution of Montezuma. It was in vain that the unhappy prince looked around for sympathy or support. As his eyes wandered over the stern visages and iron forms of the Spaniards, he felt that his hour was indeed come; and, with a voice scarcely audible from emotion, he consented to accompany the strangers,—to quit the palace, whither he was never more to return. Had he possessed the spirit of the first Montezuma, he would have called his guards around him, and left his life-blood on the threshold, sooner than have been dragged a dishonored captive across it. But his courage sunk under circumstances. He felt he was the instrument of an irresistible Fate!

No sooner had the Spaniards got his consent, than orders were given for the royal litter. The nobles, who bore and attended it, could scarcely believe their senses, when they learned their master's purpose. But pride now came to Montezuma's aid, and, since he must go, he preferred that it should appear to be with his own free will. As the royal retinue, escorted by the Spaniards, marched through the street with downcast eyes and dejected mien, the people assembled in crowds, and a rumor ran among them, that the emperor was carried off by force to the quarters of the white men. A tumult would have soon arisen but for the intervention of Montezuma himself, who called out to the people to disperse, as he was visiting his friends of his own accord; thus sealing his ignominy by a declaration which deprived his subjects of the only excuse for resistance. On reaching the quarters, he sent out his nobles with similar assurances to the mob, and renewed orders to return to their homes.

He was received with ostentatious respect by the Spaniards, and selected the suite of apartments which best pleased him. They were soon furnished with fine cotton tapestries, feather-work, and all the elegancies of Indian upholstery. He was attended by such of his household as he chose, his wives and his pages, and was served with his usual pomp and luxury at his meals. He gave audience, as in his own palace, to his subjects, who were admitted to his presence, few, indeed, at a time, under the pretext of greater order and decorum. From the Spaniards themselves he met with a formal deference. No one, not even the general himself, approached him without doffing his casque, and rendering the obeisance due to his rank. Nor did they ever sit in his presence, without being invited by him to do so.

With all this studied ceremony and show of homage, there was one circumstance which too clearly proclaimed to his people that their sovereign was a prisoner. In the front of the palace a patrol of sixty men was established, and the same number in the rear. Twenty of each corps mounted guard at once, maintaining a careful watch, day and night. Another body, under command of Velásquez de León, was stationed in the royal antechamber. Cortés punished any departure from duty, or relaxation of vigilance, in these sentinels, with the utmost severity. He felt, as, indeed, every Spaniard must have felt, that the escape of the emperor now would be their ruin. Yet the task of this unintermitting watch sorely added to their fatigues. "Better this dog of a king should die," cried a soldier one day, "than that we should wear out our lives in this manner." The words were uttered in the hearing of Montezuma, who gathered something of their import, and the offender was severely chastised by order of the general. Such instances of disrespect, however, were very rare. Indeed, the amiable deportment of the monarch, who seemed to take pleasure in the society of his jailers, and who never allowed a favor or attention from the meanest soldier to go unrequited, inspired the Spaniards with as much attachment as they were capable of feeling—for a barbarian.

Things were in this posture, when the arrival of Quauhpopoca from the coast was announced. He was accompanied by his son and fifteen Aztec chiefs. He had travelled all the way, borne, as became his high rank, in a litter. On entering Montezuma's presence, he threw over his dress the coarse robe of *nequén*, and made the usual humiliating acts of obeisance. The poor parade of courtly ceremony was the more striking, when placed in contrast with the actual condition of the parties.

The Aztec governor was coldly received by his master, who referred the affair (had he the power to do otherwise?) to the examination of Cortés. It was, doubtless, conducted in a sufficiently summary manner. To the general's query, whether the cacique was the subject of Montezuma, he replied, "And what other sovereign could I serve?" implying that his sway was universal. He did not deny his share in the transaction, nor did he seek to shelter himself under the royal authority, till sentence of death was passed on him and his followers, when they all laid the blame of their proceedings on Montezuma. They were condemned to be burnt alive in the area before the palace. The funeral piles were made of heaps of arrows, javelins, and other weapons, drawn by the emperor's permission from the arsenals round the great *teocalli*, where they had been stored to supply means of defence in times of civic tumult or insurrection. By this politic precaution, Cortés proposed to remove a ready means of annoyance in case of hostilities with the citizens.

To crown the whole of the extraordinary proceedings, Cortés, while preparations for the execution were going on, entered the emperor's apartment, attended by a soldier bearing fetters in his hands. With a severe aspect, he charged the monarch with being the original contriver of the violence offered to the Spaniards, as was now proved by the declaration of his own instruments. Such a crime, which merited death in a subject, could not be atoned for, even by a sovereign, without some punishment. So saying, he ordered the soldier to fasten the fetters on Montezuma's ankles. He coolly waited till it was done; then, turning his back on the monarch, quitted the room.

Montezuma was speechless under the infliction of this last insult. He was like one struck down by a heavy blow, that deprives him of all his faculties. He offered no resistance. But, though he spoke not a word, low, ill-suppressed moans, from time to time, intimated the anguish of his spirit. His attendants, bathed in tears, offered him their consolations. They tenderly held his feet in their arms, and endeavoured, by inserting their shawls and mantles, to relieve them from the pressure of the iron. But they could not reach the iron which had penetrated into his soul. He felt that he was no more a king.

Meanwhile, the execution of the dreadful doom was going forward in the court-yard. The whole Spanish force was under arms, to check any interruption that might be offered by the Mexicans. But none was attempted. The populace gazed in silent wonder, regarding it as the sentence of the emperor. The manner of the execution, too, excited less surprise, from their familiarity with similar spectacles, aggravated, indeed, by additional horrors, in their own diabolical sacrifices. The Aztec lord and his companions, bound hand and foot to the blazing piles, submitted without a cry or a complaint to their terrible fate. Passive fortitude is the virtue of the Indian warrior; and it was the glory of the Aztec, as of the other races on the North American continent, to show how the spirit of the brave man may triumph over torture and the agonies of death.

When the dismal tragedy was ended, Cortés reentered Montezuma's apartment. Kneeling down, he unclasped his shackles with his own hand, expressing at the same time his regret that so disagreeable a duty as that of subjecting him to such a punishment had been imposed on him. This last indignity had entirely crushed the spirit of Montezuma; and the monarch, whose frown, but a week since, would have made the nations of Anahuac tremble to their remotest borders, was now craven enough to thank his deliverer for his freedom, as for a great and unmerited boon!

Not long after, the Spanish general, conceiving that his royal captive was sufficiently humbled, expressed his willingness that he should return, if he inclined, to his own palace. Montezuma declined it; alleging, it is said, that his nobles had more than once importuned him to resent his injuries by taking arms against the Spaniards; and that, were he in the midst of them, it would be difficult to avoid it, or to save his capital from bloodshed and anarchy. The reason did honor to his heart, if it was the one which influenced him. It is probable that he did not care to trust his safety to those haughty and ferocious chieftains, who had witnessed the degradation of their master, and must despise his pusillanimity, as a thing unprecedented in an Aztec monarch. It is also said, that, when Marina conveyed to him the permission of Cortés, the other interpreter, Aguilar, gave him to understand the Spanish officers never would consent that he should avail himself of it.

Whatever were his reasons, it is certain that he declined the offer; and the general, in a well-feigned, or real ecstasy, embraced him, declaring, "that he loved him as a brother, and that every Spaniard would be zealously devoted to his interests, since he had shown himself so mindful of theirs!" Honeyed words, "which," says the shrewd old chronicler who was present, "Montezuma was wise enough to know the worth of."

The events recorded in this chapter are certainly some of the most extraordinary on the page of history. That a small body of men, like the Spaniards, should have entered the palace of a mighty prince, have seized his person in the midst of his vassals, have borne him off a captive to their quarters,—that they should have put to an ignominious death before his face his high officers, for executing, probably, his own commands, and have crowned the whole by putting the monarch in irons like a common malefactor,—that this should have been done, not to a drivelling dotard in the decay of his fortunes, but to a proud monarch in the plenitude of his power, in the very heart of his capital, surrounded by thousands and tens of thousands, who trembled at his nod, and would have poured out their blood like water in his defence,—that all this should have been done by a mere handful of adventurers, is a thing too extravagant, altogether too improbable, for the pages of romance! It is, nevertheless, literally true. Yet we shall not be prepared to acquiesce in the judgments of contemporaries who ·regarded these acts with admiration. We may well distrust any grounds on which it is attempted to justify the kidnapping of a friendly sovereign,— by those very persons, too, who were reaping the full benefit of his favors.

To view the matter differently, we must take the position of the Conquerors, and assume with them the original right of conquest. Regarded from this point of view, many difficulties vanish. If conquest were a duty, whatever was necessary to effect it was right also. Right and expedient become convertible terms. And it can hardly be denied, that the capture of the monarch was expedient, if the Spaniards would maintain their hold on the empire.

The execution of the Aztec governor suggests other considerations. If he were really guilty of the perfidious act imputed to him by Cortés, and if Montezuma disavowed it, the governor deserved death, and the general was justified by the law of nations in inflicting it. It is by no means so clear, however, why he should have involved so many in this sentence; most, perhaps all, of whom must have acted under his authority. The cruel manner of the death will less startle those who are familiar with the established penal codes in most civilized nations in the sixteenth century.

But, if the governor deserved death, what pretence was there for the outrage on the person of Montezuma? If the former was guilty, the latter surely was not. But, if the cacique only acted in obedience to orders, the responsibility was transferred to the sovereign who gave the orders. They could not both stand in the same category.

It is vain, however, to reason on the matter, on any abstract principles of right and wrong, or to suppose that the Conquerors troubled themselves with the refinements of casuistry. Their standard of right and wrong, in reference to the natives, was a very simple one. Despising them as an outlawed race, without God in the world, they, in common with their age, held it to be their "mission" (to borrow the cant phrase of our own day) to conquer and to convert. The measures they adopted certainly facilitated the first great work of conquest. By the execution of the caciques, they struck terror not only into the capital, but throughout the country. It proclaimed that not a hair of a Spaniard was to be touched with impunity! By rendering Montezuma contemptible in his own eyes and those of his subjects, Cortés deprived him of the support of his people, and forced him to lean on the arm of the stranger. It was a politic proceeding,—to which few men could have been equal, who had a touch of humanity in their natures.

A good criterion of the moral sense of the actors in these events is afforded by the reflections of Bernal Díaz, made some fifty years, it will be remembered, after the events themselves, when the fire of youth had become extinct, and the eye, glancing back through the vista of half a century, might be supposed to be unclouded by the passions and prejudices which throw their mist over the present. "Now that I am an old man," says the veteran, "I often entertain myself with calling to mind the heroical deeds of early days, till they are as fresh as the events of yesterday. I think of the seizure of the Indian monarch, his confinement in irons, and the execution of his officers, till all these things seem actually passing before me. And, as I ponder on our exploits, I feel that it was not of ourselves that we performed them, but that it was the providence of God which guided us. Much food is there here for meditation!" There is so, indeed, and for a meditation not unpleasing, as we reflect on the advance, in speculative morality, at least, which the nineteenth century has made over the sixteenth. But should not the consciousness of this teach us charity? Should it not make us the more distrustful of applying the standard of the present to measure the actions of the past?

THE *captive ruler settled into a routine in the quarters
of the Spaniards, and life in the native metropolis continued on an even tenor. The conquistadors amassed
more loot and distributed it in a manner which left a
number of them thoroughly disgruntled. Christian
worship was instituted atop one of the teocallis. In
time, the change of events so bore in upon the natives
that their ill will, once concealed, increasingly evi-
denced itself.*

*Meanwhile the affairs of Cortés outside Mexico had
worsened. In Spain the studied delay of Charles V
blocked the requests of Cortés' agents; in Cuba Governor Velásquez' rage induced that administrator to
put a punitive force of nine hundred Spaniards with
eighteen vessels and eighty horses under the command
of Pánfilo de Narváez. When the expedition disem-
barked, in late April, 1520, near Vera Cruz, Cortés'
commander of the coastal garrison, youthful Gonzalo
de Sandoval, proved equal to the situation.*

III

A Challenge Met

SANDOVAL meanwhile had not been inattentive to the movements of Narváez. From the time of his first appearance on the
coast, that vigilant officer, distrusting the object of the armament, had kept his eye on him. No sooner was he apprized of
the landing of the Spaniards, than the commander of Villa Rica
sent off his few disabled soldiers to a place of safety in the
neighbourhood. He then put his works in the best posture of
defence that he could, and prepared to maintain the place to
the last extremity. His men promised to stand by him, and, the
more effectually to fortify the resolution of any who might
falter, he ordered a gallows to be set up in a conspicuous part
of the town! The constancy of his men was not put to the trial.

The only invaders of the place were a priest, a notary, and

four other Spaniards, selected for the mission, already noticed, by Narváez. The ecclesiastic's name was Guevara. On coming before Sandoval, he made him a formal address, in which he pompously enumerated the services and claims of Velásquez, taxed Cortés and his adherents with rebellion, and demanded of Sandoval to tender his submission, as a loyal subject, to the newly constituted authority of Narváez.

The commander of La Villa Rica was so much incensed at this unceremonious mention of his companions in arms, that he assured the reverend envoy that nothing but respect for his cloth saved him from the chastisement he merited. Guevara now waxed wroth in his turn, and called on the notary to read the proclamation. But Sandoval interposed, promising that functionary, that, if he attempted to do so, without first producing a warrant of his authority from the Crown, he should be soundly flogged. Guevara lost all command of himself at this, and stamping on the ground repeated his orders in a more peremptory tone than before. Sandoval was not a man of many words. He simply remarked, that the instrument should be read to the general himself in Mexico. At the same time, he ordered his men to procure a number of sturdy *tamanes,* or Indian porters, on whose backs the unfortunate priest and his companions were bound like so many bales of goods. They were then placed under a guard of twenty Spaniards, and the whole caravan took its march for the capital. Day and night they travelled, stopping only to obtain fresh relays of carriers; and as they passed through populous towns, forests, and cultivated fields, vanishing as soon as seen, the Spaniards, bewildered by the strangeness of the scene, as well as of their novel mode of conveyance, hardly knew whether they were awake or in a dream. In this way, at the end of the fourth day, they reached the Tezcucan lake in view of the Aztec capital.

Its inhabitants had already been made acquainted with the fresh arrival of white men on the coast. Indeed, directly on their landing, intelligence had been communicated to Montezuma, who is said (it does not seem probable) to have con-

cealed it some days from Cortés. At length, inviting him to an
interview, he told him there was no longer any obstacle to his
leaving the country, as a fleet was ready for him. To the inquiries of the astonished general, Montezuma replied by point-
ing to a hieroglyphical map sent him from the coast, on which
the ships, the Spaniards themselves, and their whole equipment,
were minutely delineated. Cortés, suppressing all emotions but
those of pleasure, exclaimed, "Blessed be the Redeemer for his
mercies!" On returning to his quarters, the tidings were received by the troops with loud shouts, the firing of cannon,
and other demonstrations of joy. They hailed the new comers
as a reinforcement from Spain. Not so their commander. From
the first, he suspected them to be sent by his enemy, the governor of Cuba. He communicated his suspicions to his officers,
through whom they gradually found their way among the men.
The tide of joy was instantly checked. Alarming apprehensions
succeeded, as they dwelt on the probability of this suggestion,
and on the strength of the invaders. Yet their constancy did
not desert them; and they pledged themselves to remain true to
their cause, and, come what might, to stand by their leader.
It was one of those occasions that proved the entire influence
which Cortés held over these wild adventurers. All doubts were
soon dispelled by the arrival of the prisoners from Villa Rica.

One of the convoy, leaving the party in the suburbs, entered
the city, and delivered a letter to the general from Sandoval,
acquainting him with all the particulars. Cortés instantly sent
to the prisoners, ordered them to be released, and furnished
them with horses to make their entrance into the capital,—a
more creditable conveyance than the backs of *tamanes*. On their
arrival, he received them with marked courtesy, apologized for
the rude conduct of his officers, and seemed desirous by the most
assiduous attentions to soothe the irritation of their minds.
He showed his good-will still further by lavishing presents on
Guevara and his associates, until he gradually wrought such a
change in their dispositions, that, from enemies, he converted
them into friends, and drew forth many important particulars

respecting not merely the designs of their leader, but the feelings of his army. The soldiers, in general, they said, far from desiring a rupture with those of Cortés, would willingly coöperate with them, were it not for their commander. They had no feelings of resentment to gratify. Their object was gold. The personal influence of Narváez was not great, and his arrogance and penurious temper had already gone far to alienate from him the affections of his followers. These hints were not lost on the general.

He addressed a letter to his rival in the most conciliatory terms. He besought him not to proclaim their animosity to the world, and, by kindling a spirit of insubordination in the natives, unsettle all that had been so far secured. A violent collision must be prejudicial even to the victor, and might be fatal to both. It was only in union that they could look for success. He was ready to greet Narváez as a brother in arms, to share with him the fruits of conquest, and, if he could produce a royal commission, to submit to his authority.—Cortés well knew he had no such commission to show.

Soon after the departure of Guevara and his comrades, the general determined to send a special envoy of his own. The person selected for this delicate office was father Olmedo, who, through the campaign, had shown a practical good sense, and a talent for affairs, not always to be found in persons of his spiritual calling. He was intrusted with another epistle to Narváez, of similar import with the preceding. Cortés wrote, also, to the licentiate Ayllón, with whose departure he was not acquainted, and to Andrés de Duero, former secretary of Velásquez, and his own friend, who had come over in the present fleet. Olmedo was instructed to converse with these persons in private, as well as with the principal officers and soldiers, and, as far as possible, to infuse into them a spirit of accommodation. To give greater weight to his arguments, he was furnished with a liberal supply of gold.

During this time, Narváez had abandoned his original design of planting a colony on the sea-coast, and had crossed the country to Cempoalla, where he had taken up his quarters. He was here, when Guevara returned, and presented the letter of Cortés.

Narváez glanced over it with a look of contempt, which was changed into one of stern displeasure, as his envoy enlarged on the resources and formidable character of his rival, counselling him, by all means, to accept his proffers of amity. A different effect was produced on the troops, who listened with greedy ears to the accounts given of Cortés, his frank and liberal manners, which they involuntarily contrasted with those of their own commander, the wealth in his camp, where the humblest private could stake his ingot and chain of gold at play, where all revelled in plenty, and the life of the soldier seemed to be one long holyday. Guevara had been admitted only to the sunny side of the picture.

The impression made by these accounts was confirmed by the presence of Olmedo. The ecclesiastic delivered his missives, in like manner, to Narváez, who ran through their contents with feelings of anger which found vent in the most opprobrious invectives against his rival; while one of his captains, named Salvatierra, openly avowed his intention to cut off the rebel's ears, and broil them for his breakfast! Such impotent sallies did not alarm the stout-hearted friar, who soon entered into communication with many of the officers and soldiers, whom he found better inclined to an accommodation. His insinuating eloquence, backed by his liberal largesses, gradually opened a way into their hearts, and a party was formed, under the very eye of their chief, better affected to his rival's interests than to his own. The intrigue could not be conducted so secretly as wholly to elude the suspicions of Narváez, who would have arrested Olmedo and placed him under confinement, but for the interposition of Duero. He put a stop to his further machinations by sending him back again to his master. But the poison was left to do its work.

Narváez made the same vaunt, as at his landing, of his design to march against Cortés and apprehend him as a traitor.

The Cempoallans learned with astonishment that their new guests, though the countrymen, were enemies of their former. Narváez, also, proclaimed his intention to release Montezuma from captivity, and restore him to his throne. It is said, he received a rich present from the Aztec emperor, who entered into a correspondence with him. That Montezuma should have treated him with his usual munificence, supposing him to be the friend of Cortés, is very probable. But that he should have entered into a secret communication, hostile to the general's interests, is too repugnant to the whole tenor of his conduct, to be lightly admitted.

These proceedings did not escape the watchful eye of Sandoval. He gathered the particulars partly from deserters, who fled to Villa Rica, and partly from his own agents, who in the disguise of natives mingled in the enemy's camp. He sent a full account of them to Cortés, acquainted him with the growing defection of the Indians, and urged him to take speedy measures for the defence of Villa Rica, if he would not see it fall into the enemy's hands. The general felt that it was time to act.

Yet the selection of the course to be pursued was embarrassing in the extreme. If he remained in Mexico and awaited there the attack of his rival, it would give the latter time to gather round him the whole forces of the empire, including those of the capital itself, all willing, no doubt, to serve under the banners of a chief who proposed the liberation of their master. The odds were too great to be hazarded.

If he marched against Narváez, he must either abandon the city and the emperor, the fruit of all his toils and triumphs, or, by leaving a garrison to hold them in awe, must cripple his strength already far too weak to cope with that of his adversary. Yet on this latter course he decided. He trusted less, perhaps, to an open encounter of arms, than to the influence of his personal address and previous intrigues, to bring about an amicable arrangement. But he prepared himself for either result.

In the preceding chapter, it was mentioned that Velásquez

de León was sent with a hundred and fifty men to plant a colony on one of the great rivers emptying into the Mexican Gulf. Cortés, on learning the arrival of Narváez, had despatched a messenger to his officer, to acquaint him with the fact, and to arrest his further progress. But Velásquez had already received notice of it from Narváez himself, who, in a letter written soon after his landing, had adjured him in the name of his kinsman, the governor of Cuba, to quit the banners of Cortés, and come over to him. That officer, however, had long since buried the feelings of resentment which he had once nourished against his general, to whom he was now devotedly attached, and who had honored him throughout the campaign with particular regard. Cortés had early seen the importance of securing this cavalier to his interests. Without waiting for orders, Velásquez abandoned his expedition, and commenced a countermarch on the capital, when he received the general's commands to wait him in Cholula.

Cortés had also sent to the distant province of Chinantla, situated far to the south-east of Cholula, for a reinforcement of two thousand natives. They were a bold race, hostile to the Mexicans, and had offered their services to him since his residence in the metropolis. They used a long spear in battle, longer, indeed, than that borne by the Spanish or German infantry. Cortés ordered three hundred of their double-headed lances to be made for him, and to be tipped with copper instead of *itztli*. With this formidable weapon he proposed to foil the cavalry of his enemy.

The command of the garrison, in his absence, he intrusted to Pedro de Alvarado,—the *Tonatiuh* of the Mexicans,—a man possessed of many commanding qualities, of an intrepid, though somewhat arrogant spirit, and his warm personal friend. He inculcated on him moderation and forbearance. He was to keep a close watch on Montezuma, for on the possession of the royal person rested all their authority in the land. He was to show him the deference alike due to his high station, and demanded by policy. He was to pay uniform respect to the usages and the prejudices of the people; remembering that though his small force would be large enough to overawe them in times of quiet, yet, should they be once rouscd, it would be swept away like chaff before the whirlwind.

From Montezuma he exacted a promise to maintain the same friendly relations with his lieutenant which he had preserved towards himself. This, said Cortés, would be most grateful to his own master, the Spanish sovereign. Should the Aztec prince do otherwise, and lend himself to any hostile movement, he must be convinced that he would fall the first victim of it.

The emperor assured him of his continued good-will. He was much perplexed, however, by the recent events. Were the Spaniards at his court, or those just landed, the true representatives of their sovereign? Cortés, who had hitherto maintained a reserve on the subject, now told him that the latter were indeed his countrymen, but traitors to his master. As such, it was his painful duty to march against them, and, when he had chastised their rebellion, he should return, before his departure from the land, in triumph to the capital. Montezuma offered to support him with five thousand Aztec warriors; but the general declined it, not choosing to encumber himself with a body of doubtful, perhaps disaffected, auxiliaries.

He left in garrison, under Alvarado, one hundred and forty men, two thirds of his whole force. With these remained all the artillery, the greater part of the little body of horse, and most of the arquebusiers. He took with him only seventy soldiers, but they were men of the most mettle in the army and his stanch adherents. They were lightly armed and encumbered with as little baggage as possible. Every thing depended on celerity of movement.

Montezuma, in his royal litter borne on the shoulders of his nobles, and escorted by the whole Spanish infantry, accompanied the general to the causeway. There, embracing him in the most cordial manner, they parted, with all the external marks of mutual regard.—It was about the middle of May, 1520, more than six months since the entrance of the Spaniards into Mexico. During this time they had lorded it over the land with absolute sway. They were now leaving the city in hostile array, not against an Indian foe, but their own countrymen. It was the beginning of a long career of calamity,—chequered, indeed, by occasional triumphs,—which was yet to be run before the Conquest could be completed.

Traversing the southern causeway, by which they had entered the capital, the little party were soon on their march across the beautiful Valley. They climbed the mountain screen which Nature has so ineffectually drawn around it; passed between the huge volcanoes that, like faithless watch-dogs on their posts, have long since been buried in slumber; threaded the intricate defiles where they had before experienced such bleak and tempestuous weather; and, emerging on the other side, descended the western [eastern] slope which opens on the wide expanse of the fruitful plateau of Cholula.

They heeded little of what they saw on their rapid march, nor whether it was cold or hot. The anxiety of their minds made them indifferent to outward annoyances; and they had fortunately none to encounter from the natives, for the name of Spaniard was in itself a charm,—a better guard than helm or buckler to the bearer.

In Cholula, Cortés had the inexpressible satisfaction of meeting Velásquez de León, with the hundred and twenty soldiers intrusted to his command for the formation of a colony. That faithful officer had been some time at Cholula, waiting for the general's approach. Had he failed, the enterprise of Cortés must have failed, also. The idea of resistance, with his own handful of followers, would have been chimerical. As it was, his little band was now trebled, and acquired a confidence in proportion.

Cordially embracing their companions in arms, now knit together more closely than ever by the sense of a great and common danger, the combined troops traversed with quick step the streets of the sacred city, where many a dark pile of ruins told of their disastrous visit on the preceding autumn. They kept the high road to Tlascala; and, at not many leagues' distance from that capital, fell in with father Olmedo and his companions on their return from the camp of Narváez, to which, it will be remembered, they had been sent as envoys. The ecclesiastic bore a letter from that commander, in which he summoned Cortés and his followers to submit to his authority as captain-general of the country, menacing them with condign punishment, in case of refusal or delay. Olmedo gave many curious particulars of the state of the enemy's camp. Narváez he described as puffed up by authority, and negligent of precautions against a foe whom he held in contempt. He was surrounded by a number of pompous, conceited officers, who ministered to his vanity, and whose braggart tones, the good father, who had an eye for the ridiculous, imitated, to the no small diversion of Cortés and the soldiers. Many of the troops, he said, showed no great partiality for their commander, and were strongly disinclined to a rupture with their countrymen; a state of feeling much promoted by the accounts they had received of Cortés, by his own arguments and promises, and by the liberal distribution of the gold with which he had been provided. In addition to these matters, Cortés gathered much important intelligence respecting the position of the enemy's force, and his general plan of operations.

At Tlascala, the Spaniards were received with a frank and friendly hospitality. It is not said, whether any of the Tlascalan allies had accompanied them from Mexico. If they did, they went no further than their native city. Cortés requested a reinforcement of six hundred fresh troops to attend him on his present expedition. It was readily granted; but, before the army had proceeded many miles on its route, the Indian auxiliaries fell off, one after another, and returned to their city. They had no personal feeling of animosity to gratify in the present instance, as in a war against Mexico. It may be, too, that, although intrepid in a contest with the bravest of the Indian races, they had had too fatal experience of the prowess of the white men, to care to measure swords with them again. At any rate, they deserted in such numbers, that Cortés dismissed the remainder at once, saying, good-humoredly, "He had rather part with them then, than in the hour of trial."

The troops soon entered on that wild district in the neighbourhood of Perote, strewed with the wreck of volcanic matter, which forms so singular a contrast to the general character of beauty with which the scenery is stamped. It was not long before their eyes were gladdened by the approach of Sandoval and about sixty soldiers from the garrison of Vera Cruz, including several deserters from the enemy. It was a most important reinforcement, not more on account of the numbers of the men than of the character of the commander, in every respect one of the ablest captains in the service. He had been compelled to fetch a circuit, in order to avoid falling in with the enemy, and had forced his way through thick forests and wild mountain-passes, till he had fortunately, without accident, reached the appointed place of rendezvous, and stationed himself once more under the banner of his chieftain.

At the same place, also, Cortés was met by Tobillos, a Spaniard whom he had sent to procure the lances from Chinantla. They were perfectly well made, after the pattern which had been given; double-headed spears, tipped with copper, and of great length. Tobillos drilled the men in the exercise of this weapon, the formidable uses of which, especially against horse, had been fully demonstrated, towards the close of the last century, by the Swiss battalions, in their encounters with the Burgundian chivalry, the best in Europe.

Cortés now took a review of his army,—if so paltry a force may be called an army,—and found their numbers were two hundred and sixty-six, only five of whom were mounted. A few muskets and crossbows were sprinkled among them. In defensive armor they were sadly deficient. They were for the most part cased in the quilted doublet of the country, thickly stuffed with cotton, the *escaupil*, recommended by its superior lightness, but which, though competent to turn the arrow of the Indian, was ineffectual against a musket-ball. Most of this cotton mail was exceedingly out of repair, giving evidence, in its unsightly gaps, of much rude service, and hard blows. Few, in this emergency, but would have given almost any price—the best of the gold chains which they wore in tawdry display over their poor habiliments—for a steel morion or cuirass, to take the place of their own hacked and battered armor.

Under this coarse covering, however, they bore hearts stout and courageous as ever beat in human bosoms. For they were the heroes, still invincible, of many a hard-fought field, where the odds had been incalculably against them. They had large experience of the country and of the natives; knew well the character of their own commander, under whose eye they had been trained, till every movement was in obedience to him. The whole body seemed to constitute but a single individual, in respect of unity of design and of action. Thus its real effective force was incredibly augmented; and, what was no less important, the humblest soldier felt it to be so.

The troops now resumed their march across the table-land, until, reaching the western [eastern] slope, their labors were lightened, as they descended towards the broad plains of the *tierra caliente,* spread out like a boundless ocean of verdure below them. . . .

Coming upon an open reach of meadow, of some extent, they were, at length, stopped by a river, or rather stream, called *Río de Canoas,* "the River of Canoes," of no great volume ordinarily, but swollen at this time by excessive rains. It had rained hard that day, although at intervals the sun had broken forth with intolerable fervor, affording a good specimen of those alternations of heat and moisture, which give such activity to vegetation in the tropics, where the process of forcing seems to be always going on.

The river was about a league distant from the camp of Narváez. Before seeking out a practicable ford, by which to cross it, Cortés allowed his men to recruit their exhausted strength by stretching themselves on the ground. The shades of evening had gathered round; and the rising moon, wading through dark masses of cloud, shone with a doubtful and interrupted light. It was evident that the storm had not yet spent its fury. Cortés did not regret this. He had made up his mind to an assault that very night, and in the darkness and uproar of the tempest his movements would be most effectually concealed.

Before disclosing his design, he addressed his men in one of those stirring, soldierly harangues, to which he had recourse in emergencies of great moment, as if to sound the depths of their hearts, and, where any faltered, to reanimate them with his own heroic spirit. He briefly recapitulated the great events of the campaign, the dangers they had surmounted, the victories they had achieved over the most appalling odds, the glorious spoil they had won. But of this they were now to be defrauded; not by men holding a legal warrant from the Crown, but by adventurers, with no better title than that of superior force. They had established a claim on the gratitude of their country and their sovereign. This claim was now to be dishonored, their very services were converted into crimes, and their names branded with infamy as those of traitors. But the time had at last come for vengeance. God would not desert the soldier of the Cross. Those, whom he had carried victorious through greater dangers, would not be left to fail now. And, if they should fail, better to die like brave men on the field of battle, than, with fame and fortune cast away, to perish ignominiously like slaves on the gibbet.—This last point he urged home upon his hearers; well knowing there was not one among them so dull as not to be touched by it.

They responded with hearty acclamations, and Velásquez de León, and de Lugo, in the name of the rest, assured their commander, if they failed, it should be his fault, not theirs. They would follow wherever he led.—The general was fully satisfied with the temper of his soldiers, as he felt that his difficulty lay not in awakening their enthusiasm, but in giving it a right direction. One thing is remarkable. He made no allusion to the defection which he knew existed in the enemy's camp. He would have his soldiers, in this last pinch, rely on nothing but themselves.

He announced his purpose to attack the enemy that very night, when he should be buried in slumber, and the friendly darkness might throw a veil over their own movements, and conceal the poverty of their numbers. To this the troops, jaded though they were by incessant marching, and half famished, joyfully assented. In their situation, suspense was the worst of evils. He next distributed the commands among his captains. To Gonzalo de Sandoval he assigned the important office of taking Narváez. He was commanded, as *alguacil mayor,* to seize the person of that officer as a rebel to his sovereign, and, if he made resistance, to kill him on the spot. He was provided with sixty picked men to aid him in this difficult task, supported by several of the ablest captains, among whom were two of the Alvarados, de Ávila, and Ordaz. The largest division of the force was placed under Christóval de Olid, or, according to some authorities, of Pizarro, one of that family so renowned in the subsequent conquest of Peru. He was to get possession of the artillery, and to cover the assault of Sandoval by keeping those of the enemy at bay, who would interfere with it. Cortés reserved only a body of twenty men for himself, to act on any point that occasion might require. The watch-word was *Espíritu Santo,* it being the evening of Whitsunday. Having made these arrangements, he prepared to cross the river. . . .

Silently and stealthily they held on their way without beat of drum, or sound of trumpet, when they suddenly came on the two sentinels who had been stationed by Narváez to give notice of their approach. This had been so noiseless, that the videttes were both of them surprised on their post, and one only, with difficulty, effected his escape. The other was brought before Cortés. Every effort was made to draw from him some account of the present position of Narváez. But the man remained obstinately silent; and, though threatened with the gibbet, and having a noose actually drawn round his neck, his Spartan heroism was not to be vanquished. Fortunately no change had taken place in the arrangements of Narváez since the intelligence previously derived from Duero.

The other sentinel, who had escaped, carried the news of the enemy's approach to the camp. But his report was not credited by the lazy soldiers, whose slumbers he had disturbed. "He had been deceived by his fears," they said, "and mistaken the noise of the storm and the waving of the bushes, for the enemy. Cortés and his men were far enough on the other side of the river, which they would be slow to cross in such a night." Narváez himself shared in the same blind infatuation, and the discredited sentinel slunk abashed to his own quarters, vainly menacing them with the consequences of their incredulity.

Cortés, not doubting that the sentinel's report must alarm the enemy's camp, quickened his pace. As he drew near, he discerned a light in one of the lofty towers of the city. "It is the quarters of Narváez," he exclaimed to Sandoval, "and that light must be your beacon." On entering the suburbs, the Spaniards were surprised to find no one stirring, and no symptom of alarm. Not a sound was to be heard, except the measured tread of their own footsteps, half-drowned in the howling of the tempest. Still they could not move so stealthily as altogether to elude notice, as they defiled through the streets of this populous city. The tidings were quickly conveyed to the enemy's quarters, where, in an instant, all was bustle and confusion. The trumpets sounded to arms. The dragoons sprang to their steeds, the artillery-men to their guns. Narváez hastily buckled on his armor, called his men around him, and summoned those in the neighbouring *teocallis* to join him in the area. He gave his orders with coolness; for, however wanting in prudence, he was not deficient in presence of mind, or courage.

All this was the work of a few minutes. But in those minutes the Spaniards had reached the avenue leading to the camp. Cortés ordered his men to keep close to the walls of the buildings, that the cannon-shot might have a free range. No sooner had they presented themselves before the inclosure, than the artillery of Narváez opened a general fire. Fortunately the pieces were pointed so high that most of the balls passed over their heads, and three men only were struck down. They did not give the enemy time to reload. Cortés shouting the watch-word of the night, "Espíritu Santo! Espíritu Santo! Upon them!" in a moment Olid and his division rushed on the artillery-men, whom they pierced, or knocked down with their pikes, and got possession of their guns. Another division engaged the cavalry, and made a diversion in favor of Sandoval, who with his gallant little band sprang up the great stairway of the temple. They were received with a shower of missiles,—arrows, and musket-balls, which, in the hurried aim, and the darkness of the night, did little mischief. The next minute the assailants were on the platform, engaged hand to hand with their foes. Narváez fought bravely in the midst, encouraging his followers. His standard-bearer fell by his side, run through the body. He himself received several wounds; for his short sword was no match for the long pikes of the assailants. At length, he received a blow from a spear, which struck out his left eye. "Santa María!" exclaimed the unhappy man, "I am slain!" The cry was instantly taken up by the followers of Cortés, who shouted, "Victory!"

Disabled, and half mad with agony from his wound, Narváez was withdrawn by his men into the sanctuary. The assailants endeavoured to force an entrance, but it was stoutly defended. At length a soldier, getting possession of a torch, or firebrand, flung it on the thatched roof, and in a few moments the combustible materials of which it was composed were in a blaze. Those within were driven out by the suffocating heat and smoke. A soldier named Farfán grappled with the wounded commander, and easily brought him to the ground; when he was speedily dragged down the steps, and secured with fetters. His followers, seeing the fate of their chief, made no further resistance. . . .

IV

Rebellion in Tenochtitlán

No sooner had the struggle with his rival been decided, than Cortés despatched a courier with the tidings to the capital. In less than a fortnight, the same messenger returned with letters from Alvarado, conveying the alarming information, that the Mexicans were in arms, and had vigorously assaulted the Spaniards in their own quarters. The enemy, he added, had burned the brigantines, by which Cortés had secured the means of retreat in case of the destruction of the bridges. They had attempted to force the defences, and had succeeded in partially undermining them, and they had overwhelmed the garrison with a tempest of missiles, which had killed several, and wounded a great number. The letter concluded with beseeching his commander to hasten to their relief, if he would save them, or keep his hold on the capital.

These tidings were a heavy blow to the general,—the heavier, it seemed, coming, as they did, in the hour of triumph, when he had thought to have all his enemies at his feet. There was no room for hesitation. To lose their footing in the capital, the noblest city in the Western World, would be to lose the country itself, which looked up to it as its head. He opened the matter fully to his soldiers, calling on all who would save their countrymen to follow him. All declared their readiness to go; showing an alacrity, says Díaz, which some would have been slow to manifest, had they foreseen the future.

Cortés now made preparations for instant departure. He countermanded the orders previously given to Velásquez and Ordaz, and directed them to join him with their forces at Tlascala. He recalled the troops from Vera Cruz, leaving only a hundred men in garrison there, under command of one Rodrigo

Rangre,* for he could not spare the services of Sandoval at this crisis. He left his sick and wounded at Cempoalla, under charge of a small detachment, directing that they should follow as soon as they were in marching order. Having completed these arrangements, he set out from Cempoalla, well supplied with provisions by its hospitable cacique, who attended him some leagues on his way. The Totonac chief seems to have had an amiable facility of accommodating himself to the powers that were in the ascendant.

Nothing worthy of notice occurred during the first part of the march. The troops everywhere met with a friendly reception from the peasantry, who readily supplied their wants. Some time before reaching Tlascala, the route lay through a country thinly settled; and the army experienced considerable suffering from want of food, and still more from that of water. Their distress increased to an alarming degree, as, in the hurry of their forced march, they travelled with the meridian sun beating fiercely on their heads. Several faltered by the way, and, throwing themselves down by the road-side, seemed incapable of further effort, and almost indifferent to life.

In this extremity, Cortés sent forward a small detachment of horse to procure provisions in Tlascala, and speedily followed in person. On arriving, he found abundant supplies already prepared by the hospitable natives. They were sent back to the troops; the stragglers were collected one by one; refreshments were administered; and the army, restored in strength and spirits, entered the republican capital.

Here they gathered little additional news respecting the events in Mexico, which a popular rumor attributed to the secret encouragement and machinations of Montezuma. Cortés was commodiously lodged in the quarters of Maxixca,** one of the four chiefs of the republic. They readily furnished him with two thousand troops. There was no want of heartiness, when the war was with their ancient enemy, the Aztec.

* Rangel. C.H.G.
** Maxixcatzin. C.H.G.

The Spanish commander, on reviewing his forces, after the junction with his two captains, found that they amounted to about a thousand foot, and one hundred horse, besides the Tlascalan levies. In the infantry were nearly a hundred arquebusiers, with as many crossbow-men; and the part of the army brought over by Narváez was admirably equipped. It was inferior, however, to his own veterans in what is better than any outward appointments,—military training, and familiarity with the peculiar service in which they were engaged.

Leaving these friendly quarters, the Spaniards took a more northerly route, as more direct than that by which they had before penetrated into the Valley. It was the road to Tezcuco. It still compelled them to climb the same bold range of the Cordilleras, which attains its greatest elevation in the two mighty *volcans* at whose base they had before travelled. The sides of the sierra were clothed with dark forests of pine, cypress, and cedar, through which glimpses now and then opened into fathomless dells and valleys, whose depths, far down in the sultry climate of the tropics, were lost in a glowing wilderness of vegetation. From the crest of the mountain range the eye travelled over the broad expanse of country, which they had lately crossed, far away to the green plains of Cholula. Towards the west, they looked down on the Mexican Valley, from a point of view wholly different from that which they had before occupied, but still offering the same beautiful spectacle, with its lakes trembling in the light, its gay cities and villas floating on their bosom, its burnished *teocallis* touched with fire, its cultivated slopes and dark hills of porphyry stretching away in dim perspective to the verge of the horizon. At their feet lay the city of Tezcuco, which, modestly retiring behind her deep groves of cypress, formed a contrast to her more ambitious rival on the other side of the lake, who seemed to glory in the unveiled splendors of her charms, as Mistress of the Valley.

As they descended into the populous plains, their reception by the natives was very different from that which they had experienced on the preceding visit. There were no groups of curious peasantry to be seen gazing at them as they passed, and offering their simple hospitality. The supplies they asked were not refused, but granted with an ungracious air, that showed the blessing of the giver did not accompany them. This air of reserve became still more marked as the army entered the suburbs of the ancient capital of the Acolhuans. No one came forth to greet them, and the population seemed to have dwindled away,—so many of them were withdrawn to the neighbouring scene of hostilities at Mexico. Their cold reception was a sensible mortification to the veterans of Cortés, who, judging from the past, had boasted to their new comrades of the sensation their presence would excite among the natives. The cacique of the place, who, as it may be remembered, had been created through the influence of Cortés, was himself absent. The general drew an ill omen from all these circumstances, which even raised an uncomfortable apprehension in his mind respecting the fate of the garrison in Mexico.

But his doubts were soon dispelled by the arrival of a messenger in a canoe from that city, whence he had escaped through the remissness of the enemy, or, perhaps, with their connivance. He brought despatches from Alvarado, informing his commander that the Mexicans had for the last fortnight desisted from active hostilities, and converted their operations into a blockade. The garrison had suffered greatly, but Alvarado expressed his conviction that the siege would be raised, and tranquillity restored, on the approach of his countrymen. Montezuma sent a messenger, also, to the same effect. At the same time, he exculpated himself from any part in the late hostilities, which he said had not only been conducted without his privity, but contrary to his inclination and efforts.

The Spanish general, having halted long enough to refresh his wearied troops, took up his march along the southern margin of the lake, which led him over the same causeway by which he had before entered the capital. It was the day consecrated to St. John the Baptist, the 24th of June, 1520. But how different was the scene from that presented on his former entrance! No crowds now lined the roads, no boats swarmed on the lake, filled with admiring spectators. A single pirogue might now and then be seen in the distance, like a spy stealthily watching their movements, and darting away the moment it had attracted notice. A deathlike stillness brooded over the scene,—a stillness that spoke louder to the heart, than the acclamations of multitudes.

Cortés rode on moodily at the head of his battalions, finding abundant food for meditation, doubtless, in this change of circumstances. As if to dispel these gloomy reflections, he ordered his trumpets to sound, and their clear, shrill notes, borne across the waters, told the inhabitants of the beleaguered fortress, that their friends were at hand. They were answered by a joyous peal of artillery, which seemed to give a momentary exhilaration to the troops, as they quickened their pace, traversed the great draw-bridges, and once more found themselves within the walls of the imperial city.

The appearance of things here was not such as to allay their apprehensions. In some places they beheld the smaller bridges removed, intimating too plainly, now that their brigantines were destroyed, how easy it would be to cut off their retreat. The town seemed even more deserted than Tezcuco. Its once busy and crowded population had mysteriously vanished. And, as the Spaniards defiled through the empty streets, the tramp of their horses' feet upon the pavement was answered by dull and melancholy echoes that fell heavily on their hearts. With saddened feelings they reached the great gates of the palace of Axayacatl. The gates were thrown open, and Cortés and his veterans, rushing in, were cordially embraced by their companions in arms, while both parties soon forgot the present in the interesting recapitulation of the past.

The first inquiries of the general were respecting the origin of the tumult. The accounts were various. Some imputed it to the desire of the Mexicans to release their sovereign from confinement; others to the design of cutting off the garrison while crippled by the absence of Cortés and their countrymen. All agreed, however, in tracing the immediate cause to the violence of Alvarado. It was common for the Aztecs to celebrate an annual festival in May, in honor of their patron war-god. It was called the "incensing of Huitzilopotchli," and was commemorated by sacrifice, religious songs, and dances, in which most of the nobles engaged, for it was one of the great festivals which displayed the pomp of the Aztec ritual. As it was held in the court of the *teocalli,* in the immediate neighbourhood of the Spanish quarters, and as a part of the temple itself was reserved for a Christian chapel, the caciques asked permission of Alvarado to perform their rites there. They requested also, it is said, to be allowed the presence of Montezuma. This latter petition Alvarado declined, in obedience to the injunctions of Cortés; but acquiesced in the former, on condition that the Aztecs should celebrate no human sacrifices, and should come without weapons.

They assembled accordingly on the day appointed, to the number of six hundred, at the smallest computation. They were dressed in their most magnificent gala costumes, with their graceful mantles of feather-work, sprinkled with precious stones, and their necks, arms, and legs ornamented with collars and bracelets of gold. They had that love of gaudy splendor which belongs to semi-civilized nations, and on these occasions displayed all the pomp and profusion of their barbaric wardrobes.

Alvarado and his soldiers attended as spectators, some of them taking their station at the gates, as if by chance, and others mingling in the crowd. They were all armed, a circumstance, which, as it was usual, excited no attention. The Aztecs were soon engrossed by the exciting movement of the dance, accompanied by their religious chant and wild, discordant minstrelsy. While thus occupied, Alvarado and his men, at a concerted signal, rushed with drawn swords on their victims. Unprotected by armor or weapons of any kind, they were hewn down without resistance by their assailants, who, in their bloody work, says a contemporary, showed no touch of pity or compunction. Some fled to the gates, but were caught on the long pikes of the soldiers. Others, who attempted to scale the *Coatepantli,* or Wall of Serpents, as it was called, which surrounded the area, shared the like fate, or were cut to pieces, or shot by the ruthless soldiery. The pavement, says a writer of the age, ran with streams of blood, like water in a heavy shower. Not an Aztec, of all that gay company, was left alive! It was repeating the dreadful scene of Cholula, with the disgraceful addition, that the Spaniards, not content with slaughtering their victims, rifled them of the precious ornaments on their persons! On this sad day fell the flower of the Aztec nobility. Not a family of note, but had mourning and desolation brought within its walls. And many a doleful ballad, rehearsing the tragic incidents of the story, and adapted to the plaintive national airs, continued to be chanted by the natives long after the subjugation of the country.

Various explanations have been given of this atrocious deed. But few historians have been content to admit that of Alvarado himself. According to this, intelligence had been obtained through his spies—some of them Mexicans—of an intended rising of the Indians. The celebration of this festival was fixed on, as the period for its execution, when the caciques would be met together, and would easily rouse the people to support them. Alvarado, advised of all this, had forbidden them to wear arms at their meeting. While affecting to comply, they had secreted their weapons in the neighbouring arsenals, whence they could readily withdraw them. But his own blow, by anticipating theirs, defeated the design, and, as he confidently hoped, would deter the Aztecs from a similar attempt in future.

Such is the account of the matter given by Alvarado. But, if true, why did he not verify his assertion by exposing the arms thus secreted? Why did he not vindicate his conduct in the eyes of the Mexicans generally, by publicly avowing the treason of the nobles, as was done by Cortés at Cholula? The whole looks much like an apology devised after the commission of the deed, to cover up its atrocity.

Some contemporaries assign a very different motive for the massacre, which, according to them, originated in the cupidity of the Conquerors, as shown by their plundering the bodies of their victims. Bernal Díaz, who, though not present, had conversed familiarly with those who were, vindicates them from the charge of this unworthy motive. According to him, Alvarado struck the blow in order to intimidate the Aztecs from an insurrectionary movement. But whether he had reason to apprehend such, or even affected to do so before the massacre, the old chronicler does not inform us.

On reflection, it seems scarcely possible that so foul a deed, and one involving so much hazard to the Spaniards themselves, should have been perpetrated from the mere desire of getting possession of the bawbles worn on the persons of the natives. It is more likely this was an afterthought, suggested to the rapacious soldiery by the display of the spoil before them. It is not improbable that Alvarado may have gathered rumors of a conspiracy among the nobles,—rumors, perhaps, derived through the Tlascalans, their inveterate foes, and for that reason very little deserving of credit. He proposed to defeat it by imitating the example of his commander at Cholula. But he omitted to imitate his leader in taking precautions against the subsequent rising of the populace. And he grievously miscalculated, when he confounded the bold and warlike Aztec with the effeminate Cholulan.

No sooner was the butchery accomplished, than the tidings spread like wildfire through the capital. Men could scarcely credit their senses. All they had hitherto suffered, the desecration of their temples, the imprisonment of their sovereign, the insults heaped on his person, all were forgotten in this one act. Every feeling of long smothered hostility and rancor now burst forth in the cry for vengeance. Every former sentiment of superstitious dread was merged in that of inextinguishable hatred. It required no effort of the priests—though this was not wanting—to fan these passions into a blaze. The city rose in arms to a man; and on the following dawn, almost before the Spaniards could secure themselves in their defences, they were assaulted with desperate fury. Some of the assailants attempted to scale the walls; others succeeded in partially undermining and in setting fire to the works. Whether they would have succeeded in carrying the place by storm is doubtful. But, at the prayers of the garrison, Montezuma himself interfered, and mounting the battlements addressed the populace, whose fury he endeavoured to mitigate by urging considerations for his own safety. They respected their monarch so far as to desist from further attempts to storm the fortress, but changed their operations into a regular blockade. They threw up works around the palace to prevent the egress of the Spaniards. They susended the *tianguez,* or market, to preclude the possibility of their enemy's obtaining supplies; and they then quietly sat down, with feelings of sullen desperation, waiting for the hour when famine should throw their victims into their hands.

The condition of the besieged, meanwhile, was sufficiently distressing. Their magazines of provisions, it is true, were not exhausted; but they suffered greatly from want of water, which, within the inclosure, was exceedingly brackish, for the soil was saturated with the salt of the surrounding element. In this extremity, they discovered, it is said, a spring of fresh water in the area. Such springs were known in some other parts of the city; but, discovered first under these circumstances, it was accounted as nothing less than a miracle. Still they suffered much from their past encounters. Seven Spaniards, and many Tlascalans, had fallen, and there was scarcely one of either nation who had not received several wounds. In this situation, far from their own countrymen, without expectation of succour from abroad, they seemed to have no alternative before them, but a lingering death by famine, or one more dreadful on the altar of sacrifice. From this gloomy state they were relieved by the coming of their comrades.

Cortés calmly listened to the explanation made by Alvarado. But, before it was ended, the conviction must have forced itself on his mind, that he had made a wrong selection for this important post. Yet the mistake was natural. Alvarado was a cavalier of high family, gallant and chivalrous, and his warm personal friend. He had talents for action, was possessed of firmness and intrepidity, while his frank and dazzling manners made the *Tonatiuh* an especial favorite with the Mexicans. But, underneath this showy exterior, the future conqueror of Guatemala concealed a heart rash, rapacious, and cruel. He was altogether destitute of that moderation, which, in the delicate position he occupied, was a quality of more worth than all the rest.

When Alvarado had concluded his answers to the several interrogatories of Cortés, the brow of the latter darkened, as he said to his lieutenant, "You have done badly. You have been false to your trust. Your conduct has been that of a madman!" And, turning abruptly on his heel, he left him in undisguised displeasure.

Yet this was not a time to break with one so popular, and, in many respects, so important to him, as this captain, much less to inflict on him the punishment he merited. The Spaniards were like mariners laboring in a heavy tempest, whose bark nothing but the dexterity of the pilot, and the hearty coöperation of the crew, can save from foundering. Dissensions at such a moment must be fatal. Cortés, it is true, felt strong in his present resources. He now found himself at the head of a force which could scarcely amount to less than twelve hundred and fifty Spaniards, and eight thousand native warriors, principally Tlascalans. But, though relying on this to overawe resistance, the very augmentation of numbers increased the difficulty of subsistence. Discontented with himself, disgusted with his officer, and embarrassed by the disastrous consequences in which Alvarado's intemperance had involved him, he became irritable, and indulged in a petulance by no means common; for, though a man of lively passions, by nature, he held them habitually under control.

On the day that Cortés arrived, Montezuma had left his own quarters to welcome him. But the Spanish commander, distrusting, as it would seem, however unreasonably, his good faith, received him so coldly that the Indian monarch withdrew, displeased and dejected, to his apartment. As the Mexican populace made no show of submission, and brought no supplies to the army, the general's ill-humor with the emperor continued. When, therefore, Montezuma sent some of the nobles to ask an interview with Cortés, the latter, turning to his own officers, haughtily exclaimed, "What have I to do with this dog of a king who suffers us to starve before his eyes?"

His captains, among whom were Olid, de Ávila, and Velásquez de León, endeavoured to mitigate his anger, reminding him, in respectful terms, that, had it not been for the emperor, the garrison might even now have been overwhelmed by the enemy. This remonstrance only chafed him the more. "Did not the dog," he asked, repeating the opprobrious epithet, "betray us in his communications with Narváez? And does he not now suffer his markets to be closed, and leave us to die of famine?" Then turning fiercely to the Mexicans, he said, "Go tell your master and his people to open the markets, or we will do it for them, at their cost!" The chiefs, who had gathered the import of his previous taunt on their sovereign, from his tone and gesture, or perhaps from some comprehension of his language, left his presence swelling with resentment; and, in communicating his message, took care it should lose none of its effect.

Shortly after, Cortés, at the suggestion, it is said, of Montezuma, released his brother Cuitlahua, lord of Iztapalapan, who, it will be remembered, had been seized on suspicion of coöperating with the chief of Tezcuco in his meditated revolt. It was thought he might be of service in allaying the present tumult, and bringing the populace to a better state of feeling. But he returned no more to the fortress. He was a bold, ambitious prince, and the injuries he had received from the Spaniards rankled deep in his bosom. He was presumptive heir to the crown, which, by the Aztec laws of succession, descended much more frequently in a collateral than in a direct line. The people welcomed him as the representative of their sovereign, and chose him to supply the place of Montezuma during his captivity. Cuitlahua willingly accepted the post of honor and of danger. He was an experienced warrior, and exerted himself to reorganize the disorderly levies, and to arrange a more efficient plan of operations. The effect was soon visible.

Cortés meanwhile had so little doubt of his ability to over-awe the insurgents, that he wrote to that effect to the garrison of Villa Rica, by the same despatches in which he informed them of his safe arrival in the capital. But scarcely had his messenger been gone half an hour, when he returned breathless with terror, and covered with wounds. "The city," he said, "was all in arms! The draw-bridges were raised, and the enemy would soon be upon them!" He spoke truth. It was not long before a hoarse, sullen sound became audible, like that of the roaring of distant waters. It grew louder and louder; till, from the parapet surrounding the inclosure, the great avenues which led to it might be seen dark with the masses of warriors, who came rolling on in a confused tide towards the fortress. At the same time, the terraces and *azoteas* or flat roofs, in the neighbourhood, were thronged with combatants brandishing their missiles, who seemed to have risen up as if by magic! It was a spectacle to appall the stoutest.—But the dark storm to which it was the prelude, and which gathered deeper and deeper round the Spaniards during the remainder of their residence in the capital, must form the subject of a separate Book.

BOOK FIVE

Expulsion from Mexico

I

Assaults and Sallies

THE palace of Axayacatl, in which the Spaniards were quartered, was, as the reader may remember, a vast, irregular pile of stone buildings, having but one floor, except in the centre, where another story was added, consisting of a suite of apartments which rose like turrets on the main building of the edifice. A vast area stretched around, encompassed by a stone wall of no great height. This was supported by towers or bulwarks at certain intervals, which gave it some degree of strength, not, indeed, as compared with European fortifications, but sufficient to resist the rude battering enginery of the Indians. The parapet had been pierced here and there with embrasures for the artillery, which consisted of thirteen guns; and smaller apertures were made in other parts for the convenience of the arquebusiers. The Spanish forces found accommodations within the great building; but the numerous body of Tlascalan auxiliaries could have had no other shelter than what was afforded by barracks or sheds hastily constructed for the purpose in the spacious courtyard. Most of them, probably, bivouacked under the open sky, in a climate milder than that to which they were accustomed among the rude hills of their native land. Thus crowded into a small and compact compass, the whole army could be assembled at a moment's notice; and, as the Spanish commander was careful to enforce the strictest discipline and vigilance, it was scarcely possible that he could be taken by surprise. No sooner, therefore, did the trumpet call to arms, as the approach of the enemy was announced, than every soldier was at his post, the cavalry mounted, the artillery-men at their guns, and the archers and arquebusiers stationed so as to give the assailants a warm reception.

On they came, with the companies, or irregular masses, into which the multitude was divided, rushing forward each in its own dense column, with many a gay banner displayed, and many a bright gleam of light reflected from helmet, arrow, and spear-head, as they were tossed about in their disorderly array. As they drew near the inclosure, the Aztecs set up a hideous yell, or rather that shrill whistle used in fight by the nations of Anahuac, which rose far above the sound of shell and atabal, and their other rude instruments of warlike melody. They followed this by a tempest of missiles,—stones, darts, and arrows,—which fell thick as rain on the besieged, while volleys of the same kind descended from the crowded terraces in the neighbourhood.

The Spaniards waited until the foremost column had arrived within the best distance for giving effect to their fire, when a general discharge of artillery and arquebuses swept the ranks of the assailants, and mowed them down by hundreds. The Mexicans were familiar with the report of these formidable engines, as they had been harmlessly discharged on some holy-day festival; but never till now had they witnessed their murderous power. They stood aghast for a moment, as with bewildered looks they staggered under the fury of the fire; but, soon rallying, the bold barbarians uttered a piercing cry, and rushed forward over the prostrate bodies of their comrades. A second and a third volley checked their career, and threw them into disorder, but still they pressed on, letting off clouds of arrows; while their comrades on the roofs of the houses took more deliberate aim at the combatants in the court-yard. The Mexicans were particularly expert in the use of the sling; and the stones which they hurled from their elevated positions on the heads of their enemies did even greater execution than the arrows. They glanced, indeed, from the mail-covered bodies of the cavaliers, and from those who were sheltered under the cotton panoply, or *escaupil*. But some of the soldiers, especially the veterans of Cortés, and many of their Indian allies, had but slight defences, and suffered greatly under this stony tempest.

The Aztecs, meanwhile, had advanced close under the walls of the intrenchment; their ranks broken and disordered, and their limbs mangled by the unintermitting fire of the Christians. But they still pressed on, under the very muzzle of the guns. They endeavoured to scale the parapet, which, from its moderate height, was in itself a work of no great difficulty. But the moment they showed their heads above the rampart, they were shot down by the unerring marksmen within, or stretched on the ground by a blow of a Tlascalan *maquahuitl*. Nothing daunted, others soon appeared to take the place of the fallen, and strove, by raising themselves on the writhing bodies of their dying comrades, or by fixing their spears in the crevices of the wall, to surmount the barrier. But the attempt proved equally vain.

Defeated here, they tried to effect a breach in the parapet by battering it with heavy pieces of timber. The works were not constructed on those scientific principles by which one part is made to overlook and protect another. The besiegers, therefore, might operate at their pleasure, with but little molestation from the garrison within, whose guns could not be brought into a position to bear on them, and who could mount no part of their own works for their defence, without exposing their persons to the missiles of the whole besieging army. The parapet, however, proved too strong for the efforts of the assailants. In their despair, they endeavoured to set the Christian quarters on fire, shooting burning arrows into them, and climbing up so as to dart their firebrands through the embrasures. The principal edifice was of stone. But the temporary defences of the Indian allies, and other parts of the exterior works, were of wood. Several of these took fire, and the flame spread rapidly among the light, combustible materials. This was a disaster for which the besieged were wholly unprepared. They had little water, scarcely enough for their own consumption. They endeavoured to extinguish the flames by heaping on earth. But in vain. Fortunately the great building was of materials which defied the destroying element. But the fire raged in some of the outworks, connected with the parapet, with a fury which could only be checked by throwing down a part of the wall itself, thus laying open a formidable breach. This, by the general's order, was speedily protected by a battery of heavy guns, and a file of arquebusiers, who kept up an incessant volley through the opening on the assailants.

The fight now raged with fury on both sides. The walls around the palace belched forth an unintermitting sheet of flame and smoke. The groans of the wounded and dying were lost in the fiercer battle-cries of the combatants, the roar of the artillery, the sharper rattle of the musketry, and the hissing sound of Indian missiles. It was the conflict of the European with the American; of civilized man with the barbarian; of the science of the one with the rude weapons and warfare of the other. And as the ancient walls of Tenochtitlán shook under the thunders of the artillery,—it announced that the white man, the destroyer, had set his foot within her precincts.

Night at length came, and drew her friendly mantle over the contest. The Aztec seldom fought by night. It brought little repose, however, to the Spaniards, in hourly expectation of an assault; and they found abundant occupation in restoring the breaches in their defences, and in repairing their battered armor. The beleaguering host lay on their arms through the night, giving token of their presence, now and then, by sending a stone or shaft over the battlements, or by a solitary cry of defiance from some warrior more determined than the rest, till all other sounds were lost in the vague, indistinct murmurs which float upon the air in the neighbourhood of a vast assembly.

The ferocity shown by the Mexicans seems to have been a thing for which Cortés was wholly unprepared. His past experience, his uninterrupted career of victory with a much feebler force at his command, had led him to underrate the military efficiency, if not the valor, of the Indians. The apparent facility, with which the Mexicans had acquiesced in the outrages on their sovereign and themselves, had led him to hold their courage, in particular, too lightly. He could not believe the present assault to be any thing more than a temporary ebullition of the populace, which would soon waste itself by its own fury. And he proposed, on the following day, to sally out and inflict such chastisement on his foes as should bring them to their senses, and show who was master in the capital.

With early dawn, the Spaniards were up and under arms; but not before their enemies had given evidence of their hostility by the random missiles, which, from time to time, were sent into the inclosure. As the grey light of morning advanced, it showed the besieging army far from being diminished in numbers, filling up the great square and neighbouring avenues in more dense array than on the preceding evening. Instead of a confused, disorderly rabble, it had the appearance of something like a regular force, with its battalions distributed under their respective banners, the devices of which showed a contribution from the principal cities and districts in the Valley. High above the rest was conspicuous the ancient standard of Mexico, with its well known cognizance, an eagle pouncing on an ocelot, emblazoned on a rich mantle of feather-work. Here and there priests might be seen mingling in the ranks of the besiegers, and, with frantic gestures, animating them to avenge their insulted deities.

The greater part of the enemy had little clothing save the *maxtlatl*, or sash round the loins. They were variously armed, with long spears tipped with copper, or flint, or sometimes merely pointed and hardened in the fire. Some were provided with slings, and others with darts having two or three points, with long strings attached to them, by which, when discharged, they could be torn away again from the body of the wounded. This was a formidable weapon, much dreaded by the Spaniards. Those of a higher order wielded the terrible *maquahuitl*, with its sharp and brittle blades of obsidian. Amidst the motley bands of warriors, were seen many whose showy dress and air of authority intimated persons of high military consequence. Their breasts were protected by plates of metal, over which was thrown the gay surcoat of feather-work. They wore casques resembling, in their form, the head of some wild and ferocious animal, crested with bristly hair, or overshadowed by tall and graceful plumes of many a brilliant color. Some few were decorated with the red fillet bound round the hair, having tufts of cotton attached to it, which denoted by their number that of the victories they had won, and their own preëminent rank among the warriors of the nation. The motley assembly plainly showed that priest, warrior, and citizen had all united to swell the tumult.

Before the sun had shot his beams into the Castilian quarters, the enemy were in motion, evidently preparing to renew the assault of the preceding day. The Spanish commander determined to anticipate them by a vigorous sortie, for which he had already made the necessary dispositions. A general discharge of ordnance and musketry sent death far and wide into the enemy's ranks, and, before they had time to recover from their confusion, the gates were thrown open, and Cortés, sallying out at the head of his cavalry, supported by a large body of infantry and several thousand Tlascalans, rode at full gallop against them. Taken thus by surprise, it was scarcely possible to offer much resistance. Those who did were trampled down under the horses' feet, cut to pieces with the broadswords, or pierced with the lances of the riders. The infantry followed up the blow, and the rout for the moment was general.

But the Aztecs fled only to take refuge behind a barricade, or strong work of timber and earth, which had been thrown across the great street through which they were pursued. Rallying on the other side, they made a gallant stand, and poured in turn a volley of their light weapons on the Spaniards, who, saluted with a storm of missiles at the same time, from the terraces of the houses, were checked in their career, and thrown into some disorder.

Cortés, thus impeded, ordered up a few pieces of heavy ordnance, which soon swept away the barricades and cleared a passage for the army. But it had lost the momentum acquired in its rapid advance. The enemy had time to rally and to meet the Spaniards on more equal terms. They were attacked in flank, too, as they advanced, by fresh battalions, who swarmed in from the adjoining streets and lanes. The canals were alive with boats filled with warriors, who, with their formidable darts searched every crevice or weak place in the armor of proof, and made havoc on the unprotected bodies of the Tlascalans. By repeated and vigorous charges, the Spaniards succeeded in driving the Indians before them; though many, with a desperation which showed they loved vengeance better than life, sought to embarrass the movements of their horses by clinging to their legs, or, more successfully, strove to pull the riders from their saddles. And woe to the unfortunate cavalier who was thus dismounted,—to be despatched by the brutal *maquahuitl,* or to be dragged on board a canoe to the bloody altar of sacrifice!

But the greatest annoyance which the Spaniards endured was from the missiles from the *azoteas,* consisting often of large stones, hurled with a force that would tumble the stoutest rider from his saddle. Galled in the extreme by these discharges, against which even their shields afforded no adequate protection, Cortés ordered fire to be set to the buildings. This was no very difficult matter, since, although chiefly of stone, they were filled with mats, cane-work, and other combustible materials, which were soon in a blaze. But the buildings stood separated from one another by canals and draw-bridges, so that the flames did not easily communicate to the neighbouring edifices. Hence, the labor of the Spaniards was incalculably increased, and their progress in the work of destruction—fortunately for the city—was comparatively slow. They did not relax their efforts, however, till several hundred houses had been consumed, and the miseries of a conflagration, in which the wretched inmates perished equally with the defenders, were added to the other horrors of the scene.

The day was now far spent. The Spaniards had been everywhere victorious. But the enemy, though driven back on every point, still kept the field. When broken by the furious charges of the cavalry, he soon rallied behind the temporary defences, which, at different intervals, had been thrown across the streets, and, facing about, renewed the fight with undiminished courage, till the sweeping away of the barriers by the cannon of the assailants left a free passage for the movements of their horse. Thus the action was a succession of rallying and retreating, in which both parties suffered much, although the loss inflicted on the Indians was probably tenfold greater than that of the Spaniards. But the Aztecs could better afford the loss of a hundred lives than their antagonists that of one. And, while the Spaniards showed an array broken, and obviously thinned in numbers, the Mexican army, swelled by the tributary levies which flowed in upon it from the neighbouring streets, exhibited, with all its losses, no sign of diminution. At length, sated with carnage, and exhausted by toil and hunger, the Spanish commander drew off his men, and sounded a retreat.

On his way back to his quarters, he beheld his friend, the secretary Duero, in a street adjoining, unhorsed, and hotly engaged with a body of Mexicans, against whom he was desperately defending himself with his poniard. Cortés, roused at the sight, shouted his war-cry, and, dashing into the midst of the enemy, scattered them like chaff by the fury of his onset; then, recovering his friend's horse, he enabled him to remount, and the two cavaliers, striking their spurs into their steeds, burst through their opponents and joined the main body of the army. Such displays of generous gallantry were not uncommon in these engagements, which called forth more feats of personal adventure than battles with antagonists better skilled in the science of war. The chivalrous bearing of the general was emulated in full measure by Sandoval, De León, Olid, Alvarado, Ordaz, and his other brave companions, who won such glory under the eye of their leader, as prepared the way for the independent commands which afterwards placed provinces and kingdoms at their disposal.

The undaunted Aztecs hung on the rear of their retreating foes, annoying them at every step by fresh flights of stones and arrows; and, when the Spaniards had reëntered their fortress, the Indian host encamped around it, showing the same dogged resolution as on the preceding evening. Though true to their ancient habits of inaction during the night, they broke the stillness of the hour by insulting cries and menaces, which reached the ears of the besieged. "The gods have delivered you, at last, into our hands," they said; "Huitzilopotchli has long cried for his victims. The stone of sacrifice is ready. The knives are sharpened. The wild beasts in the palace are roaring for their offal. And the cages," they added, taunting the Tlascalans with their leanness, "are waiting for the false sons of Anahuac, who are to be fattened for the festival!" These dismal menaces, which sounded fearfully in the ears of the besieged, who understood too well their import, were mingled with piteous lamentations for their sovereign, whom they called on the Spaniards to deliver up to them.

Cortés suffered much from a severe wound which he had received in the hand in the late action. But the anguish of his mind must have been still greater, as he brooded over the dark prospect before him. He had mistaken the character of the Mexicans. Their long and patient endurance had been a violence to their natural temper, which, as their whole history proves, was arrogant and ferocious beyond that of most of the races of Anahuac. The restraint, which, in deference to their monarch, more than to their own fears, they had so long put on their natures, being once removed, their passions burst forth with accumulated violence. The Spaniards had encountered in the Tlascalan an open enemy, who had no grievance to complain of, no wrong to redress. He fought under the vague apprehension only of some coming evil to his country. But the Aztec, hitherto the proud lord of the land, was goaded by insult and injury, till he had reached that pitch of self-devotion, which made life cheap, in comparison with revenge. Armed thus with the energy of despair, the savage is almost a match for the civilized man; and a whole nation, moved to its depths by a common feeling, which swallows up all selfish considerations of personal interest and safety, becomes, whatever be its resources, like the earthquake and the tornado, the most formidable among the agencies of nature.

Considerations of this kind may have passed through the mind of Cortés, as he reflected on his own impotence to restrain the fury of the Mexicans, and resolved, in despite of his late supercilious treatment of Montezuma, to employ his authority to allay the tumult,—an authority so successfully exerted in behalf of Alvarado, at an earlier stage of the insurrection. He was the more confirmed in his purpose, on the following morning, when the assailants, redoubling their efforts, succeeded in scaling the works in one quarter, and effecting an entrance into the inclosure. It is true, they were met with so resolute a spirit, that not a man, of those who entered, was left alive. But, in the impetuosity of the assault, it seemed, for a few moments, as if the place was to be carried by storm.

Cortés now sent to the Aztec emperor to request his interposition with his subjects in behalf of the Spaniards. But Montezuma was not in the humor to comply. He had remained moodily in his quarters ever since the general's return. Disgusted with the treatment he had received, he had still further cause for mortification in finding himself the ally of those who were the open enemies of his nation. From his apartment he had beheld the tragical scenes in his capital, and seen another, the presumptive heir to his throne, taking the place which he should have occupied at the head of his warriors, and fighting the battles of his country. Distressed by his position, indignant at those who had placed him in it, he coldly answered, "What have I to do with Malinche? I do not wish to hear from him. I desire only to die. To what a state has my willingness to serve him reduced me!" When urged still further to comply by Olid and father Olmedo, he added, "It is of no use. They will neither believe me, nor the false words and promises of Malinche. You will never leave these walls alive." On being assured, however, that the Spaniards would willingly depart, if a way were opened to them by their enemies, he at length—moved, probably, more by the desire to spare the blood of his subjects, than of the Christians—consented to expostulate with his people.

In order to give the greater effect to his presence, he put on his imperial robes. The *tilmatli,* his mantle of white and blue, flowed over his shoulders, held together by its rich clasp of green *chalchivitl.* The same precious gem, with emeralds of uncommon size, set in gold, profusely ornamented other parts of his dress. His feet were shod with the golden sandals, and his brows covered by the *copilli,* or Mexican diadem, resembling in form the pontifical tiara. Thus attired, and surrounded by a guard of Spaniards and several Aztec nobles, and preceded by the golden wand, the symbol of sovereignty, the Indian monarch ascended the central turret of the palace. His presence was instantly recognised by the people, and, as the royal retinue advanced along the battlements, a change, as if by magic, came over the scene. The clang of instruments, the fierce cries of the assailants, were hushed, and a deathlike stillness pervaded the whole assembly, so fiercely agitated, but a few moments before, by the wild tumult of war! Many prostrated themselves on the ground; others bent the knee; and all turned with eager expectation towards the monarch, whom they had been taught to reverence with slavish awe, and from whose countenance they had been wont to turn away as from the intolerable splendors of divinity! Montezuma saw his advantage; and, while he stood thus confronted with his awestruck people, he seemed to recover all his former authority and confidence, as he felt himself to be still a king. With a calm voice, easily heard over the silent assembly, he is said by the Castilian writers to have thus addressed them.

"Why do I see my people here in arms against the palace of my fathers? Is it that you think your sovereign a prisoner, and wish to release him? If so, you have acted rightly. But you are mistaken. I am no prisoner. The strangers are my guests. I remain with them only from choice, and can leave them when I list. Have you come to drive them from the city? That is unnecessary. They will depart of their own accord, if you will open a way for them. Return to your homes, then. Lay down your arms. Show your obedience to me who have a right to it. The white men shall go back to their own land; and all shall be well again within the walls of Tenochtitlán."

As Montezuma announced himself the friend of the detested strangers, a murmur ran through the multitude; a murmur of contempt for the pusillanimous prince who could show himself so insensible to the insults and injuries for which the nation was in arms! The swollen tide of their passions swept away all the barriers of ancient reverence, and, taking a new direction, descended on the head of the unfortunate monarch, so far degenerated from his warlike ancestors. "Base Aztec," they exclaimed, "woman, coward, the white men have made you a woman,—fit only to weave and spin!" These bitter taunts were soon followed by still more hostile demonstrations. A chief, it is said, of high rank, bent a bow or brandished a javelin with an air of defiance against the emperor, when, in an instant, a cloud of stones and arrows descended on the spot where the royal train was gathered. The Spaniards appointed to protect his person had been thrown off their guard by the respectful deportment of the people during their lord's address. They now hastily interposed their bucklers. But it was too late Montezuma was wounded by three of the missiles, one of which, a stone, fell with such violence on his head, near the temple, as brought him senseless to the ground. The Mexicans, shocked at their own sacrilegious act, experienced a sudden revulsion of feeling, and, setting up a dismal cry, dispersed panic-struck, in different directions. Not one of the multitudinous array remained in the great square before the palace!

The unhappy prince, meanwhile, was borne by his attendants to his apartments below. On recovering from the insensibility caused by the blow, the wretchedness of his condition broke upon him. He had tasted the last bitterness of degradation. He had been reviled, rejected, by his people. The meanest of the rabble had raised their hands against him. He had nothing more to live for. It was in vain that Cortés and his officers endeavoured to soothe the anguish of his spirit and fill him with better thoughts. He spoke not a word in answer. His wound, though dangerous, might still, with skilful treatment, not prove mortal. But Montezuma refused all the remedies for it. He tore off the bandages as often as they were applied, maintaining, all the while, the most determined silence. He sat with eyes dejected, brooding over his fallen fortunes, over the image of ancient majesty, and present humiliation. He had survived his honor. But a spark of his ancient spirit seemed to kindle in his bosom, as it was clear he did not mean to survive his disgrace.—From this painful scene the Spanish general and his followers were soon called away by the new dangers which menaced the garrison.

II

Distress and Death

OPPOSITE to the Spanish quarters, at only a few rods distance, stood the great *teocalli* of Huitzilopotchli. This pyramidal mound, with the sanctuaries that crowned it, rising altogether to the height of near a hundred and fifty feet, afforded an elevated position that completely commanded the palace of Axayacatl, occupied by the Christians. A body of five or six hundred Mexicans, many of them nobles and warriors of the highest rank, had got possession of the *teocalli*, whence they discharged such a tempest of arrows on the garrison, that no one could leave his defences for a moment without imminent danger; while the Mexicans, under shelter of the sanctuaries, were entirely covered from the fire of the besieged. It was obviously necessary to dislodge the enemy, if the Spaniards would remain longer in their quarters.

Cortés assigned this service to his chamberlain, Escobar, giving him a hundred men for the purpose, with orders to storm the *teocalli*, and set fire to the sanctuaries. But that officer was thrice repulsed in the attempt, and, after the most desperate efforts was obliged to return with considerable loss, and without accomplishing his object.

Cortés, who saw the immediate necessity of carrying the place, determined to lead the storming party himself. He was then suffering much from the wound in his left hand, which had disabled it for the present. He made the arm serviceable, however, by fastening his buckler to it, and, thus crippled, sallied out at the head of three hundred chosen cavaliers, and several thousand of his auxiliaries.

In the court-yard of the temple he found a numerous body of Indians prepared to dispute his passage. He briskly charged them, but the flat, smooth stones of the pavement were so slippery, that the horses lost their footing, and many of them fell. Hastily dismounting, they sent back the animals to their quarters, and, renewing the assault, the Spaniards succeeded without much difficulty in dispersing the Indian warriors, and opening a free passage for themselves to the *teocalli*. This building, as the reader may remember, was a huge pyramidal structure, about three hundred feet square at the base. A flight of stone steps on the outside, at one of the angles of the mound, led to a platform, or terraced walk, which passed round the building until it reached a similar flight of stairs directly over the preceding, that conducted to another landing as before. As there were five bodies or divisions of the *teocalli*, it became necessary to pass round its whole extent four times, or nearly a mile, in order to reach the summit, which, it may be recollected, was an open area, crowned only by the two sanctuaries dedicated to the Aztec deities.

Cortés, having cleared a way for the assault, sprang up the lower stairway, followed by Alvarado, Sandoval, Ordaz, and the other gallant cavaliers of his little band, leaving a file of arquebusiers and a strong corps of Indian allies to hold the enemy in check at the foot of the monument. On the first landing, as well as on the several galleries above, and on the summit, the Aztec warriors were drawn up to dispute his passage. From their elevated position they showered down volleys of lighter missiles, together with heavy stones, beams, and burning rafters, which, thundering along the stairway, overturned the ascending Spaniards, and carried desolation through their ranks. The more fortunate, eluding or springing over these obstacles, succeeded in gaining the first terrace; where, throwing themselves on their enemies, they compelled them, after a short resistance, to fall back. The assailants pressed on, effectually supported by a brisk fire of the musketeers from below, which so much galled the Mexicans in their exposed situation, that they were glad to take shelter on the broad summit of the *teocalli*.

Cortés and his comrades were close upon their rear, and the two parties soon found themselves face to face on this aërial battle-field, engaged in mortal combat in presence of the whole

city, as well as of the troops in the court-yard, who paused, as
if by mutual consent, from their own hostilities, gazing in
silent expectation on the issue of those above. The area, though
somewhat smaller than the base of the *teocalli,* was large
enough to afford a fair field of fight for a thousand combatants.
It was paved with broad, flat stones. No impediment occurred
over its surface, except the huge sacrificial block, and the temples of stone which rose to the height of forty feet, at the further
extremity of the arena. One of these had been consecrated to
the Cross. The other was still occupied by the Mexican war-
god. The Christian and the Aztec contended for their religions
under the very shadow of their respective shrines; while the
Indian priests, running to and fro, with their hair wildly
streaming over their sable mantles, seemed hovering in mid
air, like so many demons of darkness urging on the work of
slaughter!

The parties closed with the desperate fury of men who had
no hope but in victory. Quarter was neither asked nor given;
and to fly was impossible. The edge of the area was unprotected
by parapet or battlement. The least slip would be fatal; and
the combatants, as they struggled in mortal agony, were sometimes seen to roll over the sheer sides of the precipice together.
Cortés himself is said to have had a narrow escape from this
dreadful fate. Two warriors, of strong, muscular frames, seized
on him, and were dragging him violently towards the brink of
the pyramid. Aware of their intention, he struggled with all his
force, and, before they could accomplish their purpose, succeeded in tearing himself from their grasp, and hurling one of
them over the walls with his own arm! The story is not improbable in itself, for Cortés was a man of uncommon agility
and strength. It has been often repeated; but not by contemporary history.

The battle lasted with unintermitting fury for three hours.
The number of the enemy was double that of the Christians;
and it seemed as if it were a contest which must be determined
by numbers and brute force, rather than by superior science.

But it was not so. The invulnerable armor of the Spaniard, his sword of matchless temper, and his skill in the use of it, gave him advantages which far outweighed the odds of physical strength and numbers. After doing all that the courage of despair could enable men to do, resistance grew fainter and fainter on the side of the Aztecs. One after another they had fallen. Two or three priests only survived to be led away in triumph by the victors. Every other combatant was stretched a corpse on the bloody arena, or had been hurled from the giddy heights. Yet the loss of the Spaniards was not inconsiderable. It amounted to forty-five of their best men, and nearly all the remainder were more or less injured in the desperate conflict.

The victorious cavaliers now rushed towards the sanctuaries. The lower story was of stone; the two upper were of wood. Penetrating into their recesses, they had the mortification to find the image of the Virgin and the Cross removed. But in the other edifice they still beheld the grim figure of Huitzilopotchli, with his censer of smoking hearts, and the walls of his oratory reeking with gore,—not improbably of their own countrymen! With shouts of triumph the Christians tore the uncouth monster from his niche, and tumbled him, in the presence of the horror-struck Aztecs, down the steps of the *teocalli*. They then set fire to the accursed building. The flames speedily ran up the slender towers, sending forth an ominous light over city, lake, and valley, to the remotest hut among the mountains. It was the funeral pyre of Paganism, and proclaimed the fall of that sanguinary religion which had so long hung like a dark cloud over the fair regions of Anahuac!

Having accomplished this good work, the Spaniards descended the winding slopes of the *teocalli* with more free and buoyant step, as if conscious that the blessing of Heaven now rested on their arms. They passed through the dusky files of Indian warriors in the court-yard, too much dismayed by the appalling scenes they had witnessed to offer resistance; and reached their own quarters in safety. That very night they followed up the blow by a sortie on the sleeping town, and burned three hundred houses, the horrors of conflagration being made still more impressive by occurring at the hour when the Aztecs, from their own system of warfare, were least prepared for them.

Hoping to find the temper of the natives somewhat subdued by these reverses, Cortés now determined, with his usual policy, to make them a vantage-ground for proposing terms of accommodation. He accordingly invited the enemy to a parley, and, as the principal chiefs, attended by their followers, assembled in the great square, he mounted the turret before occupied by Montezuma, and made signs that he would address them. Marina, as usual, took her place by his side, as his interpreter. The multitude gazed with earnest curiosity on the Indian girl, whose influence with the Spaniards was well known, and whose connexion with the general, in particular, had led the Aztecs to designate him by her Mexican name of Malinche. Cortés, speaking through the soft, musical tones of his mistress, told his audience they must now be convinced, that they had nothing further to hope from opposition to the Spaniards. They had seen their gods trampled in the dust, their altars broken, their dwellings burned, their warriors falling on all sides. "All this," continued he, "you have brought on yourselves by your rebellion. Yet for the affection the sovereign, whom you have so unworthily treated, still bears you, I would willingly stay my hand, if you will lay down your arms, and return once more to your obedience. But, if you do not," he concluded, "I will make your city a heap of ruins, and leave not a soul alive to mourn over it!"

But the Spanish commander did not yet comprehend the character of the Aztecs, if he thought to intimidate them by menaces. Calm in their exterior and slow to move, they were the more difficult to pacify when roused; and now that they had been stirred to their inmost depths, it was no human voice that could still the tempest. It may be, however, that Cortés did not so much misconceive the character of the people. He may have felt that an authoritative tone was the only one he could assume with any chance of effect, in his present position, in which milder and more conciliatory language would, by intimating a consciousness of inferiority, have too certainly defeated its own object.

It was true, they answered, he had destroyed their temples, broken in pieces their gods, massacred their countrymen. Many more, doubtless, were yet to fall under their terrible swords. But they were content so long as for every thousand Mexicans they could shed the blood of a single white man! "Look out," they continued, "on our terraces and streets, see them still thronged with warriors as far as your eyes can reach. Our numbers are scarcely diminished by our losses. Yours, on the contrary, are lessening every hour. You are perishing from hunger and sickness. Your provisions and water are failing. You must soon fall into our hands. *The bridges are broken down, and you cannot escape!* There will be too few of you left to glut the vengeance of our Gods!" As they concluded, they sent a volley of arrows over the battlements, which compelled the Spaniards to descend and take refuge in their defences.

The fierce and indomitable spirit of the Aztecs filled the besieged with dismay. All, then, that they had done and suffered, their battles by day, their vigils by night, the perils they had braved, even the victories they had won, were of no avail. It was too evident that they had no longer the spring of ancient superstition to work upon, in the breasts of the natives, who, like some wild beast that has burst the bonds of his keeper, seemed now to swell and exult in the full consciousness of their strength. The annunciation respecting the bridges fell like a knell on the ears of the Christians. All that they had heard was too true,—and they gazed on one another with looks of anxiety and dismay.

The same consequences followed, which sometimes take place among the crew of a shipwrecked vessel. Subordination was lost in the dreadful sense of danger. A spirit of mutiny broke out, especially among the recent levies drawn from the army of

Narváez. They had come into the country from no motive of ambition, but attracted simply by the glowing reports of its opulence, and they had fondly hoped to return in a few months with their pockets well lined with the gold of the Aztec monarch. But how different had been their lot! From the first hour of their landing, they had experienced only trouble and disaster, privations of every description, sufferings unexampled, and they now beheld in perspective a fate yet more appalling. Bitterly did they lament the hour when they left the sunny fields of Cuba for these cannibal regions! And heartily did they curse their own folly in listening to the call of Velásquez, and still more, in embarking under the banner of Cortés!

They now demanded with noisy vehemence to be led instantly from the city, and refused to serve longer in defence of a place where they were cooped up like sheep in the shambles, waiting only to be dragged to slaughter. In all this they were rebuked by the more orderly, soldierlike conduct of the veterans of Cortés. These latter had shared with their general the day of his prosperity, and they were not disposed to desert him in the tempest. It was, indeed, obvious, on a little reflection, that the only chance of safety, in the existing crisis, rested on subordination and union; and that even this chance must be greatly diminished under any other leader than their present one.

Thus pressed by enemies without and by factions within, that leader was found, as usual, true to himself. Circumstances so appalling, as would have paralyzed a common mind, only stimulated his to higher action, and drew forth all its resources. He combined what is most rare, singular coolness and constancy of purpose, with a spirit of enterprise that might well be called romantic. His presence of mind did not now desert him. He calmly surveyed his condition, and weighed the difficulties which surrounded him, before coming to a decision. Independently of the hazard of a retreat in the face of a watchful and desperate foe, it was a deep mortification to surrender up the city, where he had so long lorded it as a master; to abandon the rich treasures which he had secured to himself and his followers; to forego the very means by which he had hoped to propitiate the favor of his sovereign, and secure an amnesty for his irregular proceedings. This, he well knew, must, after all, be dependent on success. To fly now was to acknowledge himself further removed from the conquest than ever. What a close was this to a career so auspiciously begun! What a contrast to his magnificent vaunts! What a triumph would it afford to his enemies! The governor of Cuba would be amply revenged.

But, if such humiliating reflections crowded on his mind, the alternative of remaining, in his present crippled condition, seemed yet more desperate. With his men daily diminishing in strength and numbers, their provisions reduced so low that a small daily ration of bread was all the sustenance afforded to the soldier under his extraordinary fatigues, with the breaches every day widening in his feeble fortifications, with his ammunition, in fine, nearly expended, it would be impossible to maintain the place much longer—and none but men of iron constitutions and tempers, like the Spaniards, could have held it out so long—against the enemy. The chief embarrassment was as to the time and manner in which it would be expedient to evacuate the city. The best route seemed to be that of Tlacopan (Tacuba). For the causeway, the most dangerous part of the road, was but two miles long in that direction, and would, therefore, place the fugitives, much sooner than either of the other great avenues, on terra firma. Before his final departure, however, he proposed to make another sally in that direction, in order to reconnoitre the ground, and, at the same time, divert the enemy's attention from his real purpose by a show of active operations.

For some days, his workmen had been employed in constructing a military machine of his own invention. It was called a *manta*, and was contrived somewhat on the principle of the mantelets used in the wars of the Middle Ages. It was, however, more complicated, consisting of a tower made of light beams and planks, having two chambers, one over the other. These were to be filled with musketeers, and the sides were provided with loop-holes, through which a fire could be kept up on the enemy. The great advantage proposed by this contrivance was, to afford a defence to the troops against the missiles hurled from the terraces. These machines, three of which were made, rested on rollers, and were provided with strong ropes, by which they were to be dragged along the streets by the Tlascalan auxiliaries.

The Mexicans gazed with astonishment on this warlike machinery, and, as the rolling fortresses advanced, belching forth fire and smoke from their entrails, the enemy, incapable of making an impression on those within, fell back in dismay. By bringing the *mantas* under the walls of the houses, the Spaniards were enabled to fire with effect on the mischievous tenants of the *azoteas,* and when this did not silence them, by letting a ladder, or light draw-bridge, fall on the roof from the top of the *manta,* they opened a passage to the terrace, and closed with the combatants hand to hand. They could not, however, thus approach the higher buildings, from which the Indian warriors threw down such heavy masses of stone and timber as dislodged the planks that covered the machines, or, thundering against their sides, shook the frail edifices to their foundations, threatening all within with indiscriminate ruin. Indeed, the success of the experiment was doubtful, when the intervention of a canal put a stop to their further progress.

The Spaniards now found the assertion of their enemies too well confirmed. The bridge which traversed the opening had been demolished; and, although the canals which intersected the city were, in general, of no great width or depth, the removal of the bridges not only impeded the movements of the general's clumsy machines, but effectually disconcerted those of his cavalry. Resolving to abandon the *mantas,* he gave orders to fill up the chasm with stone, timber, and other rubbish drawn from the ruined buildings, and to make a new passage-way for the army. While this labor was going on, the Aztec slingers and archers on the other side of the opening kept up a galling discharge on the Christians, the more defenceless from the nature of their occupation. When the work was completed, and a safe passage secured, the Spanish cavaliers rode briskly against the enemy, who, unable to resist the shock of the steel-clad column, fell back with precipitation to where another canal afforded a similar strong position for defence.

There were no less than seven of these canals, intersecting the great street of Tlacopan, and at every one the same scene was renewed, the Mexicans making a gallant stand, and inflicting some loss, at each, on their persevering antagonists. These operations consumed two days, when, after incredible toil, the Spanish general had the satisfaction to find the line of communication completely reëstablished through the whole length of the avenue, and the principal bridges placed under strong detachments of infantry. At this juncture, when he had driven the foe before him to the furthest extremity of the street, where it touches on the causeway, he was informed, that the Mexicans, disheartened by their reverses, desired to open a parley with him respecting the terms of an accommodation, and that their chiefs awaited his return for that purpose at the fortress. Overjoyed at the intelligence, he instantly rode back, attended by Alvarado, Sandoval, and about sixty of the cavaliers, to his quarters.

The Mexicans proposed that he should release the two priests captured in the temple, who might be the bearers of his terms, and serve as agents for conducting the negotiation. They were accordingly sent with the requisite instructions to their countrymen. But they did not return. The whole was an artifice of the enemy, anxious to procure the liberation of their religious leaders, one of whom was their *teoteuctli,* or high-priest, whose presence was indispensable in the probable event of a new coronation.

Cortés, meanwhile, relying on the prospects of a speedy arrangement, was hastily taking some refreshment with his officers, after the fatigues of the day; when he received the alarming tidings, that the enemy were in arms again, with more fury than ever; that they had overpowered the detachments posted under Alvarado at three of the bridges, and were busily occupied in demolishing them. Stung with shame at the facility with which he had been duped by his wily foe, or rather by his own sanguine hopes, Cortés threw himself into the saddle, and, followed by his brave companions, galloped back at full speed to the scene of action. The Mexicans recoiled before the impetuous charge of the Spaniards. The bridges were again restored; and Cortés and his chivalry rode down the whole extent of the great street, driving the enemy, like frightened deer, at the points of their lances. But, before he could return on his steps, he had the mortification to find that the indefatigable foe, gathering from the adjoining lanes and streets, had again closed on his infantry, who, worn down by fatigue, were unable to maintain their position at one of the principal bridges. New swarms of warriors now poured in on all sides, overwhelming the little band of Christian cavaliers with a storm of stones, darts, and arrows, which rattled like hail on their armor and on that of their well-barbed horses. Most of the missiles, indeed, glanced harmless from the good panoplies of steel, or thick quilted cotton, but, now and then, one better aimed penetrated the joints of the harness, and stretched the rider on the ground.

The confusion became greater around the broken bridge. Some of the horsemen were thrown into the canal, and their steeds floundered wildly about without a rider. Cortés himself, at this crisis, did more than any other to cover the retreat of his followers. While the bridge was repairing, he plunged boldly into the midst of the barbarians, striking down an enemy at every vault of his charger, cheering on his own men, and spreading terror through the ranks of his opponents by the well-known sound of his battle-cry. Never did he display greater hardihood, or more freely expose his person, emulating, says an old chronicler, the feats of the Roman Cocles. In this way he stayed the tide of assailants, till the last man had crossed the bridge, when, some of the planks having given way, he was compelled to leap a chasm of full six feet in width, amidst a cloud of missiles, before he could place himself in safety. A report ran through the army that the general was slain. It soon spread through the city, to the great joy of the Mexicans, and reached the fortress, where the besieged were thrown into no less consternation. But, happily for them, it was false. He, indeed, received two severe contusions on the knee, but in other respects remained uninjured. At no time, however, had he been in such extreme danger; and his escape, and that of his companions, were esteemed little less than a miracle. More than one grave historian refers the preservation of the Spaniards to the watchful care of their patron Apostle, St. James, who, in these desperate conflicts, was beheld careering on his milk-white steed at the head of the Christian squadrons, with his sword flashing lightning, while a lady robed in white—supposed to be the Virgin—was distinctly seen by his side, throwing dust in the eyes of the infidel! The fact is attested both by Spaniards and Mexicans,—by the latter after their conversion to Christianity. Surely, never was there a time when the interposition of their tutelar saint was more strongly demanded.

The coming of night dispersed the Indian battalions, which, vanishing like birds of ill omen from the field, left the well-contested pass in possession of the Spaniards. They returned, however, with none of the joyous feelings of conquerors to their citadel, but with slow step and dispirited, with weapons hacked, armor battered, and fainting under the loss of blood, fasting, and fatigue. In this condition they had yet to learn the tidings of a fresh misfortune in the death of Montezuma.

The Indian monarch had rapidly declined, since he had received his injury, sinking, however, quite as much under the anguish of a wounded spirit, as under disease. He continued in the same moody state of insensibility as that already described; holding little communication with those around him, deaf to consolation, obstinately rejecting all medical remedies as well as nourishment. Perceiving his end approach, some of the cavaliers present in the fortress, whom the kindness of his manners had personally attached to him, were anxious to save the soul of the dying prince from the sad doom of those who perish in the darkness of unbelief. They accordingly waited on him, with father Olmedo at their head, and in the most earnest manner implored him to open his eyes to the error of his creed, and consent to be baptized. But Montezuma—whatever may have been suggested to the contrary—seems never to have faltered in his hereditary faith, or to have contemplated becoming an apostate; for surely he merits that name in its most odious application, who, whether Christian or Pagan, renounces his religion without conviction of its falsehood. Indeed, it was a too implicit reliance on its oracles, which had led him to give such easy confidence to the Spaniards. His intercourse with them had, doubtless, not sharpened his desire to embrace their communion; and the calamities of his country he might consider as sent by his gods to punish him for his hospitality to those who had desecrated and destroyed their shrines.

When father Olmedo, therefore, kneeling at his side, with the uplifted crucifix, affectionately besought him to embrace the sign of man's redemption, he coldly repulsed the priest, exclaiming, "I have but a few moments to live; and will not at this hour desert the faith of my fathers." One things, however, seemed to press heavily on Montezuma's mind. This was the fate of his children, especially of three daughters, whom he had by his two wives; for there were certain rites of marriage, which distinguished the lawful wife from the concubine. Calling Cortés to his bedside, he earnestly commended these children to his care, as "the most precious jewels that he could leave him." He besought the general to interest his master, the emperor, in their behalf, and to see that they should not be left destitute, but be allowed some portion of their rightful inheritance. "Your lord will do this," he concluded, "if it were only for the friendly offices I have rendered the Spaniards, and for the love I have shown them,—though it has brought me to this condition! But for this I bear them no ill-will." Such, according to Cortés himself, were the words of the dying monarch. Not long after, on the 30th of June, 1520, he expired in the arms of some of his own nobles, who still remained faithful in their attendance on his person. . . .

III

La Noche Triste

THERE was no longer any question as to the expediency of
evacuating the capital. The only doubt was as to the time of
doing so, and the route. The Spanish commander called a
council of officers to deliberate on these matters. It was his
purpose to retreat on Tlascala, and in that capital to decide
according to circumstances on his future operations. After
some discussion, they agreed on the causeway of Tlacopan as
the avenue by which to leave the city. It would, indeed, take
them back by a circuitous route, considerably longer than either
of those by which they had approached the capital. But, for
that reason, it would be less likely to be guarded, as least
suspected; and the causeway itself, being shorter than either
of the other entrances, would sooner place the army in comparative security on the main land.

There was some difference of opinion in respect to the hour
of departure. The day-time, it was argued by some, would be
preferable, since it would enable them to see the nature and
extent of their danger, and to provide against it. Darkness
would be much more likely to embarrass their own movements
than those of the enemy, who were familiar with the ground.
A thousand impediments would occur in the night, which might
prevent their acting in concert, or obeying, or even ascertain-
ing, the orders of the commander. But, on the other hand, it
was urged, that the night presented many obvious advantages
in dealing with a foe who rarely carried his hostilities beyond
the day. The late active operations of the Spaniards had thrown
the Mexicans off their guard, and it was improbable they would
anticipate so speedy a departure of their enemies. With celerity
and caution, they might succeed, therefore, in making their
escape from the town, possibly over the causeway, before their

retreat should be discovered; and, could they once get beyond
that pass of peril, they felt little apprehension for the rest.

These views were fortified, it is said, by the counsels of a
soldier named Botello, who professed the mysterious science
of judicial astrology. He had gained credit with the army by
some predictions which had been verified by the events; those
lucky hits which make chance pass for calculation with the
credulous multitude. This man recommended to his countrymen by all means to evacuate the place in the night, as the hour
most propitious to them, although he should perish in it. The
event proved the astrologer better acquainted with his own
horoscope than with that of others.

It is possible Botello's predictions had some weight in determining the opinion of Cortés. Superstition was the feature of
the age, and the Spanish general, as we have seen, had a full
measure of its bigotry. Seasons of gloom, moreover, dispose
the mind to a ready acquiescence in the marvellous. It is, however, quite as probable that he made use of the astrologer's
opinion, finding it coincided with his own, to influence that of
his men, and inspire them with higher confidence. At all events,
it was decided to abandon the city that very night.

The general's first care was to provide for the safe transportation of the treasure. Many of the common soldiers had converted their share of the prize, as we have seen, into gold chains,
collars, or other ornaments, which they easily carried about
their persons. But the royal fifth, together with that of Cortés
himself, and much of the rich booty of the principal cavaliers,
had been converted into bars and wedges of solid gold, and
deposited in one of the strong apartments of the palace. Cortés
delivered the share belonging to the Crown to the royal officers,
assigning them one of the strongest horses, and a guard of
Castilian soldiers, to transport it. Still, much of the treasure,
belonging both to the Crown and to individuals, was necessarily abandoned, from the want of adequate means of conveyance. The metal lay scattered in shining heaps along the
floor, exciting the cupidity of the soldiers. "Take what you will

of it," said Cortés to his men. "Better you should have it, than these Mexican hounds. But be careful not to overload yourselves. He travels safest in the dark night who travels lightest." His own more wary followers took heed to his counsel, helping themselves to a few articles of least bulk, though, it might be, of greatest value. But the troops of Narváez, pining for riches, of which they had heard so much, and hitherto seen so little, showed no such discretion. To them it seemed as if the very mines of Mexico were turned up before them, and, rushing on the treacherous spoil, they greedily loaded themselves with as much of it, not merely as they could accommodate about their persons, but as they could stow away in wallets, boxes, or any other mode of conveyance at their disposal.

Cortés next arranged the order of march. The van, composed of two hundred Spanish foot, he placed under the command of the valiant Gonzalo de Sandoval, supported by Diego de Ordaz, Francisco de Lujo, and about twenty other cavaliers. The rear-guard, constituting the strength of the infantry, was intrusted to Pedro de Alvarado, and Velásquez de León. The general himself took charge of the "battle," or centre, in which went the baggage, some of the heavy guns, most of which, however, remained in the rear, the treasure, and the prisoners. These consisted of a son and two daughters of Montezuma, Cacama, the deposed lord of Tezcuco, and several other nobles, whom Cortés retained as important pledges in his future negotiations with the enemy. The Tlascalans were distributed pretty equally among the three divisions; and Cortés had under his immediate command a hundred picked soldiers, his own veterans most attached to his service, who, with Christóval de Olid, Francisco de Morla, Alonso de Ávila, and two or three other cavaliers, formed a select corps, to act wherever occasion might require.

The general had already superintended the construction of a portable bridge to be laid over the open canals in the causeway. This was given in charge to an officer named Magariño, with forty soldiers under his orders, all pledged to defend the passage to the last extremity. The bridge was to be taken up when the entire army had crossed one of the breaches, and transported to the next. There were three of these openings in the causeway, and most fortunate would it have been for the expedition, if the foresight of the commander had provided the same number of bridges. But the labor would have been great, and time was short.

At midnight the troops were under arms, in readiness for the march. Mass was performed by father Olmedo, who invoked the protection of the Almighty through the awful perils of the night. The gates were thrown open, and, on the first of July, 1520, the Spaniards for the last time sallied forth from the walls of the ancient fortress, the scene of so much suffering and such indomitable courage.

The night was cloudy, and a drizzling rain, which fell without intermission, added to the obscurity. The great square before the palace was deserted, as, indeed, it had been since the fall of Montezuma. Steadily, and as noiselessly as possible, the Spaniards held their way along the great street of Tlacopan, which so lately had resounded to the tumult of battle. All was now hushed in silence; and they were only reminded of the past by the occasional presence of some solitary corpse, or a dark heap of the slain, which too plainly told where the strife had been hottest. As they passed along the lanes and alleys which opened into the great street, or looked down the canals, whose polished surface gleamed with a sort of ebon lustre through the obscurity of night, they easily fancied that they discerned the shadowy forms of their foe lurking in ambush, and ready to spring on them. But it was only fancy; and the city slept undisturbed even by the prolonged echoes of the tramp of the horses, and the hoarse rumbling of the artillery and baggage trains. At length, a lighter space beyond the dusky line of buildings showed the van of the army that it was emerging on the open causeway. They might well have congratulated themselves on having thus escaped the dangers of an assault in the city itself, and that a brief time would place them in comparative safety on the opposite shore.—But the Mexicans were not all asleep.

As the Spaniards drew near the spot where the street opened
on the causeway, and were preparing to lay the portable bridge
across the uncovered breach, which now met their eyes, several
Indian sentinels, who had been stationed at this, as at the other
approaches to the city, took the alarm, and fled, rousing their
countrymen by their cries. The priests, keeping their night
watch on the summit of the *teocallis,* instantly caught the tidings and sounded their shells, while the huge drum in the
desolate temple of the war-god sent forth those solemn tones,
which, heard only in seasons of calamity, vibrated through
every corner of the capital. The Spaniards saw that no time
was to be lost. The bridge was brought forward and fitted with
all possible expedition. Sandoval was the first to try its strength,
and, riding across, was followed by his little body of chivalry,
his infantry, and Tlascalan allies, who formed the first division
of the army. Then came Cortés and his squadrons, with the
baggage, ammunition wagons, and a part of the artillery. But
before they had time to defile across the narrow passage, a
gathering sound was heard, like that of a mighty forest agitated
by the winds. It grew louder and louder, while on the dark
waters of the lake was heard a plashing noise, as of many oars.
Then came a few stones and arrows striking at random among
the hurrying troops. They fell every moment faster and more
furious, till they thickened into a terrible tempest, while the
very heavens were rent with the yells and war-cries of myriads
of combatants, who seemed all at once to be swarming over
land and lake!

The Spaniards pushed steadily on through this arrowy sleet,
though the barbarians, dashing their canoes against the sides
of the causeway, clambered up and broke in upon their ranks.
But the Christians, anxious only to make the escape, declined
all combat except for self-preservation. The cavaliers, spurring
forward their steeds, shook off their assailants, and rode over
their prostrate bodies, while the men on foot with their good
swords or the butts of their pieces drove them headlong again
down the sides of the dike.

But the advance of several thousand men, marching, probably, on a front of not more than fifteen or twenty abreast, necessarily required much time, and the leading files had already reached the second breach in the causeway before those in the rear had entirely traversed the first. Here they halted; as they had no means of effecting a passage, smarting all the while under unintermitting volleys from the enemy, who were clustered thick on the waters around this second opening. Sorely distressed, the van-guard sent repeated messages to the rear to demand the portable bridge. At length the last of the army had crossed, and Magariño and his sturdy followers endeavoured to raise the ponderous frame-work. But it stuck fast in the sides of the dike. In vain they strained every nerve. The weight of so many men and horses, and above all of the heavy artillery, had wedged the timbers so firmly in the stones and earth, that it was beyond their power to dislodge them. Still they labored amidst a torrent of missiles, until, many of them slain, and all wounded, they were obliged to abandon the attempt.

The tidings soon spread from man to man, and no sooner was their dreadful import comprehended, than a cry of despair arose, which for a moment drowned all the noise of conflict. All means of retreat were cut off. Scarcely hope was left. The only hope was in such desperate exertions as each could make for himself. Order and subordination were at an end. Intense danger produced intense selfishness. Each thought only of his own life. Pressing forward, he trampled down the weak and the wounded, heedless whether it were friend or foe. The leading files, urged on by the rear, were crowded on the brink of the gulf. Sandoval, Ordaz, and the other cavaliers dashed into the water. Some succeeded in swimming their horses across. Others failed, and some, who reached the opposite bank, being overturned in the ascent, rolled headlong with their steeds into the lake. The infantry followed pellmell, heaped promiscuously on one another, frequently pierced by the shafts, or struck down by the war-clubs of the Aztecs; while many an unfortunate victim was dragged half-stunned on board their canoes, to be reserved for a protracted, but more dreadful death.

The carnage raged fearfully along the length of the causeway. Its shadowy bulk presented a mark of sufficient distinctness for the enemy's missiles, which often prostrated their own countrymen in the blind fury of the tempest. Those nearest the dike, running their canoes alongside, with a force that shattered them to pieces, leaped on the land, and grappled with the Christians, until both came rolling down the side of the causeway together. But the Aztec fell among his friends, while his antagonist was borne away in triumph to the sacrifice. The struggle was long and deadly. The Mexicans were recognised by their white cotton tunics, which showed faint through the darkness. Above the combatants rose a wild and discordant clamor, in which horrid shouts of vengeance were mingled with groans of agony, with invocations of the saints and the blessed Virgin, and with the screams of women; for there were several women, both natives and Spaniards, who had accompanied the Christian camp. Among these, one named María de Estrada is particularly noticed for the courage she displayed, battling with broadsword and target like the stanchest of the warriors.

The opening in the causeway, meanwhile, was filled up with the wreck of matter which had been forced into it, ammunition-wagons, heavy guns, bales of rich stuffs scattered over the waters, chests of solid ingots, and bodies of men and horses, till over this dismal ruin a passage was gradually formed, by which those in the rear were enabled to clamber to the other side. Cortés, it is said, found a place that was fordable, where, halting, with the water up to his saddle-girths, he endeavoured to check the confusion, and lead his followers by a safer path to the opposite bank. But his voice was lost in the wild uproar, and finally, hurrying on with the tide, he pressed forwards with a few trusty cavaliers, who remained near his person, to the van; but not before he had seen his favorite page, Juan de Salazar, struck down, a corpse, by his side. Here he found Sandoval and his companions, halting before the third and last breach, endeavouring to cheer on their followers to surmount it. But their resolution faltered. It was wide and deep; though the passage was not so closely beset by the enemy as the preceding ones. The cavaliers again set the example by plunging into the water. Horse and foot followed as they could, some swimming, others with dying grasp clinging to the manes and tails of the struggling animals. Those fared best, as the general had predicted, who travelled lightest; and many were the unfortunate wretches, who, weighed down by the fatal gold which they loved so well, were buried with it in the salt flat floods of the lake. Cortés, with his gallant comrades, Olid, Morla, Sandoval, and some few others, still kept in the advance, leading his broken remnant off the fatal causeway. The din of battle lessened in the distance; when the rumor reached them, that the rear-guard would be wholly, overwhelmed without speedy relief. It seemed almost an act of desperation; but the generous hearts of the Spanish cavaliers did not stop to calculate danger, when the cry for succour reached them. Turning their horses' bridles, they galloped back to the theatre of action, worked their way through the press, swam the canal, and placed themselves in the thick of the *melée* on the opposite bank.

The first grey of the morning was now coming over the waters. It showed the hideous confusion of the scene which had been shrouded in the obscurity of night. The dark masses of combatants, stretching along the dike, were seen struggling for mastery, until the very causeway on which they stood appeared to tremble, and reel to and fro, as if shaken by an earthquake; while the bosom of the lake, as far as the eye could reach, was darkened by canoes crowded with warriors, whose spears and bludgeons, armed with blades of "volcanic glass," gleamed in the morning light.

The cavaliers found Alvarado unhorsed, and defending himself with a poor handful of followers against an overwhelming tide of the enemy. His good steed, which had borne him through many a hard fight, had fallen under him. He was himself wounded in several places, and was striving in vain to rally his scattered column, which was driven to the verge of the canal by the fury of the enemy, then in possession of the whole

rear of the causeway, where they were reinforced every hour
by fresh combatants from the city. The artillery in the earlier
part of the engagement had not been idle, and its iron shower,
sweeping along the dike, had mowed down the assailants by
hundreds. But nothing could resist their impetuosity. The
front ranks, pushed on by those behind, were at length forced
up to the pieces, and, pouring over them like a torrent, over-
threw men and guns in one general ruin. The resolute charge of
the Spanish cavaliers, who had now arrived, created a temporary check, and gave time for their countrymen to make a
feeble rally. But they were speedily borne down by the returning flood. Cortés and his companions were compelled to plunge
again into the lake,—though all did not escape. Alvarado stood
on the brink for a moment, hesitating what to do. Unhorsed
as he was, to throw himself into the water, in the face of the
hostile canoes that now swarmed around the opening, afforded
but a desperate chance of safety. He had but a second for
thought. He was a man of powerful frame, and despair gave
him unnatural energy. Setting his long lance firmly on the
wreck which strewed the bottom of the lake, he sprung forward
with all his might, and cleared the wide gap at a leap! Aztecs
and Tlascalans gazed in stupid amazement, exclaiming, as
they beheld the incredible feat, "This is truly the *Tonatiuh*,—
the child of the Sun!"—The breadth of the opening is not given.
But it was so great, that the valorous captain Díaz, who well
remembered the place, says the leap was impossible to any
man. Other contemporaries, however, do not discredit the story.
It was, beyond doubt, matter of popular belief at the time; it
is to this day familiarly known to every inhabitant of the
capital; and the name of the *Salto de Alvarado,* "Alvarado's
Leap," given to the spot, still commemorates an exploit which
rivalled those of the demi-gods of Grecian fable.

Cortés and his companions now rode forward to the front,
where the troops, in a loose, disorderly manner, were marching
off the fatal causeway. A few only of the enemy hung on their
rear, or annoyed them by occasional flights of arrows from the

lake. The attention of the Aztecs was diverted by the rich spoil that strewed the battle-ground, fortunately for the Spaniards, who, had their enemy pursued with the same ferocity with which he had fought, would, in their crippled condition, have been cut off, probably, to a man. But little molested, therefore, they were allowed to defile through the adjacent village, or suburbs, it might be called, of Popotla.

The Spanish commander there dismounted from his jaded steed, and, sitting down on the steps of an Indian temple, gazed mournfully on the broken files as they passed before him. What a spectacle did they present! The cavalry, most of them dismounted, were mingled with the infantry, who dragged their feeble limbs along with difficulty; their shattered mail and tattered garments dripping with the salt ooze, showing through their rents many a bruise and ghastly wound; their bright arms soiled, their proud crests and banners gone, the baggage, artillery, all, in short, that constitutes the pride and panoply of glorious war, for ever lost. Cortés, as he looked wistfully on their thinned and disordered ranks, sought in vain for many a familiar face, and missed more than one dear companion who had stood side by side with him through all the perils of the Conquest. Though accustomed to control his emotions, or, at least, to conceal them, the sight was too much for him. He covered his face with his hands, and the tears, which trickled down, revealed too plainly the anguish of his soul.

He found some consolation, however, in the sight of several of the cavaliers on whom he most relied. Alvarado, Sandoval, Olid, Ordaz, Ávila, were yet safe. He had the inexpressible satisfaction, also, of learning the safety of the Indian interpreter, Marina, so dear to him, and so important to the army. She had been committed, with a daughter of a Tlascalan chief, to several of that nation. She was fortunately placed in the van, and her faithful escort had carried her securely through all the dangers of the night. Aguilar, the other interpreter, had also escaped. And it was with no less satisfaction, that Cortés learned the safety of the ship-builder, Martín López. The general's solicitude for the fate of this man, so indispensable, as he proved, to the success of his subsequent operations, showed, that, amidst all his affliction, his indomitable spirit was looking forward to the hour of vengeance.

Meanwhile, the advancing column had reached the neighbouring city of Tlacopan, (Tacuba,) once the capital of an independent principality. There it halted in the great street, as if bewildered and altogether uncertain what course to take; like a herd of panic-struck deer, who, flying from the hunters, with the cry of hound and horn still ringing in their ears, look wildly around for some glen or copse in which to plunge for concealment. Cortés, who had hastily mounted and rode on to the front again, saw the danger of remaining in a populous place, where the inhabitants might sorely annoy the troops from the *azoteas*, with little risk to themselves. Pushing forward, therefore, he soon led them into the country. There he endeavoured to reform his disorganized battalions, and bring them to something like order.

Hard by, at no great distance on the left, rose an eminence, looking towards a chain of mountains which fences in the Valley on the west. It was called the Hill of Otoncalpolco, and sometimes the Hill of Montezuma. It was crowned with an Indian *teocalli*, with its large outworks of stone covering an ample space, and by its strong position, which commanded the neighbouring plain, promised a good place of refuge for the exhausted troops. But the men, disheartened and stupefied by their late reverses, seemed for the moment incapable of further exertion; and the place was held by a body of armed Indians. Cortés saw the necessity of dislodging them, if he would save the remains of his army from entire destruction. The event showed he still held a control over their wills stronger than circumstances themselves. Cheering them on, and supported by his gallant cavaliers, he succeeded in infusing into the most sluggish something of his own intrepid temper, and led them up the ascent in face of the enemy. But the latter made slight resistance, and, after a few feeble volleys of missiles which did little injury, left the ground to the assailants.

It was covered by a building of considerable size, and furnished ample accommodations for the diminished numbers of the Spaniards. They found there some provisions; and more, it is said, were brought to them, in the course of the day, from some friendly Otomie villages in the neighbourhood. There was, also, a quantity of fuel in the courts, destined to the uses of the temple. With this they made fires to dry their drenched garments, and busily employed themselves in dressing one another's wounds, stiff and extremely painful from exposure and long exertion. Thus refreshed, the weary soldiers threw themselves down on the floor and courts of the temple, and soon found the temporary oblivion,—which Nature seldom denies even in the greatest extremity of suffering.

There was one eye in that assembly, however, which we may well believe did not so speedily close. For what agitating thoughts must have crowded on the mind of their commander, as he beheld his poor remnant of followers thus huddled together in this miserable bivouac! And this was all that survived of the brilliant array with which but a few weeks since he had entered the capital of Mexico! Where now were his dreams of conquest and empire? And what was he but a luckless adventurer, at whom the finger of scorn would be uplifted as a madman? Whichever way he turned, the horizon was almost equally gloomy, with scarcely one light spot to cheer him. He had still a weary journey before him, through perilous and unknown paths, with guides of whose fidelity he could not be assured. And how could he rely on his reception at Tlascala, the place of his destination; the land of his ancient enemies; where, formerly as a foe, and now as a friend, he had brought desolation to every family within its borders?

Yet these agitating and gloomy reflections, which might have crushed a common mind, had no power over that of Cortés; or rather, they only served to renew his energies, and quicken his perceptions, as the war of the elements purifies and gives elasticity to the atmosphere. He looked with an unblenching eye on his past reverses; but, confident in his own resources, he saw a light through the gloom which others could not. Even in the shattered relics which lay around him, resembling in their haggard aspect and wild attire a horde of famished outlaws, he discerned the materials out of which to reconstruct his ruined fortunes. In the very hour of discomfiture and general despondency, there is no doubt that his heroic spirit was meditating the plan of operations which he afterwards pursued with such dauntless constancy.

The loss sustained by the Spaniards on this fatal night, like every other event in the history of the Conquest, is reported with the greatest discrepancy. If we believe Cortés' own letter, it did not exceed one hundred and fifty Spaniards, and two thousand Indians. But the general's bulletins, while they do full justice to the difficulties to be overcome, and the importance of the results, are less scrupulous in stating the extent either of his means or of his losses. Thoan Cano,* one of the cavaliers present, estimates the slain at eleven hundred and seventy Spaniards, and eight thousand allies. But this is a greater number than we have allowed for the whole army. Perhaps we may come nearest the truth by taking the computation of Gómara, who was the chaplain of Cortés, and who had free access, doubtless, not only to the general's papers, but to other authentic sources of information. According to him, the number of Christians killed and missing was four hundred and fifty, and that of natives four thousand. This, was the loss sustained in the conflicts of the previous week, may have reduced the former to something more than a third, and the latter to a fourth, or, perhaps, fifth, of the original force with which they entered the capital. The brunt of the action fell on the rearguard, few of whom escaped. It was formed chiefly of the soldiers of Narváez, who fell the victims, in some measure, of their cupidity. Forty-six of the cavalry were cut off, which with

*Juan Cano. C.H.G.

previous losses reduced the number in this branch of the service to twenty-three, and some of these in very poor condition. The greater part of the treasure, the baggage, the general's papers, including his accounts, and a minute diary of transactions since leaving Cuba,—which, to posterity, at least, would have been of more worth than the gold,—had been swallowed up by the waters. The ammunition, the beautiful little train of artillery, with which Cortés had entered the city, were all gone. Not a musket even remained, the men having thrown them away, eager to disencumber themselves of all that might retard their escape on that disastrous night. Nothing, in short, of their military apparatus was left, but their swords, their crippled cavalry, and a few damaged crossbows, to assert the superiority of the European over the barbarian.

The prisoners, including, as already noticed, the children of Montezuma and the cacique of Tezcuco, all perished by the hands of their ignorant countrymen, it is said, in the indiscriminate fury of the assault. There were, also, some persons of consideration among the Spaniards, whose names were inscribed on the same bloody roll of slaughter. Such was Francisco de Morla, who fell by the side of Cortés, on returning with him to the rescue. But the greatest loss was that of Juan Velásquez de León, who, with Alvarado, had command of the rear. It was the post of danger on that night, and he fell, bravely defending it, at an early part of the retreat. He was an excellent officer, possessed of many knightly qualities, though somewhat haughty in his bearing, being one of the best connected cavaliers in the army. The near relation of the governor of Cuba, he looked coldly, at first, on the pretensions of Cortés; but, whether from a conviction that the latter had been wronged, or from personal preference, he afterwards attached himself zealously to his leader's interests. The general requited this with a generous confidence, assigning him, as we have seen, a separate and independent command, where misconduct, or even a mistake, would have been fatal to the expedition. Velásquez proved himself worthy of the trust; and there was no cavalier in the army, with the exception, perhaps, of Sandoval and Alvarado, whose loss would have been so deeply deplored by the commander.—Such were the disastrous results of this terrible passage of the causeway; more disastrous than those occasioned by any other reverse which has stained the Spanish arms in the New World; and which have branded the night on which it happened, in the national annals, with the name of the *noche triste,* "the sad or melancholy night."

IV

Retreat and Battle

THE Mexicans, during the day which followed the retreat of the Spaniards, remained, for the most part, quiet in their own capital, where they found occupation in cleansing the streets and causeways from the dead, which lay festering in heaps that might have bred a pestilence. They may have been employed, also, in paying the last honors to such of their warriors as had fallen, solemnizing the funeral rites by the sacrifice of their wretched prisoners, who, as they contemplated their own destiny, may well have envied the fate of their companions who left their bones on the battle-field. It was most fortunate for the Spaniards, in their extremity, that they had this breathing-time allowed them by the enemy. But Cortés knew that he could not calculate on its continuance, and, feeling how important it was to get the start of his vigilant foe, he ordered his troops to be in readiness to resume their march by midnight. Fires were left burning, the better to deceive the enemy; and at the appointed hour, the little army, without sound of drum or trumpet, but with renewed spirits, sallied forth from the gates of the *teocalli,* within whose hospitable walls they had found such seasonable succour. The place is now indicated by a Christian church, dedicated to the Virgin, under the title of *Nuestra Señora de los Remedios,* whose miraculous image— the very same, *it is said,* brought over by the followers of Cortés—still extends her beneficent sway over the neighbouring capital; and the traveller, who pauses within the precincts of the consecrated fane, may feel that he is standing on the spot made memorable by the refuge it afforded to the Conquerors in the hour of their deepest despondency.

It was arranged that the sick and wounded should occupy the centre, transported on litters, or on the backs of the *tamanes,* while those who were strong enough to keep their seats should mount behind the cavalry. The able-bodied soldiers were ordered to the front and rear, while others protected the flanks, thus affording all the security possible to the invalids.

The retreating army held on its way unmolested under cover of the darkness. But, as morning dawned, they beheld parties of the natives moving over the heights, or hanging at a distance, like a cloud of locusts, on their rear. They did not belong to the capital; but were gathered from the neighbouring country, where the tidings of their rout had already penetrated. The charm, which had hitherto covered the white men, was gone. The dread *Teules* were no longer invincible.

The Spaniards, under the conduct of their Tlascalan guides, took a circuitous route to the north, passing through Quauhtitlan, and round lake Tzompanco, (Zumpango,) thus lengthening their march, but keeping at a distance from the capital. From the eminences, as they passed along, the Indians rolled down heavy stones, mingled with volleys of darts and arrows, on the heads of the soldiers. Some were even bold enough to descend into the plain and assault the extremities of the column. But they were soon beaten off by the horse, and compelled to take refuge among the hills, where the ground was too rough for the rider to follow. Indeed, the Spaniards did not care to do so, their object being rather to fly than to fight.

In this way they slowly advanced, halting at intervals to drive off their assailants when they became too importunate, and greatly distressed by their missiles and their desultory attacks. At night, the troops usually found shelter in some town or hamlet, whence the inhabitants, in anticipation of their approach, had been careful to carry off all the provisions. The Spaniards were soon reduced to the greatest straits for subsistence. Their principal food was the wild cherry, which grew in the woods, or by the roadside. Fortunate were they, if they found a few ears of corn unplucked. More frequently nothing was left but the stalks; and with them, and the like unwholesome fare, they were fain to supply the cravings of the appetite. When a horse happened to be killed, it furnished an extraordinary banquet; and Cortés himself records the fact of his having made one of a party who thus sumptuously regaled themselves, devouring the animal even to his hide.

The wretched soldiers, faint with famine and fatigue, were sometimes seen to drop down lifeless on the road. Others loitered behind, unable to keep up with the march, and fell into the hands of the enemy, who followed in the track of the army like a flock of famished vultures, eager to pounce on the dying and the dead. Others, again, who strayed too far, in their eagerness to procure sustenance, shared the same fate. The number of these, at length, and the consciousness of the cruel lot for which they were reserved, compelled Cortés to introduce stricter discipline, and to enforce it by sterner punishments than he had hitherto done,—though too often ineffectually, such was the indifference to danger, under the overwhelming pressure of present calamity.

In their prolonged distresses, the soldiers ceased to set a value on those very things for which they had once been content to hazard life itself. More than one, who had brought his golden treasure safe through the perils of the *noche triste*, now abandoned it as an intolerable burden; and the rude Indian peasant gleaned up, with wondering delight, the bright fragments of the spoils of the capital.

Through these weary days Cortés displayed his usual serenity and fortitude. He was ever in the post of danger, freely exposing himself in encounters with the enemy; in one of which he received a severe wound in the head, that afterwards gave him much trouble. He fared no better than the humblest soldier, and strove, by his own cheerful countenance and counsels, to fortify the courage of those who faltered assuring them that their sufferings would soon be ended by their arrival in the hospitable "land of bread." His faithful officers coöperated with him in these efforts; and the common file, indeed, especially his own veterans, must be allowed, for the most part, to have shown a full measure of the constancy and power of endurance so characteristic of their nation,—justifying the honest boast of an old chronicler, "that there was no people capable of supporting hunger as the Spaniards, and none of them who were ever more severely tried than the soldiers of Cortés." A similar fortitude was shown by the Tlascalans, trained in a rough school that made them familiar with hardship and privations. Although they sometimes threw themselves on the ground, in the extremity of famine, imploring their gods not to abandon them, they did their duty as warriors, and, far from manifesting coldness towards the Spaniards as the cause of their distress, seemed only the more firmly knit to them by the sense of a common suffering.

On the seventh morning, the army had reached the mountain rampart which overlooks the plains of Otompan, or Otumba, as commonly called, from the Indian city,—now a village,—situated in them. The distance from the capital is hardly nine leagues. But the Spaniards had travelled more than thrice that distance, in their circuitous march round the lakes. This had been performed so slowly, that it consumed a week; two nights of which had been passed in the same quarters, from the absolute necessity of rest. It was not, therefore, till the 7th of July, that they reached the heights commanding the plains which stretched far away towards the territory of Tlascala, in full view of the venerable pyramids of Teotihuacán, two of the most remarkable monuments of the antique American civilization now existing north of the Isthmus. During all the preceding day, they had seen parties of the enemy hovering like dark clouds above the highlands, brandishing their weapons, and calling out in vindictive tones, "Hasten on! You will soon find yourselves where you cannot escape!" words of mysterious import, which they were made fully to comprehend on the following morning. . . .

As the army was climbing the mountain steeps which shut in the Valley of Otompan, the videttes came in with the intelligence, that a powerful body was encamped on the other side, apparently awaiting their approach. The intelligence was soon confirmed by their own eyes, as they turned the crest of the sierra, and saw spread out, below, a mighty host, filling up the whole depth of the valley, and giving to it the appearance, from the white cotton mail of the warriors, of being covered with snow. It consisted of levies from the surrounding country, and especially the populous territory of Tezcuco, drawn together at the instance of Cuitlahua, Montezuma's successor, and now concentrated on this point to dispute the passage of the Spaniards. Every chief of note had taken the field with his whole array gathered under his standard, proudly displaying all the pomp and rude splendor of his military equiment. As far as the eye could reach, were to be seen shields and waving banners, fantastic helmets, forests of shining spears, the bright feather-mail of the chief, and the coarse cotton panoply of his follower, all mingled together in wild confusion, and tossing to and fro like the billows of a troubled ocean. It was a sight to fill the stoutest heart among the Christians with dismay, heightened by the previous expectation of soon reaching the friendly land which was to terminate their wearisome pilgrimage. Even Cortés, as he contrasted the tremendous array before him with his own diminished squadrons, wasted by disease and enfeebled by hunger and fatigue, could not escape the conviction that his last hour had arrived.

But his was not the heart to despond; and he gathered strength from the very extremity of his situation. He had no room for hesitation; for there was no alternative left to him. To escape was impossible. He could not retreat on the capital, from which he had been expelled. He must advance,—cut through the enemy, or perish. He hastily made his dispositions for the fight. He gave his force as broad a front as possible, protecting it on each flank by his little body of horse, now reduced to twenty. Fortunately, he had not allowed the invalids, for the last two days, to mount behind the riders, from a desire to spare the horses, so that these were now in tolerable condition; and, indeed, the whole army had been refreshed by halting, as we have seen, two nights and a day in the same place, a delay, however, which had allowed the enemy time to assemble in such force to dispute its progress.

Cortés instructed his cavaliers not to part with their lances, and to direct them at the face. The infantry were to thrust, not strike, with their swords; passing them, at once through the bodies of their enemies. They were, above all, to aim at the leaders, as the general well knew how much depends on the life of the commander in the wars of barbarians, whose want of subordination makes them impatient of any control but that to which they are accustomed.

He then addressed to his troops a few words of encouragement, as customary with him on the eve of an engagement. He reminded them of the victories they had won with odds nearly as discouraging as the present; thus establishing the superiority of science and discipline over numbers. Numbers, indeed, were of no account, where the arm of the Almighty was on their side. And he bade them have full confidence, that He, who had carried them safely through so many perils, would not now abandon them and his own good cause, to perish by the hand of the infidel. His address was brief, for he read in their looks that settled resolve which rendered words unnecessary. The circumstances of their position spoke more forcibly to the heart of every soldier than any eloquence could have done, filling it with that feeling of desperation, which makes the weak arm strong, and turns the coward into a hero. After they had earnestly commended themselves, therefore, to the protection of God, the Virgin, and St. James, Cortés led his battalions straight against the enemy.

It was a solemn moment,—that, in which the devoted little band, with steadfast countenances, and their usual intrepid step, descended on the plain, to be swallowed up, as it were, in the vast ocean of their enemies. The latter rushed on with impetuosity to meet them, making the mountains ring to their discordant yells and battle-cries, and sending forth volleys of stones and arrows which for a moment shut out the light of day.

But, when the leading files of the two armies closed, the superiority of the Christians was felt, as their antagonists, falling back before the charges of cavalry, were thrown into confusion by their own numbers who pressed on them from behind. The Spanish infantry followed up the blow, and a wide lane was opened in the ranks of the enemy, who, receding on all sides, seemed willing to allow a free passage for their opponents. But it was to return on them with accumulated force, as rallying they poured upon the Christians, enveloping the little army on all sides, which, with its bristling array of long swords and javelins, stood firm,—in the words of a contemporary,—like an islet against which the breakers, roaring and surging, spend their fury in vain. The struggle was desperate of man against man. The Tlascalan seemed to renew his strength, as he fought almost in view of his own native hills; as did the Spaniard, with the horrible doom of the captive before his eyes. Well did the cavaliers do their duty on that day; charging, in little bodies of four of five abreast, deep into the enemy's ranks, riding over the broken files, and by this temporary advantage giving strength and courage to the infantry. Not a lance was there which did not reek with the blood of the infidel. Among the rest, the young captain Sandoval is particularly commemorated for his daring prowess. Managing his fiery steed with easy horsemanship, he darted, when least expected, into the thickest of the *mêlée,* overturning the stanchest warriors, and rejoicing in danger, as if it were his natural element.

But these gallant displays of heroism served only to ingulf the Spaniards deeper and deeper in the mass of the enemy, with scarcely any more chance of cutting their way through his dense and interminable battalions, than of hewing a passage with their swords through the mountains. Many of the Tlascalans and some of the Spaniards had fallen, and not one but had been wounded. Cortés himself had received a second cut on the head, and his horse was so much injured that he was compelled to dismount, and take one from the baggage train, a strong-boned animal, who carried him well through the turmoil of the day. The contest had now lasted several hours. The sun rode high in the heavens, and shed an intolerable fervor over the plain. The Christians, weakened by previous sufferings, and faint with loss of blood, began to relax in their desperate exertions. Their enemies, constantly supported by fresh relays from the rear, were still in good heart, and, quick to perceive their advantage, pressed with redoubled force on the Spaniards. The horse fell back, crowded on the foot; and the latter, in vain seeking a passage amidst the dusky throngs of the enemy, who now closed up the rear, were thrown into some disorder. The tide of battle was setting rapidly against the Christians. The fate of the day would soon be decided; and all that now remained for them seemed to be to sell their lives as dearly as possible.

At this critical moment, Cortés, whose restless eye had been roving round the field in quest of any object that might offer him the means of arresting the coming ruin, rising in his stirrups, descried at a distance, in the midst of the throng, the chief who from his dress and military *cortége* he knew must be the commander of the barbarian forces. He was covered with a rich surcoat of feather-work; and a panache of beautiful plumes, gorgeously set in gold and precious stones, floated above his head. Rising above this, and attached to his back, between the shoulders, was a short staff bearing a golden net for a banner, the singular, but customary, symbol of authority for an Aztec commander. The cacique, whose name was Cihuaca, was borne on a litter, and a body of young warriors, whose gay and ornamented dress showed them to be the flower of the Indian nobles, stood round as a guard of his person and the sacred emblem.

The eagle eye of Cortés no sooner fell on this personage, than it lighted up with triumph. Turning quickly round to the cavaliers at his side, among whom were Sandoval, Olid, Alvarado, and Ávila, he pointed out the chief, exclaiming, "There is our mark! Follow and support me!" Then crying his war-cry, and striking his iron heel into his weary steed, he plunged headlong into the thickest of the press. His enemies fell back, taken by surprise and daunted by the ferocity of the attack. Those who did not were pierced through with his lance, or borne down by the weight of his charger. The cavaliers followed close in the rear. On they swept, with the fury of a thunderbolt, cleaving the solid ranks asunder, strewing their path with the dying and the dead, and bounding over every obstacle in their way. In a few minutes they were in the presence of the Indian commander, and Cortés, overturning his supporters, sprung forward with the strength of a lion, and, striking him through with his lance, hurled him to the ground. A young cavalier, Juan de Salamanca, who had kept close by his general's side, quickly dismounted and despatched the fallen chief. Then tearing away his banner, he presented it to Cortés, as a trophy to which he had the best claim. It was all the work of a moment. The guard, overpowered by the suddenness of the onset, made little resistance, but, flying, communicated their own panic to their comrades. The tidings of the loss soon spread over the field. The Indians, filled with consternation, now thought only of escape. In their blind terror, their numbers augmented their confusion. They trampled on one another, fancying it was the enemy in their rear.

The Spaniards and Tlascalans were not slow to avail themselves of the marvellous change in their affairs. Their fatigue, their wounds, hunger, thirst, all were forgotton in the eagerness for vengeance; and they followed up the flying foe, dealing death at every stroke, and taking ample retribution for all they had suffered in the bloody marshes of Mexico. Long did they pursue, till, the enemy having abandoned the field, they returned sated with slaughter to glean the booty which he had left. It was great, for the ground was covered with the bodies of chiefs, at whom the Spaniards, in obedience to the general's instructions, had particularly aimed; and their dresses displayed all the barbaric pomp of ornament, in which the Indian warrior delighted. When his men had thus indemnified themselves, in some degree, for their late reverses, Cortés called them again under their banners; and, after offering up a grateful acknowledgement to the Lord of Hosts for their miraculous preservation, they renewed their march across the now deserted valley. The sun was declining in the heavens, but, before the shades of evening had gathered around, they reached an Indian temple on an eminence, which afforded a strong and commodious position for the night.

Such was the famous battle of Otompan,—or Otumba, as commonly called, from the Spanish corruption of the name. It was fought on the 8th of July, 1520. The whole amount of the Indian force is reckoned by Castilian writers at two hundred thousand! that of the slain at twenty thousand! Those who admit to the first part of the estimate will find no difficulty in receiving the last. It is about as difficult to form an accurate calculation of the numbers of a disorderly savage multitude, as of the pebbles on the beach, or the scattered leaves in autumn. Yet it was, undoubtedly, one of the most remarkable victories ever achieved in the New World. And this, not merely on account of the disparity of the forces, but of their unequal condition. For the Indians were in all their strength, while the Christians were wasted by disease, famine, and long protracted sufferings; without cannon or fire-arms, and deficient in the military apparatus which had so often struck terror into their barbarian foe,—deficient even in the terrors of a victorious name. But they had discipline on their side, desperate resolve, and implicit confidence in their commander. That they should have triumphed against such odds furnishes an inference of the same kind as that established by the victories of the European over the semi-civilized hordes of Asia.

Yet even here all must not be referred to superior discipline and tactics. For the battle would certainly have been lost, had it not been for the fortunate death of the Indian general. And, although the selection of the victim may be called the result of calculation, yet it was by the most precarious chance that he was thrown in the way of the Spaniards. It is, indeed, one among many examples of the influence of fortune in determining the fate of military operations. The star of Cortés was in the ascendant. Had it been otherwise, not a Spaniard would have survived that day, to tell the bloody tale of the battle of Otumba.

V

Refuge in Tlaxcala

ON the following morning, the army broke up its encampment at an early hour. The enemy do not seem to have made an attempt to rally. Clouds of skirmishers, however, were seen during the morning, keeping at a respectful distance, though, occasionally venturing near enough to salute the Spaniards with a volley of missiles.

On a rising ground they discovered a fountain, a blessing not too often met with in these arid regions, and gratefully commemorated by the Christians, for the refreshment afforded by its cool and abundant waters. A little further on they described the rude works which served as the bulwark and boundary of the Tlascalan territory. At the sight, the allies sent up a joyous shout of congratulation, in which the Spaniards heartily joined, as they felt they were soon to be on friendly and hospitable ground.

But these feelings were speedily followed by others of a different nature; and, as they drew nearer the territory, their minds were disturbed with the most painful apprehensions as to their reception by the people among whom they were bringing desolation and mourning, and who might so easily, if ill-disposed, take advantage of their present crippled condition. "Thoughts like these," says Cortés, "weighed as heavily on my spirit as any which I ever experienced in going to battle with the Aztecs." Still he put, as usual, a good face on the matter, and encouraged his men to confide in their allies, whose past conduct had afforded every ground for trusting to their fidelity in future. He cautioned them, however, as their own strength was much impaired, to be most careful to give no umbrage, or ground for jealousy, to their high-spirited allies. "Be but on your guard," continued the intrepid general, "and we have still stout hearts and strong hands to carry us through the midst of them!" With these anxious surmises, bidding adieu to the Aztec domain, the Christian army crossed the frontier, and once more trod the soil of the Republic.

The first place at which they halted was the town of Huejotlipán, a place of about twelve or fifteen thousand inhabitants. They were kindly greeted by the people, who came out to receive them, inviting the troops to their habitations, and administering all the relief of their simple hospitality. Yet this was not so disinterested, according to some of the Spaniards, as to prevent their expecting in requital a share of the plunder taken in the late action. Here the weary forces remained two or three days, when the news of their arrival having reached the capital, not more than four or five leagues distant, the old chief, Maxixca, their efficient friend on their former visit, and Xicotencatl, the young warrior, who, it will be remembered, had commanded the troops of his nation in their bloody encounters with the Spaniards, came with a numerous concourse of the citizens to welcome the fugitives to Tlascala. Maxixca, cordially embracing the Spanish commander, testified the deepest sympathy for his misfortunes. That the white men could so long have withstood the confederated power of the Aztecs was proof enough of their marvellous prowess. "We have made common cause together," said the lord of Tlascala, " and we have common injuries to avenge; and, come weal or come woe, be assured we will prove true and loyal friends, and stand by you to the death."

This cordial assurance and sympathy, from one who exercised a control over the public counsels beyond any other ruler, effectually dispelled the doubts that lingered in the mind of Cortés. He readily accepted his invitation to continue his march, at once, to the capital, where he would find so much better accommodations for his army, than in a small town on the frontier. The sick and wounded, placed in hammocks, were borne on the shoulders of the friendly natives; and, as the troops drew near the city, the inhabitants came flocking out in crowds to meet them, rending the air with joyous acclamations, and wild bursts of their rude Indian minstrelsy. Amidst the general jubilee, however, were heard sounds of wailing and sad lament, as some unhappy relative or friend, looking earnestly into the diminished files of their countrymen, sought in vain for some dear and familiar countenance, and, as they turned disappointed away, gave utterance to their sorrow in tones that touched the heart of every soldier in the army. With these mingled accompaniments of joy and woe,—the motley web of human life,—the way-worn columns of Cortés at length reëntered the republican capital.

The general and his suite were lodged in the rude, but spacious, palace of Maxixca. The rest of the army took up their quarters in the district over which the Tlascalan lord presided. Here they continued several weeks, until, by the attentions of the hospitable citizens, and such medical treatment as their humble science could supply, the wounds of the soldiers were healed, and they recovered from the debility to which they had been reduced by their long and unparalleled sufferings. Cortés was one of those who suffered severely. He lost the use of two of the fingers of his left hand. He had received, besides, two injuries on the head; one of which was so much exasperated by his subsequent fatigues and excitement of mind, that it assumed an alarming appearance. A part of the bone was obliged to be removed. A fever ensued, and for several days the hero, who had braved danger and death in their most terrible forms, lay stretched on his bed, as helpless as an infant. His excellent constitution, however, got the better of disease, and he was, at length, once more enabled to resume his customary activity.—The Spaniards, with politic generosity, requited the hospitality of their hosts by sharing with them the spoils of their recent victory, and Cortés especially rejoiced the heart of Maxixca, by presenting him with the military trophy which he had won from the Indian commander.

But while the Spaniards were thus recruiting their health and spirits under the friendly treatment of their allies, and recovering the confidence and tranquillity of mind which had

sunk under their hard reverses, they received tidings, from time
to time, which showed that their late disaster had not been
confined to the Mexican capital. On his descent from Mexico
to encounter Narváez, Cortés had brought with him a quantity
of gold, which he left for safe keeping at Tlascala. To this
was added a considerable sum, collected by the unfortunate
Velásquez de León, in his expedition to the coast, as well as
contributions from other sources. From the unquiet state of
the capital, the general thought it best, on his return there,
still to leave the treasure under the care of a number of
invalid soldiers, who, when in marching condition, were to
rejoin him in Mexico. A party from Vera Cruz, consisting of
five horsemen and forty foot, had since arrived at Tlascala, and,
taking charge of the invalids and treasure, undertook to escort
them to the capital. He now learned that they had been in-
ercepted on the route, and all cut off, with the entire loss of
the treasure. Twelve other soldiers, marching in the same
direction, had been massacred in the neighbouring province of
Tepeaca; and accounts continually arrived of some unfortunate Castilian, who, presuming on the respect hitherto shown
to his countrymen, and ignorant of the disasters in the capital,
had fallen a victim to the fury of the enemy.

These dismal tidings filled the mind of Cortés with gloomy
apprehensions for the fate of the settlement at Villa Rica,—
the last stay of their hopes. He despatched a trusty messenger, at once, to that place; and had the inexpressible satisfaction
to receive a letter in return from the commander of the garrison, acquainting him with the safety of the colony, and its
friendly relations with the neighbouring Totonacs. It was the
best guaranty of the fidelity of the latter, that they had offended
the Mexicans too deeply to be forgiven.

While the affairs of Cortés wore so gloomy an aspect without,
he had to experience an annoyance scarcely less serious from
the discontents of his followers. Many of them had fancied
that their late appalling reverses would put an end to the
expedition; or at least, postpone all thoughts of resuming it

for the present. But they knew little of Cortés who reasoned thus. Even while tossing on his bed of sickness, he was ripening in his mind fresh schemes for retrieving his honor, and for recovering the empire which had been lost more by another's rashness than his own. This was apparent, as he become convalescent, from the new regulations he made respecting the army, as well as from the orders sent to Vera Cruz for fresh reinforcements.

The knowledge of all this occasioned much disquietude to the disaffected soldiers. They were, for the most part, the ancient followers of Narváez, on whom, as we have seen, the brunt of the war had fallen the heaviest. Many of them possessed property in the Islands, and had embarked on this expedition chiefly from the desire of increasing it. But they had gathered neither gold nor glory in Mexico. Their present service filled them only with disgust; and the few, comparatively, who had been so fortunate as to survive, languished to return to their rich mines and pleasant farms in Cuba, bitterly cursing the day when they had left them.

Finding their complaints little heeded by the general, they prepared a written remonstrance, in which they made their demand more formally. They represented the rashness of persisting in the enterprise in his present impoverished state, without arms or ammunition, almost without men; and this, too, against a powerful enemy, who had been more than a match for him with all the strength of his late resources. It was madness to think of it. The attempt would bring them all to the sacrifice-block. Their only course was to continue their march to Vera Cruz. Every hour of delay might be fatal. The garrison in that place might be overwhelmed from want of strength to defend itself; and thus their last hope would be annihilated. But, once there, they might wait in comparative security for such reinforcements as would join them from abroad; while in case of failure they could the more easily make their escape. They concluded, with insisting on being permitted to return, at once, to the port of Villa Rica. This

petition, or rather remonstrance, was signed by all the disaffected soldiers, and, after being formally attested by the
royal notary, was presented to Cortés.

It was a trying circumstance for him. What touched him
most nearly was, to find the name of his friend, the secretary
Duero, to whose good offices he had chiefly owed his command,
at the head of the paper. He was not, however, to be shaken
from his purpose for a moment; and while all outward resources seemed to be fading away, and his own friends faltered,
or failed him, he was still true to himself. He knew that to
retreat to Vera Cruz would be to abandon the enterprise. Once
there, his army would soon find a pretext and a way for breaking up and returning to the Islands. All his ambitious schemes
would be blasted. The great prize, already once in his grasp,
would then be lost for ever. He would be a ruined man.

In his celebrated letter to Charles the Fifth, he says, that, in
reflecting on his position, he felt the truth of the old adage,
"that fortune favors the brave. The Spaniards were the followers of the Cross; and, trusting in the infinite goodness and
mercy of God, he could not believe that He would suffer them
and his own good cause thus to perish among the heathen. He
was resolved, therefore, not to descend to the coast, but at
all hazards to retrace his steps and beard the enemy again in
his capital." . . . .

DISCONTENT once more raised its voice among the Spaniards, especially among the Narváez men. Scarcely had Cortés met this challenge with a stirring appeal to their pride, loyalty, and honor when friction arose between Indians and Spaniards. Once this new storm of discontent subsided and he found his men recuperated from their wounds, Cortés had plans which he wanted to put into effect.

VI

Campaigns and Plans

THE Spanish commander, reassured by the result of the deliberations in the Tlascalan senate, now resolved on active operations, as the best means of dissipating the spirit of faction and discontent inevitably fostered by a life of idleness. He proposed to exercise his troops, at first, against some of the neighbouring tribes who had laid violent hands on such of the Spaniards as, confiding in their friendly spirit, had passed through their territories. Among these were the Tepeacans, a people often engaged in hostility with the Tlascalans, and who, as mentioned in a preceding Chapter, had lately massacred twelve Spaniards in their march to the capital. An expedition, against them would receive the ready support of his allies, and would assert the dignity of the Spanish name, much dimmed in the estimation of the natives by the late disasters.

The Tepeacans were a powerful tribe of the same primitive stock as the Aztecs, to whom they acknowledged allegiance. They had transferred this to the Spaniards, on their first march into the country, intimidated by the bloody defeats of their Tlascalan neighbours. But, since the troubles in the capital, they had again submitted to the Aztec sceptre. Their capital, now a petty village, was a flourishing city at the time of the Conquest, situated in the fruitful plains that stretch far away towards the base of Orizaba. The province contained, moreover,

several towns of considerable size, filled with a bold and warlike population.

As these Indians had once acknowledged the authority of
Castile, Cortés and his officers regarded their present conduct
in the light of the rebellion, and, in a council of war, it was decided that those engaged in the late massacre had fairly incurred the doom of slavery. Before proceeding against them,
however, the general sent a summons requiring their submission, and offering full pardon for the past, but, in case of refusal, menacing them with the severest retribution. To this the
Indians, now in arms, returned a contemptuous answer, challenging the Spaniards to meet them in fight, as they were in
want of victims for their sacrifices.

Cortés, without further delay, put himself at the head of
his small corps of Spaniards, and a large reinforcement of Tlascalan warriors. They were led by the younger Xicotencatl, who
now appeared willing to bury his recent animosity, and desirous to take a lesson in war under the chief who had so often
foiled him in the field.

The Tepeacans received their enemy on their borders. A
bloody battle followed, in which the Spanish horse were somewhat embarrassed by the tall maize that covered part of the
plain. They were successful in the end, and the Tepeacans,
after holding their ground like good warriors, were at length
routed with great slaughter. A second engagement, which took
place a few days after, was followed by like decisive results;
and victorious Spaniards with their allies, marching straightway on the city of Tepeaca, entered it in triumph. No further
resistance was attempted by the enemy, and he whole province, to avoid further calamities, eagerly tendered its submission. Cortés, however, inflicted the meditated chastisements
on the places implicated in the massacre. The inhabitants were
branded with a hot iron as slaves, and, after the royal fifth had
been reserved, were distributed between his own men and the
allies. The Spaniards were familiar with the system of *repartimientos* established in the Islands: but this was the first ex-

ample of slavery in New Spain. It was justified, in the opinion of the general and his military casuists, by the aggravated offences of the party. The sentence, however, was not countenanced by the Crown, which as the colonial legislation abundantly shows, was ever at issue with the craving and mercenary spirit of the colonist.

Satisfied with this display of his vengeance, Cortés now established his head-quarters at Tepeaca, which, situated in a cultivated country, afforded easy means for maintaining an army, while its position on the Mexican frontier made it a good *point d'appui* for future operations.

The Aztec government, since it had learned the issue of its negotiations at Tlascala, had been diligent in fortifying its frontier in that quarter. The garrisons usually maintained there were strengthened, and large bodies of men were marched in the same direction, with orders to occupy the strong positions on the borders. The conduct of these troops was in their usual style of arrogance and extortion, and greatly disgusted the inhabitants of the country.

Among the places thus garrisoned by the Aztecs was Quauhquechollan,* a city containing thirty thousand inhabitants, according to the historians, and lying to the south-west twelve leagues or more from the Spanish quarters. It stood at the extremity of a deep valley, resting against a bold range of hills, or rather, mountains, and flanked by two rivers with exceedingly high and precipitous banks. The only avenue, by which the town could be easily approached, was protected by a stone wall more than twenty feet high and of great thickness. Into this place, thus strongly defended by art as well as by nature, the Aztec emperor had thrown a garrison of several thousand warriors, while a much more formidable force occupied the heights commanding the city.

The cacique of this strong post, impatient of the Mexican yoke, sent to Cortés, inviting him to march to his relief, and promising a coöperation of the citizens in an assault on the Az-

* Guacachula. C.H.G.

tec quarters. The general eagerly embraced the proposal, and detached Christóval de Olid, with two hundred Spaniards and a strong body of Tlascalans, to support the friendly cacique. On the way, Olid was joined by many volunteers from the Indian city and from the neighbouring capital of Cholula, all equally pressing their services. The number and eagerness of these auxiliaries excited suspicions in the bosom of the cavalier. They were strengthened by the surmises of the soldiers of Narváez, whose imaginations were still haunted, it seems, by the horrors of the *noche triste,* and who saw in the friendly alacrity of their new allies evidence of an insidious understanding with the Aztecs. Olid, catching this distrust, made a countermarch on Cholula, where he seized the suspected chiefs, who had been most forward in offering their services, and sent them under a strong guard to Cortés.

The general, after a careful examination, was satisfied of the integrity of the suspected parties. He, expressing his deep regret at the treatment they had received, made them such amends as he could by liberal presents; and, as he now saw the impropriety of committing an affair of such importance to other hands, put himself at the head of his remaining force, and effected a junction with his officer in Cholula.

He had arranged with the cacique of the city against which he was marching, that, on the appearance of the Spaniards, the inhabitants should rise on the garrison. Every thing succeeded as he had planned. No sooner had the Christian battalions defiled on the plain before the town, than the inhabitants attacked the garrison with the utmost fury. The latter, abandoning the outer defences of the place, retreated to their own quarters in the principal *teocalli,* where they maintained a hard struggle with their adversaries. In the heat of it, Cortés, at the head of his little body of horse, rode into the place, and directed the assault in person. The Aztecs made a fierce defence. But fresh troops constantly arriving to support the assailants, the works were stormed, and every one of the garrison was put to the sword.

The Mexican forces, meanwhile, stationed on the neighbouring eminences, had marched down to the support of their countrymen in the town, and formed in order of battle in the suburbs, where they were encountered by the Tlascalan levies.
"They mustered," says Cortés, speaking of the enemy, "at least,
thirty thousand men, and it was a brave sight for the eye to
look on,—such a beautiful array of warriors glistening with
gold and jewels and variegated feather-work!" The action was
well contested between the two Indian armies. The suburbs
were set on fire, and, in the midst of the flames, Cortés and
his squadrons, rushing on the enemy, at length broke their
array, and compelled them to fall back in disorder into the
narrow gorge of the mountain, from which they had lately
descended. The pass was rough and precipitous. Spaniards and
Tlascalans followed close in the rear, and the light troops, scaling the high wall of the valley, poured down on the enemy's
flanks. The heat was intense, and both parties were so much
exhausted by their efforts, that it was with difficulty, says the
chronicler, that the one could pursue, or the other fly. They
were not too weary, however, to slay. The Mexicans were routed
with terrible slaughter. They found no pity from their Indian foes, who had a long account of injuries to settle with them.
Some few sought refuge by flying higher up into the fastnesses
of the sierra. They were followed by their indefatigable enemy,
until, on the bald summit of the ridge, they reached the Mexican encampment. It covered a wide tract of ground. Various
utensils, ornamented dresses, and articles of luxury, were scattered round, and the number of slaves in attendance showed
the barbaric pomp with which the nobles of Mexico went to
their campaigns. It was a rich booty for the victors, who spread
over the deserted camp, and loaded themselves with the spoil,
until the gathering darkness warned them to descend.

Cortés followed up the blow by assaulting the strong town
of Itzocan,* held, also by a Mexican garrison and situated in
the depths of a green valley watered by artificial canals, and

* Izucar. C.H.G.

smiling in all the rich abundance of this fruitful region of the plateau. The place, though stoutly defended, was stormed and carried; the Aztecs were driven across a river which ran below the town, and, although the light bridges that traversed it were broken down in the flight, whether by design or accident, the Spaniards, fording and swimming the stream as they could, found their way to the opposite bank, following up the chase with the eagerness of bloodhounds. Here, too, the booty was great; and the Indian auxiliaries flocked by thousands to the banners of the chief who so surely led them on to victory and plunder.

Soon afterwards, Cortés returned to his headquarters at Tepeaca. Thence he detached his officers on expeditions which were usually successful. Sandoval, in particular, marched against a large body of the enemy lying between the camp and Vera Cruz; defeated them in two decisive battles, and thus restored the communications with the port.

The result of these operations was the reduction of that populous and cultivated territory which lies between the great *volcán,* on the west, and the mighty skirts of Orizaba, on the east. Many places, also, in the neighbouring province of Mixtecapán acknowledged the authority of the Spaniards, and others from the remote region of Oaxaca sent to claim their protection. The conduct of Cortés towards his allies had gained him great credit for disinterestedness and equity. The Indian cities in the adjacent territory appealed to him, as their umpire, in their differences with one another, and cases of disputed succession in their governments were referred to his arbitration. By his discreet and moderate policy, he insensibly acquired an ascendency over their counsels, which had been denied to the ferocious Aztec. His authority extended wider and wider every day; and a new empire grew up, in the very heart of the land, forming a counterpoise to the colossal power which had so long overshadowed it.

Cortés now felt himself strong enough to put in execution

the plans for recovering the capital, over which he had been brooding ever since the hour of his expulsion. He had greatly undervalued the resources of the Aztec monarchy. He was now aware, from bitter experience, that, tŏ vanquish it, his own forces, and all he could hope to muster, would be incompetent, without a very extensive support from the Indians themselves. A large army would, moreover, require large supplies for its maintenance, and these could not be regularly obtained, during a protracted siege, without the friendly coöperation of the natives. On such support he might now safely calculate from Tlascala, and the other Indian territories, whose warriors were so eager to serve under his banners. His past acquaintance with them had instructed him in their national character and system of war; while the natives who had fought under his command, if they had caught little of the Spanish tactics, had learned to act in concert with the white men, and to obey him implicitly as their commander. This was a considerable improvement in such wild and disorderly levies, and greatly augmented the strength derived from numbers.

Experience showed, that, in a future conflict with the capital, it would not do to trust to the causeways, but that, to succeed, he must command the lake. He proposed, therefore, to build a number of vessels like those constructed under his orders in Montezuma's time, and afterwards destroyed by the inhabitants. For this he had still the services of the same experienced ship-builder, Martín López, who, as we have seen, had fortunately escaped the slaughter of the "Melancholy Night." Cortés now sent this man to Tlascala, with orders to build thirteen brigantines, which might be taken to pieces and carried on the shoulders of the Indians to be launched on the waters of Lake Tezcuco. The sails, rigging, and iron work, were to be brought from Vera Cruz, where they had been stored since their removal from the dismantled ships. It was a bold conception, that of constructing a fleet to be transported across forest and mountain before it was launched on its destined waters! But it suited the daring genius of Cortés, who, with the coöperation of his stanch Tlascalan confederates, did not doubt his ability to carry it into execution. . . .

> LUCKILY *reinforcements by the shipload landed upon the coast of Mexico in this period. As the army grew in numbers, it reëstablished its confidence by campaigning in the vicinity of Tlaxcala. Thus the campaigns not only gave tone to the invading army, they also reaffirmed Tlaxcalan loyalty to the Spaniards. In the offing loomed a renewal of hostilities between Spaniard and Aztec.*

While the events related in the preceding Chapter were passing, an important change had taken place in the Aztec monarchy. Montezuma's brother and successor, Cuitlahua, had suddenly died of the small-pox, after a brief reign of four months,—brief, but glorious, for it had witnessed the overthrow of the Spaniards and their expulsion from Mexico. On the death of their warlike chief, the electors were convened, as usual, to supply the vacant throne. It was an office of great responsibility in the dark hour of their fortunes. The *teoteuctli,* or high-priest, invoked the blessing of the supreme God on their deliberations. His prayer is still extant. It was the last one ever made on a similar occasion in Anahuac, and a few extracts from it may interest the reader, as a specimen of Aztec eloquence.

"O Lord! thou knowest that the days of our sovereign are at an end, for thou hast placed him beneath thy feet. He abides in the place of his retreat; he has trodden the path which we are all to tread; he has gone to the house whither we are all to follow,—the house of eternal darkness, where no light cometh. He is gathered to his rest, and no one henceforth shall disquiet him. . . . All these were the princes, his predecessors, who sat on the imperial throne, directing the affairs of thy kingdom; for thou art the universal lord and emperor, by whose will and movement the whole world is directed; thou needest not the counsel of another. They laid down the intolerable burden of government, and left it to him, their successor. Yet he sojourned but a few days in his kingdom,—but a few days had we enjoyed his presence, when thou summonedst him away to follow those who had ruled over the land before him. And great cause has he for thankfulness, that thou hast relieved him from so grievous a load, and placed him in tranquillity and rest. ... Who now shall order matters for the good of the people and the realm? Who shall appoint the judges to administer justice to thy people? Who now shall bid the drum and the flute to sound, and gather together the veteran soldiers and the men mighty in battle? Our Lord and our Defence! wilt thou, in thy wisdom, elect one who shall be worthy to sit on the throne of thy kingdom; one who shall bear the grievous burden of government; who shall comfort and cherish thy poor people, even as the mother cherisheth her offspring? ... O Lord most merciful! pour forth thy light and thy splendor over this thine empire! ... Order it so that thou shalt be served in all, and through all."

The choice fell on Quauhtemotzin, or Guatemozin,* as euphoniously corrupted by the Spaniards. He was nephew to the two last monarchs, and married his cousin, the beautiful princess Tecuichpo, Montezuma's daughter. "He was not more than twenty-five years old, and elegant in his person for an Indian," says one who had seen him often; "valiant, and so terrible, that his followers trembled in his presence." He did not shrink from the perilous post that was offered to him; and, as he saw the tempest gathering darkly around, he prepared to meet it like a man. Though young, he had ample experience in military matters, and had distinguished himself above all others in the bloody conflicts of the capital. He bore a sort of religious hatred to the Spaniards, like that which Hannibal is said to have sworn, and which he certainly cherished, against his Roman foes.

By means of his spies, Guatemozin made himself acquainted

* Cuauhtémoc. C.H.G.

with the movements of the Spaniards, and their design to besiege the capital. He prepared for it by sending away the useless part of the population, while he called in his potent vassals from the neighbourhood. He continued the plans of his predecessor for strengthening the defences of the city, reviewed his troops, and stimulated them by prizes to excel in their exercises. He made harangues to his soldiers to rouse them to a spirit of desperate resistance. He encouraged his vassals throughout the empire to attack the white men wherever they were to be met with, setting a price on their heads, as well as on the persons of all who should be brought alive to him in Mexico. And it was no uncommon thing for the Spaniards to find hanging up in the temples of the conquered places the arms and accoutrements of their unfortunate countrymen who had been seized and sent to the capital for sacrifice.—Such was the young monarch who was now called to the tottering throne of the Aztecs; worthy, by his bold and magnanimous nature, to sway the sceptre of his country, in the most flourishing period of her renown; and now, in her distress, devoting himself in the true spirit of a patriot prince to uphold her falling fortunes, or bravely perish with them.

We must now return to the Spaniards in Tlascala, where we left them preparing to resume their march on Mexico. Their commander had the satisfaction to see his troops tolerably complete in their appointments; varying, indeed, according to the condition of the different reinforcements which had arrived from time to time; but, on the whole, superior to those of the army with which he had first invaded the country. His whole force fell little short of six hundred men; forty of whom were cavalry, together with eighty arquebusiers and crossbow-men. The rest were armed with sword and target, and with the copper-headed pike of Chinantla. He had nine cannon of a moderate calibre, and was indifferently supplied with powder.

As his forces were drawn up in order of march, Cortés rode through the ranks, exhorting his soldiers, as usual with him on these occasions, to be true to themselves, and the enterprise in which they were embarked. He told them, they were to march against *rebels*, who had once acknowledged allegiance to the Spanish sovereign; against barbarians, the enemies of their religion. They were to fight the battles of the Cross and of the crown; to fight their own battles, to wipe away the stain from their arms, to avenge their injuries, and the loss of the dear companions who had been butchered on the field or on the accursed altar of sacrifice. Never was there a war which offered higher incentives to the Christian cavalier; a war which opened to him riches and renown in this life, and an imperishable glory in that to come.

Thus did the politic chief touch all the secret springs of devotion, honor, and ambition in the bosoms of his martial audience, waking the mettle of the most sluggish before leading him on the perilous emprise. They answered with acclamations, that they were ready to die in defence of the Faith; and would either conquer, or leave their bones with those of their countrymen in the waters of the Tezcuco.

The army of the allies next passed in review before the general. It is variously estimated by writers from a hundred and ten to a hundred and fifty thousand soldiers! The palpable exaggeration, no less than the discrepancy, shows that little reliance can be placed on any estimate. It is certain, however, that it was a multitudinous array, consisting not only of the flower of the Tlascalan warriors, but of those of Cholula, Tepeaca, and the neighbouring territories, which had submitted to the Castilian crown.

They were armed, after the Indian fashion, with bows and arrows, the glassy *maquahuitl*, and the long pike, which formidable weapon, Cortés, as we have seen, had introduced among his own troops. They were divided into battalions, each having its own banner, displaying the appropriate arms or emblem of its company. The four great chiefs of the nation marched in the van; three of them venerable for their years, and showing, in the insignia which decorated their persons, the evidence of many a glorious feat in arms. The panache of many-colored plumes floated from their casques, set in emeralds or other precious stones. Their *escaupil,* or stuffed doublet of cotton, was covered with the graceful surcoat of feather-work, and their feet were protected by sandals embossed with gold. Four young pages followed, bearing their weapons, and four others supported as many standards, on which were emblazoned the armorial bearings of the four great divisions of the republic. The Tlascalans, though frugal in the extreme, and rude in their way of life, were as ambitious of display in their military attire as any of the races on the plateau. As they defiled before Cortés, they saluted him by waving their banners and by a flourish of their wild music, which the general acknowledged by courteously raising his cap as they passed. The Tlascalan warriors, and especially the younger Xicotencatl, their commander, affected to imitate their European masters, not merely in their tactics, but in minuter matters of military etiquette.

Cortés, with the aid of Marina, made a brief address to his Indian allies. He reminded them that he was going to fight their battles against their ancient enemies. He called on them to support him in a manner worthy of their renowned republic. To those who remained at home, he committed the charge of aiding in the completion of the brigantines, on which the success of the expedition so much depended; and he requested that none would follow his banner, who were not prepared to remain till the final reduction of the capital. This address was answered by shouts, or rather yells, of defiance, showing the exultation felt by his Indian confederates at the prospect of at last avenging their manifold wrongs, and humbling their haughty enemy.

Before setting out on the expedition, Cortés published a code of ordinances, as he terms them, or regulations for the army, too remarkable to be passed over in silence. The preamble sets forth, that in all institutions, whether divine or human,—if the latter have any worth,—order is the great law. The ancient chronicles inform us, that the greatest captains in past times owed their successes quite as much to the wisdom of their ordinances, as to their own valor and virtue. The situation of the Spaniards eminently demanded such a code; a mere handful of men as they were, in the midst of countless enemies, most cunning in the management of thēir weapons and in thc art of war. The instrument then reminds the army that the conversion of the heathen is the work most acceptable in the eye of the Almighty, and one that will be sure to receive his support. It calls on every soldier to regard this as the prime object of the expedition, *without which the war would be manifestly unjust, and every acquisition made by it, a robbery.*

The general solemnly protests, that the principal motive, which operates in his own bosom, is the desire to wean the natives from their gloomy idolatry, and to impart to them the knowledge of a purer faith; and next, to recover for his master, the emperor, the dominions which of right belong to him.

The ordinances then prohibit all blasphemy against God or the saints; a vice much more frequent among Catholic than Protestant nations, arising, perhaps, less from difference of religion, than of physical temperament,—for the warm sun of the South, under which Catholicism prevails, stimulates the sensibilities to the more violent expression of passion.

Another law is directed against gaming, to which thc Spaniards, in all ages, have been peculiarly addicted. Cortés, making allowance for the strong national propensity, authorizes it under certain limitations; but prohibits the use of dice altogether. Then follow other laws against brawls and private combats, against personal taunts and the irritating sarcasms of rival companies; rules for the more perfect discipline of the troops, whether in camp or the field. Among others, is one prohibiting any captain, under pain of death, from charging the enemy without orders; a practice, noticed as most pernicious and of too frequent occurrence,—showing the impetuous spirit and want of true military subordination in· the bold cavaliers who followed the standard of Cortés.

The last ordinance prohibits any man, officer or private, from securing to his own use any of the booty taken from the enemy, whether it be gold, silver, precious stones, feather-work, stuffs, slaves, or other commodity, however or wherever obtained, in the city or in the field; and requires him to bring it forthwith to the presence of the general, or the officer appointed to receive it. The violation of this law was punished with death and confiscation of property. So severe an edict may be thought to prove, that, however much the *Conquistador* may have been influenced by spiritual considerations, he was by no means insensible to those of a temporal character. . . .

BOOK SIX

Siege and Surrender of Mexico

THE military ordinances were proclaimed to the as-
sembled troops on December 26, 1520, and two days
later Cortés led his determined army westward. At
this time their objective in the Valley of Mexico was
the populous city of Texcoco on the eastern shore of
the lake of the same name. This became the forward
base of the invaders.

I

The Return to the Valley of Mexico

IT was the plan of Cortés, on entering the Valley, to commence
operations by reducing the subordinate cities before striking
at the capital itself, which, like some goodly tree, whose roots
had been severed one after another, would be thus left without
support against the fury of the tempest. The first point of
attack which he selected was the ancient city of Iztapalapan;
a place containing fifty thousand inhabitants, according to his
own account, and situated about six leagues distant, on the
narrow tongue of land, which divides the waters of the great
salt lake from those of the fresh. It was the private domain of
the last sovereign of Mexico; where, as the reader may remember, he entertained the white men, the night before their entrance into the capital, and astonished them by the display of
his princely gardens. To this monarch they owed no good-will,
for he had conducted the operations on the *noche triste.* He
was, indeed, no more; but the people of his city entered heartily
into his hatred of the strangers, and were now the most loyal
vassals of the Mexican crown.

In a week after his arrival at his new quarters, Cortés, leaving the command of the garrison to Sandoval, marched against
this Indian city, at the head of two hundred Spanish foot, eighteen horse, and between three and four thousand Tlascalans.
Their route lay along the eastern border of the lake, gemmed

with many a bright town and hamlet, or, unlike its condition at the present day, darkened with overhanging groves of cypress and cedar, and occasionally opening a broad expanse to their view, with the Queen of the Valley rising gloriously from the waters, as if proudly conscious of her supremacy over the fair cities around her. Further on, the eye ranged along the dark line of causeway connecting Mexico with the mainland, and suggesting many a bitter recollection to the Spaniards.

They quickened their step, and had advanced within two leagues of their point of destination, when they were encountered by a strong Aztec force, drawn up to dispute their progress. Cortés instantly gave them battle. The barbarians showed their usual courage; but, after some hard fighting, were compelled to give way before the steady valor of the Spanish infantry, backed by the desperate fury of the Tlascalans, whom the sight of an Aztec seemed to inflame almost to madness. The enemy retreated in disorder, closely followed by the Spaniards. When they had arrived within half a league of Iztapalapan, they observed a number of canoes filled with Indians, who appeared to be laboring on the mole which hemmed in the waters of the salt lake. Swept along in the tide of pursuit, they gave little heed to it, but, following up the chase, entered pell-mell with the fugitives into the city.

The houses stood some of them on dry ground, some on piles in the water. The former were deserted by the inhabitants, most of whom had escaped in canoes across the lake, leaving, in their haste, their effects behind them. The Tlascalans poured at once into the vacant dwellings and loaded themselves with booty; while the enemy, making the best of their way through this part of the town, sought shelter in the buildings erected over the water, or among the reeds which sprung from its shallow bottom. In the houses were many of the citizens also, who still lingered with their wives and children, unable to find the means of transporting themselves from the scene of danger.

Cortés, supported by his own men, and by such of the allies as could be brought to obey his orders, attacked the enemy in this last place of their retreat. Both parties fought up to their girdles in the water. A desperate struggle ensued; as the Aztec fought with the fury of a tiger driven to bay by the huntsmen. It was all in vain. The enemy was overpowered in every quarter. The citizen shared the fate of the soldier, and a pitiless massacre succeeded, without regard to sex or age. Cortés endeavoured to stop it. But it would have been as easy to call away the starving wolf from the carcass he was devouring, as the Tlascalan who had once tasted the blood of an enemy. More than six thousand, including women and children, according to the Conqueror's own statement, perished in the conflict.

Darkness meanwhile had set in; but it was dispelled in some measure by the light of the burning houses, which the troops had set on fire in different parts of the town. Their insulated position, it is true, prevented the flames from spreading from one building to another, but the solitary masses threw a strong and lurid glare over their own neighbourhood, which gave additional horror to the scene. As resistance was now at an end, the soldiers abandoned themselves to pillage, and soon stripped the dwellings of every portable article of any value.

While engaged in this work of devastation, a murmuring sound was heard as of the hoarse rippling of waters, and a cry soon arose among the Indians that the dikes were broken! Cortés now comprehended the business of the men whom he had seen in the canoes at work on the mole which fenced in the great basin of Lake Tezcuco. It had been pierced by the desperate Indians, who thus laid the country under an inundation, by suffering the waters of the salt lake to spread themselves over the lower level, through the opening. Greatly alarmed, the general called his men together, and made all haste to evacuate the city. Had they remained three hours longer, he says, not a soul could have escaped. They came staggering under the weight of booty, wading with difficulty through the water, which was fast gaining upon them. For some distance, their path was illumined by the glare of the burning buildings. But, as the light faded away in distance, they wandered with uncertain steps, sometimes up to their knees, at others up to their waists, in the water, through which they floundered on with the greatest difficulty. As they reached the opening in the dike, the stream became deeper, and flowed out with such a current that the men were unable to maintain their footing. The Spaniards, breasting the flood, forced their way through; but many of the Indians, unable to swim, were borne down by the waters. All the plunder was lost. The powder was spoiled; the arms and clothes of the soldiers were saturated with the brine, and the cold nightwind, as it blew over them, benumbed their weary limbs till they could scarcely drag them along. At dawn they beheld the lake swarming with canoes, full of Indians, who had anticipated their disaster, and who now saluted them with showers of stones, arrows, and other deadly missiles. Bodies of light troops, hovering in the distance, disquieted the flanks of the army in like manner. The Spaniards had no desire to close with the enemy. They only wished to regain their comfortable quarters in Tezcuco, where they arrived on the same day, more disconsolate and fatigued than after many a long march and hard-fought battle.

The close of the expedition, so different from its brilliant commencement, greatly disappointed Cortés. His numerical loss had, indeed, not been great; but this affair convinced him how much he had to apprehend from the resolution of a people, who, with a spirit worthy of the ancient Hollanders, were prepared to bury their country under water, rather than to submit. Still the enemy had little cause for congratulation; since, independently of the number of slain, they had seen one of their most flourishing cities sacked, and in part, at least, laid in ruins,— one of those, too, which in its public works displayed the nearest approach to civilization. Such are the triumphs of war!

The expedition of Cortés, notwithstanding the disasters which chequered it, was favorable to the Spanish cause. The fate of Iztapalapan struck a terror throughout the Valley. The consequences were soon apparent in the deputations sent by the different places eager to offer their submission. Its influence was visible, indeed, beyond the mountains. Among others, the people of Otumba, the town near which the Spaniards had gained their famous victory, sent to tender their allegiance and to request the protection of the powerful strangers. They excused themselves, as usual, for the part they had taken in the late hostilities, by throwing the blame on the Aztecs.

But the place of most importance, which thus claimed their protection, was Chalco, situated on the eastern extremity of the lake of that name. It was an ancient city, peopled by a kindred tribe of the Aztecs, and once their formidable rival. The Mexican emperor, distrusting their loyalty, had placed a garrison within their walls to hold them in check. The rulers of the city now sent a message secretly to Cortés, proposing to put themselves under his protection, if he would enable them to expel the garrison.

The Spanish commander did not hesitate; but instantly detached a considerable force under Sandoval for this object. On the march, his rear-guard, composed of Tlascalans, was roughly handled by some light troops of the Mexicans. But he took his revenge in a pitched battle which took place with the main body of the enemy at no great distance from Chalco. They were drawn up on a level ground, covered with green crops of maize and maguey. The field is traversed by the road which at this day leads from the last mentioned city to Tezcuco. Sandoval, charging the enemy at the head of his cavalry, threw them into disorder. But they quickly rallied, formed again, and renewed the battle with greater spirit than ever. In a second attempt he was more fortunate; and, breaking through their lines by a desperate onset, the brave cavalier succeeded, after a warm, but ineffectual, struggle on their part, in completely routing and driving them from the field. The conquering army continued its march to Chalco, which the Mexican garrison had already evacuated, and was received in triumph by the assembled citizens, who seemed eager to testify their gratitude for their deliverance from the Aztec yoke. After taking such measures as he could for the permanent security of the place, Sandoval returned to Tezcuco, accompanied by the two young lords of the city, sons of the late cacique.

They were courteously received by Cortés; and they informed him that their father had died full of years, a short time before. With his last breath he had expressed his regret that he should not have lived to see Malinche. He believed that the white men were the beings predicted by the oracles, as one day to come from the East and take possession of the land; and he enjoined it on his children, should the strangers return to the Valley, to render them their homage and allegiance. The young caciques expressed their readiness to do so; but, as this must bring on them the vengeance of the Aztecs, they implored the general to furnish a sufficient force for their protection.

Cortés received a similar application from various other towns, which were disposed, could they do so with safety, to throw off the Mexican yoke. But he was in no situation to comply with their request. He now felt, more sensibly than ever, the incompetency of his means to his undertaking. "I assure your Majesty," he writes in his letter to the Emperor, "the greatest uneasiness which I feel, after all my labors and fatigues, is from my inability to succour and support our Indian friends, your Majesty's loyal vassals." Far from having a force competent to this, he had scarcely enough for his own protection. His vigilant enemy had an eye on all his movements, and, should he cripple his strength by sending away too many detachments or by employing them at too great a distance, would be prompt to take advantage of it. His only expeditions, hitherto, had been in the neighbourhood, where the troops, after striking some sudden and decisive blow, might speedily regain their quarters. The utmost watchfulness was maintained there, and the Spaniards lived in as constant preparation for an assault, as if their camp was pitched under the walls of Mexico.

On two occasions the general had sallied forth and engaged the enemy in the environs of Tezcuco. At one time a thousand canoes, filled with Aztecs, crossed the lake to gather in a large crop of Indian corn nearly ripe, on its borders. Cortés thought it important to secure this for himself. He accordingly marched out and gave battle to the enemy, drove them from the field, and swept away the rich harvest to the granaries of Tezcuco. Another time a strong body of Mexicans had established themselves in some neighbouring towns friendly to their interests. Cortés, again sallying, dislodged them from their quarters, beat them in several skirmishes, and reduced the places to obedience. But these enterprises demanded all his resources, and left him nothing to spare for his allies. In this exigency, his fruitful genius suggested an expedient for supplying the deficiency of his means.

Some of the friendly cities without the Valley, observing the numerous beacon-fires on the mountains, inferred that the Mexicans were mustering in great strength, and that the Spaniards must be hard pressed in their new quarters. They sent messengers to Tezcuco expressing their apprehension, and offering reinforcements, which the general, when he set out on his march, had declined. He returned many thanks for the proffered aid; but, while he declined it for himself, as unnecessary, he indicated in what manner their services might be effectual for the defence of Chalco and the other places which had invoked his protection. But his Indian allies were in deadly feud with these places, whose inhabitants had too often fought under the Aztec banner not to have been engaged in repeated wars with the people beyond the mountains.

Cortés set himself earnestly to reconcile these differences. He told the hostile parties that they should be willing to forget their mutual wrongs, since they had entered into new relations. They were now vassals of the same sovereign, engaged in a common enterprise against the formidable foe who had so long trodden them in the dust. Singly they could do little, but united they might protect each other's weakness and hold their enemy at bay, till the Spaniards could come to their assistance. These arguments finally prevailed; and the politic general had the satisfaction to see the high-spirited and hostile tribes forego their long-cherished rivalry, and, resigning the pleasures of revenge, so dear to the barbarian, embrace one another as friends and champions in a common cause. To this wise policy the Spanish commander owed quite as much of his subsequent successes, as to his arms.

Thus the foundations of the Mexican empire were hourly loosening, as the great vassals, around the capital, on whom it most relied, fell off one after another from their allegiance. The Aztecs, properly so called, formed but a small part of the population of the Valley. This was principally composed of cognate tribes, members of the same great family of the Nahuatlacs,* who had come upon the plateau at nearly the same time. They were mutual rivals, and were reduced one after another by the more warlike Mexican, who held them in subjection, often by open force, always by fear. Fear was the great principle of cohesion which bound together the discordant members of the monarchy, and this was now fast dissolving before the influence of a power more mighty than that of the Aztec. This, it is true, was not the first time that the conquered races had attempted to recover their independence. But all such attempts had failed for want of concert. It was reserved for the commanding genius of Cortés to extinguish their old hereditary feuds, and, combining their scattered energies, to animate them with a common principle of action.

Encouraged by this state of things, the Spanish general thought it a favorable moment to press his negotiations with the capital. He availed himself of the presence of some noble Mexicans, taken in the late action with Sandoval, to send another message to their master. It was in substance a repetition of the first, with a renewed assurance, that, if the city would return to its allegiance to the Spanish crown, the authority of Guatemozin should be confirmed, and the persons and property of his subjects be respected. To this communication no reply was made. The young Indian emperor had a spirit as dauntless as that of Cortés himself. On his head descended the full effects

* Nahuatl. C.H.G.

of that vicious system of government bequeathed to him by his ancestors. But, as he saw his empire crumbling beneath him, he sought to uphold it by his own energy and resources. He anticipated the defection of some vassals by establishing garrisons within their walls. Others he conciliated by exempting them from tributes or greatly lightening their burdens, or by advancing them to posts of honor and authority in the state. He showed, at the same time, his implacable animosity towards the Christians, by commanding that every one taken within his dominions should be straightway sent to the capital, where he was sacrificed, with all the barbarous ceremonies prescribed by the Aztec ritual.

While these occurrences were passing, Cortés received the welcome intelligence, that the brigantines were completed and waiting to be transported to Tezcuco. He detached a body for the service, consisting of two hundred Spanish foot and fifteen horse, which he placed under the command of Sandoval. This cavalier had been rising daily in the estimation both of the general and of the army. Though one of the youngest officers in the service, he possessed a cool head and a ripe judgment, which fitted him for the most delicate and difficult undertakings. . . .

There were thirteen vessels in all, of different sizes. They had been constructed under the direction of the experienced ship-builder, Martín López, aided by three or four Spanish carpenters and the friendly natives, some of whom showed no mean degree of imitative skill. The brigantines, when completed, had been fairly tried on the waters of the Zahuapan. They were then taken to pieces, and, as López was impatient of delay, the several parts, the timbers, anchors, iron-work, sails, and cordage were placed on the shoulders of the *tamanes*, and, under a numerous military escort, were thus far advanced on the way to Tezcuco. Sandoval dismissed a part of the Indian convoy, as superfluous.

Twenty thousand warriors he retained, dividing them into two equal bodies for the protection of the *tamanes* in the centre.

His own little body of Spaniards he distributed in like manner. The Tlascalans in the van marched under the command of a chief who gloried in the name of Chichemecatl.* For some reason Sandoval afterwards changed the order of march, and placed this division in the rear,—an arrangement which gave great umbrage to the doughty warrior that led it, who asserted his right to the front, the place which he and his ancestors had always occupied, as the post of danger. He was somewhat appeased by Sandoval's assurance that it was for that very reason he had been transferred to the rear, the quarter most likely to be assailed by the enemy. But even then he was greatly dissatisfied, on finding that the Spanish commander was to march by his side, grudging, it would seem, that any other should share the laurel with himself.

Slowly and painfully, encumbered with their heavy burden, the troops worked their way over steep eminences and rough mountain-passes, presenting, one might suppose, in their long line of march, many a vulnerable point to an enemy. But, although small parties of warriors were seen hovering, at times, on their flanks and rear, they kept at a respectful distance, not caring to encounter so formidable a foe. On the fourth day the warlike caravan arrived in safety before Tezcuco.

Their approach was beheld with joy by Cortés and the soldiers, who hailed it as the signal of a speedy termination of the war. The general, attended by his officers, all dressed in their richest attire, came out to welcome the convoy. It extended over a space of two leagues, and so slow was its progress that six hours elapsed before the closing files had entered the city. The Tlascalan chiefs displayed all their wonted bravery of apparel, and the whole array, composed of the flower of their warriors, made a brilliant appearance. They marched by the sound of atabal and cornet, and, as they traversed the streets of the capital amidst the acclamations of the soldiery, they made the city ring with the shouts of "Castile and Tlascala, long live our sovereign, the emperor!"

* Chichimecatecle. C.H.G.

"It was a marvellous thing," exclaims the Conqueror, in his Letters, "that few have seen, or even heard of,—this transportation of thirteen vessels of war on the shoulders of men, for nearly twenty leagues across the mountains!" It was, indeed, a stupendous achievement, and not easily matched in ancient or modern story; one which only a genius like that of Cortés could have devised, or a daring spirit like his have so successfully executed. Little did he foresee, when he ordered the destruction of the fleet which first brought him to the country, and with his usual forecast commanded the preservation of the iron-work and rigging,—little did he foresee the important uses for which they were to be reserved. So important, that on their preservation may be said to have depended the successful issue of his great enterprise.

He greeted his Indian allies with the greatest cordiality, testifying his sense of their services by those honors and attentions which he knew would be most grateful to their ambitious spirits. "We come," exclaimed the hardy warriors, "to fight under your banner; to avenge our common quarrel, or to fall by your side"; and, with their usual impatience, they urged him to lead them at once against the enemy. "Wait," replied the general, bluntly, "till you are rested, and you shall have your hands full."

II

Reconnaissance, Mop-up and Build-up

IN the course of three or four days, the Spanish general furnished the Tlascalans with the opportunity so much coveted, and allowed their boiling spirits to effervesce in active operations. He had, for some time, meditated an expedition to reconnoitre the capital and its environs, and to chastise, on the way, certain places, which had sent him insulting messages of defiance, and which were particularly active in their hostilities. He disclosed his design to a few only of his principal officers, from his distrust of the Tezcucans, whom he suspected to be in correspondence with the enemy.

Early in the spring, he left Tezcuco, at the head of three hundred and fifty Spaniards and the whole strength of his allies. He took with him Alvarado and Olid, and entrusted the charge of the garrison to Sandoval. Cortés had had practical acquaintance with the incompetence of the first of these cavaliers for so delicate a post, during his short, but disastrous, rule in Mexico.

But all his precautions had not availed to shroud his designs from the vigilant foe, whose eye was on all his movements; who seemed even to divine his thoughts, and to be prepared to thwart their execution. He had advanced but a few leagues, when he was met by a considerable body of Mexicans, drawn up to dispute his progress. A sharp skirmish took place, in which the enemy were driven from the ground, and the way was left open to the Christians. They held a circuitous route to the north, and their first point of attack was the insular town of Xaltocan, situated on the northern extremity of the lake of that name, now called San Christóbal. The town was entirely surrounded by water, and communicated with the main land by means of causeways, in the same manner as the Mexican capital. Cortés, riding at the head of his cavalry, advanced along the dike, till he was brought to a stand by finding a wide opening in it, through which the waters poured so as to be altogether impracticable, not only for horse, but for infantry. The lake was covered with canoes, filled with Aztec warriors, who, anticipating the movement of the Spaniards, had come to the aid of the city. They now began a furious discharge of stones and arrows on the assailants, while they were themselves tolerably well protected from the musketry of the enemy by the light bulwarks, with which, for that purpose, they had fortified their canoes.

The severe volleys of the Mexicans did some injury to the Spaniards and their allies, and began to throw them into disorder, crowded as they were on the narrow causeway, without the means of advancing, when Cortés ordered a retreat. This was followed by renewed tempests of missiles, accompanied by taunts and fierce yells of defiance. The battle-cry of the Aztec, like the war-whoop of the North American Indian, was an appalling note, according to the Conqueror's own acknowledgment, in the ears of the Spaniards. At this juncture, the general fortunately obtained information from a deserter, one of the Mexican allies, of a ford, by which the army might traverse the shallow lake, and penetrate into the place. He instantly detached the greater part of the infantry on the service, posting himself with the remainder and with the horse at the entrance of the passage, to cover the attack and prevent any interruption in the rear.

The soldiers, under the direction of the Indian guide, forded the lake without much difficulty, though in some places the water came above their girdles. During the passage, they were annoyed by the enemy's missiles; but, when they had gained the dry level, they took ample revenge, and speedily put all who resisted to the sword. The greater part, together with the townsmen, made their escape in the boats. The place was now abandoned to pillage. The troops found in it many women, who had been left to their fate; and these, together with a considerable quantity of cotton stuffs, gold, and articles of food, fell into the hands of the victors, who, setting fire to the deserted city, returned in triumph to their comrades.

Continuing his circuitous route, Cortés presented himself successively before three other places, each of which had been deserted by the inhabitants in anticipation of his arrival. The principal of these, Azcapozalco, had once been the capital of an independent state. It was now the great slave-market of the Aztecs, where their unfortunate captives were brought, and disposed of at public sale. It was also the quarter occupied by the jewellers; and the place whence the Spaniards obtained the goldsmiths who melted down the rich treasures received from Montezuma. But they found there only a small supply of the precious metals, or, indeed, of any thing else of value, as the people had been careful to remove their effects. They spared the buildings, however, in consideration of their having met with no resistance.

During the nights, the troops bivouacked in the open fields, maintaining the strictest watch, for the country was all in arms, and beacons were flaming on every hill-top, while dark masses of the enemy were occasionally descried in the distance. The Spaniards were now traversing the most opulent region of Anahuac. Cities and villages were scattered over hill and valley, with cultivated environs blooming around them, all giving token of a dense and industrious population. In the centre of this brilliant circumference stood the Indian metropolis, with its gorgeous tiara of pyramids and temples, attracting the eye of the soldier from every other object, as he wound round the borders of the lake. Every inch of ground, which the army trod, was familiar to them,—familiar as the scenes of childhood, though with very different associations, for it had been written on their memories in characters of blood. On the right rose the Hill of Montezuma, crowned by the *teocalli*, under the roof of which the shattered relics of the army had been gathered, on the day following the flight from the capital. In front lay the city of Tacuba, through whose inhospitable streets they had hurried in fear and consternation; and away to the east of it, stretched the melancholy causeway.

In was the general's purpose to march at once on Tacuba, and establish his quarters in that ancient capital for the present. He found a strong force encamped under its walls, prepared to dispute his entrance. Without waiting for their advance, he rode at full gallop against them with his little body of horse. The arquebuses and crossbows opened a lively volley on their extended wings, and the infantry, armed with their swords and copper-headed lances, and supported by the Indian battalions, followed up the attack of the horse with an alacrity which soon put the enemy to flight. The Spaniards usually opened the combat with a charge of cavalry. But, had the science of the Aztecs been equal to their courage, they might with their long spears have turned the scale of battle, sometimes at least, in their own favor; for it was with the same formidable weapon, that the Swiss mountaineers, but a few years before this period of our history, broke and completely foiled the famous *ordonnance* of Charles the Bold, the best appointed cavalry of their day. But the barbarians were ignorant of the value of this weapon when opposed to cavalry. And, indeed, the appalling apparition of the war-horse and his rider still held a mysterious power over their imaginations, which contributed, perhaps, quite as much as the effective force of the cavalry itself, to their discomfiture.—Cortés led his troops without further opposition into the suburbs of Tacuba, the ancient Tlacopan, where he established himself for the night.

On the following morning, he found the indefatigable Aztecs again under arms, and, on the open ground before the city, prepared to give him battle. He marched out against them, and, after an action, hotly contested, though of no long duration, again routed them. They fled towards the town, but were driven through the streets at the point of the lance, and were compelled, together with the inhabitants, to evacuate the place. The city was then delivered over to pillage; and the Indian allies, not content with plundering the houses of every thing portable within them, set them on fire, and in a short time a quarter of the town—the poorer dwellings, probably, built of light, combustible materials—was in flames. Cortés and his troops did all in their power to stop the conflagration, but the Tlascalans were a fierce race, not easily guided at any time, and, when their passions were once kindled, it was impossible, even for the general himself, to control them. They were a terrible auxiliary, and, from their insubordination, as terrible sometimes to friend as to foe.

Cortés proposed to remain in his present quarters for some days, during which time he established his own residence in the ancient palace of the lords of Tlacopan. It was a long range of low buildings, like most of the royal residences in the country, and offered good accommodations for the Spanish forces. During his halt here, there was not a day on which the army was not engaged in one or more rencontres with the enemy. They terminated almost uniformly in favor of the Spaniards, though with more or less injury to them and to their allies. One encounter, indeed, had nearly been attended with more fatal consequences.

The Spanish general, in the heat of pursuit, had allowed himself to be decoyed upon the great causeway,—the same which had once been so fatal to his army. He followed the flying foe, until he had gained the further side of the nearest bridge, which had been repaired since the disastrous action of the *noche triste.* When thus far advanced, the Aztecs, with the rapidity of lightning, turned on him, and he beheld a large reinforcement in their rear, all fresh on the field, prepared to support their countrymen. At the same time, swarms of boats, unobserved in the eagerness of the chase, seemed to start up as if by magic, covering the waters around. The Spaniards were now exposed to a perfect hail-storm of missiles, both from the causeway and the lake; but they stood unmoved amidst the tempest, when Cortés, too late perceiving his error, gave orders for the retreat. Slowly, and with admirable coolness, his men receded, step by step, offering a resolute front to the enemy. The Mexicans came on with their usual vociferation, making the shores echo to their war-cries, and striking at the Spaniards with their long pikes, and with poles, to which the swords taken from the Christians had been fastened. A cavalier, named Volante, bearing the standard of Cortés, was felled by one of their weapons, and, tumbling into the lake, was picked up by the Mexican boats. He was a man of a muscular frame, and, as the enemy were dragging him off, he succeeded in extricating himself from their grasp, and, clenching his colors in his hand, with a desperate effort sprang back upon the causeway. At length, after some hard fighting, in which many of the Spaniards were wounded, and many of their allies slain, the troops regained the land, where Cortés, with a full heart, returned thanks to Heaven for what he might well regard as a providential deliverance. It was a salutary lesson; though he should scarcely have needed one, so soon after the affair of Iztapalapan, to warn him of the wily tactics of his enemy.

It had been one of Cortés' principal objects in this expedition to obtain an interview, if possible, with the Aztec emperor, or with some of the great lords at his court, and to try if some means for an accommodation could not be found, by which he might avoid the appeal to arms. An occasion for such a parley presented itself, when his forces were one day confronted with those of the enemy, with a broken bridge interposed between them. Cortés, riding in advance of his people, intimated by signs his peaceful intent, and that he wished to confer with the Aztecs. They respected the signal, and, with the aid of his interpreter, he requested, that, if there were any great chief among them, he would come forward and hold a parley with him. The Mexicans replied, in derision, they were all chiefs, and bade him speak openly whatever he had to tell them. As the general returned no answer, they asked, why he did not make another visit to the capital, and, tauntingly, added, "Perhaps Malinche does not expect to find there another Montezuma, as obedient to his commands as the former." Some of them complimented the Tlascalans with the epithet of *women*, who, they said, would never have ventured so near the capital, but for the protection of the white men.

The animosity of the two nations was not confined to these

harmless, though bitter, jests, but showed itself in regular cartels of defiance, which daily passed between the principal chieftains. These were followed by combats, in which one or more champions fought on a side, to vindicate the honor of their respective countries. A fair field of fight was given to the warriors, who conducted those combats, *à l'outrance,* with the punctilio of a European tourney; displaying a valor worthy of the two boldest of the races of Anahuac, and a skill in the management of their weapons, which drew forth the admiration of the Spaniards.

Cortés had now been six days in Tacuba. There was nothing further to detain him, as he had accomplished the chief objects of his expedition. He had humbled several of the places which had been most active in their hostility; and he had revived the credit of the Castilian arms, which had been much tarnished by their former reverses in this quarter of the Valley. He had also made himself acquainted with the condition of the capital, which he found in a better posture of defence than he had imagined. All the ravages of the preceding year seemed to be repaired, and there was no evidence, even to his experienced eye, that the wasting hand of war had so lately swept over the land. The Aztec troops, which swarmed through the Valley, seemed to be well appointed, and showed an invincible spirit, as if prepared to resist to the last. It is true, they had been beaten in every encounter. In the open field they were no match for the Spaniards, whose cavalry they could never comprehend, and whose fire-arms easily penetrated the cotton mail, which formed the stoutest defence of the Indian warrior. But, entangled in the long streets and narrow lanes of the metropolis, where every house was a citadel, the Spaniards, as experience had shown, would lose much of their superiority. With the Mexican emperor, confident in the strength of his preparations, the general saw there was no probability of effecting an accommodation. He saw, too, the necessity of the most careful preparations on his own part, indeed, that he must strain his resources to the utmost, before he could safely venture to rouse the lion in his lair.

The Spaniards returned by the same route by which they had come. Their retreat was interpreted into a flight by the natives, who hung on the rear of the army, uttering vainglorious vaunts, and saluting the troops with showers of arrows, which did some mischief. Cortés resorted to one of their own stratagems to rid himself of this annoyance. He divided his cavalry into two or three small parties, and concealed them among some thick shrubbery, which fringed both sides of the road. The rest of the army continued its march. The Mexicans followed, unsuspicious of the ambuscade, when the horse, suddently darting from their place of concealment, threw the enemy's flanks into confusion, and the retreating columns of infantry, facing about suddenly, commenced a brisk attack, which completed their consternation. It was a broad and level plain, over which the panic-struck Mexicans made the best of their way, without attempting resistance; while the cavalry, riding them down and piercing the fugitives with their lances, followed up the chase for several miles, in what Cortés calls a truly beautiful style. The army experienced no further annoyance from the enemy.

On their arrival at Tezcuco, they were greeted with joy by their comrades, who had received no tidings of them during the fortnight which had elapsed since their departure. The Tlascalans, immediately on their return, requested the general's permission to carry back to their own country the valuable booty which they had gathered in their foray,—a request, which, however unpalatable, he could not refuse.

The troops had not been in quarters more than two or three days, when an embassy arrived from Chalco, again soliciting the protection of the Spaniards against the Mexicans, who menaced them from several points in their neighbourhood. But the soldiers were so much exhausted by unintermitted vigils, forced marches, battles, and wounds, that Cortés wished to give them a breathing-time to recruit, before engaging in a new expedition. He answered the application of the Chalcans, by sending his missives to the allied cities, calling on them to march to the assistance of their confederate. It is not to be supposed, that they could comprehend the import of his despatches. But the paper, with its mysterious characters, served for a warrant to the officer who bore it, as the interpreter of the general's commands.

But, although these were implicitly obeyed, the Chalcans felt the danger so pressing, that they soon repeated their petition for the Spaniards to come in person to their relief. Cortés no longer hesitated; for he was well aware of the importance of Chalco, not merely on its own account, but from its position, which commanded one of the great avenues to Tlascala, and to Vera Cruz, the intercourse with which should run no risk of interruption. Without further loss of time, therefore, he detached a body of three hundred Spanish foot and twenty horse, under the command of Sandoval, for the protection of the city.

That active officer soon presented himself before Chalco, and, strengthened by the reinforcement of its own troops and those of the confederate towns, directed his first operations against Huaxtepec, a place of some importance, lying five leagues or more to the south among the mountains. It was held by a strong Mexican force, watching their opportunity to make a descent upon Chalco. The Spaniards found the enemy drawn up at a distance from the town, prepared to receive them. The ground was broken and tangled with bushes, unfavorable to the cavalry, which, in consequence, soon fell into disorder; and Sandoval, finding himself embarrassed by their movements, ordered them, after sustaining some loss, from the field. In their place he brought up his musketeers and crossbow-men, who poured a rapid fire into the thick columns of the Indians. The rest of the infantry, with sword and pike, charged the flanks of the enemy, who, bewildered by the shock, after sustaining considerable slaughter, fell back in an irregular manner, leaving the field of battle to the Spaniards.

The victors proposed to bivouac there, for the night. But, while engaged in preparations for their evening meal, they were aroused by the cry of "To arms, to arms! the enemy is upon us!" In an instant, the trooper was in his saddle, the soldier grasped his musket or his good Toledo, and the action was renewed with greater fury than before. The Mexicans had received a reinforcement from the city. But their second attempt was not more fortunate than their first; and the victorious Spaniards, driving their antagonists before them, entered and took possession of the town itself, which had already been evacuated by the inhabitants.

Sandoval took up his quarters in the dwelling of the lord of the place, surrounded by gardens, which rivalled those of Iztapalapan in magnificence, and surpassed them in extent. They are said to have been two leagues in circumference, having pleasure houses, and numerous tanks stocked with various kinds of fish; and they were embellished with trees, shrubs, and plants, native and exotic, some selected for their beauty and fragrance, others for their medicinal properties. They were scientifically arranged; and the whole establishment displayed a degree of horticultural taste and knowledge, of which it would not have been easy to find a counterpart, at that day, in the more civilized communities of Europe. Such is the testimony not only of the rude Conquerors, but of men of science, who visited these beautiful repositories in the day of their glory.

After halting two days to refresh his forces in this agreeable spot, Sandoval marched on Jacapichtla, about twelve miles to the eastward. It was a town, or rather fortress, perched on a rocky eminence, almost inaccessible from its steepness. It was garrisoned by a Mexican force, who rolled down on the assailants, as they attempted to scale the heights, huge fragments of rock, which, thundering over the sides of the precipice, carried ruin and desolation in their path. The Indian confederates fell back in dismay from the attempt. But Sandoval, indignant that any achievement should be too difficult for a Spaniard, commanded his cavaliers to dismount, and, declaring that he "would carry the place or die in the attempt," led on his men with the cheering cry of "St. Iago." With renewed courage, they now followed their gallant leader up the ascent, under a storm of lighter missiles, mingled with huge masses of stone, which, breaking into splinters, overturned the assailants, and made fearful havoc in their ranks. Sandoval, who had been wounded on the preceding day, received a severe contusion on the head, while more than one of his brave comrades were struck down by his side. Still they clambered up, sustaining themselves by the bushes or projecting pieces of rock, and seemed to force themselves onward as much by the energy of their wills, as by the strength of their bodies.

After incredible toil, they stood on the summit, face to face with the astonished garrison. For a moment they paused to recover breath, then sprang furiously on their foes. The struggle was short, but desperate. Most ,of the Aztecs were put to the sword. Some were thrown headlong over the battlements, and others, letting themselves down the precipice, were killed on the borders of a little stream that wound round its base, the waters of which were so polluted with blood, that the victors were unable to slake their thirst with them for a full hour!

Sandoval, having now accomplished the object of his expedition, by reducing the strong-holds which had so long held the Chalcans in awe, returned in triumph to Tezcuco. Meanwhile, the Aztec emperor, whose vigilant eye had been attentive to all that had passed, thought that the absence of so many of its warriors afforded a favorable opportunity for recovering Chalco. He sent a fleet of boats, for this purpose, across the lake, with a numerous force under the command of some of his most valiant chiefs. Fortunately the absent Chalcans reached their city before the arrival of the enemy; but, though supported by their Indian allies, they were so much alarmed by the magnitude of the hostile array, that they sent again to the Spaniards, invoking their aid.

The messengers arrived at the same time with Sandoval and his army. Cortés was much puzzled by the contradictory accounts. He suspected some negligence in his lieutenant, and, displeased with his precipitate return in this unsettled state of the affair, ordered him back at once, with such of his forces as were in fighting condition. Sandoval felt deeply injured by this proceeding, but he made no attempt at exculpation, and, obeying his commander in silence, put himself at the head of his troops, and made a rapid countermarch on the Indian city.

Before he reached it, a battle had been fought between the Mexicans and the confederates, in which the latter, who had acquired unwonted confidence from their recent successes, were victorious. A number of Aztec nobles fell into their hands in the engagement, whom they delivered to Sandoval to be carried off as prisoners to Tezcuco. On his arrival there, the cavalier, wounded by the unworthy treatment he had received, retired to his own quarters without presenting himself before his chief.

During his absence, the inquiries of Cortés had satisfied him of his own precipitate conduct, and of the great injustice he had done his lieutenant. There was no man in the army, on whose services he set so high a value, as the responsible situations in which he had placed him plainly showed; and there was none, for whom he seemed to have entertained a greater personal regard. On Sandoval's return, therefore, Cortés instantly sent to request his attendance; when, with a soldier's frankness, he made such an explanation, as soothed the irritated spirit of the cavalier,—a matter of no great difficulty, as the latter had too generous a nature, and too earnest a devotion to his commander and the cause in which they were embarked, to harbour a petty feeling of resentment in his bosom.

During the occurrence of these events, the work was going forward actively on the canal, and the brigantines were within a fortnight of their completion. The greatest vigilance was required, in the mean time, to prevent their destruction by the enemy, who had already made three ineffectual attempts to burn them on the stocks. The precautions, which Cortés thought it necessary to take against the Tezcucans themselves, added not a little to his embarrassment.

At this time he received embassies from different Indian states, some of them on the remote shores of the Mexican Gulf, tendering their allegiance and soliciting his protection. For this he was partly indebted to the good offices of Ixtlilxochitl, who, in consequence of his brother's death, was now advanced to the sovereignty of Tezcuco. This important position greatly increased his consideration and authority through the country, of which he freely availed himself to bring the natives under the dominion of the Spaniards.

The general received also at this time the welcome intelligence of the arrival of three vessels at Villa Rica, with two hundred men on board, well provided with arms and ammunition, and with seventy or eighty horses. It was a most seasonable reinforcement. From what quarter it came is uncertain; most probably, from Hispaniola. Cortés, it may be remembered, had sent for supplies to that place; and the authorities of the island, who had general jurisdiction over the affairs of the colonies, had shown themselves, on more than one occasion, well inclined towards him, probably considering him, under all circumstances, as better fitted than any other man to achieve the conquest of the country.

The new recruits soon found their way to Tezcuco; as the communications with the port were now open and unobstructed. Among them were several cavaliers of consideration, one of whom, Julián de Alderete, the royal treasurer, came over to superintend the interests of the Crown.

There was also in the number a Dominican friar, who brought a quantity of pontifical bulls, offering indulgences to those engaged in war against the infidel. The soldiers were not slow to fortify themselves with the good graces of the Church; and the worthy father, after driving a prosperous traffic with his spiritual wares, had the satisfaction to return home, at the end of a few months, well freighted, in exchange, with the more substantial treasures of the Indies.

WHILE *the navy was under construction at Texcoco, additional forays in the Valley of Mexico permitted Cortés to reduce the number of allies of the Aztecs and to gain valuable information concerning the enemy and his position. As a final preparation, Cortés made a rapid clockwise circuit of Lake Texcoco. However, every obstacle confronting Cortés was not in the Valley of Mexico.*

III

Final Preparations

AT the very time when Cortés was occupied with reconnoitring the Valley, preparatory to his siege of the capital, a busy faction in Castile was laboring to subvert his authority and defeat his plans of conquest altogether. The fame of his brilliant exploits had spread not only through the Isles, but to Spain and many parts of Europe, where a general admiration was felt for the invincible energy of the man, who, with his single arm, as it were, could so long maintain a contest with the powerful Indian empire. The absence of the Spanish monarch from his dominions, and the troubles of the country, can alone explain the supine indifference shown by the government to the prosecution of this great enterprise. To the same causes it may be ascribed, that no action was had in regard to the suits of Velásquez and Narváez, backed, as they were, by so potent an advocate as Bishop Fonseca, president of the Council of the Indies. The reins of government had fallen into the hands of Adrian of Utrecht, Charles's preceptor, and afterwards Pope,—a man of learning, and not without sagacity, but slow and timid in his policy, and altogether incapable of that decisive action which suited the bold genius of his predecessor, Cardinal Ximénes.

In the spring of 1521, however, a number of ordinances

passed the Council of the Indies, which threatened an important innovation in the affairs of New Spain. It was decreed, that the Royal Audience of Hispaniola should abandon the proceedings already instituted against Narváez, for his treatment of the commissioner Ayllón; that that unfortunate commander should be released from his confinement at Vera Cruz; and that an arbitrator should be sent to Mexico, with authority to investigate the affairs and conduct of Cortés, and to render ample justice to the governor of Cuba. There were not wanting persons at court, who looked with dissatisfaction on these proceedings, as an unworthy requital of the services of Cortés, and who thought the present moment, at any rate, not the most suitable for taking measures, which might discourage the general, and, perhaps, render him desperate. But the arrogant temper of the bishop of Burgos overruled all objections; and the ordinances having been approved by the Regency, were signed by that body, April 11, 1521. A person named Tapia, one of the functionaries of the Audience at St. Domingo, was selected as the new commissioner to be despatched to Vera Cruz. Fortunately circumstances occurred, which postponed the execution of the design for the present, and permitted Cortés to go forward unmolested in his career of conquest.

But, while thus allowed to remain, for the present at least, in possession of authority, he was assailed by a danger nearer home, which menaced not only his authority, but his life. This was a conspiracy in the army, of a more dark and dangerous character than any hitherto formed there. It was set on foot by a common soldier, named Antonio Villafaña, a native of Old Castile, of whom nothing is known but his share in this transaction. He was one of the troop of Narváez,—that leaven of disaffection, which had remained with the army, swelling with discontent on every light occasion, and ready, at all times to rise into mutiny. They had voluntarily continued in the service, after the secession of their comrades at Tlascala; but it was from the same mercenary hopes with which they had originally embarked in the expedition,—and in these they were destined still to be disappointed. They had little of the true spirit of adventure, which distinguished the old companions of Cortés; and they found the barren laurels of victory but a sorry recompense for all their toils and sufferings.

With these men were joined others, who had causes of personal disgust with the general; and others, again, who looked with distrust on the result of the war. The gloomy fate of their countrymen, who had fallen into the enemy's hands, filled them with dismay. They felt themselves the victims of a chimerical spirit in their leader, who, with such inadequate means, was urging to extremity so ferocious and formidable a foe; and they shrunk with something like apprehension from thus pursuing the enemy into his own haunts, where he would gather tenfold energy from despair.

These men would have willingly abandoned the enterprise, and returned to Cuba; but how could they do it? Cortés had control over the whole route from the city to the sea-coast; and not a vessel could leave its ports without his warrant. Even if he were put out of the way, there were others, his principal officers, ready to step into his place, and avenge the death of their commander. It was necessary to embrace these, also, in the scheme of destruction; and it was proposed, therefore, together with Cortés, to assassinate Sandoval, Olid, Alvarado, and two or three others most devoted to his interests. The conspirators would then raise the cry of liberty, and doubted not that they should be joined by the greater part of the army, or enough, at least, to enable them to work their own pleasure. They proposed to offer the command, on Cortés death, to Francisco Verdugo, a brother-in-law of Velásquez. He was an honorable cavalier, and not privy to their design. But they had little doubt that he would acquiesce in the command, thus, in a manner, forced upon him, and this would secure them the protection of the governor of Cuba, who, indeed, from his own hatred of Cortés, would be disposed to look with a lenient eye on their proceedings.

The conspirators even went so far as to appoint the subordinate officers, an *alguacil mayor* in place of Sandoval, a quartermaster general to succeed Olid, and some others. The time fixed for the execution of the plot was soon after the return of Cortés from his expedition. A parcel, pretended to have come by a fresh arrival from Castile, was to be presented to him while at table, and, when he was engaged in breaking open the letters, the conspirators were to fall on him and his officers, and despatch them with their poniards. Such was the iniquitous scheme devised for the destruction of Cortés and the expedition. But a conspiracy, to be successful, especially when numbers are concerned, should allow but little time to elapse between its conception and its execution.

On the day previous to that appointed for the perpetration of the deed, one of the party, feeling a natural compunction at the commission of the crime, went to the general's quarters, and solicited a private interview with him. He threw himself at his commander's feet, and revealed all the particulars relating to the conspiracy, adding, that in Villafaña's possession a paper would be found, containing the names of his accomplices. Cortés, thunder-struck at the disclosure, lost not a moment in profiting by it. He sent for Alvarado, Sandoval, and one of two other officers marked out by the conspirator, and, after communicating the affair to them, went at once with them to Villafaña's quarters, attended by four alguacils.

They found him in conference with three or four friends, who were instantly taken from the apartment, and placed in custody. Villafaña, confounded at this sudden apparition of his commander, had barely time to snatch a paper, containing the signatures of the confederates, from his bosom, and attempt to swallow it. But Cortés arrested his arm, and seized the paper. As he glanced his eye rapidly over the fatal list, he was much moved at finding there the names of more than one, who had some claim to consideration in the army. He tore the scroll in pieces, and ordered Villafaña to be taken into custody. He was immediately tried by a military court hastily

got together, at which the general himself presided. There
seems to have been no doubt of the man's guilt. He was condemned to death, and, after allowing him time for confession
and absolution, the sentence was executed by hanging him
from the window of his own quarters.

Those ignorant of the affair were astonished at the spectacle; and the remaining conspirators were filled with consternation, when they saw that their plot was detected, and anticipated a similar fate for themselves. But they were mistaken.
Cortés pursued the matter no further. A little reflection convinced him, that to do so would involve him in the most disagreeable, and even dangerous, perplexities. And, however
much the parties implicated in so foul a deed might deserve
death, he could ill afford the loss even of the guilty, with his
present limited numbers. He resolved, therefore, to content himself with the punishment of the ringleader. . . .

This attempt on the life of their commander excited a strong
sensation in the army, with whom his many dazzling qualities and brilliant military talents had made him a general
favorite. They were anxious to testify reprobation of so foul
a deed, coming from their own body, and they felt the necessity
of taking some effectual measures for watching over the safety
of one, with whom their own destinies, as well as the fate of
the enterprise, were so intimately connected. It was arranged,
therefore, that he should be provided with a guard of soldiers,
who were placed under the direction of a trusty cavalier named
Antonio de Quiñones. They constituted the general's body-
guard, during the rest of the campaign, watching over him day
and night, and protecting him from domestic treason, no less
than from the sword of the enemy.

As was stated at the close of the last Chapter, the Spaniards,
on their return to quarters, found the construction of the
brigantines completed, and that they were fully rigged,
equipped, and ready for service. The canal, also, after having
occupied eight thousand men for nearly two months, was
finished.

It was a work of great labor; for it extended half a league in length, was twelve feet wide, and as many deep. The sides were strengthened by palisades of wood, or solid masonry. At intervals, dams and locks were constructed, and part of the opening was through the hard rock. By this avenue the brigantines might now be safely introduced on the lake.

Cortés was resolved that so auspicious an event should be celebrated with due solemnity. On the 28th of April, the troops were drawn up under arms, and the whole population of Tezcuco assembled to witness the ceremony. Mass was performed, and every man in the army, together with the general, confessed and received the sacrament. Prayers were offered up by father Olmedo, and a benediction invoked on the little navy, the first—worthy of the name—ever launched on American waters. The signal was given by the firing of a cannon, when the vessels, dropping down the canal, one after another, reached the lake in good order; and, as they emerged on its ample bosom, with music sounding, and the royal ensign of Castile proudly floating from their masts, a shout of admiration arose from the countless multitudes of spectators, which mingled with the roar of artillery and musketry from the vessels and the shore! It was a novel spectacle to the simple natives; and they gazed with wonder on the gallant ships, which, fluttering like sea-birds on their snowy pinions, bounded lightly over the waters, as if rejoicing in their element. It touched the stern hearts of the Conquerors with a glow of rapture, and, as they felt that Heaven had blessed their undertaking, they broke forth, by general accord, into the noble anthem of the *Te Deum*. But there was no one of that vast multitude for whom the sight had deeper interest than their commander. For he looked on it as the work, in a manner, of his own hands; and his bosom swelled with exultation, as he felt he was now possessed of a power strong enough to command the lake, and to shake the haughty towers of Tenochtitlán.

The general's next step was to muster his forces in the great square of the capital. He found they amounted to eighty-seven horse, and eight hundred and eighteen foot, of which one hundred and eighteen were arquebusiers and crossbow-men. He had three large field-pieces of iron, and fifteen lighter guns or falconets of brass. The heavier cannon had been transported from Vera Cruz to Tezcuco, a little while before, by the faithful Tlascalans. He was well supplied with shot and balls, with about ten hundred weight of powder, and fifty thousand copper-headed arrows, made after a pattern furnished by him to the natives. The number and appointment of the army much exceeded what they had been at any time since the flight from Mexico, and showed the good effects of the late arrivals from the Islands. Indeed, taking the fleet into the account, Cortés had never before been in so good a condition for carrying on his operations. Three hundred of the men were sent to man the vessels, thirteen, or rather twelve, in number, one of the smallest having been found, on trial, too dull a sailer to be of service. Half of the crews were required to navigate the ships. There was some difficulty in finding hands for this, as the men were adverse to the employment. Cortés selected those who came from Palos, Moguer, and other maritime towns, and, notwithstanding their frequent claims of exemption, as hidalgos, from this menial occupation, he pressed them into service. Each vessel mounted a piece of heavy ordnance, and was placed under an officer of respectability, to whom Cortés gave a general code of instructions for the government of the little navy, of which he proposed to take the command in person.

He had already sent to his Indian confederates, announcing his purpose of immediately laying siege to Mexico, and called on them to furnish their promised levies, within the space of ten days at furthest. The Tlascalans he ordered to join him in Tezcuco; the others were to assemble at Chalco, a more convenient place of rendezvous for the operations in the southern quarter of the Valley. The Tlascalans arrived within the time prescribed, led by the younger Xicotencatl, supported by Chichemecatl, the same doughty warrior who had convoyed the brigantines to Tezcuco. They came fifty thousand strong, according to Cortés, making a brilliant show with their military finery, and marching proudly forward under the great national banner, emblazoned with a spread eagle, the arms of the republic. With as blithe and manly a step, as if they were going to the battle-ground, they defiled through the gates of the capital, making its walls ring with the friendly shouts of "Castile and Tlascala."

The observations, which Cortés had made in his late tour of *reconnaissance,* had determined him to begin the siege by distributing his forces into three separate camps, which he proposed to establish at the extremities of the principal causeways. By this arrangement the troops would be enabled to move in concert on the capital, and be in the best position to intercept its supplies from the surrounding country. The first of these points was Tacuba, commanding the fatal causeway of the *noche triste.* This was assigned to Pedro de Alvarado, with a force consisting, according to Cortés own statement, of thirty horse, one hundred and sixty-eight Spanish infantry, and five and twenty thousand Tlascalans. Christóval de Olid had command of the second army, of much the same magnitude, which was to take up its position at Cojohuacan,* the city, it will be remembered, overlooking the short causeway connected with that of Iztapalapan. Gonzalo de Sandoval had charge of the third division, of equal strength with each of the two preceding, but which was to draw its Indian levies from the forces assembled at Chalco. This officer was to march on Iztapalapan, and complete the destruction of that city, begun by Cortés soon after his entrance into the Valley. It was too formidable a post to remain in the rear of the army. The general intended to support the attack with his brigantines, after which the subsequent movements of Sandoval would be determined by circumstances.

Having announced his intended dispositions to his officers,

* Coyoacán. C.H.G.

the Spanish commander called his troops together, and made one of those brief and stirring harangues, with which he was wont on great occasions to kindle the hearts of his soldiery. "I have taken the last step," he said. "I have brought you to the goal for which you have so long panted. A few days will place you before the gates of Mexico,—the capital from which you were driven with so much ignominy. But we now go forward under the smiles of Providence. Does any one doubt it? Let him but compare our present condition with that in which we found ourselves not twelve months since, when, broken and dispirited, we sought shelter within the walls of Tlascala; nay, with that in which we were but a few months since, when we took up our quarters in Tezcuco. Since that time our strength has been nearly doubled. We are fighting the battles of the Faith, fighting for our honor, for riches, for revenge. I have brought you face to face with your foe. It is for you to do the rest."

The address of the bold chief was answered by the thundering acclamations of his followers, who declared that every man would do his duty under such a leader; and they only asked to be led against the enemy. Cortés then caused the regulations for the army, published at Tlascala, to be read again to the troops, with the assurance that they should be enforced to the letter.

It was arranged, that the Indian forces should precede the Spanish by a day's march, and should halt for their confederates on the borders of the Tezcucan territory. A circumstance occurred soon after their departure, which gave bad augury for the future. A quarrel had arisen in the camp at Tezcuco, between a Spanish soldier and a Tlascalan chief, in which the latter was badly hurt. He was sent back to Tlascala, and the matter was hushed up, that it might not reach the ears of the general, who, it was known, would not pass it over lightly. Xicotencatl was a near relative of the injured party, and, on the first day's halt, he took the opportunity to leave the army, with a number of his followers, and set off for Tlascala. Other causes are assigned for his desertion. It is certain, that, from the first, he had looked on the expedition with an evil eye, and had predicted that no good would come of it. He came into it with reluctance, as, indeed, he detested the Spaniards in his heart.

His partner in the command instantly sent information of the affair to the Spanish general, still encamped at Tezcuco. Cortés, who saw at once the mischievous consequences of this defection at such a time, detached a party of Tlascalan and Tezcucan Indians after the fugitive, with instructions to prevail upon him, if possible to return to his duty. They overtook him on the road, and remonstrated with him on his conduct, contrasting it with that of his countrymen generally, and of his own father in particular, the steady friend of the white men. "So much the worse," replied the chieftain; "if they had taken my counsel, they would never have become the dupes of the perfidious strangers." Finding their remonstrances received only with anger or contemptuous taunts, the emissaries returned without accomplishing their object.

Cortés did not hesitate on the course he was to pursue. "Xicotencatl," he said, "had always been the enemy of the Spaniards, first in the field, and since in the council-chamber; openly, or in secret, still the same,—their implacable enemy. There was no use in parleying with the false-hearted Indian." He instantly despatched a small body of horse with an alguacil to arrest the chief, wherever he might be found, even though it were in the streets of Tlascala, and to bring him back to Tezcuco. At the same time, he sent information of Xicotencatl's proceedings to the Tlascalan senate, adding, that desertion among the Spaniards was punishable with death.

The emissaries of Cortés punctually fulfilled his orders. They arrested the fugitive chief,—whether in Tlascala or in its neighbourhood is uncertain,—and brought him a prisoner to Tezcuco, where a high gallows, erected in the great square, was prepared for his reception. He was instantly led to the place of execution; his sentence and the cause for which he suffered were publicly proclaimed, and the unfortunate cacique expiated his offence by the vile death of a malefactor. His ample property, consisting of lands, slaves, and some gold, was all confiscated to the Castilian crown.

Thus perished Xicotencatl, in the flower of his age,—as dauntless a warrior as ever led an Indian army to battle. He was the first chief who successfully resisted the arms of the invaders; and, had the natives of Anahuac, generally, been animated with a spirit like his, Cortés would probably never have set foot in the capital of Montezuma. He was gifted with a clearer insight into the future than his countrymen; for he saw that the European was an enemy far more to be dreaded than the Aztec. Yet, when he consented to fight under the banner of the white men, he had no right to desert it, and he incurred the penalty prescribed by the code of savage as well as of civilized nations. It is said, indeed, that the Tlascalan senate aided in apprehending him, having previously answered Cortés, that his crime was punishable with death by their own laws. It was a bold act, however, thus to execute him in the midst of his own people. For he was a powerful chief, heir to one of the four seigniories of the republic. His chivalrous qualities made him popular, especially with the younger part of his countrymen; and his garments were torn into shreds at his death, and distributed as sacred relics among them. Still, no resistance was offered to the execution of the sentence, and no commotion followed it. He was the only Tlascalan who ever swerved from his loyalty to the Spaniards.

According to the plan of operations settled by Cortés, Sandoval, with his division, was to take a southern direction, while Alvarado and Olid would make the northern circuit of the lakes. These two cavaliers, after getting possession of Tacuba, were to advance to Chapoltepec, and demolish the great aqueduct there, which supplied Mexico with water. On the 10th of May, they commenced their march; but at Acolman, where they halted for the night, a dispute arose between the soldiers of the two divisions, respecting their quarters. From words they came to blows, and a defiance was even exchanged between the leaders, who entered into the angry feelings of their followers. Intelligence of this was soon communicated to Cortés, who sent at once to the fiery chiefs, imploring them, by their regard for him and the common cause, to lay aside their differences, which must end in their own ruin, and that of the expedition. His remonstrance prevailed, at least, so far as to establish a show of reconciliation between the parties. But Olid was not a man to forget, or easily to forgive; and Alvarado, though frank and liberal, had an impatient temper much more easily excited than appeased. They were never afterwards friends.

The Spaniards met with no opposition on their march. The principal towns were all abandoned by the inhabitants, who had gone to strengthen the garrison of Mexico, or taken refuge with their families among the mountains. Tacuba was in like manner deserted, and the troops once more established themselves in their old quarters in the lordly city of the Tepanecs.

Their first undertaking was, to cut off the pipes that conducted the water from the royal streams of Chapoltepec to feed the numerous tanks and fountains which sparkled in the court-yards of the capital. The aqueduct, partly constructed of brickwork, and partly of stone and mortar, was raised on a strong, though narrow, dike, which transported it across an arm of the lake; and the whole work was one of the most pleasing monuments of Mexican civilization. The Indians, well aware of its importance, had stationed a large body of troops for its protection. A battle followed, in which both sides suffered considerably, but the Spaniards were victorious. A part of the aqueduct was demolished, and during the siege no water found its way again to the capital through this channel.

On the following day, the combined forces descended on the fatal causeway, to make themselves masters, if possible, of the nearest bridge. They found the dike covered with a swarm of warriors, as numerous as on the night of their disaster, while the surface of the lake was dark with the multitude of canoes. The intrepid Christians strove to advance under a perfect hurricane of missiles from the water and the land, but they made slow progress. Barricades thrown across the causeway embarrassed the cavalry, and rendered it nearly useless. The sides of the Indian boats were fortified with bulwarks, which shielded the crews from the arquebuses and crossbows; and, when the warriors on the dike were hard pushed by the pike-men, they threw themselves fearlessly into the water, as if it were their native element, and, reappearing along the sides of the dike, shot off their arrows and javelins with fatal execution. After a long and obstinate struggle, the Christians were compelled to fall back on their own quarters with disgrace, and—including the allies—with nearly as much damage as they had inflicted on the enemy. Olid, disgusted with the result of the engagement, inveighed against his companion, as having involved them in it by his wanton temerity, and drew off his own forces the next morning to his own station at Cojohuacan.

The camps, separated by only two leagues, maintained an easy communication with each other. They found abundant employment in foraging the neighbouring country for provisions, and in repelling the active sallies of the enemy; on whom they took their revenge by cutting off his supplies. But their own position was precarious, and they looked with impatience for the arrival of the brigantines under Cortés. It was in the latter part of May, that Olid took up his quarters at Cojohuacan; and from that time may be dated the commencement of the siege of Mexico.

IV

The Siege: Patterns of Conflict

No sooner had Cortés received intelligence that his two officers had established themselves in their respective posts, than he ordered Sandoval to march on Iztapalapan. The cavalier's route led him through a country for the most part friendly; and at Chalco his little body of Spaniards was swelled by the formidable muster of Indian levies who awaited there his approach. After this junction, he continued his march without opposition till he arrived before the hostile city, under whose walls he found a large force drawn up to receive him. A battle followed, and the natives, after maintaining their ground sturdily for some time, were compelled to give way, and to seek refuge either on the water, or in that part of the town which hung over it. The remainder was speedily occupied by the Spaniards.

Meanwhile Cortés had set sail with his flotilla, intending to support his lieutenant's attack by water. On drawing near the southern shore of the lake, he passed under the shadow of an insulated peak, since named from him the "Rock of the Marquess." It was held by a body of Indians, who saluted the fleet, as it passed with showers of stones and arrows. Cortés, resolving to punish their audacity, and to clear the lake of his troublesome enemy, instantly landed with a hundred and fifty of his followers. He placed himself at their head, scaled the steep ascent, in the fact of a driving storm of missiles, and, reaching the summit, put the garrison to the sword. There was a number of women and children, also, gathered in the place, whom he spared.

On the top of the eminence was a blazing beacon, serving to notify to the inhabitants of the capital when the Spanish fleet weighed anchor. Before Cortés had regained his brigantine, the canoes and *piraguas* of the enemy had left the harbours of Mexico, and were seen darkening the lake for many a rood. There were several hundred of them, all crowded with warriors, and advancing rapidly by means of their oars over the calm bosom of the waters.

Cortés, who regarded his fleet, to use his own language, as "the key of the war," felt the importance of striking a decisive blow in the first encounter with the enemy. It was with chagrin, therefore, that he found his sails rendered useless by the want of wind. He calmly waited the approach of the Indian squadron, which, however, lay on their oars, at something more than musket-shot distance, as if hesitating to encounter these leviathans of their waters. At this moment, a light air from land rippled the surface of the lake; it gradually freshened into a breeze, and Cortés, taking advantage of the friendly succour, which he may be excused, under all the circumstances, for regarding as especially sent him by Heaven, extended his line of battle, and bore down, under full press of canvass, on the enemy.

The latter no sooner encountered the bows of their formidable opponents, than they were overturned and sent to the bottom by the shock, or so much damaged that they speedily filled and sank. The water was covered with the wreck of broken canoes, and with the bodies of men struggling for life in the waves, and vainly imploring their companions to take them on board their over-crowded vessels. The Spanish fleet, as it dashed through the mob of boats, sent off its volleys to the right and left with a terrible effect, completing the discomfiture of the Aztecs. The latter made no attempt at resistance, scarcely venturing a single flight of arrows, but strove with all their strength to regain the port from which they had so lately issued. They were no match in the chase, any more than in the fight, for their terrible antagonist, who, borne on the wings of the wind, careered to and fro at his pleasure, dealing death widely around him, and making the shores ring with the thunders of his ordnance. A few only of the Indian flotilla succeeded in recovering the port, and, gliding up the canals, found a shelter in the bosom of the city, where the heavier burden of the brigantines made it impossible for them to follow. This victory, more complete than even the sanguine temper of Cortés had prognosticated, proved the superiority of the Spaniards, and left them, henceforth, undisputed masters of the Aztec sea.

It was nearly dusk, when the squadron, coasting along the great southern causeway, anchored off the point of junction, called Xoloc, where the branch from Cojohuacan meets the principal dike. The avenue widened at this point, so as to afford room for two towers, or turreted temples, built of stone, and surrounded by walls of the same material, which presented altogether a position of some strength, and, at the present moment, was garrisoned by a body of Aztecs. They were not numerous, and Cortés, landing with his soldiers, succeeded without much difficulty in dislodging the enemy, and in getting possession of the works.

It seems to have been originally the general's design, to take up his own quarters with Olid at Cojohuacan. But, if so, he now changed his purpose, and wisely fixed on this spot, as the best position for his encampment. It was but half a league distant from the capital; and, while it commanded its great southern avenue, had a direct communication with the garrison at Cojohuacan, through which he might receive supplies from the surrounding country. Here, then, he determined to establish his headquarters. He at once caused his heavy iron cannon to be transferred from the brigantines to the causeway, and sent orders to Olid to join him with half his force, while Sandoval was instructed to abandon his present quarters, and advance to Cojohuacan, whence he was to detach fifty picked men of his infantry to the camp of Cortés. Having made these arrangements, the general busily occupied himself with strengthening the works at Xoloc, and putting them in the best posture of defence.

During the first five or six days after their encampment, the Spaniards experienced much annoyance from the enemy, who too late endeavoured to prevent their taking up a position so near the capital, and which, had they known much of the science of war, they would have taken better care themselves to secure. Contrary to their usual practice, the Indians made their attacks by night as well as by day. The water swarmed with canoes, which hovered at a distance in terror of the brigantines, but still approached near enough, especially under cover of the darkness, to send showers of arrows into the Christian camp, that fell so thick as to hide the surface of the ground, and impede the movements of the soldiers. Others ran along the western side of the causeway, unprotected, as it was, by the Spanish fleet, and plied their archery with such galling effect, that the Spaniards were forced to make a temporary breach in the dike, wide enough to admit two of their own smaller vessels, which, passing through, soon obtained as entire command of the interior basin, as they before had of the outer. . . .

THE SPANIARDS *launched assault after assault along the causeways—Cortés and Olid from the south, Alvarado from the west, and Sandoval from the north— aided by the brigantines which additionally tightened the blockade of the island-citadel. The fighting was bitter and the retreats at nightfall nullified considerably the gains by day. Cortés' Indian allies performed many services, the most important of which, surely, was the acquisition of the provisions needed by the invaders. Determination and system on the part of the attackers were matched by the defenders. Ambushes and counter-ambushes demonstrated the ingenuity of Cortés and Cuauhtémoc. In view of the insular position of the defenders and the strategy and tactics of the invaders, time was the ally of Cortés.*

Famine was now gradually working its way into the heart of the beleaguered city. It seemed certain, that, with this strict blockade, the crowded population must in the end be driven to capitulate, though no arm should be raised against them.

But it required time; and the Spaniards, though constant and enduring by nature, began to be impatient of hardships scarcely inferior to those experienced by the besieged. In some respects their condition was even worse, exposed, as they were, to the cold, drenching rains, which fell with little intermission, rendering their situation dreary and disastrous in the extreme.

In this state of things, there were many who would willingly have shortened their sufferings, and taken the chance of carrying the place by a *coup de main*. Others thought it would be best to get possession of the great market of Tlatelolco, which, from its situation in the north-western part of the city, might afford the means of communication with the camps of both Alvarado and Sandoval. This place, encompassed by spacious porticos, would furnish accommodations for a numerous host; and, once established in the capital, the Spaniards would be in a position to follow up the blow with far more effect than at a distance.

These arguments were pressed by several of the officers, particularly by Alderete, the royal treasurer, a person of much consideration, not only from his rank, but from the capacity and zeal he had shown in the service. In deference to their wishes, Cortés summoned a council of war, and laid the matter before it. The treasurer's views were espoused by most of the high-mettled cavaliers, who looked with eagerness to any change of their present forlorn and wearisome life; and Cortés, thinking it, probably, more prudent to adopt the less expedient course, than to enforce a cold and reluctant obedience to his own opinion, suffered himself to be overruled.

A day was fixed for the assault, which was to be made simultaneously by the two divisions under Alvarado and the commander-in-chief. Sandoval was instructed to draw off the greater part of his forces from the northern causeway, and to unite himself with Alvarado, while seventy picked soldiers were to be detached to the support of Cortés.

On the appointed morning, the two armies, after the usual celebration of mass, advanced along their respective causeways against the city. They were supported, in addition to the brigantines, by a numerous fleet of Indian boats, which were to force a passage up the canals, and by a countless multitude of allies, whose very numbers served in the end to embarrass their operations. After clearing the suburbs, three avenues presented themselves, which all terminated in the square of Tlatelolco. The principal one, being of much greater width than the other two, might rather be called a causeway than a street, since it was flanked by deep canals on either side. Cortés divided his force into three bodies. One of them he placed under Alderete, with orders to occupy the principal street. A second he gave in charge to Andrés de Tapia and Jorge de Alvarado; the former a cavalier of courage and capacity, the latter, a younger brother of Don Pedro, and possessed of the intrepid spirit which belonged to that chivalrous family. These were to penetrate by one of the parallel streets, while the general himself, at the head of the third division, was to occupy the other. A small body of cavalry, with two or three field-pieces, was stationed as a reserve in front of the great street of Tacuba, which was designated as the rallying point for the different divisions.

Cortés gave the most positive instructions to his captains, not to advance a step without securing the means of retreat, by carefully filling up the ditches, and the openings in the causeway. The neglect of this precaution by Alvarado, in an assault which he had made on the city but a few days before, had been attended with such serious consequences to his army, that Cortés rode over, himself, to his officer's quarters, for the purpose of publicly reprimanding him for his disobedience of orders. On his arrival at the camp, however, he found that his offending captain had conducted the affair with so much gallantry, that the intended reprimand—though well deserved—subsided into a mild rebuke.

The arrangements being completed, the three divisions marched at once up the several streets. Cortés, dismounting, took the van of his own squadron, at the head of his infantry.

The Mexicans fell back as he advanced, making less resistance than usual. The Spaniards pushed on, carrying one barricade after another, and carefully filling up the gaps with rubbish, so as to secure themselves a footing. The canoes supported the attack, by moving along the canals, and grappling with those of the enemy; while numbers of the nimble-footed Tlascalans, scaling the terraces, passed on from one house to another, where they were connected, hurling the defenders into the streets below. The enemy, taken apparently by surprise, seemed incapable of withstanding for a moment the fury of the assault; and the victorious Christians, cheered on by the shouts of triumph which arose from their companions in the adjoining streets, were only the more eager to be first at the destined goal.

Indeed, the facility of his success led the general to suspect that he might be advancing too fast; that it might be a device of the enemy to draw them into the heart of the city, and then surround or attack them in the rear. He had some misgivings, moreover, lest his too ardent officers, in the heart of the chase, should, notwithstanding his commands, have overlooked the necessary precaution of filling up the breaches. He, accordingly, brought his squadron to a halt, prepared to baffle any insidious movement of his adversary. Meanwhile he received more than one message from Alderete, informing him that he had nearly gained the market. This only increased the general's apprehension, that, in the rapidity of his advance, he might have neglected to secure the ground. He determined to trust no eyes but his own, and, taking a small body of troops, proceeded at once to reconnoitre the route followed by the treasurer.

He had not proceeded far along the great street, or causeway, when his progress was arrested by an opening ten or twelve paces wide, and filled with water, at least two fathoms deep, by which a communication was formed between the canals on the opposite sides. A feeble attempt had been made to stop the gap with the rubbish of the causeway, but in too careless a manner to be of the least service; and a few straggling stones and pieces of timber only showed that the work had been abandoned almost as soon as begun. To add to his consternation, the general observed that the sides of the causeway in this neighbourhood had been pared off, and, as was evident, very recently. He saw in all this the artifice of the cunning enemy; and had little doubt that his hot-headed officer had rushed into a snare deliberately laid for him. Deeply alarmed, he set about repairing the mischief as fast as possible, by ordering his men to fill up the yawning chasm.

But they had scarcely begun their labors, when the hoarse echoes of conflict in the distance were succeeded by a hideous sound of mingled yells and war-whoops, that seemed to rend the very heavens. This was followed by a rushing noise, as of the tread of thronging multitudes, showing that the tide of battle was turned back from its former course, and was rolling on towards the spot where Cortés and his little band of cavaliers were planted.

His conjecture proved too true. Alderete had followed the retreating Aztecs with an eagerness which increased with every step of his advance. He had carried the barricades, which had defended the breach, without much difficulty, and, as he swept on, gave orders that the opening should be stopped. But the blood of the high-spirited cavaliers was warmed by the chase, and no one cared to be detained by the ignoble occupation of filling up the ditches, while he could gather laurels so easily in the fight; and they all pressed on, exhorting and cheering one another with the assurance of being the first to reach the square of Tlatelolco. In this way they suffered themselves to be decoyed into the heart of the city; when suddenly the horn of Guatemozin—the sacred symbol, heard only in seasons of extraordinary peril—sent forth a long and piercing note from the summit of a neighbouring *teocalli*. In an instant, the flying Aztecs, as if maddened by the blast, wheeled about, and turned on their pursuers. At the same time, countless swarms of warriors from the adjoining streets and lanes poured in upon the flanks of the assailants, filling the air with the fierce, unearthly cries which had reached the ears of Cortés, and drowning, for a moment, the wild dissonance which reigned in the other quarters of the capital.

The army, taken by surprise, and shaken by the fury of the assault, were thrown into the utmost disorder. Friends and foes, white men and Indians, were mingled together in one promiscuous mass. Spears, swords, and war-clubs were brandished together in the air. Blows fell at random. In their eagerness to escape, they trod down one another. Blinded by the missiles, which now rained on them from the *azoteas,* they staggered on, scarcely knowing in what direction, or fell, struck down by hands which they could not see. On they came like a rushing torrent sweeping along some steep declivity, and rolling in one confused tide towards the open breach, on the further side of which stood Cortés and his companions, horror-struck at the sight of the approaching ruin. The foremost files soon plunged into the gulf, treading one another under the flood, some striving ineffectually to swim, others, with more success, to clamber over the heaps of their suffocated comrades. Many, as they attempted to scale the opposite sides of the slippery dike, fell into the water, or were hurried off by the warriors in the canoes, who added to the horrors of the rout by the fresh storm of darts and javelins, which they poured on the fugitives.

Cortés, meanwhile, with his brave followers, kept his station undaunted on the other side of the breach. "I had made up my mind," he says, "to die, rather than desert my poor followers in their extremity! With outstretched hands he endeavoured to rescue as many as he could from the watery grave, and from the more appalling fate of captivity. He as vainly tried to restore something like presence of mind and order among the distracted fugitives. His person was too well known to the Aztecs, and his position now made him a conspicuous mark for their weapons. Darts, stones, and arrows fell around him thick as hail, but glanced harmless from his steel helmet and armor of proof. At length a cry of "Malinche," "Malinche," arose among the enemy; and six of their number, strong and athletic warriors, rushing on him at once, made a violent effort to drag him

on board their boat. In the struggle he received a severe wound
in the leg, which, for the time, disabled it. There seemed to be
no hope for him; when a faithful follower, Christóval de Olea,
perceiving his general's extremity, threw himself on the Aztecs,
and with a blow cut off the arm of one savage, and then plunged
his sword in the body of another. He was quickly supported by
a comrade named Lerma, and by a Tlascalan chief, who, fighting over the prostrate body of Cortés, despatched three more
of the assailants, though the heroic Olea paid dearly for his
self-devotion, as he fell mortally wounded by the side of his
general.

The report soon spread among the soldiers, that the commander was taken; and Quiñones, the captain of his guard,
with several others, pouring in to the rescue, succeeded in dis-
entangling Cortés from the grasp of his enemies who were
struggling with him in the water, and, raising him in their arms,
placed him again on the causeway. One of his pages, meanwhile, had advanced some way through the press, leading a
horse for his master to mount. But the youth received a wound
in the throat from a javelin, which prevented him from effecting his object. Another of his attendants was more successful.
It was Guzmán, his chamberlain; but, as he held the bridle,
while Cortés was assisted into the saddle, he was snatched away
by the Aztecs, and, with the swiftness of thought, hurried off
by their canoes. The general still lingered, unwilling to leave
the spot, while his presence could be of the least service. But
the faithful Quiñones, taking his horse by the bridle, turned
his head from the breach, exclaiming, at the same time, that
"his master's life was too important to the army to be thrown
away there."

Yet it was no easy matter to force a passage through the
press. The surface of the causeway, cut up by the feet of men
and horses, was knee-deep in mud, and in some parts was so
much broken, that the water from the canals flowed over it.
The crowded mass, in their efforts to extricate themselves from
their perilous position, staggered to and fro like a drunken

man. Those on the flanks were often forced by the lateral pressure of their comrades down the slippery sides of the dike, where they were picked up by the canoes of the enemy, whose shouts of triumph proclaimed the savage joy with which they gathered in every new victim for the sacrifice. Two cavaliers, riding by the general's side, lost their footing, and rolled down the declivity into the water. One was taken and his horse killed. The other was happy enough to escape. The valiant ensign, Corral, had a similar piece of good fortune. He slipped into the canal, and the enemy felt sure of their prize, when he again succeeded in recovering the causeway with the tattered banner of Castile still flying above his head. The barbarians set up a cry of disappointed rage, as they lost possession of a trophy, to which the people of Anahuac attached, as we have seen, the highest importance, hardly inferior in their eyes to the capture of the commander-in-chief himself.

Cortés at length succeeded in regaining the firm ground, and reaching the open place before the great street of Tacuba. Here, under a sharp fire of the artillery, he rallied his broken squadrons, and, charging at the head of the little body of horse, which, not having been brought into action, were still fresh, he beat off the enemy. He then commanded the retreat of the two other divisions. The scattered forces again united; and the general, sending forward his Indian confederates, took the rear with a chosen body of cavalry to cover the retreat of the army, which was effected with but little additional loss.

Andrés de Tapia was despatched to the western causeway to acquaint Alvarado and Sandoval with the failure of the enterprise. Meanwhile the two captains had penetrated far into the city. Cheered by the triumphant shouts of their countrymen in the adjacent streets, they had pushed on with extraordinary vigor, that they might not be outstripped in the race of glory. They had almost reached the market-place, which lay nearer to their quarters than to the general's, when they heard the blast from the dread horn of Guatemozin, followed by the overpowering yell of the barbarians, which had so startled the ears of Cortés; till at length the sounds of the receding conflict died away in the distance. The two captains now understood that the day must have gone hard with their countrymen. They soon had further proof of it, when the victorious Aztecs, returning from the pursuit of Cortés, joined their forces to those engaged with Sandoval and Alvarado, and fell on them with redoubled fury. At the same time they rolled on the ground two or three of the bloody heads of the Spaniards, shouting the name of "Malinche." The captains, struck with horror at the spectacle,—though they gave little credit to the words of the enemy,—instantly ordered a retreat. Indeed, it was not in their power to maintain their ground against the furious assaults of the besieged, who poured on them, swarm after swarm, with a desperation, of which, says one who was there, "although it seems as if it were now present to my eyes, I can give but a faint idea to the reader. God alone could have brought us off safe from the perils of that day." The fierce barbarians followed up the Spaniards to their very intrenchments. But here they were met, first by the cross fire of the brigantines, which, dashing through the palisades planted to obstruct their movements, completely enfiladed the causeway, and next by that of the small battery erected in front of the camp, which, under the management of a skilful engineer, named Medrano, swept the whole length of the defile. Thus galled in front and on flank, the shattered columns of the Aztecs were compelled to give way and take shelter under the defences of the city.

The greatest anxiety now prevailed in the camp, regarding the fate of Cortés; for Tapia had been detained on the road by scattered parties of the enemy, whom Guatemozin had stationed there to interrupt the communications between the camps. He arrived, at length, however, though bleeding from several wounds. His intelligence, while it reassured the Spaniards as to the general's personal safety, was not calculated to allay their uneasiness in other respects. . . .

ON both sides the bloody losses mounted. Captured Spaniards served the defenders as sacrifices to their gods. At times the siege approached stalemate, and in the face of Spanish losses, native allies defected from Cortés' camp. The core of the invading force, however, stood steadfast. When a Spanish embassy proved fruitless, the demolition of the city, stone by stone, became the battle plan of the invaders.

V

The Siege: Climax and Conclusion

CORTÉS now steadily pursued the plan he had laid down for the devastation of the city. Day after day the several armies entered by their respective quarters, Sandoval probably directing his operations against the north-eastern district. The buildings, made of the porous *tetzontli*, though generally low, were so massy and extensive, and the canals were so numerous, that their progress was necessarily slow. They, however, gathered fresh accessions of strength every day from the numbers who flocked to the camp from the surrounding country, and who joined in the work of destruction with a hearty good-will, which showed their eagerness to break the detested yoke of the Aztecs. The latter raged with impotent anger, as they beheld their lordly edifices, their temples, all they had been accustomed to venerate, thus ruthlessly swept away; their canals, constructed with so much labor, and what to them seemed science, filled up with rubbish; their flourishing city, in short, turned into a desert, over which the insulting foe now rode triumphant. They heaped many a taunt on the Indian allies. "Go on," they said, bitterly; "the more you destroy, the more you will have to build up again hereafter. If we conquer, you shall build for us; and, if your white friends conquer, they will make you do as much for them." The event justified the prediction.

In their rage they rushed blindly on the corps which covered the Indian pioneers. But they were as often driven back by the impetuous charge of the cavalry, or received on the long pikes of Chinantla, which did good service to the besiegers in their operations. At the close of day, however, when the Spaniards drew off their forces, taking care to send the multitudinous host of confederates first from the ground, the Mexicans usually rallied for a more formidable attack. Then they poured out from every lane and by-way, like so many mountain streams, sweeping over the broad level cleared by the enemy, and falling impetuously on their flanks and rear. At such times, they inflicted considerable loss in their turn, till an ambush, which Cortés laid for them among the buildings adjoining the great temple, did them so much mischief, that they were compelled to act with more reserve.

At times the war displayed something of a chivalrous character, in the personal rencontres of the combatants. Challenges passed between them, and especially between the native warriors. These combats were usually conducted on the *azoteas,* whose broad and level surface afforded a good field of fight. On one occasion, a Mexican of powerful frame, brandishing a sword and buckler, which he had won from the Christians, defied his enemies to meet him in single fight. A young page of Cortés', named Núñez, obtained his master's permission to accept the vaunting challenge of the Aztec; and, springing on the *azotea,* succeeded after a hard struggle in discomfiting his antagonist, who fought at a disadvantage with weapons in which he was unpractised, and, running him through the body, brought off his spoils in triumph, and laid them at the general's feet.

The division of Cortés had now worked its way as far north as the great street of Tacuba, which opened a communication with Alvarado's camp, and near which stood the palace of Guatemozin. It was a spacious stone pile, that might well be called a fortress. Though deserted by its royal master, it was held by a strong body of Aztecs, who made a temporary defence, but of little avail against the battering enginery of the besiegers. It was soon set on fire, and its crumbling walls were levelled in the dust, like those other stately edifices of the capital, the boast and admiration of the Aztecs, and some of the fairest fruits of their civilization. "It was a sad thing to witness their destruction," exclaims Cortés; "but it was part of our plan of operations, and we had no alternative."

These operations had consumed several weeks, so that it was now drawing towards the latter part of July. During this time, the blockade had been maintained with the utmost rigor, and the wretched inhabitants were suffering all the extremities of famine. Some few stragglers were taken, from time to time, in the neighbourhood of the Christian camp, whither they had wandered in search of food. They were kindly treated by command of Cortés, who was in hopes to induce others to follow their example, and thus to afford a means of conciliating the inhabitants, which might open the way to their submission. But few were found willing to leave the shelter of the capital, and they preferred to take their chance with their suffering countrymen, rather than trust themselves to the mercies of the besiegers.

From these few stragglers, however, the Spaniards heard a dismal tale of woe, respecting the crowded population in the interior of the city. All the ordinary means of sustenance had long since failed, and they now supported life as they could, by means of such roots as they could dig from the earth, by gnawing the bark of trees, by feeding on the grass,—on anything, in short, however loathsome, that could allay the craving of appetite. Their only drink was the brackish water of the soil saturated with the salt lake. Under this unwholesome diet, and the diseases engendered by it, the population was gradually wasting away. Men sickened and died every day, in all the excruciating torments produced by hunger, and the wan and emaciated survivors seemed only to be waiting for their time.

The Spaniards had visible confirmation of all this, as they penetrated deeper into the city and approached the district of Tlatelolco, now occupied by the besieged. They found the ground turned up in quest of roots and weeds, the trees stripped of their green stems, their foliage, and their bark. Troops of famished Indians flitted in the distance, gliding like ghosts among the scenes of their former residence. Dead bodies lay unburied in the streets and court-yards, or filled up the canals. It was a sure sign of the extremity of the Aztecs; for they held the burial of the dead as a solemn and imperative duty. In the early part of the siege, they had religiously attended to it. In its later stages, they were still careful to withdraw the dead from the public eye, by bringing their remains within the houses. But the number of these, and their own sufferings, had now so fearfully increased, that they had grown indifferent to this, and they suffered their friends and their kinsmen to lie and moulder on the spot where they drew their last breath!

As the invaders entered the dwellings, a more appalling spectacle presented itself;—the floors covered with the prostrate forms of the miserable inmates, some in the agonies of death, others festering in their corruption; men, women, and children, inhaling the poisonous atmosphere, and mingled promiscuously together; mothers, with their infants in their arms perishing of hunger before their eyes, while they were unable to afford them the nourishment of nature; men crippled by their wounds, with their bodies frightfully mangled, vainly attempting to crawl away, as the enemy entered. Yet, even in this state, they scorned to ask for mercy, and glared on the invaders with the sullen ferocity of the wounded tiger, that the huntsmen have tracked to his forest cave. The Spanish commander issued strict orders that mercy should be shown to these poor and disabled victims. But the Indian allies made no distinction. An Aztec, under whatever circumstances, was an enemy; and, with hideous shouts of triumph, they pulled down the burning buildings on their heads, consuming the living and the dead in one common funeral pile!

Yet the sufferings of the Aztecs, terrible as they were, did not incline them to submission. There were many, indeed, who, from greater strength of constitution, or from the more favorable circumstances in which they were placed, still showed all their wonted energy of body and mind, and maintained the same undaunted and resolute demeanour as before. They fiercely rejected all the overtures of Cortés, declaring they would rather die than surrender, and adding, with a bitter tone of exultation, that the invaders would be at least disappointed in their expectations of treasure, for it was buried where they could never find it!

The women, it is said, shared in this desperate—it should rather be called heroic—spirit. They were indefatigable in nursing the sick, and dressing their wounds; they aided the warriors in battle, by supplying them with the Indian ammunition of stones and arrows, prepared their slings, strung their bows, and displayed, in short, all the constancy and courage shown by the noble maidens of Saragossa in our day, and by those of Carthage in the days of antiquity.

Cortés had now entered one of the great avenues leading to the market-place of Tlatelolco, the quarter, towards which the movements of Alvarado were also directed. A single canal only lay in his way, but this was of great width and stoutly defended by the Mexican archery. At this crisis, the army one evening, while in their intrenchments on the causeway, were surprised by an uncommon light, that arose from the huge *teocalli* in that part of the city, which, being at the north, was the most distant from their own position. This temple, dedicated to the dread war-god, was inferior only to the pyramid in the great square; and on it the Spaniards had more than once seen their unhappy countrymen led to slaughter. They now supposed that the enemy were employed in some of their diabolical ceremonies, when the flame, mounting higher and higher, showed that the sanctuaries themselves were on fire. A shout of exultation at the sight broke forth from the assembled soldiers, as they assured one another that their countrymen under Alvarado had got possession of the building.

It was indeed true. That gallant officer, whose position on

the western causeway placed him near the district of Tlatelolco, had obeyed his commander's instructions to the letter, razing every building to the ground in his progress, and filling up the ditches with their ruins. He, at length, found himself before the great *teocalli* in the neighbourhood of the market. He ordered a company, under a cavalier named Gutierre de Badajoz, to storm the place, which was defended by a body of warriors, mingled with priests, still more wild and ferocious than the soldiery. The garrison, rushing down the winding terraces, fell on the assailants with such fury, as compelled them to retreat in confusion, and with some loss. Alvarado ordered another detachment to their support. This last was engaged, at the moment, with a body of Aztecs, who hung on its rear as it wound up the galleries of the *teocalli*. Thus hemmed in between two enemies, above and below, the position of the Spaniards was critical. With sword and buckler, they plunged desperately on the ascending Mexicans, and drove them into the court-yard below, where Alvarado plied them with such lively volleys of musketry, as soon threw them into disorder and compelled them to abandon the ground. Being thus rid of annoyance in the rear, the Spaniards returned to the charge. They drove the enemy up the heights of the pyramid, and, reaching the broad summit, a fierce encounter followed in mid-air,—such an encounter as takes place where death is the certain consequence of defeat. It ended, as usual, in the discomfiture of the Aztecs, who were either slaughtered on the spot still wet with the blood of their own victims, or pitched headlong down the sides of the pyramid.

The area was covered with the various symbols of the barbarous worship of the country, and with two lofty sanctuaries, before whose grinning idols were displayed the heads of several Christian captives, who had been immolated on their altars. Although overgrown by their long, matted hair and bushy beards, the Spaniards could recognise, in the livid countenances, their comrades who had fallen into the hands of the enemy. Tears fell from their eyes, as they gazed on the melancholy spectacle, and thought of the hideous death which their countrymen had suffered. They removed the sad relics with decent care, and after the Conquest deposited them in consecrated ground, on a spot since covered by the Church of the Martyrs.

They completed their work by firing the sanctuaries, that the place might be no more polluted by these abominable rites. The flame crept slowly up the lofty pinnacles, in which stone was mingled with wood, till, at length, bursting into one bright blaze, it shot up its spiral volume to such a height, that it was seen from the most distant quarters of the Valley. It was this which had been hailed by the soldiery of Cortés, and it served as the beacon-light to both friend and foe, intimating the progress of the Christian arms.

The commander-in-chief and his division, animated by the spectacle, made, in their entrance on the following day, more determined efforts to place themselves alongside of their companions under Alvarado. The broad canal, above noticed as the only impediment now lying in his way, was to be traversed; and on the further side the emaciated figures of the Aztec warriors were gathered in numbers to dispute the passage, like the gloomy shades that wander—as ancient poets tell us— on the banks of the infernal river. They poured down, however, a storm of missiles, which were no shades, on the heads of the Indian laborers, while occupied with filling up the wide gap with the ruins of the surrounding buildings. Still they toiled on in defiance of the arrowy shower, fresh numbers taking the place of those who fell. And when at length the work was completed, the cavalry rode over the rough plain at full charge against the enemy, followed by the deep array of spearmen, who bore down all opposition with their invincible phalanx.

The Spaniards now found themselves on the same ground with Alvarado's division. Soon afterwards, that chief, attended by several of his staff, rode into their lines, and cordially embraced his countrymen and companions in arms, for the first time since the beginning of the siege. They were now in the neighbourhood of the market. Cortés, taking with him a few of his cavaliers, galloped into it. It was a vast inclosure, as the reader has already seen, covering many an acre. Its dimensions were suited to the immense multitudes who gathered there from all parts of the Valley in the flourishing days of the Aztec monarchy. It was surrounded by porticos and pavilions for the accommodation of the artisans and traders, who there displayed their various fabrics and articles of merchandise. The flat roofs of the piazzas were now covered with crowds of men and women, who gazed in silent dismay on the steel-clad horsemen, that profaned these precincts with their presence, for the first time since their expulsion from the capital. The multitude, composed, for the most part, probably, of unarmed citizens, seemed taken by surprise; at least, they made no show of resistance; and the general, after leisurely viewing the ground, was permitted to ride back unmolested to the army.

On arriving there, he ascended the *teocalli,* from which the standard of Castile, supplanting the memorials of Aztec superstition, was now triumphantly floating. The Conqueror, as he strode among the smoking embers on the summit, calmly surveyed the scene of desolation below. The palaces, the temples, the busy marts of industry and trade, the glittering canals, covered with their rich freights from the surrounding country, the royal pomp of groves and gardens, all the splendors of the imperial city, the capital of the Western World, forever gone,— and in their place a barren wilderness! How different the spectacle which the year before had met his eye, as it wandered over the same scenes from the heights of the neighbouring *teocalli,* with Montezuma at his side! Seven eighths of the city were laid in ruins, with the occasional exception, perhaps, of some colossal temple, that it would have required too much time to demolish. The remaining eighth, comprehending the district of Tlatelolco, was all that now remained to the Aztecs, whose population—still large after all its losses—was crowded into a compass that would hardly have afforded accommodations for a third of their numbers. It was the quarter lying between the great northern and western causeways, and is recognised in the modern capital as the *Barrio de San Jago* and its vicinity. It was the favorite residence of the Indians after the Conquest, though at the present day thinly covered with humble dwellings, forming the straggling suburbs, as it were, of the metropolis. Yet it still affords some faint vestiges of what it was in its prouder days; and the curious antiquary, and occasionally the laborer, as he turns up the soil, encounters a glittering fragment of obsidian, or the mouldering head of a lance, or arrow, or some other warlike relic, attesting that on this spot the retreating Aztecs made their last stand for the independence of their country.

On the day following, Cortés, at the head of his battalions, made a second entry into the great *tianguez*. But this time the Mexicans were better prepared for his coming. They were assembled in considerable force in the spacious square. A sharp encounted followed; but it was short. Their strength was not equal to their spirit, and they melted away before the rolling fire of musketry, and left the Spaniards masters of the inclosure.

The first act was to set fire to some temples of no great size within the market-place, or more probably on its borders. As the flames ascended, the Aztecs, horror-struck, broke forth into piteous lamentations at the destruction of the deities on whom they relied for protection.

The general's next step was at the suggestion of a soldier named Sotelo, a man who had served under the Great Captain in the Italian wars, where he professed to have gathered knowledge of the science of engineering, as it was then practised. He offered his services to construct a sort of catapult, a machine for discharging stones of great size, which might take the place of the regular battering-train, in demolishing the buildings. As the ammunition, notwithstanding the liberal supplies, which, from time to time, had found their way into the camp, now began to fail, Cortés eagerly acceded to a proposal so well suited to his exigences. Timber and stone were furnished, and a number of hands were employed, under the direction of the self-styled engineer, in constructing the ponderous apparatus, which was erected on a solid platform of masonry, thirty paces square, and seven or eight feet high, that covered the centre of the market-place.- It was the work of the Aztec princes, and was used as a scaffolding, on which mountebanks and jugglers might exhibit their marvellous feats for the amusement of the populace, who took great delight in these performances.

The erection of the machine consumed several days, during which hostilities were suspended, while the artisans were protected from interruption by a strong corps of infantry. At length the work was completed; and the besieged, who, with silent awe, had beheld from the neighbouring *azoteas* the progress of the mysterious engine, which was to lay the remainder of their capital in ruins, now looked with terror for its operation. A stone of huge size was deposited on the timber. The machinery was set in motion; and the rocky fragment was discharged with a tremendous force from the catapult. But, instead of taking the direction of the Aztec buildings, it rose high and perpendicularly into the air, and, descending whence it sprung, broke the ill-omened machine into splinters! It was a total failure. The Aztecs were released from their apprehensions, and the soldiery made many a merry jest on the catastrophe, somewhat at the expense of their commander, who testified no little vexation at the disappointment, and still more at his own credulity.

There was no occasion to resort to artificial means to precipitate the ruin of the Aztecs. It was accelerated every hour by causes more potent than those arising from mere human agency. There they were,—pent up in their close and suffocating quarters, nobles, commoners, and slaves, men, women, and children, some in houses, more frequently in hovels,—for this part of the city was not the best,—others in the open air in canoes, or in the streets, shivering in the cold rains of night, and scorched by the burning heat of day. An old chronicler mentions the fact of two women of rank remaining three days and nights up to their necks in the water among the reeds, with only a handful of maize for their support. The ordinary means of sustaining life were long since gone. They wandered about in search of any thing, however unwholesome or revolting, that might mitigate the fierce gnawings of hunger. Some hunted for insects and worms on the borders of the lake, or gathered the salt weeds and moss from its bottom, while at times they might be seen casting a wistful look at the green hills beyond, which many of them had left to share the fate of their brethren in the capital.

To their credit, it is said by the Spanish writers, that they were not driven, in their extremity, to violate the laws of nature by feeding on one another. But unhappily this is contradicted by the Indian authorities, who state that many a mother, in her agony, devoured the offspring which she had no longer the means of supporting. This is recorded of more than one siege in history; and it is the more probable here, where the sensibilities must have been blunted by familiarity with the brutal practices of the national superstition.

But all was not sufficient, and hundreds of famished wretches died every day from extremity of suffering. Some dragged themselves into the houses, and drew their last breath alone, and in silence. Others sank down in the public streets. Wherever they died, there they were left. There was no one to bury, or to remove them. Familiarity with the spectacle made the men indifferent to it. They looked on in dumb despair, waiting for their own turn. There was no complaint, no lamentation, but deep, unutterable woe.

If in other quarters of the town the corpses might be seen scattered over the streets, here they were gathered in heaps. "They lay so thick," says Bernal Díaz, "that one could not tread except among the bodies." "A man could not set his foot down," says Cortés, yet more strongly, "unless on the corpse of an Indian!" They were piled one upon another, the living mingled with the dead. They stretched themselves on the bodies of their friends, and lay down to sleep there. Death was everywhere. The city was a vast charnel-house, in which all was hastening to decay and decomposition. A poisonous steam arose from the mass of putrefaction, under the action of alternate rain and heat, which so tainted the whole atmosphere, that the Spaniards, including the general himself, in their brief visits to the quarter, were made ill by it, and it bred a pestilence that swept off even greater numbers than the famine.

Men's minds were unsettled by these strange and accumulated horrors. They resorted to all the superstitious rites prescribed by the religion, to stay the pestilence. They called on their priests to invoke the gods in their behalf. But the oracles were dumb, or gave only gloomy responses. Their deities had deserted them, and in their place they saw signs of celestial wrath, telling of still greater woes in reserve. Many, after the siege, declared, that, among other prodigies, they beheld a stream of light, of a blood-red color, coming from the north in the direction of Tepejacac,* with a rushing noise, like that of a whirlwind, which swept round the district of Tlatelolco, darting out sparkles and flakes of fire, till it shot far into the centre of the lake! In the disordered state of their nerves, a mysterious fear took possession of their senses. Prodigies were of familiar occurence, and the most familiar phenomena of nature were converted into prodigies. Stunned by their calamities, reason was bewildered, and they became the sport of the wildest, and most superstitious fancies.

In the midst of these scenes, the young emperor of the Aztecs remained, according to all accounts, calm and courageous. With his fair capital laid in ruins before his eyes, his nobles and faithful subjects dying around him, his territory rent away, foot by foot, till scarce enough remained for him to stand on, he rejected every invitation to capitulate, and showed the same indomitable spirit, as at the commencement of the siege. When Cortés, in the hope that the extremities of·the besieged would incline them to listen to an accommodation, persuaded a noble prisoner to bear to Guatemozin his proposals to that effect; the

* Tepeyac. C.H.G.

fierce young monarch, according to the general, ordered him at once to be sacrificed. It is a Spaniard, we must remember, who tells the story.

Cortés, who had suspended hostilities for several days, in the vain hope that the distresses of the Mexicans would bend them to submission, now determined to drive them to it by a general assault. Cooped up, as they were, within a narrow quarter of the city, their position favored such an attempt. He commanded Alvarado to hold himself in readiness, and directed Sandoval—who, besides the causeway, had charge of the fleet, which lay off the Tlatelolcan district—to support the attack by a cannonade on the houses near the water. He then led his forces into the city, or rather across the horrid waste that now encircled it.

On entering the Indian precincts, he was met by several of the chiefs, who, stretching forth their emaciated arms, exclaimed, "You are the children of the Sun. But the Sun is swift in his course. Why are you, then, so tardy? Why do you delay so long to put an end to our miseries? Rather kill us at once, that we may go to our god Huitzilopochtli, who waits for us in heaven to give us rest from our sufferings!"

Cortés was moved by their piteous appeal, and answered, that he desired not their death, but their submission. "Why does your master refuse to treat with me," he said, "when a single hour will suffice for me to crush him and all his people?" He then urged them to request Guatemozin to confer with him, with the assurance that he might do it in safety, as his person should not be molested.

The nobles, after some persuasion, undertook the mission; and it was received by the young monarch in a manner which showed—if the anecdote before related of him be true—that misfortune had, at length, asserted some power over his haughty spirit. He consented to the interview, though not to have it take place on that day, but the following, in the great square of Tlatelolco. Cortés, well satisfied, immediately withdrew from the city, and resumed his position on the causeway.

The next morning he presented himself at the place appointed, having previously stationed Alvarado there with a strong corps of infantry, to guard against treachery. The stone platform in the centre of the square was covered with mats and carpets, and a banquet was prepared to refresh the famished monarch, and his nobles. Having made these arrangements, he awaited the hour of the interview.

But Guatemozin, instead of appearing himself, sent his nobles, the same who had brought to him the general's invitation, and who now excused their master's absence on the plea of illness. Cortés, though disappointed, gave a courteous reception to the envoys, considering that it might still afford the means of opening a communication with the emperor. He persuaded them, without much entreaty, to partake of the good cheer spread before them, which they did with a voracity that told how severe had been their abstinence. He then dismissed them with a seasonable supply of provisions for their master, pressing him to consent to an interview, without which it was impossible their differences could be adjusted.

The Indian envoys returned in a short time, bearing with them a present of fine cotton fabrics, of no great value, from Guatemozin, who still declined to meet the Spanish general. Cortés, though deeply chagrined, was unwilling to give up the point. "He will surely come," he said to the envoys "when he sees that I suffer you to go and come unharmed, you who have been my steady enemies, no less than himself, throughout the war. He has nothing to fear from me." He again parted with them, promising to receive their answer the following day.

On the next morning, the Aztec chiefs, entering the Christian quarters, announced to Cortés that Guatemozin would confer with him at noon in the market-place. The general was punctual at the hour; but without success. Neither monarch, nor ministers appeared there. It was plain that the Indian prince did not care to trust the promises of his enemy. A thought of Montezuma may have passed across his mind. After he had waited three hours, the general's patience was exhausted, and, as he learned that the Mexicans were busy in preparations for defence, he made immediate dispositions for the assault.

The confederates had been left without the walls, for he did not care to bring them in sight of the quarry, before he was ready to slip the leash. He now ordered them to join him; and, supported by Alvarado's division, marched at once into the enemy's quarters. He found them prepared to receive him. Their most able-bodied warriors were thrown into the van, covering their feeble and crippled comrades. Women were seen occasionally mingling in the ranks, and, as well as children, thronged the *azoteas*, where, with famine-stricken visages, and haggard eyes, they scowled defiance and hatred on their invaders.

As the Spaniards advanced, the Mexicans set up a fierce war-cry, and sent off clouds of arrows with their accustomed spirit, while the women and boys rained down darts and stones from their elevated position on the terraces. But the missiles were sent by hands too feeble to do much damage; and, when the squadrons closed, the loss of strength became still more sensible in the Aztecs. Their blows fell feebly and with doubtful aim, though some, it is true, of stronger constitution, or gathering strength from despair, maintained to the last a desperate fight.

The arquebusiers now poured in a deadly fire. The brigantines replied by successive volleys, in the opposite quarter. The besieged, hemmed in, like deer surrounded by the huntsmen, were brought down on every side. The carnage was horrible. The ground was heaped up with the slain, until the maddened combatants were obliged to climb over the human mounds to get at one another. The miry soil was saturated with blood, which ran off like water, and dyed the canals themselves with crimson. All was uproar and terrible confusion. The hideous yells of the barbarians; the oaths and execrations of the Spaniards; the cries of the wounded; the shrieks of women and children; the heavy blows of the Conquerors; the death-struggle of their victims; the rapid, reverberating echoes of musketry;

the hissing of innumerable missiles; the crash and crackling of blazing buildings, crushing hundreds in their ruins; the blinding volumes of dust and sulphurous smoke shrouding all in their gloomy canopy,—made a scene appalling even to the soldiers of Cortés, steeled as they were by many a rough passage of war, and by long familiarity with blood and violence. "The piteous cries of the women and children, in particularly," says the general, "were enough to break one's heart." He commanded that they should be spared, and that all, who asked it, should receive quarter. He particularly urged this on the confederates, and placed men among them to restrain their violence. But he had set an engine in motion too terrible to be controlled. It were as easy to curb the hurricane in its fury, as the passions of an infuriated horde of savages. "Never did I see so pitiless a race," he exclaims, "or any thing wearing the form of man so destitute of humanity." They made no distinction of sex or age, and in this hour of vengeance seemed to be requiting the hoarded wrongs of a century. At length, sated with slaughter, the Spanish commander sounded a retreat. It was full time, if, according to his own statement,—we may hope it is an exaggeration,—forty thousand souls had perished! Yet their fate was to be envied, in comparison with that of those who survived.

Through the long night which followed, no movement was perceptible in the Aztec quarter. No light was seen there, no sound was heard, save the low moaning of some wounded or dying wretch, writhing in his agony. All was dark and silent,— the darkness of the grave. The last blow seemed to have completely stunned them. They had parted with hope, and sat in sullen despair, like men waiting in silence the stroke of the executioner. Yet, for all this, they showed no disposition to submit. Every new injury had sunk deeper into their souls, and filled them with a deeper hatred of their enemy. Fortune, friends, kindred, home,—all were gone. They were content to throw away life itself, now that they had nothing more to live for.

Far different was the scene in the Christian camp, where, elated with their recent successes, all was alive with bustle, and preparation for the morrow. Bonfires were seen blazing along the causeways, lights gleamed from tents and barracks, and the sounds of music and merriment, borne over the waters, proclaimed the joy of the soldiers, at the prospect of so soon terminating their wearisome campaign.

On the following morning the Spanish commander again mustered his forces, having decided to follow up the blow of the preceding day, before the enemy should have time to rally, and, at once to put an end to the war. He had arranged with Alvarado, on the evening previous, to occupy the market-place of Tlatelolco; and the discharge of an arquebuse was to be the signal for a simultaneous assault. Sandoval was to hold the northern causeway, and, with the fleet, to watch the movements of the Indian emperor, and to intercept the flight to the main land, which Cortés knew he meditated. To allow him to effect this would be to leave a formidable enemy in his own neighbourhood, who might at any time kindle the flame of insurrection throughout the country. He ordered Sandoval, however, to do no harm to the royal person, and not to fire on the enemy at all, except in self-defence.

It was the memorable 13th of August, 1521, the day of St. Hypolito,—from this circumstance selected as the patron saint of modern Mexico,—that Cortés led his warlike array for the last time across the black and blasted environs which lay around the Indian capital. On entering the Aztec precincts, he paused, willing to afford its wretched inmates one more chance of escape, before striking the fatal blow. He obtained an interview with some of the principal chiefs, and expostulated with them on the conduct of their prince. "He surely will not," said the general, "see you all perish, when he can so easily save you." He then urged them to prevail on Guatemozin to hold a conference with him, repeating the assurances of his personal safety.

The messengers went on their mission, and soon returned

with the *cihuacoatl* at their head, a magistrate of high authority among the Mexicans. He said, with a melancholy air, in which his own disappointment was visible, that "Guatemozin was ready to die where he was, but would hold no interview with the Spanish commander"; adding, in a tone of resignation, "it is for you to work your pleasure." "Go then," replied the stern Conqueror, "and prepare your countrymen for death. Their hour is come."

He still postponed the assault for several hours. But the impatience of his troops at this delay was heightened by the rumor, that Guatemozin and his nobles were preparing to escape with their effects in the *piraguas* and canoes which were moored on the margin of the lake. Convinced of the fruitlessness and impolicy of further procrastination, Cortés made his final dispositions for the attack, and took his own station on an *azotea,* which commanded the theatre of operations.

When he assailants came into presence of the enemy, they found them huddled together in the utmost confusion, all ages and sexes, in masses so dense that they nearly forced one another over the brink of the causeways into the water below. Some had climbed on the terraces, others feebly supported themselves against the walls of the buildings. Their squalid and tattered garments gave a wildness to their appearance, which still further heightened the ferocity of their expression, as they glared on their enemy with eyes in which hate was mingled with despair. When the Spaniards had approached within bowshot, the Aztecs let off a flight of impotent missiles, showing, to the last, the resolute spirit, though they had lost the strength, of their better days. The fatal signal was then given by the discharge of an arquebuse,—speedily followed by peals of heavy ordnance, the rattle of fire-arms, and the hellish shouts of the confederates, as they sprang upon their victims. It is unnecessary to stain the page with a repetition of the horrors of the preceding day. Some of the wretched Aztecs threw themselves into the water, and were picked up by the canoes. Others sunk and were suffocated in the canals. The number of these became so great, that a bridge was made of their dead bodies, over which the assailants could climb to the opposite banks. Others again, especially the women, begged for mercy, which, as the chroniclers assure us, was everywhere granted by the Spaniards, and, contrary to the instructions and entreaties of Cortés, everywhere refused by the confederates.

While this work of butchery was going on, numbers were observed pushing off in the barks that lined the shore, and making the best of their way across the lake. They were constantly intercepted by the brigantines, which broke through the flimsy array of boats; sending off their volleys to the right and left, as the crews of the latter hotly assailed them. The battle raged as fiercely on the lake as on the land. Many of the Indian vessels were shattered and overturned. Some few, however, under cover of the smoke, which rolled darkly over the waters, succeeded in clearing themselves of the turmoil, and were fast nearing the opposite shore.

Sandoval had particularly charged his captains to keep an eye on the movements of any vessel in which it was at all probable that Guatemozin might be concealed. At this crisis, three or four of the largest *piraguas* were seen skimming over the water, and making their way rapidly across the lake. A captain, named Garcí Holguín, who had command of one of the best sailers in the fleet, instantly gave them chase. The wind was favorable, and, every moment, he gained on the fugitives, who pulled their oars with a vigor that despair alone could have given. But it was in vain; and, after a short race, Holguín, coming alongside of one of the *piraguas,* which, whether from its appearance, or from information he had received, he conjectured might bear the Indian emperor, ordered his men to level their crossbows at the boat. But, before they could discharge them, a cry arose from those in it, that their lord was on board. At the same moment, a young warrior, armed with buckler and *maquahuitl,* rose up, as if to beat off the assailants. But, as the Spanish captain ordered his men not to shoot, he dropped his weapons, and exclaimed, "I am Guatemozin; lead me to Malinche, I am his prisoner; but let no harm come to my wife and my followers."

Holguín assured him, that his wishes should be respected, and assisted him to get on board the brigantine, followed by his wife and attendants. These were twenty in number, consisting of Coanaco, the deposed lord of Tezcuco, the lord of Tlacopan, and several other caciques and dignitaries, whose rank, probably, had secured them some exemption from the general calamities of the siege. When the captives were seated on the deck of his vessel, Holguín requested the Aztec prince to put an end to the combat by commanding his people in the other canoes to surrender. But, with a dejected air, he replied, "It is not necessary. They will fight no longer, when they see that their prince is taken." He spoke truth. The news of Guatemozin's capture spread rapidly through the fleet, and on shore, where the Mexicans were still engaged in conflict with their enemies. It ceased, however, at once. They made no further resistance; and those on the water quickly followed the brigantines, which conveyed their captive monarch to land. It seemed as if the fight had been maintained thus long, the better to divert the enemy's attention, and cover their master's retreat.

Meanwhile Sandoval, on receiving tidings of the capture, brought his own brigantine alongside of Holguín's, and demanded the royal prisoner to be surrendered to him. But his captain claimed him as his prize. A dispute arose between the parties, each anxious to have the glory of the deed, and perhaps the privilege of commemorating it on his escutcheon. The controversy continued so long that it reached the ears of Cortés, who, in his station on the *azotea*, had learned, with no little satisfaction, the capture of his enemy. He instantly sent orders to his wrangling officers, to bring Guatemozin before him, that he might adjust the difference between them. He charged them, at the same time, to treat their prisoner with respect. He then made preparations for the interview; caused the terrace to be carpeted with crimson cloth and matting, and a table to be spread with provisions, of which the unhappy Aztec stood so much in need. His lovely Indian mistress, Doña Marina, was present to act as interpreter. She had stood by his side through all the troubled scenes of the Conquest, and she was there now to witness its triumphant termination.

Guatemozin, on landing, was escorted by a company of infantry to the presence of the Spanish commander. He mounted the *azotea* with a calm and steady step, and was easily to be distinguished from his attendant nobles, though his full, dark eye was no longer lighted up with its accustomed fire, and his features wore an expression of passive resignation, that told little of the fierce and fiery spirit that burned within. His head was large, his limbs well proportioned, his complexion, fairer than those of his bronze-colored nation, and his whole deportment singularly mild and engaging.

Cortés came forward with a dignified and studied courtesy to receive him. The Aztec monarch probably knew the person of his conqueror, for he first broke silence by saying; "I have done all that I could, to defend myself and my people. I am now reduced to this state. You will deal with me, Malinche, as you list." Then, laying his hand on the hilt of a poniard, stuck in the general's belt, he added, with vehemence, "Better despatch me with this, and rid me of life at once." Cortés was filled with admiration at the proud bearing of the young barbarian, showing in his reverses a spirit worthy of an ancient Roman. "Fear not," he replied, "you shall be treated with all honor. You have defended your capital like a brave warrior. A Spaniard knows how to respect valor even in an enemy. He then inquired of him, where he had left the princess, his wife; and, being informed that she still remained under protection of a Spanish guard on board the brigantine, the general sent to have her escorted to his presence.

She was the youngest daughter of Montezuma; and was hardly yet on the verge of womanhood. On the accession of her cousin, Guatemozin, to the throne, she had been wedded to him as his lawful wife. She is celebrated by her contemporaries for her personal charms; and the beautiful princess, Tecuichpo, is

still commemorated by the Spaniards, since from her, by a subsequent marriage, are descended some of the illustrious families
of their own nation. She was kindly received by Cortés, who
showed her the respectful attentions suited to her rank. Her
birth, no doubt, gave her an additional interest in his eyes, and
he may have felt some touch of compunction, as he gazed on the
daughter of the unfortunate Montezuma. He invited his royal
captives to partake of the refreshments, which their exhausted
condition rendered so necessary. Meanwhile the Spanish commander made his dispositions for the night, ordering Sandoval to escort the prisoners to Cojohuacan, whither he proposed, himself, immediately to follow. The other captains, Olid
and Alvarado, were to draw off their forces to their respective
quarters. It was impossible for them to continue in the capital,
where the poisonous effluvia from the unburied carcasses loaded
the air with infection. A small guard only was stationed to keep
order in the wasted suburbs.—It was the hour of vespers when
Guatemozin surrendered, and the siege might be considered as
then concluded. The evening set in dark, and the rain began to
fall, before the several parties had evacuated the city.

During the night, a tremendous tempest, such as the Spaniards had rarely witnessed, and such as is known only within the
tropics, burst over the Mexican Valley. The thunder, reverberating from the rocky amphitheatre of hills, bellowed over the
waste of waters, and shook the *teocallis* and crazy tenements
of Tenochtitlán—the few that yet survived—to their foundations. The lightning seemed to cleave asunder the vault of
heaven, as its vivid flashes wrapped the whole scene in a ghastly
glare, for a moment, to be again swallowed up in darkness.
The war of elements was in unison with the fortunes of the
ruined city. It seemed as if the deities of Anahuac, scared from
their ancient abodes, were borne along shrieking and howling
in the blast, as they abandoned the fallen capital to its fate!

On the day following the surrender, Guatemozin requested
the Spanish commander to allow the Mexicans to leave the
city, and to pass unmolested into the open country. To this

Cortés readily assented, as, indeed, without it he could take no steps for purifying the capital. He gave his orders, accordingly, for the evacuation of the place, commanding that no one, Spaniard or confederate, should offer violence to the Aztecs, or in any way obstruct their departure. The whole number of these is variously estimated at from thirty to seventy thousand, beside women and children, who had survived the sword, pestilence, and famine. It is certain they were three days in defiling along the several causeways,—a mournful train; husbands and wives, parents and children, the sick and the wounded, leaning on one another for support, as they feebly tottered along, squalid, and but half covered with rags, that disclosed at every step hideous gashes, some recently received, others festering from long neglect, and carrying with them an atmosphere of contagion. Their wasted forms and famine-stricken faces told the whole history of the siege; and, as the straggling files gained the opposite shore, they were observed to pause from time to time, as if to take one more look at the spot so lately crowned by the imperial city, once their pleasant home, and endeared to them by many a glorious recollection.

On the departure of the inhabitants, measures were immediately taken to purify the place, by means of numerous fires kept burning day and night, especially in the infected quarter of Tlatelolco, and by collecting the heaps of dead, which lay mouldering in the streets, and consigning them to the earth.— Of the whole number, who perished in the course of the siege, it is impossible to form any probable computation. The accounts range widely from one hundred and twenty thousand, the lowest estimate, to two hundred and forty thousand. The number of the Spaniards who fell was comparatively small, but that of the allies must have been large, if the historian of Tezcuco is correct in asserting, that thirty thousand perished of his own countrymen alone. That the number of those destroyed within the city was immense cannot be doubted, when we consider that, besides its own redundant population, it was thronged with that of the neighbouring towns, who, distrusting their strength to resist the enemy, sought protection within its walls.

The booty found there—that is, the treasures of gold and jewels, the only booty of much value in the eyes of the Spaniards—fell far below their expectations. It did not exceed, according to the general's statement, a hundred and thirty thousand *castellanos* of gold, including the sovereign's share, which, indeed, taking into account many articles of curious and costly workmanship, voluntarily relinquished by the army, greatly exceeded his legitimate fifth. Yet the Aztecs must have been in possession of a much larger treasure, if it were only the wreck of that recovered from the Spaniards on the night of the memorable flight from Mexico. Some of the spoil may have been sent away from the capital; some spent in preparations for defence, and more of it buried in the earth, or sunk in the water of the lake. Their menaces were not without a meaning. They had, at least, the satisfaction of disappointing the avarice of their enemies.

Cortés had no further occasion for the presence of his Indian allies. He assembled the chiefs of the different squadrons, thanked them for their services, noticed their valor in flattering terms, and, after distributing presents among them, with the assurance that his master, the Emperor, would recompense their fidelity yet more largely, dismissed them to their own homes. They carried off a liberal share of the spoils, of which they had plundered the dwellings,—not of a kind to excite the cupidity of the Spaniards,—and returned in triumph, shortsighted triumph! at the success of their expedition, and the downfall of the Aztec dynasty.

Great, also, was the satisfaction of the Spaniards at this brilliant termination of their long and laborious campaign. They were, indeed, disappointed at the small amount of treasure found in the conquered city. But the soldier is usually too much absorbed in the present to give much heed to the future; and, though their discontent showed itself afterwards in a more clamorous form, they now thought only of their triumph, and abandoned themselves to jubilee. Cortés celebrated the event by a banquet, as sumptuous as circumstances would permit, to which all the cavaliers and officers were invited. Loud and long was their revelry, which was carried to such an excess, as provoked the animadversion of father Olmedo, who intimated that this was not the fitting way to testify their sense of the favors shown them by the Almighty. Cortés admitted the justice of the rebuke, but craved some indulgence for a soldier's license in the hour of victory. The following day was appointed for the commemoration of their successes in a more suitable manner.

A procession of the whole army was then formed with father Olmedo at its head. The soiled and tattered banners of Castile, which had waved over many a field of battle, now threw their shadows on the peaceful array of the soldiery, as they slowly moved along, rehearsing the litany, and displaying the image of the Virgin and the blessed symbol of man's redemption. The reverend father pronounced a discourse, in which he briefly reminded the troops of their great cause for thankfulness to Providence for conducting them safe through their long and perilous pilgrimage; and, dwelling on the responsibility incurred by their present position, he besought them not to abuse the rights of conquest, but to treat the unfortunate Indians with humanity. The sacrament was then administered to the commander-in-chief and the principal cavaliers, and the services concluded with a solemn thanksgiving to the God of battles, who had enabled them to carry the banner of the Cross triumphant over this barbaric empire.

Thus, after a siege of nearly three months' duration, unmatched in history for the constancy and courage of the besieged, seldom surpassed for the severity of its sufferings, fell the renowned capital of the Aztecs. Unmatched, it may be truly said, for constancy and courage, when we recollect that the door of capitulation on the most honorable terms was left open to them throughout the whole blockade, and that, sternly rejecting every proposal of their enemy, they, to a man, preferred to die rather than surrender. More than three centuries had elapsed, since the Aztecs, a poor and wandering tribe from the far North-west had come on the plateau. There they built their miserable collection of huts on the spot—as tradition tells us— prescribed by the oracle. Their conquests, at first confined to their immediate neighbourhood, gradually covered the Valley, then, crossing the mountains, swept over the broad extent of the table-land, descended its precipitous sides, and rolled onwards to the Mexican Gulf, and the distant confines of Central America. Their wretched capital, meanwhile, keeping pace with the enlargement of the territory, had grown into a flourishing city, filled with buildings, monuments of art, and a numerous population, that gave it the first rank among the capitals of the Western World. At this crisis, came over another race from the remote East, strangers like themselves, whose coming had also been predicted by the oracle, and, appearing on the plateau, assailed them in the very zenith of their prosperity, and blotted them out from the map of nations for ever! The whole story has the air of fable, rather than of history! a legend of romance, —a tale of the genii!

Yet we cannot regret the fall of an empire, which did so little to promote the happiness of its subjects, or the real interests of humanity. Notwithstanding the lustre thrown over its latter days by the glorious defence of its capital, by the mild munificence of Montezuma, by the dauntless heroism of Guatemozin, the Aztecs were emphatically a fierce and brutal race, little calculated, in their best aspects, to excite our sympathy and regard. Their civilization, such as it was, was not their own, but reflected, perhaps imperfectly, from a race whom they had succeeded in the land. It was, in respect to the Aztecs, a generous graft on a vicious stock, and could have brought no fruit to perfection. They ruled over their wide domains with a sword, instead of a sceptre. They did nothing to ameliorate the condition, or in any way promote the progress, of their vassals. Their vassals were serfs, used only to minister to their pleasure, held in awe by armed garrisons, ground to the dust by imposts in peace, by military conscriptions in war. They did not, like the Romans, whom they resembled in the nature of their conquests, extend the rights of citizenship to the conquered. They did not amalgamate them into one great nation, with common rights and interests. They held them as aliens,— even those, who in the Valley were gathered round the very walls of the capital. The Aztec metropolis, the heart of the monarchy, had not a sympathy, not a pulsation, in common with the rest of the body politic. It was a stranger in its own land.

The Aztecs not only did not advance the condition of their vassals, but, morally speaking, they did much to degrade it. How can a nation, where human sacrifices prevail, and especially when combined with cannibalism, further the march of civilization? How can the interests of humanity be consulted, where man is levelled to the rank of the brutes that perish? The influence of the Aztecs introduced their gloomy superstition into lands before unacquainted with it, or where, at least, it was not established in any great strength. The example of the capital was contagious. As the latter increased in opulence, the religious celebrations were conducted with still more terrible magnificence; in the same manner, as the gladiator shows of the Romans increased in pomp with the increasing splendor of the capital. Men became familiar with scenes of horror and the most loathsome abominations. Women and children—the whole nation became familiar with, and assisted at them. The heart was hardened, the manners were made ferocious, the feeble light of civilization, transmitted from a milder race, was growing fainter and fainter, as thousands and thousands of miserable victims, throughout the empire, were yearly fattened in its cages, sacrificed on its altars, dressed and served at its banquets! The whole land was converted into a vast human shambles! The empire of the Aztecs did not fall before its time.

Whether these unparalleled outrages furnish a sufficient plea to the Spaniards for their invasion, whether, with the Protestant, we are content to find a warrant for it in the natural rights and demands of civilization, or, with the Roman Catholic, in the good pleasure of the Pope,—on the one or other of which grounds, the conquests by most Christian nations in the East and the West have been defended,—it is unnecessary to discuss, as it has already been considered in a former Chapter. It is more material to inquire, whether, assuming the right, the conquest of Mexico was conducted with a proper regard to the claims of humanity. And here we must admit, that, with all allowance for the ferocity of the age and the laxity of its principles, there are passages which every Spaniard, who cherishes the fame of his countrymen, would be glad to see expunged from their history; passages not to be vindicated on the score of self-defence, or of necessity of any kind, and which must for ever leave a dark spot on the annals of the Conquest. And yet, taken as a whole, the invasion, up to the capture of the capital, was conducted on principles less revolting to humanity, than most, perhaps than any, of the other conquests of the Castilian crown in the New World.

It may seem slight praise to say, that the followers of Cortés used no blood-hounds to hunt down their wretched victims, as in some other parts of the Continent, nor exterminated a peaceful and submissive population in mere wantonness of cruelty, as in the Islands. Yet it is something, that they were not so far infected by the spirit of the age, and that their swords were rarely stained with blood, unless it was indispensable to the success of their enterprise. Even in the last siege of the capital, the sufferings of the Aztecs, terrible as they were, do not imply any unusual cruelty in the victors; they were not greater than those inflicted on their own countrymen at home, in many a memorable instance, by the most polished nations, not merely of ancient times, but of our own. They were the inevitable consequences which follow from war, when, instead of being confined to its legitimate field, it is brought home to the hearthstone, to the peaceful community of the city,—its burghers untrained to arms, its women and children yet more defenceless. In the present instance, indeed, the sufferings of the besieged were in a great degree to be charged on themselves,—on their patriotic, but desperate, self-devotion. It was not the desire, as certainly it was not the interest, of the Spaniards, to destroy the capital, or its inhabitants. When any of these fell into their hands, they were kindly entertained, their wants supplied, and every means taken to infuse into them a spirit of conciliation; and this, too, it should be remembered, in despite of the dreadful doom to which they consigned their Christian captives. The gates of a fair capitulation were kept open, though unavailingly, to the last hour.

The right of conquest necessarily implies that of using whatever force may be necessary for overcoming resistance to the assertion of that right. For the Spaniards to have done otherwise than they did would have been to abandon the siege, and, with it, the conquest of the country. To have suffered the inhabitants, with their high-spirited monarch, to escape, would have prolonged the miseries of the war by transferring it to another and more inaccessible quarter. They literally, as far as the success of the expedition was concerned, had no choice. If our imagination is struck with the amount of suffering in this, and in similar scenes of the Conquest, it should be borne in mind, that it is a natural result of the great masses of men engaged in the conflict. The amount of suffering does not of itself show the amount of cruelty which caused it; and it is but justice to the Conquerors of Mexico to say, that the very brilliancy and importance of their exploits have given a melancholy celebrity to their misdeeds, and thrown them into somewhat bolder relief than strictly belongs to them.—It is proper that thus much should be stated, not to excuse their excesses, but that we may be enabled to make a more impartial estimate of their conduct, as compared with that of other nations under similar circumstances, and that we may not visit them with peculiar obloquy for evils which necessarily flow from the condition of war. I have not drawn a veil over these evils; for the historian should not shrink from depicting, in their true colors, the atrocities of a condition, over which success is apt to throw a false halo of glory, but which, bursting asunder the strong bonds of human fellowship, purchases its triumphs by arming the hand of man against his brother, makes a savage of the civilized, and kindles the fires of hell in the bosom of the savage.

Whatever may be thought of the Conquest in a moral view, regarded as a military achivement it must fill us with astonishment. That a handful of adventurers, indifferently armed and equipped, should have landed on the shores of a powerful empire inhabited by a fierce and warlike race, and, in defiance of the reiterated prohibitions of its sovereign, have forced their way into the interior;—that they should have done this, without knowledge of the language or of the land, without chart or compass to guide them, without any of the difficulties they were to encounter, totally uncertain whether the next step might bring them on a hostile nation, or on a desert, feeling their way along in the dark, as it were;—that, though nearly overwhelmed by their first encounter with the inhabitants, they should have still pressed on to the capital of the empire, and, having reached it, thrown themselves unhesitatingly into the midst of their enemies;—that, so far from being daunted by the extraordinary spectacle there exhibited of power and civilization, they should have been but more confirmed in their original design;— that they should have seized the monarch, have executed his ministers before the eyes of his subjects, and, when driven forth with ruin from the gates, have gathered their scattered wreck together, and, after a system of operations, pursued with consummate policy and daring, have succeeded in overturning the capital, and establishing their sway over the country;—that all this should have been so effected by a mere handful of indigent adventurers, is a fact little short of the miraculous,—too startling for the probabilities demanded by fiction, and without a parallel in the pages of history.

Yet this must not be understood too literally; for it would be unjust to the Aztecs themselves, at least to their military prowess, to regard the Conquest as directly achieved by the Spaniards alone. This would indeed be to arm the latter with the charmed shield of Ruggiero, and the magic lance of Astolfo, overturning its hundreds at a touch. The Indian empire was in a manner conquered by Indians. The first terrible encounter of the Spaniards with the Tlascalans, which had nearly proved their ruin, did in fact insure their success. It secured to them a strong native support, on which to retreat in the hour of trouble, and round which they could rally the kindred races of the land for one great and overwhelming assault. The Aztec monarchy fell by the hands of its own subjects, under the direction of European sagacity and science. Had it been united, it might have bidden defiance to the invaders. As it was, the capital was dissevered from the rest of the country, and the bolt, which might have passed off comparatively harmless, had the empire been cemented by a common principle of loyalty and patriotism, now found its way into every crack and crevice of the ill-compacted fabric, and buried it in its own ruins.— Its fate may serve as a striking proof, that a government, which does not rest on the sympathies of its subjects, cannot long abide; that human institutions, when not connected with human prosperity and progress, must fall,—if not before the increasing light of civilization, by the hand of violence; by violence from within, if not from without. And who shall lament their fall?

BOOK SEVEN

Subsequent Career of Cortés

> EVER *mindful of narrative, Prescott considered the*
> *fall of Tenochtitlán synonymous with the Conquest*
> *of Mexico. Accordingly his afterpiece was intended*
> *simply to round out the career of Cortés. But it does*
> *more than that because later chapters of that Span-*
> *iard's life are related to the widening conquest of*
> *Mexico.*

I

Expanding the Conquest

THE tidings of the fall of Mexico were borne on the wings of the wind over the plateau, and down the broad sides of the Cordilleras. Many an envoy made his appearance from the remote Indian tribes, anxious to learn the truth of the astounding intelligence, and to gaze with their own eyes on the ruins of the detested city. Among these were ambassadors from the kingdom of Michuacan,* a powerful and independent state, inhabited by one of the kindred Nahuatlac races, and lying between the Mexican Valley and the Pacific. The embassy was soon followed by the king of the country in person, who came in great state to the Castilian quarters. Cortés received him with equal parade, astonished him by the brilliant evolutions of his cavalry and by the thunders of his ordnance, and escorted him in one of the brigantines round the fallen city, whose pile of smouldering palaces and temples was all that now remained of the once dread capital of Anahuac. The Indian monarch gazed with silent awe on the scene of desolation, and eagerly craved the protection of the invincible beings who had caused it. His example was followed by ambassadors from the remote regions which had never yet had intercourse with the Spaniards. Cortés, who saw the boundaries of his empire thus rapidly enlarging, availed himself of the favorable dispositions

* Michoacán. C.H.G.

of the natives to ascertain the products and resources of their several countries.

Two small detachments were sent into the friendly state of Michuacan, through which country they penetrated to the borders of the great Southern ocean. No European had as yet descended on its shores so far north of the equator. The Spaniards eagerly advanced into its waters, erected a cross on the sandy margin, and took possession of it, with all the usual formalities, in the name of their Most Catholic Majesties. On their return, they visited some of the rich districts towards the north, since celebrated for their mineral treasures, and brought back samples of gold and Californian pearls, with an account of their discovery of the Ocean. The imagination of Cortés was kindled, and his soul swelled with exultation at the splendid prospects which their discoveries unfolded. "Most of all," he writes to the emperor, "do I exult in the tidings brought me of the Great Ocean. For in it, as cosmographers, and those learned men who know most about the Indies, inform us, are scattered the rich isles teeming with gold and spices of precious stones." He at once sought a favorite spot for a colony on the shores of the Pacific, and made arrangements for the construction of four vessels to explore the mysteries of these unknown seas. This was the beginning of his noble enterprises for discovery in the Gulf of California.

Although the greater part of Anahuac, overawed by the successes of the Spaniards, had tendered their allegiance, there were some, especially on the southern slopes of the Cordilleras, who showed a less submissive disposition. Cortés instantly sent out strong detachments under Sandoval and Alvarado to reduce the enemy and establish colonies in the conquered provinces. The highly colored reports, which Alvarado, who had a quick scent for gold, gave of the mineral wealth of Oaxaca, no doubt operated with Cortés in determining him to select this region for his own particular domain.

The commander-in-chief, with his little band of Spaniards, now daily recruited by reinforcements from the Islands, still occupied the quarters of Cojohuacan, which they had taken up at the termination of the siege. Cortés did not immediately decide in what quarter of the Valley to establish the new capital which was to take the place of the ancient Tenochtitlán. The situation of the latter, surrounded by water and exposed to occasional inundations, had some obvious disadvantages. But there was no doubt that in some part of the elevated and central plateau of the Valley the new metropolis should be built, to which both European and Indian might look up as to the head of the colonial empire of Spain. At length he decided on retaining the site of the ancient city, moved to it, as he says, "by its past renown, and the memory"—not an enviable one, surely —"in which it was held among the nations"; and he made preparations for the reconstruction of the capital on a scale of magnificence, which should, in his own language, "raise her to the rank of Queen of the surrounding provinces, in the same manner as she had been of yore."

The labor was to be performed by the Indian population, drawn from all quarters of the Valley, and including the Mexicans themselves, great numbers of whom still lingered in the neighbourhood of their ancient residence. At first they showed reluctance, and even symptoms of hostility, when called to this work of humiliation by their conquerors. But Cortés had the address to secure some of the principal chiefs in his interests, and, under their authority and direction, the labor of their countrymen was conducted. The deep groves of the Valley and the forests of the neighbouring hills supplied cedar, cypress, and other durable woods, for the interior of the buildings, and the quarries of *tetzontli* and the ruins of the ancient edifices furnished abundance of stone. As there were no beasts of draught employed by the Aztecs, an immense number of hands was necessarily required for the work. All within the immediate control of Cortés were pressed into the service. The spot so recently deserted now swarmed with multitudes of Indians of various tribes, and with Europeans, the latter directing, while the others labored. The prophecy of the Aztecs was accomplished. And the work of reconstruction went forward with a rapidity like that shown by an Asiatic despot, who concentrates the population of an empire on the erection of a favorite capital.

Yet the condition of Cortés, notwithstanding the success of his arms, suggested many causes for anxiety. He had not received a word of encouragement from home,—not a word, indeed, of encouragement or censure. In what light his irregular course was regarded by the government or the nation was still matter of painful uncertainty. He now prepared another Letter to the emperor, the Third in the published series, written in the same simple and energetic style which has entitled his Commentaries, as they may be called, to a comparison with those of Cæsar. It was dated at Cojohuacan, May 15th, 1522, and in it he recapitulated the events of the final siege of the capital, and his subsequent operations, accomplished by many sagacious reflections, as usual, on the character and resources of the country. With this letter he purposed to send the royal fifth of the spoils of Mexico, and a rich collection of fabrics, especially of gold and jewelry wrought into many rare and fanciful forms. One of the jewels was an emerald, cut in a pyramidal shape, of so extraordinary a size, that the base was as broad as the palm of the hand! The collection was still further augmented by specimens of many of the natural products, as well as of animals peculiar to the country.

The army wrote a letter to accompany that of Cortés, in which they expatiated on his manifold services, and besought the emperor to ratify his proceedings and confirm him in his present authority. The important mission was intrusted to two of the general's confidential officers, Quiñones and Ávila. It proved to be unfortunate. The agents touched at the Azores, where Quiñones lost his life in a brawl. Ávila, resuming his voyage, was captured by a French privateer, and the rich spoils of the Aztecs went into the treasury of his Most Christian Majesty. Francis the First gazed with pardonable envy on the treasures which his Imperial rival drew from his colonial domains; and he intimated his discontent by peevishly expressing a desire "to see the clause in Adam's testament which entitled his brothers of Castile and Portugal to divide the New World between them." Ávila found means, through a private hand, of transmitting his letters, the most important part of his charge, to Spain, where they reached the court in safety. . . .

> WHILE *Cortés' prospects darkened in Europe, the first person charged with investigating his conduct of the Conquest of Mexico, Cristóbal de Tapia, arrived, succumbed to his own avarice, and departed. Based in Coyoacán, Cortés caused the city of Mexico to rise on the site of rubble-strewn Tenochtitlán. At the same time more regional campaigning by his captains took place.*
>
> *Belatedly Charles V confirmed Cortés as governor, captain-general, and chief justice of the immense area which increasingly often carried the name New Spain. To encourage settlement and guarantee permanent control by Spain, Cortés distributed grants of land to the conquistadors and the more recent arrivals from the Old World.*

The attention of Cortés was not confined to the capital. He was careful to establish settlements in every part of the country which afforded a favorable position for them. He founded Zacatula on the shores of the miscalled Pacific, Coliman in the territory of Michuacan, San Esteban on the Atlantic coast, probably not far from the site of Tampico, Medellín (so called after his own birth-place) in the neighbourhood of the modern Vera Cruz, and a port near the river Antigua, from which it derived its name. It was designed to take the place of Villa Rica, which, as experience had shown, from its exposed situation, afforded no protection to shipping against the winds that sweep over the Mexican Gulf. Antigua, sheltered within the recesses of the bay, presented a more advantageous position. Cortés established there a board of trade, connected the settlement by a highway with the capital, and fondly pre-

dicted that his new city would become the great emporium of
the country. But in this he was mistaken. From some cause not
very obvious, the port of entry was removed, at the close of
the sixteenth century, to the modern Vera Cruz; which, without any superiority, probably, of topographical position or
even of salubrity of climate, has remained ever since the great
commercial capital of New Spain.

Cortés stimulated the settlement of his several colonies by
liberal grants of land and municipal privileges. The great difficulty was to induce women to reside in the country, and without them he felt that the colonies, like a tree without roots,
must soon perish. By a singular provision he required every
settler, if a married man, to bring over his wife within eighteen
months, on pain of forfeiting his estate. If he were too poor
to do this himself, the government would assist him. Another
law imposed the same penalty on all bachelors who did not
provide themselves with wives within the same period! The
general seems to have considered celibacy as too great a luxury
for a young country.

His own wife, Doña Catalina Xuárez, was among those who
came over from the Islands to New Spain. According to Bernal
Díaz, her coming gave him no particular satisfaction. It is
possible; since his marriage with her seems to have been entered
into with reluctance, and her lowly condition and connexions
stood somewhat in the way of his future advancement. Yet
they lived happily together for several years, according to the
testimony of Las Casas; and, whatever he may have felt, he had
the generosity, or the prudence, not to betray his feelings to
the world. On landing, Doña Catalina was escorted by Sandoval to the capital, where she was kindly received by her husband, and all the respect paid to her, to which she was entitled
by her elevated rank. But the climate of the table-land was not
suited to her constitution, and she died in three months after
her arrival. An event so auspicious to his worldly prospects
did not fail, as we shall see hereafter, to provoke the tongue of
scandal to the most malicious, but it is scarcely necessary to
say, unfounded inferences.

In the distribution of the soil among the Conquerors, Cortés adopted the vicious system of *repartimientos,* universally practised among his countrymen. In a letter to the emperor, he states, that the superior capacity of the Indians in New Spain had made him regard it as a grievous thing to condemn them to servitude, as had been done in the Islands. But, on further trial, he found the Spaniards so much harassed and impoverished, that they could not hope to maintain themselves in the land without enforcing the services of the natives, and for this reason he had at length waived his own scruples in compliance with their repeated remonstrances. This was the wretched pretext used on the like occasions by his countrymen to cover up this flagrant act of injustice. The Crown, however, in its instructions to the general, disavowed the act and annulled the *repartimientos.* It was all in vain. The necessities, or rather the cupidity, of the colonists, easily evaded the royal ordinances. The colonial legislation of Spain shows, in the repetition of enactments against slavery, the perpetual struggle that subsisted between the Crown and the colonists, and the impotence of the former to enforce measures repugnant to the interests, at all events to the avarice, of the latter. New Spain furnishes no exception to the general fact.

The Tlascalans, in gratitude for their signal services, were exempted, at the recommendation of Cortés, from the doom of slavery. It should be added, that the general, in granting the *repartimientos,* made many humane regulations for limiting the power of the master, and for securing as many privileges to the native as were compatible with any degree of compulsory service. These limitations, it is true, were too often disregarded; and in the mining districts, in particular, the situation of the poor Indian was often deplorable. Yet the Indian population, clustering together in their own villages, and living under their own magistrates, have continued to prove by their numbers, fallen as these have below their primitive amount, how far superior was their condition to that in most other parts of the vast colonial empire of Spain. This condition has been gradually ameliorated, under the influence of higher moral views and larger ideas of government; until the servile descendants of the ancient lords of the soil have been permitted, in republican Mexico, to rise—nominally, at least—to a level with the children of their conquerors.

Whatever disregard he may have shown to the political rights of the natives, Cortés manifested a commendable solicitude for their spiritual welfare. He requested the emperor to send out holy men to the country; not bishops and pampered prelates, who too often squandered the substance of the Church in riotous living, but godly persons, members of religious fraternities, whose lives might be a fitting commentary on their teaching. Thus only, he adds,—and the remark is worthy of note,—can they exercise any influence over the natives, who have been accustomed to see the least departure from morals in their own priesthood punished with the utmost rigor of the law. In obedience to these suggestions twelve Franciscan friars embarked for New Spain, which they reached early in 1524. They were men of unblemished purity of life, nourished with the learning of the cloister, and, like many others whom the Romish Church has sent forth on such apostolic missions, counted all personal sacrifices as little in the sacred cause to which they were devoted.

The presence of the reverend fathers in the country was greeted with general rejoicing. The inhabitants of the towns through which they passed came out in body to welcome them; processions were formed of the natives bearing wax tapers in their hands, and the bells of the churches rung out a joyous peal in honor of their arrival. Houses of refreshment were provided for them along their route to the capital; and, when they entered it, they were met by a brilliant cavalcade of the principal cavaliers and citizens, with Cortés at their head. The general, dismounting, and bending one knee to the ground, kissed the robes of father Martín of Valencia, the principal of the fraternity. The natives, filled with amazement at the viceroy's humiliation before men whose naked feet and tattered garments gave them the aspect of mendicants, henceforth regarded them as beings of a superior nature. The Indian chronicler of Tlascala does not conceal his admiration of this edifying condescension of Cortés, which he pronounces "one of the most heroical acts of his life!"

The missionaries lost no time in the good work of conversion. They began their preaching through interpreters, until they had acquired a competent knowledge of the language themselves. They opened schools and founded colleges, in which the native youth were instructed in profane as well as Christian learning. The ardor of the Indian neophyte emulated that of his teacher. In a few years every vestige of the primitive *teocallis* was effaced from the land. The uncouth idols of the country, and unhappily the hieroglyphical manuscripts, shared the same fate. Yet the missionary and the convert did much to repair these losses by their copious accounts of the Aztec institutions, collected from the most authentic sources.

The business of conversion went on prosperously among the several tribes of the great Nahuatlac family. In about twenty years from the first advent of the missionaries, one of their body could make the pious vaunt, that nine millions of converts—a number probably exceeding the population of the country—had been admitted within the Christian fold! The Aztec worship was remarkable for its burdensome ceremonial, and prepared its votaries for the pomp and splendors of the Romish ritual. It was not difficult to pass from the fasts and festivals of one religion to the fasts and festivals of the other; to transfer their homage from the fantastic idols of their own creation to the beautiful forms in sculpture and in painting which decorated the Christian cathedral. It is true, they could have comprehended little of the dogmas of their new faith, and little, it may be, of its vital spirit. But, if the philosopher may smile at the reflection, that conversion, under these circumstances, was one of form rather than of substance, the philanthropist will console himself by considering how much the cause of humanity and good morals must have gained by the substitution of these unsullied rites for the brutal abominations of the Aztecs.

The Conquerors settled in such parts of the country as best

suited their inclinations. Many occupied the south-eastern slopes of the Cordilleras towards the rich valley of Oaxaca. Many more spread themselves over the broad surface of the table-land, which, from its elevated position, reminded them of the plateau of their own Castiles. . . .

> CORTES *remained in the Valley of Mexico, but he organized expeditions on numerous fronts. On the Pacific, at Zacatula, he had a small fleet constructed and fitted out to search for the strait between the oceans. To the east, on the waters of the Gulf of Mexico, another expedition was assembled. Under Cristóbal de Olid, it was charged with planting a colony in Honduras. To the southeast, Pedro de Alvarado led an expedition overland into the region beyond Oaxaca.*
>
> *Cortés first responded to word of Olid's defection in Honduras by sending a lieutenant there. When that commander, Francisco de las Casas, fell into the rebel's hands, a bad situation had so worsened that it demanded Cortés' personal attention.*

On the 12th of October, 1524, Cortés commenced his march. As he descended the sides of the Cordilleras, he was met by many of his old companions in arms, who greeted their commander with a hearty welcome, and some of them left their estates to join the expedition. He halted in the province of Coatzacualco, (Huasacualco), until he could receive intelligence respecting his route from the natives of Tabasco. They furnished him with a map, exhibiting the principal places whither the Indian traders, who wandered over these wild regions, were in the habit of resorting. With the aid of this map, a compass, and such guides as from time to time he could pick up on his journey, he proposed to traverse that broad level tract which forms the base of Yucatan, and spreads from the Coatzacualco river to the head of the Gulf of Honduras. "I shall give your Majesty," he begins his celebrated Letter to the emperor, describing this expedition, "an account, as usual, of the most remarkable events of my journey, every one of which might form the subject of a separate narration." Cortés did not exaggerate.

The beginning of the march lay across a low and marshy level, intersected by numerous little streams, which form the headwaters of the *Río de Tabasco,* and of the other rivers that discharge themselves, to the north, into the Mexican Gulf. The smaller streams they forded, or passed in canoes, suffering their horses to swim across as they held them by the bridle. Rivers of more formidable size they crossed on floating bridges. It gives one some idea of the difficulties they had to encounter in this way, when it is stated, that the Spaniards were obliged to construct no less than fifty of these bridges in a distance of less than a hundred miles! One of them was more than nine hundred paces in length. Their troubles were much augmented by the difficulty of obtaining subsistence, as the natives frequently set fire to the villages on their approach, leaving to the way-worn adventurers only a pile of smoking ruins.

It would be useless to encumber the page with the names of Indian towns which lay in the route of the army, but which may be now obsolete, and, at all events, have never found their way into a map of the country. The first considerable place which they reached was Iztapan, pleasantly situated in the midst of a fruitful region, on the banks of one of the tributaries of the Río de Tabasco. Such was the extremity to which the Spaniards had already, in the course of a few weeks, been reduced by hunger and fatigue, that the sight of a village in these dreary solitudes was welcomed by his followers, says Cortés, "with a shout of joy that was echoed back from all the surrounding woods." The army was now at no great distance from the ancient city of Palenque, the subject of so much speculation in our time. The village of *Las Tres Cruzes,* indeed, situated between twenty and thirty miles from Palenque, is said still to commemorate the passage of the Conquerors by the existence of three crosses which they left there. Yet no allusion is made to the ancient capital. Was it then the abode of a populous and flourishing community, such as once occupied it, to judge from the extent and magnificence of its remains? Or was it, even then, a heap of mouldering ruins, buried in a wilderness of vegetation, and thus hidden from the knowledge of the surrounding country? If the former, the silence of Cortés is not easy to be explained.

On quitting Iztapan, the Spaniards struck across a country having the same character of a low and marshy soil, chequered by occasional patches of cultivation, and covered with forests of cedar and Brazil wood, which seemed absolutely intermin-able. The overhanging foliage threw so deep a shade, that, as Cortés says, the soldiers could not see where to set their feet. To add to their perplexity, their guides deserted them; and, when they climbed to the summits of the tallest trees, they could see only the same cheerless, interminable line of waving woods. The compass and the map furnished the only clue to extricate them from this gloomy labyrinth; and Cortés and his officers, among whom was the constant Sandoval, spread-ing out their chart on the ground, anxiously studied the prob-able direction of their route. Their scanty supplies meanwhile had entirely failed them, and they appeased the cravings of ap-petite by such roots as they dug out of the earth, or by the nuts and berries that grew wild in the woods. Numbers fell sick, and many of the Indians sank by the way, and died of absolute starvation.

When, at length, the troops emerged from these dismal for-ests, their path was crossed by a river of great depth, and far wider than any which they had hitherto traversed. The soldiers, disheartened, broke out into murmers against their leader, who was plunging them deeper and deeper in a boundless wilder-ness, where they must lay their bones. It was in vain that Cortés encouraged them to construct a floating bridge, which might take them to the opposite bank of the river. It seemed a work of appalling magnitude, to which their wasted strength was unequal. He was more successful in his appeal to the Indian auxiliaries, till his own men, put to shame by the ready obedi-ence of the latter, engaged in the work with a hearty good-will, which enabled them, although ready to drop from fatigue, to accomplish it at the end of four days. It was, indeed, the only expedient by which they could hope to extricate themselves from their perilous situation. The bridge consisted of one thousand pieces of timber, each of the thickness of a man's body and sixty feet long. When we consider that the timber was all standing in the forest at the commencement of the labor, it must be admitted to have been an achievement worthy of the Spaniards. The well-compacted beams presented a solid structure, which nothing, says Cortés, but fire could destroy. It excited the admiration of the natives, who came from a great distance to see it; and "the bridge of Cortés" remained for many a year the enduring monument of that commander's energy and perseverance.

The arrival of the army on the opposite bank of the river involved them in new difficulties. The ground was so soft and saturated with water, that the horses floundered up to their girths, and, sometimes plunging into quagmires, were nearly buried in the mud. It was with the greatest difficulty that they could be extricated by covering the wet soil with the foliage and the boughs of trees, when a stream of water, which forced its way through the heart of the morass, furnished the jaded animals with the means of effecting their escape by swimming. As the Spaniards emerged from these slimy depths, they came on a broad and rising ground, which, by its cultivated fields teeming with maize, *agi,* or pepper of the country, and the *yuca* plant, intimated their approach to the capital of the fruitful province of Aculan. . . .

DURING *this most arduous of all of Cortés' marches, Cuauhtémoc, present as a hostage, was hanged because of his complicity in a rumored plot to massacre the Spaniards.*

It would be wearisome to recount all the perils and hardships endured by the Spaniards in the remainder of their journey. It would be repeating only the incidents of the preceding narrative; the same obstacles in their path, the same extremities of famine and fatigue,—hardships more wearing on the spirits than encounters with an enemy, which, if more hazardous, are also more exciting. It is easier to contend with man than with Nature. Yet I must not omit to mention the passage of the *Sierra de los Pedernales,* "the Mountain of Flints," which, though only twenty-four miles in extent, consumed no less than twelve days in crossing it! The sharp stones cut the horses' feet to pieces, while many were lost down the precipices and ravines; so that, when they had reached the opposite side, sixty-eight of these valuable animals had perished, and the remainder were, for the most part, in an unserviceable condition!

The rainy season had now set in, and the torrents of water, falling day and night, drenched the adventurers to the skin, and added greatly to their distresses. The rivers, swollen beyond their usual volume, poured along with a terrible impetuosity that defied the construction of bridges; and it was with the greatest difficulty, that, by laying trunks of trees from one huge rock to another, with which these streams were studded, they effected a perilous passage to the opposite banks.

At length the shattered train drew near the Golfo Dolce, at the head of the Bay of Honduras. Their route could not have been far from the site of Copán, the celebrated city whose architectural ruins have furnished such noble illustrations for the pencil of Catherwood. But the Spaniards passed on in silence. Nor, indeed, can we wonder, that, at this stage of the enterprise, they should have passed on without heeding the vicinity of a city in the wilderness, though it were as glorious as the capital of Zenobia; for they were arrived almost within view of the Spanish settlements, the object of their long and wearisome pilgrimage.

The place which they were now approaching was Naco, or San Gil de Buena Vista, a Spanish settlement on the Golfo Dolce. Cortés advanced cautiously, prepared to fall on the town by surprise. He had held on his way with the undeviating step of the North American Indian, who, traversing morass and mountain and the most intricate forests, guided by the instinct of revenge, presses straight towards the mark, and, when he has reached it, springs at once on his unsuspecting victim. Before Cortés made his assault, his scouts fortunately fell in with some of the inhabitants of the place, from whom they received tidings of the death of Olid, and of the reëstablishment of his own authority. Cortés, therefore, entered the place like a friend, and was cordially welcomed by his countrymen, greatly astonished, says Díaz, "by the presence among them of the general so renowned throughout these countries."

The colony was at this time sorely suffering from famine; and to such extremity was it soon reduced, that the troops would probably have found a grave in the very spot to which they had looked forward as the goal of their labors, but for the seasonable arrival of a vessel with supplies from Cuba. With a perseverance which nothing could daunt, Cortés made an examination of the surrounding country, and occupied a month more in exploring dismal swamps, steaming with unwholesome exhalations, and infected with bilious fevers, and with swarms of venomous insects which left peace neither by day nor night. At length he embarked with a part of his forces on board of two brigantines, and, after touching at one or two ports in the Bay, anchored off Truxillo, the principal Spanish settlement on that coast. The surf was too high for him easily to effect a landing; but the inhabitants, overjoyed at his arrival, rushed into the shallow water and eagerly bore back the general in their arms to the shore.

After he had restored the strength and spirits of his men, the indefatigable commander prepared for a new expedition, the object of which was to explore and to reduce the extensive province of Nicaragua. One may well feel astonished at the adventurous spirit of the man, who, unsubdued by the terrible sufferings of his recent march, should so soon be prepared for another enterprise, equally appalling. It is difficult, in this age of sober sense, to conceive the character of a Castilian cavalier of the sixteenth century, a true counterpart of which it would not have been easy to find in any other nation, even at that time,—or anywhere, indeed, save in those tales of chivalry, which, however wild and extravagant they may seem, were much more true to character than to situation. The mere excitement of exploring the strange and the unknown was a sufficient compensation to the Spanish adventurer for all his toils and trials. It seems to have been ordered by Providence, that such a race of men should exist contemporaneously with the discovery of the New World, that those regions should be brought to light which were beset with dangers and difficulties so appalling as might have tended to overawe and discourage the ordinary spirit of adventure. Yet Cortés, though filled with this spirit, proposed nobler ends to himself than those of the mere vulgar adventurer. In the expedition to Nicaragua, he designed, as he had done in that to Honduras, to ascertain the resources of the country in general, and, above all, the existence of any means of communication between the great oceans on its borders. If none such existed, it would at least establish this fact, the knowledge of which, to borrow his own language, was scarcely less important.

The general proposed to himself the further object of enlarging the colonial empire of Castile. The conquest of Mexico was but the commencement of a series of conquests. To the warrior who had achieved this nothing seemed impracticable; and scarcely would any thing have been so, had he been properly sustained. It is no great stretch of imagination, to see the Conqueror of Mexico advancing along the provinces of the vast Isthmus,—Nicaragua, Costa Rica, and Darien, until he had planted his victorious banner on the shores of the Gulf of Panamá; and, while it was there fanned by the breezes from the golden South, the land of the Incas, to see him gathering such intelligence of this land as would stimulate him to carry his arms still further, and to anticipate, it might be, the splendid career of Pizarro!

But from these dreams of ambition Cortés was suddenly aroused by such tidings as convinced him that his absence from Mexico was already too far prolonged, and that he must return without delay, if he would save the capital or the country.

IN *June, 1526, Cortés reëntered Mexico. For a time*
the local factionalism subsided. Then another inves-
tigator arrived and Cortés' enemies reëmerged. As
royal rule moved in, Cortés, proud and angered, real-
ized that his position might be completely under-
mined. Accordingly he prepared an early return to
Spain. Arriving in his homeland in the spring of 1528,
the conqueror proceeded to Toledo, the seat of his
emperor's court. Charles V honored his famous sub-
ject by designating him Marquess of the Valley of
Oaxaca. Cortés also was confirmed as captain-gen-
eral of New Spain. Gone, however, was any role in
the political affairs of the land that he had won.
Marrying for a second time, Cortés took as his wife
Juana de Zúñiga, daughter of a count and niece of
a duke. Wearying of the idleness and luxury that
characterized his stay in Spain, he soon prepared to
return to the land of his triumphs.

II

The Closing Years

EARLY in the spring of 1530, Cortés embarked for New Spain.
He was accompanied by the marchioness, his wife, together
with his aged mother, who had the good fortune to live to see
her son's elevation, and by a magnificent retinue of pages and
attendants, such as belonged to the household of a powerful
noble. How different from the forlorn condition, in which,
twenty-six years before, he had been cast loose, as a wild adventurer, to seek his bread upon the waters!

The first point of his destination was Hispaniola, where he
was to remain until he received tidings of the organization of
the new government that was to take charge of Mexico. In the
preceding Chapter it was stated, that the administration of the
country had been intrusted to a body called the Royal Audience; one of whose first duties it was to investigate the charges
brought against Cortés. Nuñez de Guzmán, his avowed enemy,

was placed at the head of this board; and the investigation was conducted with all the rancor of personal hostility. A remarkable document still exists, called the *Pesquisa Secreta,* or "Secret Inquiry," which contains a record of the proceedings against Cortés. It was prepared by the secretary of the Audience, and signed by the several members. The document is very long, embracing nearly a hundred folio pages. The name and the testimony of every witness are given, and the whole forms a mass of loathsome details such as might better suit a prosecution in a petty municipal court than that of a great officer of the Crown.

The charges are eight in number; involving, among other crimes, that of a deliberate design to cast off his allegiance to the Crown; that of the murder of two of the commissioners who had been sent out to supersede him; of the murder of his own wife, Catalina Xuárez; of extortion, and of licentious practices, —of offences, in short, which, from their private nature, would seem to have little to do with his conduct as a public man. The testimony is vague and often contradictory; the witnesses are for the most part obscure individuals, and the few persons of consideration among them appear to have been taken from the ranks of his decided enemies. When it is considered, that the inquiry was conducted in the absence of Cortés, before a court, the members of which were personally unfriendly to him, and that he was furnished with no specification of the charges, and had no opportunity, consequently, of disproving them, it is impossible, at this distance of time, to attach any importance to this paper as a legal document. When it is added, that no action was taken on it by the government, to whom it was sent, we may be disposed to regard it simply as a monument of the malice of his enemies. It has been drawn by the curious antiquary from the obscurity to which it had been so long consigned in the Indian archives at Seville; but it can be of no further use to the historian, than to show, that a great name in the sixteenth century exposed its possessor to calumnies as malignant as it has at any time since.

The high-handed measures of the Audience, and the oppressive conduct of Guzmán, especially towards the Indians, excited general indignation in the colony, and led to serious apprehensions of an insurrection. It became necessary to supersede an administration so reckless and unprincipled. But Cortés was detained two months at the island, by the slow movements of the Castilian court, before tidings reached him of the appointment of a new Audience for the government of the country. The person selected to preside over it was the bishop of St. Domingo, a prelate whose acknowledged wisdom and virtue gave favorable augury for the conduct of his administration. After this, Cortés resumed his voyage, and landed at Villa Rica on the 15th of July, 1530.

After remaining for a time in the neighbourhood, where he received some petty annoyances from the Audience, he proceeded to Tlascala, and publicly proclaimed his powers as Captain-General of New Spain and the South Sea. An edict, issued by the empress during her husband's absence, had interdicted Cortés from approaching within ten leagues of the Mexican capital, while the present authorities were there. The empress was afraid of a collision between the parties. Cortés, however, took up his residence on the opposite side of the lake, at Tezcuco.

No sooner was his arrival there known in the metropolis, than multitudes, both of Spaniards and natives, crossed the lake to pay their respects to their old commander, to offer him their services, and to complain of their manifold grievances. It seemed as if the whole population of the capital was pouring into the neighboring city, where the marquess maintained the state of an independent potentate. The members of the Audience, indignant at the mortifying contrast which their own diminished court presented, imposed heavy penalties on such of the natives as should be found in Tezcuco; and, affecting to consider themselves in danger, made preparations for the defence of the city. But these belligerent movements were terminated by the arrival of the new Audience; though Guzmán had the address to maintain his hold on the northern province, where he earned a reputation for cruelty and extortion, unrivalled even in the annals of the New World.

Every thing seemed now to assure a tranquil residence to Cortés. The new magistrates treated him with marked respect, and took his advice on the most important measures of government. Unhappily this state of things did not long continue; and a misunderstanding arose between the parties, in respect to the enumeration of the vassals assigned by the Crown to Cortés, which the marquess thought was made on principles prejudicial to his interests, and repugnant to the intentions of the grant. He was still further displeased by finding that the Audience were intrusted, by their commission, with a concurrent jurisdiction with himself in military affairs. This led, occasionally, to an interference, which the proud spirit of Cortés, so long accustomed to independent rule, could ill brook. After submitting to it for a time, he left the capital in disgust, no more to return there, and took up his residence in his city of Cuernavaca.

It was the place won by his own sword from the Aztecs, previous to the siege of Mexico. It stood on the southern slope of the Cordilleras, and overlooked a wide expanse of country, the fairest and most flourishing portion of his own domain. He had erected a stately palace on the spot, and henceforth made this city his favorite residence. It was well situated for superintending his vast estates, and he now devoted himself to bring them into proper cultivation. He introduced the sugar-cane from Cuba, and it grew luxuriantly in the rich soil of the neighbouring lowlands. He imported large numbers of merino sheep and other cattle, which found abundant pastures in the country around Tehuantepec. His lands were thickly sprinkled with groves of mulberry-trees, which furnished nourishment for the silk-worm. He encouraged the cultivation of hemp and flax, and, by his judicious and enterprising husbandry, showed the capacity of the soil for the culture of valuable products before unknown in the land; and he turned these products to the best account, by the erection of sugar-mills, and other works for the manufacture of the raw material. He thus laid the foundation of an opulence for his family, as substantial, if not as speedy, as that derived from the mines. Yet this latter source of wealth was not neglected by him; and he drew gold from the region of Tehuantepec, and silver from that of Zacatecas. The amount derived from these mines was not so abundant as at a later day. But the expense of working them, on the other hand, was much less in the earlier stages of the operation, when the metal lay so much nearer the surface.

But this tranquil way of life did not long content his restless and adventurous spirit; and it sought a vent by availing itself of his new charter of discovery to explore the mysteries of the great Southern Ocean. In 1527, two years before his return to Spain, he had sent a little squadron to the Moluccas. The expedition was attended with some important consequences; but, as they do not relate to Cortés, an account of it will find a more suitable place in the maritime annals of Spain, where it has been given by the able hand which has done so much for the country in this department.

Cortés was preparing to send another squadron of four vessels in the same direction, when his plans were interrupted by his visit to Spain; and his unfinished little navy, owing to the malice of the Royal Audience, who drew off the hands employed in building it, went to pieces on the stocks. Two other squadrons were now fitted out by Cortés, in the years 1532 and 1533, and sent on a voyage of discovery to the North-west. They were unfortunate, though, in the latter expedition, the Californian peninsula was reached, and a landing effected on its southern extremity at Santa Cruz, probably the modern port of La Paz. One of the vessels, thrown on the coast of New Galicia, was seized by Guzmán, the old enemy of Cortés, who ruled over that territory; the crew were plundered, and the ship detained as a lawful prize. Cortés, indignant at the outrage, de-

manded justice from the Royal Audience; and, as that body was
too feeble to enforce its own decrees in his favor, he took redress
into his own hands.

He made a rapid but difficult march on Chiametla, the scene
of Guzmán's spoliation; and, as the latter did not care to face
his incensed antagonist, Cortés recovered his vessel, though not
the cargo. He was then joined by the little squadron which he
had fitted out from his own port of Tehuantepec,—a port,
which, in the sixteenth century, promised to hold the place since
occupied by that of Acapulco. The vessels were provided with
every thing requisite for planting a colony in the newly discovered region, and transported four hundred Spaniards and
three hundred negro slaves, which Cortés had assembled for
that purpose. With this intention he crossed the Gulf, the Adri-
atic—to which an old writer compares it—of the Western
World.

Our limits will not allow us to go into the details of this
disastrous expedition, which was attended with no important
results either to its projector or to science. It may suffice to say,
that, in the prosecution of it, Cortés and his followers were
driven to the last extremity by famine; that he again crossed
the Gulf, was tossed about by terrible tempests, without a pilot
to guide him, was thrown upon the rocks, where his shattered
vessel nearly went to pieces, and after a succession of dangers
and disasters as formidable as any which he had ever encountered on land, succeeded, by means of his indomitable energy,
in bringing his crazy bark safe into the same port of Santa Cruz
from which he had started.

While these occurrences were passing, the new Royal Audience, after a faithful discharge of its commission, had been
superseded by the arrival of a Viceroy, the first ever sent to
New Spain. Cortés, though invested with similar powers, had
the title only of Governor. This was the commencement of the
system, afterwards pursued by the Crown, of intrusting the
colonial administration to some other individual, whose high
rank and personal consideration might make him the fitting

representative of majesty. The jealousy of the Court did not allow the subject clothed with such ample authority to remain long enough in the same station to form dangerous schemes of ambition, but at the expiration of a few years he was usually recalled, or transferred to some other province of the vast colonial empire. The person now sent to Mexico was Don Antonio de Mendoza, a man of moderation and practical good sense, and one of that illustrious family who in the preceding reign furnished so many distinguished ornaments to the Church, to the camp, and to letters.

The long absence of Cortés had caused the deepest anxiety in the mind of his wife, the marchioness of the Valley. She wrote to the viceroy immediately on his arrival, beseeching him to ascertain, if possible, the fate of her husband, and, if he could be found, to urge his return. The viceroy, in consequence, despatched two ships in search of Cortés, but whether they reached him before his departure from Santa Cruz is doubtful. It is certain, that he returned safe, after his long absence, to Acapulco, and was soon followed by the survivors of his wretched colony.

Undismayed by these repeated reverses, Cortés, still bent on some discovery worthy of his reputation, fitted out three more vessels, and placed them under the command of an officer named Ulloa. This expedition, which took its departure in July, 1539, was attended with more important results. Ulloa penetrated to the head of the Gulf; then, returning and winding round the coast of the peninsula, doubled its southern point, and ascended as high as the twenty-eighth or twenty-ninth degree of north latitude on its western borders. After this, sending home one of the squadron, the bold navigator held on his course to the north, but was never more heard of.

Thus ended the maritime enterprises of Cortés; sufficiently disastrous in a pecuniary view, since they cost him three hundred thousand *castellanos* of gold, without the return of a ducat. He was even obliged to borrow money, and to pawn his wife's jewels, to procure funds for the last enterprise; thus incurring a debt, which, increased by the great charges of his princely establishment, hung about him during the remainder of his life. But, though disastrous in an economical view, his generous efforts added important contributions to science. In the course of these expeditions, and those undertaken by Cortés previous to his visit to Spain, the Pacific had been coasted from the Bay of Panamá to the Río Colorado. The great peninsula of California had been circumnavigated as far as the isle of Cedros, or Cerros, into which the name has since been corrupted. This vast tract, which had been supposed to be an archipelago of islands, was now discovered to be a part of the continent; and its general outline, as appears from the maps of the time, was nearly as well understood as at the present day. Lastly, the navigator had explored the recesses of the Californian Gulf, or *Sea of Cortés,* as, in honor of the great discoverer, it is with more propriety named by the Spaniards; and he had ascertained, that, instead of the outlet before supposed to exist towards the north, this unknown ocean was locked up within the arms of the mighty continent. These were results that might have made the glory and satisfied the ambition of a common man; but they are lost in the brilliant renown of the former achievements of Cortés.

Notwithstanding the embarrassment of the marquess of the Valley, he still made new efforts to enlarge the limits of discovery, and prepared to fit out another squadron of five vessels, which he proposed to place under the command of a natural son, Don Luis. But the viceroy Mendoza, whose imagination had been inflamed by the reports of an itinerant monk respecting an *El Dorado* in the north, claimed the right of discovery in that direction. Cortés protested against this, as an unwarrantable interference with his own powers. Other subjects of collision arose between them; till the marquess, disgusted with this perpetual check on his authority and his enterprises, applied for redress to Castile. He finally determined to go there to support his claims in person, and to obtain, if possible, remuneration for the heavy charges he had incurred by his maritime expeditions, as well as for the spoliation of his property by the Royal Audience, during his absence from the country; and lastly, to procure an assignment of his vassals on principles more conformable to the original intentions of the grant. With these objects in view, he bade adieu to his family, and, taking with him his eldest son and heir, Don Martín, then only eight years of age, he embarked at Mexico in 1540, and, after a favorable voyage, again set foot on the shores of his native land.

The emperor was absent from the country. But Cortés was honorably received in the capital, where ample accommodations were provided for him and his retinue. When he attended the Royal Council of the Indies, to urge his suit, he was distinguished by uncommon marks of respect. The president went to the door of the hall to receive him, and a seat was provided for him among the members of the Council. But all evaporated in this barren show of courtesy. Justice, proverbially slow in Spain, did not mend her gait for Cortés; and at the expiration of a year, he found himself no nearer the attainment of his object than on the first week after his arrival in the capital.

In the following year, 1541, we find the marquess of the Valley embarked as a volunteer in the memorable expedition against Algiers. Charles the Fifth, on his return to his dominions, laid siege to that strong-hold of the Mediterranean corsairs. Cortés accompanied the forces destined to meet the emperor, and embarked on board the vessel of the Admiral of Castile. But a furious tempest scattered the navy, and the admiral's ship was driven a wreck upon the coast. Cortés and his son escaped by swimming, but the former, in the confusion of the scene, lost the inestimable set of jewels noticed in the preceding chapter; "a loss," says an old writer, "that made the expedition fall more heavily on the marquess of the Valley, than on any other man in the kingdom, except the emperor.

It is not necessary to recount the particulars of this disastrous siege, in which Moslem valor, aided by the elements, set at defiance the combined forces of the Christians. A council of war was called, and its was decided to abandon the enterprise and return to Castile. This determination was indignantly received by Cortés, who offered, with the support of the army, to reduce the place himself; and he only expressed the regret, that he had not a handful of those gallant veterans by his side who had served him in the conquest of Mexico. But his offers were derided, as those of a romantic enthusiast. He had not been invited to take part in the discussions of the council of war. It was a marked indignity; but the courtiers, weary of the service, were too much bent on an immediate return to Spain, to hazard the opposition of a man, who, when he had once planted his foot, was never known to raise it again, till he had accomplished his object.

On arriving in Castile, Cortés lost no time in laying his suit before the emperor. His applications were received by the monarch with civility,—a cold civility, which carried no conviction of its sincerity. His position was materially changed since his former visit to the country. More than ten years had elapsed, and he was now too well advanced in years to give promise of serviceable enterprise in future. Indeed, his undertakings of late had been singularly unfortunate. Even his former successes suffered the disparagement natural to a man of declining fortunes. They were already eclipsed by the magnificent achievements in Peru, which had poured a golden tide into the country, that formed a striking contrast to the streams of wealth, that, as yet, had flowed in but scantily from the silver mines of Mexico. Cortés had to learn, that the gratitude of a Court has reference to the future much more than to the past. He stood in the position of an importunate suitor, whose claims, however just, are too large to be readily allowed. He found, like Columbus, that it was possible to deserve too greatly.

In the month of February, 1544, he addressed a letter to the emperor,—it was the last he ever wrote him,—soliciting his attention to his suit. He begins, by proudly alluding to his past services to the Crown. "He had hoped, that the toils of youth would have secured him repose in his old age. For forty years he had pressed his life with little sleep, bad food, and with his arms constantly by his side. He had freely exposed his person to peril, and spent his substance in exploring distant and unknown regions, that he might spread abroad the name of his sovereign, and bring under his sceptre many great and powerful nations. All this he had done, not only without assistance from home, but in the face of obstacles thrown in his way by rivals and by enemies who thirsted like leeches for his blood. He was now old, infirm, and embarrassed with debt. Better had it been for him not to have known the liberal intentions of the emperor, as intimated by his grants; since he should then have devoted himself to the care of his estates, and not have been compelled, as he now was, to contend with the officers of the Crown, against whom it was more difficult to defend himself than to win the land from the enemy." He concludes with beseeching his sovereign to "order the Council of the Indies, with the other tribunals which had cognizance of his suits, to come to a decision; since he was too old to wander about like a vagrant, but ought rather, during the brief remainder of his life, to stay at home and settle his account with Heaven, occupied with the concerns of his soul, rather than with his substance."

This appeal to his sovereign, which has something in it touching from a man of the haughty spirit of Cortés, had not the effect to quicken the determination of his suit. He still lingered at the court from week to week, and from month to month, beguiled by the deceitful hopes of the litigant, tasting all that bitterness of the soul which arises from hope deferred. After three years more, passed in this unprofitable and humiliating occupation, he resolved to leave his ungrateful country and return to Mexico.

He had proceeded as far as Seville, accompanied by his son, when he fell ill of an indigestion, caused, probably, by irritation and trouble of mind. This terminated in dysentery, and his strength sank so rapidly under the disease, that it was apparent his mortal career was drawing towards its close. He prepared for it by making the necessary arrangements for the settlement of his affairs. He had made his will some time before; and he now executed it. It is a very long document, and in some respects a remarkable one.

The bulk of his property was entailed to his son, Don Martín, then fifteen years of age. In the testament he fixes his majority at twenty-five; but at twenty his guardians were to allow him his full income, to maintain the state becoming his rank. In a paper accompanying the will, Cortés specified the names of the agents to whom he had committed the management of his vast estates scattered over many different provinces; and he requests his executors to confirm the nomination, as these agents have been selected by him from a knowledge of their peculiar qualifications. Nothing can better show the thorough supervision, which, in the midst of pressing public concerns, he had given to the details of his widely extended property.

He makes a liberal provision for his other children, and a generous allowance to several old domestics and retainers in his household. By another clause he gives away considerable sums in charity, and he applies the revenues of his estates in the city of Mexico to establish and permanently endow three public institutions,—a hospital in the capital, which was to be dedicated to Our Lady of the Conception, a college in Cojohuacan for the education of missionaries to preach the gospel among the natives, and a convent, in the same place, for nuns. To the chapel of this convent, situated in his favorite town, he orders that his own body shall be transported for burial, in whatever quarter of the world he may happen to die.

After declaring that he has taken all possible care to ascertain the amount of the tributes formerly paid by his Indian vassals to their native sovereigns, he enjoins on his heir, that, in case those which they have hitherto paid shall be found to exceed the right valuation, he shall restore them a full equivalent. In another clause, he expresses a doubt whether it is right to exact personal service from the natives; and commands that a strict inquiry shall be made into the nature and the value of such services as he had received, and that, in all cases, a fair compensation shall be allowed for them. Lastly, he makes the remarkable declaration: "It has long been a question, whether one can conscientiously hold property in Indian slaves. Since this point has not yet been determined, I enjoin it on my son Martín and his heirs, that they spare no pains to come to an exact knowledge of the truth; as a matter which deeply concerns the conscience of each of them, no less than mine."

Such scruples of conscience, not to have been expected in Cortés, were still less likely to be met with in the Spaniards of a later generation. The state of opinion in respect to the great question of slavery, in the sixteenth century, at the commencement of the system, bears some resemblance to that which exists in our time, when we may hope it is approaching its conclusion. Las Casas and the Dominicans of the former age, the abolitionists of their day, thundered out their uncompromising invectives against the system, on the broad ground of natural equity and the rights of man. The great mass of proprietors troubled their heads little about the question of right, but were satisfied with the expediency of the institution. Others more considerate and conscientious, while they admitted the evil, found an argument for its toleration in the plea of necessity, regarding the constitution of the white man as unequal, in a sultry climate, to the labor of cultivating the soil. In one important respect, the condition of slavery, in the sixteenth century, differed materially from its condition in the nineteenth. In the former, the seeds of the evil, but lately sown, might have been, with comparatively little difficulty, eradicated. But in our time they have struck their roots deep into the social system, and cannot be rudely handled without shaking the very foundations of the political fabric. It is easy to conceive, that a man, who admits all the wretchedness of the institution and its wrong to humanity, may nevertheless hesitate to adopt a remedy, until he is satisfied that the remedy itself is not worse than the disease. That such a remedy will come with time, who can doubt, that has confidence in the ultimate prevalence of the right, and the progressive civilization of his species?

Cortés names, as his executors, and as guardians of his children, the duke of Medina Sidonia, the marquess of Astorga, and the count of Aguilar. For his executors in Mexico, he appoints his wife, the marchioness, the archbishop of Toledo, and two other prelates. The will was executed at Seville, October 11th, 1547.

Finding himself much incommoded, as he grew weaker, by the presence of visiters, to which he was necessarily exposed at Seville, he withdrew to the neighbouring village of Castilleja de la Cuesta, attended by his son, who watched over his dying parent with final solicitude. Cortés seems to have contemplated his approaching end with the composure not always to be found in those who have faced death with indifference on the field of battle. At length, having devoutly confessed his sins and received his sacrament, he expired on the 2d of December, 1547, in the sixty-third year of his age.

Bibliographical Note

I N April, 1843, in his first American contract outside his beloved Boston, Prescott contracted for the publication of 5,000 copies of his *Conquest of Mexico* by Harper and Brothers of New York. Released one volume at a time, between December 6 and 21, the book was produced from stereotype plates which Prescott owned. All American editions down to 1874 were produced from these plates. Only exceedingly minor changes were made in the plates during the long interval between 1843 and 1874. For the present selections a copy of the first American edition, that of December, 1843, was employed.

Two editions of the complete text of the *Conquest of Mexico* are currently in print, the Everyman's Library edition, which has been continuously available since 1909, and the Modern Library edition, which has been continuously available since 1936.

Index